Suburban Islam

Suburban Islam

JUSTINE HOWE

OXFORD
UNIVERSITY PRESS

OXFORD
UNIVERSITY PRESS

Oxford University Press is a department of the University of Oxford. It furthers the University's objective of excellence in research, scholarship, and education by publishing worldwide. Oxford is a registered trade mark of Oxford University Press in the UK and certain other countries.

Published in the United States of America by Oxford University Press
198 Madison Avenue, New York, NY 10016, United States of America.

First issued as an Oxford University Press paperback, 2021

Library of Congress Cataloging-in-Publication Data
Names: Howe, Justine, 1981–
Title: Suburban Islam / Justine Howe.
Description: New York, NY : Oxford University Press, [2018] |
Includes bibliographical references and index. |
Identifiers: LCCN 2017028643 (print) | LCCN 2017030894 (ebook) |
ISBN 9780190258887 (updf) | ISBN 9780190258894 (online content) |
ISBN 9780190863067 (epub) | ISBN 9780190258870 (cloth) |
ISBN 9780197558539 (paper)
Subjects: LCSH: Muslims—Illinois—Chicago Metropolitan Area. |
Muslims—Illinois—Chicago Metropolitan Area—Social life and customs. |
Islam—Illinois—Chicago Metropolitan Area. | Muslims—Illinois—Ethnic identity. |
Mohammed Webb Foundation (Lombard, Illinois)
Classification: LCC BP67.I32 (ebook) | LCC BP67.I32 C454 2018 (print) |
DDC 297.09773/11—dc23
LC record available at https://lccn.loc.gov/2017028643

For Brian

Contents

Acknowledgments

I AM GRATEFUL to acknowledge the many people who have helped bring this book into being. First and foremost, I thank the members of the Webb Foundation for their generosity, hospitality, and willingness to share their stories. I came away from this project with deep admiration for the work you are doing.

This book began as a doctoral dissertation at Northwestern University, where I benefitted from a vibrant intellectual community and the guidance of a stellar committee: Rüdiger Seesemann, Robert Orsi, Kambiz GhaneaBassiri, Muhammad Sani Umar, and Brannon Ingram. My gratitude goes to Rüdiger for allowing me to shift course in graduate school and to pursue a project on American Islam. Bob shepherded the dissertation to completion and has been a steadfast supporter of my work and career ever since. Bob's combination of ethnographic storytelling and critical acumen is a model for my work. I thank Kambiz for reading many versions of this manuscript, pushing me toward more precise conclusions, and being a trusted mentor.

In the early stages of this project, a fellowship from the American Association of University Women afforded an uninterrupted year of dissertation writing and facilitated its timely completion. A graduate fellowship from Northwestern University provided additional research and writing support.

Since 2013, Case Western Reserve University has been a lively academic home, thanks in no small part to the leadership of Dean Cyrus Taylor of the College of Arts and Sciences. Conversations with my colleagues in the Department of Religious Studies have sharpened the book's arguments. I am especially indebted to the exceptional mentorship of my department chair, Timothy Beal, who provided constructive feedback on several chapters, secured me a timely teaching release, and offered practical advice and encouragement at every stage in the publication process. Outside of religious studies, Chris Haufe has been an indispensable conversation partner on American Islam. I also thank Peter Knox, Director of the Baker-Nord Center for the Humanities, for his support of my research and for the opportunities that the BNC has created for me.

Over the past several years I have learned a great deal from audiences at several institutions and conferences, including Case Western Reserve University, Northwestern University, the University of Chicago, the School of Oriental and African Studies at the University of London, University of California, Santa Barbara, California State University Northridge, the Society for the Social Scientific Study of Religion, the Society for the Study of Muslim Ethics, and the American Academy of Religion.

Working with Oxford University Press has been a rewarding and smooth experience. Cynthia Read helped me to navigate the publishing process and provided crucial support and encouragement along the way. The comments and suggestions of three anonymous readers significantly improved the manuscript. Thank you to Henry Southgate for his superb copyediting. Douglas Easton did an expert job compiling the index.

I thank the *Journal of Qur'anic Studies* and Edinburgh University Press for their permission to reprint portions of "Interpreting the Qur'an in the United States: Religious Pluralism, Tradition, and Context," *Journal of Qur'anic Studies* 18, no. 3 (2016): 34–69, in chapter 5.

Several generous colleagues and friends from around the country have provided advice, facilitated field contacts, and commented on chapter drafts. I am very grateful to Sabahat Adil, Jenan Mohajir, and Jawad Qureshi for vital conversations about Muslim communities in Chicago. Many thanks to the members of the North American Religions Workshop at Northwestern University for their many suggestions on what would later become chapter 2, especially Amanda Baugh, Christopher Cantwell, and Will Caldwell. Sylvester Johnson's guidance on critical race theory proved transformational for the book as a whole. As I finished the manuscript, I benefitted from the insights and comraderie of my Young Scholars in American Religions cohort: Brandon Bayne, Cara Burnidge, Emily Clark, Brett Grainger, Rachel Gross, M. Cooper Harriss, Elizabeth Jemison, Nicole Turner, and Daniel Vaca. Well before they became our mentors, Kathryn Lofton and Leigh Schmidt's respective approaches to religion and American consumer culture inspired my own.

This book took shape during the eight years that I spent in Chicago. Profound thanks go to the Howe family there, for their kindness and encouragement: Timothy and Eliza Earle, the late Larry and Tina Howe, and Becky Howe. To Matthew Cressler and Mary Ellen Giess, I could not have survived graduate school or the early years of parenthood without your friendship.

I also want to extend warm thanks to our Cleveland friends: Maggie Popkin and Elliot Morrison, Amanda and Michael McCarthy, Erin Benay and Matthew Feinberg, Andrea and Matthew Rager, Meghan Guegold and Shachar Israel, Stephanie and Ron Paduchak, and Abbey and Peter Brown. Thank you for making Northeast Ohio home.

My deepest gratitude goes to my family. My grandfathers, Bob Theurkauf and Snuffy Howe, passed away during the writing of this book. I wish they were here to read and talk about it. My grandmothers, Tina Theurkauf and Carmen Howe, are among my most enthusiastic advocates. I am particularly grateful to Steve, Vicki, Amber, and Brandon Clites, for all the care and love.

I offer profound thanks to my parents, Rick and Susan Howe, for their love and faith in my abilities. For as long as I can remember, they fostered a passion for learning, taught me that ideas mattered, and gave me the license to pursue whatever career I wanted, even if it took me far from sunny California. I can always count on my sister and best friend, Ellen Howe Kueterman, for affirmation and solidarity. Many thanks to my brother, Warren Howe, for much-needed doses of political satire, but mostly for the moral support and thoughtful conversations.

My sons, Liam and Rory, are the center of my world. In the years that it took to research and write, Liam has grown from an infant to an articulate, empathetic, and inquisitive person. Rory arrived as I revised the manuscript, and he has infused our family with ever more humor and affection.

Words are inadequate to express the gratitude I have for my husband, Brian, who has lived through every aspect of this book. Thank you for your sustaining love. I have come to doubt many things in this world, but never this: we have a true partnership, and it is the greatest gift of my life.

Introduction

APPROACHING AMERICAN ISLAM

IN FEBRUARY 2016, after more than seven years in office, President Barack Obama made his first visit to an American mosque. During his remarks to the Islamic Society of Baltimore, Obama both affirmed the historical presence of Muslims in the United States and denounced discrimination and Islamophobia. He also addressed the special burden of American Muslims to account for acts of violence committed by other Muslims. While acknowledging such a burden might not be fair, the President declared that American Muslims need to ramp up their efforts to make their "good works" known:

> Part of the answer is to make sure that the Muslim community in all of its variety, in all of its good works that it's doing, in all the talent that's on display, that it's out there visible on a consistent basis—not just at a certain moment. But what is also true is, is that there is a battle of hearts and minds that takes place—that is taking place right now, and American Muslims are better positioned than anybody to show that it is possible to be faithful to Islam and to be part of a pluralistic society and to be on the cutting-edge of science and to believe in democracy. And so I would urge all of you not to see this as a burden, but as a great opportunity and a great privilege to show who you are. . . . Because when you do you'll make clear that this is not a clash of civilizations between the West and Islam.[1]

Obama's remarks point to the line between hypervisibility and invisibility upon which American Muslims walk.[2] On the one hand, "terrorists" flood American television screens, constant signifiers of Islam as a dangerous threat. On the other hand, American Muslims are repeatedly criticized for not being vocal enough against violence carried out in the name of their religion. Obama's remarks suggested that American Muslims ought to transform this burden into a privilege and opportunity. Although he noted that American Muslims are already good citizens, Obama also emphasized that their efforts to demonstrate this patriotic loyalty have fallen short. American Muslims, the president insisted, must "on a consistent basis" represent their faith as peaceful, just, and democratic. Otherwise, they risk perpetuating the global perception that an insurmountable chasm exists "between the West and Islam," with all the consequences (military and otherwise) that this implies.

This book examines how one community, the Mohammed Alexander Russell Webb Foundation (Webb), has navigated these kinds of pressures since 2004. Webb's vision has been constructed within the shifting political and religious terrain of the post-9/11 United States. The community offers a case study of the ways that American Muslims have responded to the demands of proving Islam's compatibility with liberal democracy and embracing "Judeo-Christian" commonalities of their "Abrahamic" faith. For this Chicago Muslim community, the 9/11 attacks and their resultant discrimination, violence, and surveillance were especially transformative. To have their patriotism or loyalty questioned, to field endless questions about Islam and its purportedly violent nature, and to endure questioning by law enforcement agencies have been profoundly disorienting experiences. Prior to September 11, many of these American Muslims were more confident in their position as full members of middle- and upper-middle-class neighborhoods. Most of them were successful young professionals preoccupied with the daily obligations of raising their children, serving on school committees, and keeping up with the Joneses.

Almost all Webb participants are citizens, and the majority were born in the United States. In addition to their legal status, they understand themselves as having earned full "cultural citizenship."[3] Facilitated by their socioeconomic privilege, most members by and large have embodied the normative markers of Americanness: they belong to and celebrate heteronormative nuclear families; express a firm commitment to liberal principles such as individualism; extol the virtues of "spirituality" over stagnant ritualized cultures; and embrace trappings of middle-class consumerism.[4] The racialization of "the Muslim" as a category, however, suddenly marked them as foreign and antithetical to liberal democracy and global stability, which in turn cast their cultural citizenship into doubt.[5] The Webb Foundation is in large part a communal attempt to make sense of this shockwave, to restore their sense of pride as Muslims, and to publicly reassert their right to belonging as Americans. In the process, Webb members wanted to create spaces of comfort, fun, and affirmation for themselves and their children.

Everyone I interviewed for this book spoke about the day-to-day anxiety they feel over contemporary depictions of Islam and the worry they carry about their children's futures as negative representations of Islam persist in American media, policy circles, and in the broader public. Their intense anxiety reflects the meteoric rise of anti-Muslim sentiment, which renders them suspect others and presumes their association with religious violence. This rhetoric and its corollary images have become a mainstay of US discourse during the War on Terror. Indeed, representations of Muslims as uniquely threatening to the American social and political order have only intensified in recent years.

The astonishingly xenophobic rhetoric of the 2016 presidential campaign cycle was particularly instructive in terms of tracking the resilience of these negative perceptions of Islam and Muslims.[6] Then Republican Party nominee Donald Trump repeatedly called for a ban on all Muslims entering the United States.[7] Following the Bastille Day attack in Nice, France, former Speaker of the House Newt Gingrich deemed sharia (Islamic law and ethics) "incompatible with western civilization" and vowed that American Muslims who follow sharia should be deported.[8] A recent survey concluded that Muslims have fallen below atheists as the least favorable religious group as ranked by other non-Muslim Americans.[9]

The Webb Foundation thus represents one response, among many, to the persistent societal doubt about whether Muslims can make good Americans.[10] What emerges from Webb is not a singular vision. Rather, I attend to the fragmented, evolving ways that this group works out, individually and collectively, what American Islam means to them during a time in which *Muslim* and *American* are repeatedly presented as incompatible categories. Dissatisfied with the ways that mosques have led them through this increasingly troubled terrain of American religious politics, this group of families endeavored to "stop complaining" and create a space through which to address their concerns together.

Webb as a Case Study for American Islam

Webb is a third-space community in the western suburbs of Chicago. Its core membership consists of nuclear families, many of which include spouses of different ethnic and racial backgrounds who are seeking an educational, devotional, and social alternative to local mosques. As a whole, roughly half the organization's members are first- or second-generation immigrants from South Asia (with a particularly large contingent from Hyderabad, India); a quarter of participants are white converts; a quarter are Arab-American; and there are several African American or Latinx members.

In this way, Webb families illustrate the demographic diversity of American Muslims, but with fewer African Americans than the overall US Muslim population. This ethnic and racial diversity does not begin to encompass the geographic, political, and theological differences that also characterize American Muslim communities.

Webb is defined less by a coherent set of beliefs or theology than by a shared commitment to enacting American Islam through sets of overlapping relationships. These include bonds between spouses, parents and their children, friendships forged among adults and children, and relationships that participants seek with the Prophet Muhammad and God. In its early years, the community focused on fostering friendships among its members; then it gradually built up a formal set of ritual activities and educational programs. By the time I began fieldwork in early 2010, the organization had a clear mission, a fresh website, a small, permanent staff, and an official board.[11]

In order to facilitate these relationships, the Webb community engages in a variety of activities. From 2010 to 2014, about 150 people, both children and adults, gathered regularly at Webb for religious events, recreational activities, and social get-togethers. Webb's marquee event is their *mawlid*, or celebration of the Prophet Muhammad's birthday, which has drawn more than three hundred guests each year. Other major annual events include the "Welcome Home Hajji" celebration, which honors community members who recently completed the pilgrimage to Mecca, and Webb's potluck-style *iftar*, the evening meal to break the fast during Ramadan. Since its inception, Webb has also maintained a robust service agenda through its youth programs, which stresses the value of volunteerism and social justice. Webb board members organize an annual Thanksgiving Turkey drive, which partners with schools and social service organizations to provide over a thousand turkeys to needy families on the south and west sides of Chicago. Additional events and activities have included father-daughter camping, lectures on parenting, ski trips, nature walks, father-son football games, and a book club.[12] Finally, Webb also participates in a variety of interfaith projects and cosponsored events with Christian and Jewish congregations.

Webb provides a particularly important window into broader trends, especially devotional practices and communal formation outside of American mosques. According to the 2011 Pew report "Muslim Americans: No Signs of Growth in Alienation of Support for Extremism," only 47 percent of American Muslims attend mosques weekly, 34 percent attend yearly, and 19 percent never attend. Many Webb members fit this profile of "unmosqued" Muslims, as either former mosque-goers or as practitioners whose devotions center on the home, smaller reading groups, or attendance in classes led by trusted scholars, at least until they discovered the Webb Foundation. For them and many others, religious observance cannot be measured through mosque membership or attendance, just as church or synagogue attendance is an inadequate measure of religiosity among Christians and Jews.

The Webb Foundation represents but one slice of American Muslims' heterogeneous institutionalizing practices. The life histories I track here demonstrate how American Muslims' religiosity intersects with their racial, ethnic, and gendered identities, moral commitments, and motivations through various life stages. Indeed, Webb sheds indispensable light on the many communities that shape the specific contours of American Muslims' diverse experiences. In addition to mosques, American Muslims have created many other communities that align with their faith, including book clubs, Montessori preschools, support groups for new converts, artist and writers' collectives, online communities, and more. Similar groups to the Webb community, which are focused on the nuclear family and the cultivation of American identity, can be found in other major suburban areas, including northern Virginia, Long Island, and the Bay Area. Such groups deserve additional study, without which we cannot begin to account for the breadth of American Muslim lives.

Shared class affiliation undergirds the construction of religious and social belonging at Webb. Members primarily conceive of culture through terms such as "comfort" and "lifestyle." Here, class denotes more than simply wealth; it includes a multitude of material practices, epistemologies, and tastes. Despite the prevalence of scholarship on the importance of consumerism to the construction of contemporary selfhood, this lens is virtually absent from studies of American Muslims.[13] This omission reflects our tendency to cordon off religion from practices seen as worldly, mundane, and material.[14] Like other Americans, my interviewees are twenty-first-century consumers who imbue leisure activities with profound moral significance. Participants see these activities as fulfilling an obligation to embrace and instill an "indigenous" American culture in their children. Webb families implicitly recognize the cultural capital of these social rituals specific to their US context. At the same time, they see these ritual acts as part of global historical processes in which Muslims have adopted and created local cultures even as they practice a universal faith.[15]

In their appropriation of recreational rituals as quintessentially American, Webb participants also explicitly follow in the footsteps of other US immigrant faiths, such as Catholics and Jews, in understanding these activities as potentially smoothing the pathway for Islam's acceptance in the American religious landscape. Particularly in the face of bigotry, the persistence of these narratives at Webb demonstrate the optimism that many Muslims maintain in the American national project and its capacity for justice, freedom, and equality. As I explore, however, these narratives depend on the unwitting elision of structural factors that have enabled groups such as white Catholics and Jews to achieve greater parity with Protestant Americans, while rendering other groups such as African Americans as less deserving citizens.[16]

Webb exemplifies institutionalizing processes that have crystallized in American Islam after September 11, 2001, which has been a time of immense growth for American Muslim communities more broadly. It is also indebted to decades of institutional development on the part of earlier generations of Chicago's Muslims. Indeed, the Webb Foundation is part of the rich history of American religious communities built on voluntarism and lay authority. Since the early twentieth century, American Muslims have been actively engaged in building permanent institutions across the United States, which included the creation of the country's first mosques, both in immigrant and African American communities. After World War II, the proliferation of political and religious organizations picked up speed, spurred on by the activities of groups such as the Nation of Islam and the efforts of post-1965 immigrants who created communities oriented around particular national and ethnic practices, political organizations, social service agencies, university associations, and educational foundations.[17]

Tradition and Authority in American Islam

Webb is representative of a broader project among American Muslims seeking to recover "tradition" in order to address what Zareena Grewal has termed the "global crisis of authority" in contemporary Islam.[18] This crisis is rooted in a perceived lack of "coherence" in Muslim debates, disagreements over the construction of Muslim authority, and anxiety over the status of Islam in the modern world.[19] Here, I use the term "tradition" to highlight Webb's intention to recuperate an authentic Islam that they want to access through classical, premodern scholarship. Webb members contrast this mission with the modes of authority and forms of Islamic knowledge that they find in their mosques. Unlike the student-travelers in Grewal's study, who travel to the "Middle East" in order to partake in the wisdom of "traditional" scholars and their pedagogies, Webb participants affirm that the Islamic tradition can be recovered and reproduced right here in America, so long as one has the guidance of scholars who have access to the authorizing wisdom of classical bodies of Islamic knowledge. The Webb community creates the opportunity for its members to engage these intellectuals' ideas in a physical and pedagogical setting modeled on the American university classroom, with the goal of enabling members to debate and disagree with each other. At Webb, the Islamic tradition sanctions cultural diversity and internal debate, such that while Muslim communities embrace the full range of human ethnicities and cultures, participants interpret this heterogeneity as proof of Islam's intrinsic universality.

Webb members rely on this underlying narrative, and the practices it legitimates, to contest what they see as the two dominant orientations in American mosques: "cultural Islam," or ethnic particularism, and "Wahhabism," or Salafi practices and theologies. They argue that these influences have prevented American Islam from achieving its vibrant potential. Furthermore, Salafis have endangered American Muslims by their association with illiberal and potentially "extremist" forms of Islam. This engagement with the Islamic tradition is thus connected to broader constructions of authority, not just over who speaks on behalf of Islam but even more so over who speaks on behalf of America.[20] Webb members hold in tension this veneration for premodern Muslim thinkers as they rely on their individual lived experiences as the basis for their vision of American Islam writ large.

"American Islam"

Webb is a microcosm through which to explore and analyze important dynamics as they are unfolding within American Islam. I employ Juliane Hammer and Omid Safi's use of the term "American Islam" as simultaneously a "construct, a project, and a reality."[21] In doing so, I want to attend to the ongoing processes by which American Muslims enact American Islam while also situating critically these efforts within the arc of American religious history. My method adopts what Kambiz GhaneaBassiri calls a "relational approach," which underscores the historical presence of Muslims in the United States as well as the continuous, reciprocal dialogue and negotiations with Americans of varying faiths.[22] As the field of American Islam has moved beyond the immigrant/African American binary, it has become imperative for scholars to more fully account for the ways that American Muslims negotiate and encounter various forms of difference and inequality within a variety of institutional locations. [23]

I am not interested in uplifting Webb's vision of American Islam as "good" or "moderate," nor do I endorse the ritual practices I analyze here.[24] But we must also note that such assessments, particularly the rhetoric of "good" and "bad" religion, have contributed directly to Webb's imagining of American Muslim selfhood. Since the Cold War, the image of the "bad" Muslim (violent, fanatical) was paired with the representation of the "good" Muslim (tolerant, moderate).[25] This dichotomy has been deployed for a variety of political goals, with the effect of delegitimizing certain forms of Muslim practice.[26] American Muslims are both subject to these representations and have internalized them, but they do not simply replicate these categories.[27] Webb members do more with these representations (and the racialized logic upon which they are based) than merely to condemn other Muslims as suspect Americans. At Webb, these categories are appropriated, contested, and deployed in an effort to bridge the gap between their deep commitment to their faith and its overwhelmingly negative portrayal in American pop culture.[28] In their attempts to create spaces of religious belonging and to forge connections with non-Muslim Americans, Webb participants also reinscribe practices of religious exclusion, especially against other Muslims who cannot or do not wish to embrace their vision of American Islam.

I approach religion and culture as mutually constituted through social practices, relationships, material objects, institutions, and relations of power, which individuals and communities negotiate in particular times and places. I was drawn to the Webb Foundation as a field site precisely because I found what participants were doing with these categories to be so fascinating, not to mention shot through with such evident political stakes. Categories such as "Islam" and "America" require analysis because their meanings are multiple, contested, and never self-evident. As an ethnographer, I attend to the ways my conversation partners deploy and produce these categories to construct an American Islam that they seek to bring into effect through their efforts at the Webb Foundation. *Suburban Islam* examines how one group of American Muslims deliberately and intentionally sets out to enact an Islam recognizable to others as American. Even as Webb intends to build a more inclusive and welcoming community, it also produces its own boundaries, elisions of extant social hierarchies, and unresolved tensions.

On the surface, how Webb members enact American culture appears overly determined or superficially nostalgic. This is because the racialization and marginalization of American Muslims have resulted in an increasingly narrow discursive space in which these communities practice, circumscribing what they can say and how they can practice Islam, and demanding all the while that they prove their loyalty to the American state.[29] This climate has also turned American Muslims into representatives for Islam as a whole, requiring them to account for the actions of Muslims in global contexts far removed from their local circumstances.

But it would be a mistake to see the Webb Foundation as a successful domestication of American Muslims, who have merely taken up the patriotic call to render Islam an acceptable faith. To be sure, Webb participants sometimes replicate the "culture-talk" that defines so much of the discourse surrounding Islam today, for example, by criticizing the cultures of immigrants as static and by celebrating a singular American culture. But at the same time, Webb participants produce creative enactments of what it means to be an American Muslim that undermine the very foundations of the logic established by broader social and political pressures. In 2012, amid calls to ban sharia in many US states, Webb members wanted one of their adult education classes to focus on *fiqh* (Islamic jurisprudence). Conversations in that class, however, challenged the terms of popular debate by insisting on *fiqh* and sharia as everyday processes of normative reflection and action, negotiated within families and between individuals, religious scholars, and God. That is, Webb participants recuperated the Islamic tradition in order to claim that their individual experiences as American Muslims are actually essential to discerning the divine will. I analyze this and other examples of how Webb participates in and moves beyond culturist depictions of Islam in chapters 5 and 6.

Webb as a Religious Third Space

I use the term "third space" to analyze multiple aspects of the Webb community and its significance: to describe Webb's cultural and institutional location, explain its appeal, and show how it serves as a site for emerging identities by offering its members a context through which to attempt to overcome the binary division between "America" and "Islam." Like other American Muslims, Webb members occupy what Shabana Mir describes as an "in-between space awkwardly straddling recognized categories, fitting into none."[30] This in-between status is not merely repressive or constraining, but also engenders possibilities for new ways of being. That is, communities and individuals sometimes challenge dominant practices and representations of culture, while also inhabiting many of those same practices and representations. In the Webb community, members use these representations deliberately, appropriating and deploying conceptions of "Islam" and "America" in ways that both reinforce dominant narratives of American assimilation *and* produce alternative practices of belonging and exclusion within American religions.[31]

In third spaces, constructions of self and community are also highly contingent. Webb is a generative site of critique and optimistic reform, in which peer debate and discussion are a primary means to discount existing visions for American Islam, gain Islamic knowledge, and to create alternative ways to be American Muslims. The chapters that follow highlight the radical potential of third spaces, or what cultural geographer Edward Soja calls the "potentially emancipatory *praxis*" of the third space and its "creative process of restructuring that draws selectively and strategically from the two opposing categories to open new alternatives."[32] There is considerable disagreement among members about what American Islam should look like, despite a broad understanding of Webb's mission: to work for Islam's acceptance as an American faith, to create a "seamless" American Muslim identity, and to increase the visibility of women in American Muslim communities. This openness to change is partly due to the relative newness of the organization as well as the specific possibilities that emerge from the organization's creative use of space and the cultural location of American Muslims.

Webb participants are subject to and claim a doubly marginal cultural location, as Muslims cast as threatening to American society and as Muslims who feel they do not belong at their local religious institutions. This marginality is both painful and liberating. In his now classic formulation, Homi Bhabha described third space as:

> the terrain for elaborating strategies of selfhood—singular or communal—that initiate new signs of identity, and innovative sites of collaboration and contestation in the act of defining society itself . . . The right to signify from the periphery of authorized power and privilege does not depend on the persistence of tradition; it is resourced by the power of tradition to be reinscribed through the conditions of contradictoriness that attend upon the lives of those who are 'in the minority.'[33]

Webb members carry with them emotionally charged experiences of racial, gendered, and religious exclusion carried out by other Muslims as well as non-Muslim Americans. Members challenge Islam's supposed incompatibility with American culture. But they also engage in broader debates concerning Islamic authority, ritual practice, and textual interpretation. Even as members of the community occupy positions of marginality, their outsider status also confers an advantageous position through which to challenge Muslim practices and theologies in their mosques. University-educated and economically secure, Webb participants are in important ways more privileged than other Muslim communities, especially more recent immigrants who tend to have fewer financial resources. They can thus use this marginal position to far greater effect.

In doing so, Webb participants celebrate their community as an aspirational space in which they can "be themselves," where their intersecting identities come together in new ways. In this way, Webb-as-third-space offers the possibility for its members' true religious selves to emerge. Webb occupies the boundary between what Michel de Certeau calls the "tactics of practice," the everyday practices of the consumer, and the "strategies" employed by producers, who act from a position of spatial permanence and representational power. Members make religious meaning through rituals of consumerism (leisure, reading), while using those rituals to represent an alternative American Islam. De Certeau points us to the "opportunities" presented in the flux of everyday practices. Communities and individuals blur the false dichotomy between producers and consumers through consumerism's "quiet activity, in short by its quasi-invisibility, since it shows itself not in its own products (where would it place them?), but in an art of using those imposed on it."[34] For de Certeau, however, consumer acts are defined by their lack of spatial and institutional location and by their impermanence. As a third space, the Webb Foundation calls our attention to the creative potential of the everyday when it is recognized, made visible, and enacted in a more formal community.

"Third space" has gained broader currency among American Muslims more generally and is distinct from the theoretical framework outlined above. Much like Webb, increasing numbers of American Muslim movements and activists now name their institutions and activities as "third spaces" in which alternative authority structures, textual engagement, and ritual activities take shape. Such groups deserve further study because they illuminate the potentialities of Muslim being and belonging in the contemporary United States.

At Webb, members use "third space" to designate their community as an alternative to two longstanding sites for Muslim practice in the United States: the mosque and the home. That is, its members use the term to differentiate their community, as well as to affiliate themselves with a growing number of American Muslims who have begun to seek out and name "third spaces." Although "third space" can have a very broad meaning, at Webb it signals something more specific: a site that fulfills social and religious needs that members believe are missing from mosques. It would be misleading, however, to describe the Webb Foundation (and many other third spaces) as entirely separate from, or completely opposed to, mosques. Many (though not all) Webb participants retain their connections to local mosques, holding leadership positions, delivering occasional *khutbahs* or sermons, and serving on program committees. Other Webb members have severed all ties with their mosques, choosing to participate only in Webb activities or to focus their energies on religious and social events with their extended and immediate families.

As a third space, Webb orients us to multiple ways that American Muslims use space to practice Islam. Barbara Metcalf's groundbreaking edited volume

Making Muslim Space in North America and Europe rightly emphasized that American Muslims inhabit religious spaces that are not always readily apparent to outside observers. Within these varying physical spaces, its participants build what Metcalf calls the "social space" of Muslims, as well as the "cultural space" through which Muslim communities interact with the broader society.[35] Metcalf stresses the portability of Muslim ritual, which frees it from the constraints of specific physical spaces. Indeed, this spatial flexibility provides a community like Webb with the opportunity to fulfill a variety of religious functions in different locations such as community centers, football fields, hotel conference rooms, and libraries. At the same time, this flexibility is the byproduct of constraints. The creation of Muslim institutions in the United States has become more difficult in the contemporary political landscape, and the barriers to their creation—both physical and financial—have also prevented Webb from inhabiting a unified, single space for community gathering. These difficulties mirror the challenges Muslims face when building mosques and community centers across the United States.

On the whole, third spaces create possibilities of identity and community, the outcome of which remains contradictory and in flux. The close ethnographic study of one particular group allows me to explore the contours and complexities of these tensions, many of which remain salient. I intentionally do not explain these tensions away. Religion is too often presented as an integrative force that facilitates greater acceptance in American society and the ultimate fulfillment of individual selves. Robert Orsi cautions against this "causal functionalism" and the common "insistence that in religion the social and domestic life, the tension of history and psychology, find resolution."[36] For all the possibilities of being and belonging that Webb provides for its members, it also engenders new ambiguities and anxieties. The methodological tools of ethnography are essential for uncovering complex processes of community creation, the ways in which porous and contested boundaries are drawn between and within religious institutions, how authority is enacted and negotiated, and the meanings that people assign to these processes. Within this community, contestations over textual interpretations, authority, and identity mirror broader debates in American Islam. Instead of seeing the Webb Foundation as a place of closure, I theorize it as a site of possibility with all the uncertainty and complexity that entails.

It is important to point out that Webb participants mostly seem untroubled by these tensions between permanence and impermanence, flexibility and stability. More than a specific ideology or theological perspective, it is the community's embrace of process and relationship-building that sets it apart from other communities in Chicago. As the organization has grown and become more established, some of my interviewees expressed a desire for more continuity and for a dedicated physical structure. But I heard many more participants describe what they are doing as a "process" of becoming American Muslims in which there would be starts and stops along the way. In many discussions at Webb, whether about the interpretation of the Qur'an or raising their children, it seemed that participants wanted first and foremost to create a space where they felt comfortable to disagree with their friends and nuclear family members. Although sometimes these debates were exhausting and frustrating, Webb participants never wavered in their sense of accomplishment in having had created their own third space.

Narratives of Pluralism

Religious pluralism is a key practice through which Webb participants advance their vision of American Islam, appropriating and sometimes contesting the logic of religious pluralism through their interpretations of sacred texts, their interfaith endeavors, and their rituals. This engagement with pluralism reflects a broader American project of engaging religious difference. As Courtney Bender and Pamela Klassen have argued, the contemporary United States is in its "after pluralism moment."[37] Pluralism has been constituted through social, religious, and legal institutions and has become so entrenched in the American psyche that most citizens take it for granted. As a discourse, religious pluralism has helped to define the limits and possibilities of religious identity in the United States, even as its meanings have shifted over time. In the late nineteenth century, Protestantism was celebrated as inherently and uniquely compatible with the features of modernity: rationality, individualism, progress, and belief-centered faith. Until the mid-twentieth century, Catholicism posed the greatest threat to Protestant ascendancy, but during the Cold War it gained entrance alongside Judaism into what Kevin Schultz has termed "tri-faith America."[38] In the late twentieth century and especially after 9/11, Islam's compatibility with American religious pluralism has been repeatedly called into question.

Echoing colonial assertions of Islam's inherent opposition to modernity, today American Muslims are called upon to affirm that Islam recognizes Judaism and Christianity as salvific faiths through their common Abrahamic heritage and to downplay Islamic claims to superiority. However, there is an ongoing debate within local communities and among intellectuals over what religious pluralism entails, both theologically and in everyday practice. According to the 2008 Pew "Religious Landscape Survey," the majority (56 percent) of American Muslims agreed that "many religions can lead to eternal life," while 33 percent responded that "my religion is the one truth faith."[39] Scholars have increasingly turned their attention to the themes of religious tolerance and pluralism in the Qur'an and other texts, providing a fuller picture of the conceptual terrain that has helped to define the parameters of Muslim thought and practice with respect to the status of other faiths.[40] But we know very little about how most American Muslims actually construct and practice religious pluralism.

Webb members understand religious pluralism as essential to the future of American Islam, legitimated through intertwined narratives of global Muslim and American histories. Contrary to the violence associated with Islam, they point to practices of religious pluralism originally set forth by the Prophet Mohammed and the first Muslim communities, as well as to later Muslim societies, such as Muslim Spain. They pick up on arguments advanced by a variety of intellectuals and scholars, such as the common observation that prior to modernity, Muslim empires were far more tolerant of other faiths than were their Christian counterparts.[41] Most importantly, they find support for religious pluralism in sacred texts, in the lives of exemplary American Muslims such as Muhammed Alexander Russell Webb, and in the thought of scholars whom they entrust with helping them to define the boundaries and content of the Islamic tradition.

Religious pluralism also organizes Webb members' narratives of American history, as a right first enshrined in the Constitution, and then gradually expanded to include Catholicism and Judaism (and, later, the other "world religions"). That is, they invoke a teleology in which the United States moves toward greater inclusion of religious minorities, including Islam. From this perspective, recent incidents of intolerance and discrimination against Muslims are deviations from America's ever-widening commitment to freedom of religious expression and accommodation of religious difference. When my conversation partners heard that I was raised in a Catholic family with Irish and German roots, they eagerly told me about the Virgin Mary as a model of piety. The several members who attended Catholic parochial schools as children shared how nuns modeled devotion, modesty, and humility. Moreover, interviewees often drew parallels between the experiences of my German ancestors during the world wars and contemporary Muslims, both as communities associated with a foreign enemy.

Ideologies and practices of religious pluralism help to recover these dual traditions, even when they are in tension with one another. This is not because the "Islamic tradition" and the "American culture" are necessarily incommensurable. Rather it is because American Muslims do not always agree on what religious pluralism means or what it requires of them. Webb conversations produce general consensus that religious pluralism is both a moral and a civic good. At the same time, these discussions also generated anxieties about the potential political dangers of upholding the distinctiveness and superiority of Islam as American Muslims.[42]

American Muslim affirmations of religious pluralism are intended to make their communities more inclusive, by engaging with other religious groups, from interreligious dialogue to service projects. At the same time, ideologies of religious pluralism produce fault lines because many Muslims wish to maintain a certain degree of pride and confidence in the superiority of their faith. If embracing religious pluralism is an essential part of being American, then the patriotic credentials of those Muslims who cannot or do not wish to be pluralists *in this way* are called into question.

Gendered Authority and the Future of American Islam

In its governance, educational approach, and social activities, Webb works to shift gender roles typically inhabited by American Muslim men and women. At Webb, women hold a variety of ritual, pedagogical, and governance positions as board members, leaders of devotional practice, and coordinators of educational programs for children and adults alike.

In addition to the goals described above, the Webb community is focused on critiquing and reforming gendered practices they encounter as unjust and exclusionary in Chicago's religious institutions. Webb members' objectives include rectifying the lack of representation of women on mosque boards, limiting gender separation outside of ritual prayer, and including women in various aspects of ritual practices. Webb also invites its participants to discuss what many refer to as controversial issues or "hot topics," such as homosexuality. As a way to encourage women to participate fully in all dimensions of the community's activities, Webb has quite intentionally carved out positions of religious leadership for women. Indeed, female members are among the most visible Webb leaders, giving public talks, coordinating events, developing curricula, taking an active role in planning and performing rituals, and crafting the community's future goals. Webb prides itself on having a board of directors with equal representation of men and women. Its first executive director was also a woman. When asked what they like best about the Webb Foundation, women always cite its gendered practices, which include their ability to interact with men in class, to shake hands if they wish, to plan and execute events, lead programs for men and women, and to wear whatever they want, including the decision to wear the hijab. (As we will see in chapter 7, feminism is a contested category at Webb.). Webb women seek a religious space in which they can shape the direction of American Islam. Many of them spent their childhoods in local mosques, emerging from these experiences with an activist orientation and a keen purpose to re-make Islam into a set of practices and beliefs that makes sense to them. Having grown up watching their parents start Muslim institutions molded according to their own religious needs and proclivities, Webb board members and participants want to do the same. And while their mothers and grandmothers did not occupy the roles that women at Webb wish to claim for themselves, many of their female family members were instrumental in key activities at their mosques, especially youth education.

By and large, Webb women grew up in families who encouraged them to obtain college degrees and start careers. The high value placed on professional success in their extended families meant that they found themselves in what Marcia Hermansen analyzes as a form of "liminality," caught between the gendered expectations of their religious communities and the status they achieved in their professional lives. This sense of liminality, in which the seams of their multiple identities are rendered visible, is what many Webb members wish to overcome through their involvement in the organization.[43] That is, because mosque authority has often been connected to professional status, women at Webb argue for that same authority to be conferred on them. As leaders in their chosen professions, they should also assume positions of leadership within the mosque. Indeed, what Webb women seek is the Muslim authority that many professionally successful men have already attained in Chicago's Muslim institutions. Like male board members, they want this professional status and educational attainment to translate into positions of religious leadership in mosques as well as emerging communities like Webb.

Gendered concerns are not limited to practices marked as female. Members place paramount emphasis on their responsibilities as parents. Although parenting may at first seem to be a gender-neutral category, Webb's parenting initiatives place an emphasis on fatherhood and the cultivation of a particular kind of American Muslim masculinity.[44] Webb attempts to foster relationships between fathers and their children through leisure practices, such as camping trips and football games. These activities challenge the pervasive image of the patriarchal, distant, and authoritarian Muslim (especially Arab) father who is obsessed with preserving family honor, and the related designation of Muslim women as passive, secluded, and oppressed. Such representations do not resonate with Webb members' self-image nor their relationships with their own fathers, which they more often than not describe as loving and supportive. In place of these distorting and inaccurate stereotypes, these activities characterize Muslim fathers as fun-loving, compassionate, and involved in the daily labor of childrearing. By linking leisure to the moral obligation of parenting, these activities, deemed quintessentially American, are made into pious acts.

In describing these efforts, Webb participants marshal narratives of the Islamic tradition along with their personal experiences as American Muslims. On the one hand, the "Islamic tradition" functions as a legitimating force for granting women more authority and a greater public presence. Through the work and guidance of American Muslim intellectuals, including scholars working in the North American academy, Webb members conceive of the first Muslim community (the Companions of the Prophet and the first generations, or the *Salaf*) as providing a model for female leadership and gender integration and equality. On the other hand, the obligation for Muslims to embrace diverse cultures means that American Muslims ought to embody prevailing "American" gender norms that support women in public leadership roles. This argument from culture relies on an understanding of American society as exceptional, for affording women far more opportunities than in Muslim-majority societies. At the same time, Webb participants criticize common gendered practices such as dating rituals. Generally, though, they conceive of the United States as providing the conditions to achieve gendered relationships and authority structures that simultaneously emulate those at the time of the Prophet Muhammad and resonate with their professional, familial, and social practices. Economically secure and culturally cosmopolitan, Webb members assert their authority to know, represent, and embody American culture and its normative practices.

Fieldwork and Methodology

My fieldwork balanced participant observation with conversational interviews. I first encountered the Webb Foundation at a cosponsored event on interfaith environmentalism in February 2011. There I met Nadia, a founding board member, whose warm invitation to attend Webb events and her contacts paved my initial foray into the community. In addition to Nadia's assistance, other factors expedited my participation. In the summer of 2011, I began to attend the Webb book club, where the members generously introduced me to their friends and family members. The significant number of white converts and women who did not wear the hijab made my presence inconspicuous.

From 2010 through 2012, I observed a variety of Webb events, including community classes, public lectures, social gatherings, and *mawlids*. I focused on three adult classes in particular: Contemporary Issues in Islam; *Fiqh*; and the Qur'an. The instructor, Omer Mozaffar, led a biweekly seminar, where, on average, thirty-five students engaged in lively discussions. I recorded the classes and then wrote up fieldnotes before commuting back to Chicago.

I also conducted forty life-narrative interviews with some of Webb's core participants and board members, as well as people actively involved in related groups and events. Once participants agreed to be interviewed, I suggested they choose a convenient coffee shop or restaurant. Many interviewees graciously invited me to their homes. I followed a thematic script during the first third of each interview, asking the same questions about family histories, educational background, children, and participation in religious institutions, including the Webb Foundation. From there, I asked more open-ended inquiries in order to let my conversation partners discuss what was most important to them. By and large, interviewees shared stories of joy and pain from their experiences as American Muslims. Yet the most illuminating comments often came just after I switched the audio recorder off, especially when I found myself sitting at a kitchen table after a shared meal. I learned to keep my notebook handy to take down key phrases and anecdotes. In addition to formal interviews, I took notes on innumerable informal conversations.

During this first phase of fieldwork, the majority of my interviewees were women. This is not to say that men were intentionally excluded, and indeed many men floated in and out of the conversation as I spoke with their spouses. The interaction among genders at Webb events enabled me to conduct more formal interviews with men and to observe male participants in classes. But female members were—for a variety of reasons that I explain below—more eager to talk and more generous with their time. I also found that convert women were particularly interested in talking to me because they saw the interviews as an opportunity to voice their discontent and feelings of marginalization to a sympathetic ear, perhaps also identifying with me as an "outsider."

In the spring of 2011, I became pregnant with my son, and the effect on my ethnographic relationships was immediately positive. Initially I was nervous about the effect my pregnancy would have, but I soon realized that it would actually be a benefit.[45] Almost overnight, my conversation partners began to view me in a different light. They generously shared stories about their own children, they dispensed advice about parenting, and they ensured that I was more than adequately fed. One-hour interviews turned into three-hour lunches as my interviewees shared experiences with sleep, breastfeeding, and navigating family and medical complications.

Pregnancy was a visible, embodied sign of my shared investment in the nuclear family.[46] I still did not and could not share my conversation partners' experiences of marginalization and partial citizenship. But I became someone who needed care and who could benefit from the wisdom of more experienced parents. In turn, I began to share my hopes and fears, to discuss my choices about childbirth, and to talk about the kinds of issues that come up within extended families and marriages when a child is on the way. Through all of this, I realized vulnerability was a quality that I lacked in my early interactions.[47] My interviews became more relaxed conversations in which a more relational dynamic emerged.

Being an educated wife and mother was beneficial in the eyes of both men and women at Webb, as with many educated American Muslims. Webb women—some of whom are doctors and engineers, in addition to those who are full-time moms with graduate degrees, and those who work part-time—in particular began to see me as a kindred spirit, and they increasingly compared my career to the kinds of trajectories they hope their own children might pursue. Because many of the female Webb participants married during college, they completed their degrees part-time or later in life while their husbands worked. In confessing the difficulties that they endured while trying to finish their education and raise young kids, they implicitly articulated the differences between their experiences and my own. Today, more educated Muslim women are waiting to marry until their mid- to late twenties, a pattern that is consistent with broader US trends. Both men and women, but especially women, are encouraged to become successful professionally and to marry early, expectations that are often in tension with one another.

In 2014, I returned to Chicago for three follow-up research trips at Webb, to attend the annual *mawlid*, the tenth anniversary fundraising dinner, and to conduct new interviews and follow up with participants I had already interviewed. I conducted an additional ten interviews, primarily with men, who had not previously been interviewed and had numerous conversations with established contacts. These interviews were less open-ended than my initial round because I had already written extensively about my 2012 fieldwork. Moreover, Webb had grown as an organization during the two years I was absent, and its members had developed a more consistent vocabulary for describing the organization and its mission. For example, in my early interviews no one called Webb a "third space," whereas by 2014, it had become commonplace, without me ever using or suggesting the term. Furthermore, Webb had become a more established institution, and my interviews reflect its members' conviction that their organization would endure for many years to come.

I use pseudonyms to protect the identities of my interviewees and have excluded details that would reveal them. With some reluctance as an ethnographer, but in the greater interest of historical clarity, I do refer to newspaper articles and other press coverage of Webb that name and quote particular members.

Plan of the Book

The first half of the book focuses on the discursive and ritual construction of American Islam at Webb (chapters 1–4). Chapter 1 provides the history of Webb as a community, setting out its specific religious and cultural location in Chicago, and situating its vision within narratives of American religions and global developments in contemporary Islam. Chapter 2, "Imagining Religion and Culture at Webb," explores Webb members' multifaceted critique of American Muslim institutions as it dovetails with overlapping gendered, racial, and class concerns. Although Webb leaders yearn for an "indigenous" American Islam, in practice they unwittingly reinforce some of the same inequalities they seek to undermine. Chapter 3, "All-American Islam," moves from the critique of ethnic particularism to the content and performance of American culture at Webb. Here, I focus on leisure practices (ski trips, football games, apple-picking) that Webb members deem to be characteristically American. Chapter 4, "Honoring the Prophet, Performing American Islam," expands on the ritualized performance of American Muslim culture by examining the Webb Foundation's premiere public event, its annual *mawlid* honoring the birthday and legacy of the Prophet Muhammad. Webb explicitly seeks to transform the *mawlid* from a ritual primarily performed in American Muslim homes to a large public event. I highlight the ways that third spaces facilitate ritual change and offer the possibility for women to take on ritual roles denied to them elsewhere.

The second half of the book employs an "ethnography of reading" to explore the multiple interlocutors and contexts of Webb debates about sacred texts, authority, and ethics (chapters 5, 6, and 7). Chapter 5, "I Want to Know the Context," marks the transition to the second part of the book, turning our attention to the Webb adult Sunday School programs. In their study of the Qur'an, Webb students creatively employ various exegetical strategies to negotiate what religious pluralism means in practice. Chapter 6, "Islam Is

More than Halal and Haram," demonstrates how Webb debates about *fiqh* (Islamic jurisprudence) challenge anti-sharia initiatives by recasting the debate under the broad rubric of normativity and lived religious practice. Through *fiqh*, parents attempted to work out individual tactics for fulfilling their religious obligations and representing Islam, focused especially on their efforts to instill Islamic ethics in their children. The final ethnographic chapter, chapter 7, "Reading for Kernels of Truth," uses the Webb women's book club to revisit the possibilities and limitations of religious pluralism, female authority, and belonging at Webb. This chapter explores the ways in which participants negotiate and claim feminist identities within the Webb community and beyond.

1

Building the Webb Community

ON A BALMY day in October 2011, I pulled up to a two-story home on a tree-lined street in Darien, Illinois. Malika greeted me at the front door with "*salam alaykum*" and then led me into the cool, dark foyer. Eight months pregnant, I felt and probably looked more than a bit harried. I gratefully accepted a tall glass of water and then sat across from her at the long dining room table. In her early forties, Malika is a lifelong Chicagoan, whose parents emigrated from India in the 1970s. She is a founding board member of the Webb Foundation. Malika beamed with pride as she described the early days of the organization that she and her friends built from the ground up:

> We wanted a virtual space, an atmosphere, an environment. And we did that through programming. We wanted a secular and spiritual event every month. And in our mind the secular event was really a spiritual event in disguise, like taking a hike, going for a bike ride, doing community service. They have a spiritual thread that is not the prominent one, but it connects you back to the spiritual side. We held gatherings of prayer and worship. We all go to our area mosques. We're not disconnected, but we just wanted to create an environment comfortable for our families and not an emphasis on gender separation. The context of the early days in Islam, there was no segregation. It was a small community that embraced each other's strengths and weaknesses. And we thought we needed to do the same.[1]

This chapter explores the residential patterns, immigration trends, familial shifts, and educational networks out of which the Webb community emerged in the early 2000s.

The Webb Foundation represents a vision of American Islam that promotes religious pluralism, celebrates middle-class consumerism, opens up leadership opportunities for women, and reimagines the United States as the ideal location for the practice of an "authentic" Islam. It began as the collective effort of a group of married couples, including Malika and her husband. With the exception of a sole convert, the founding members were second-generation immigrants who had been raised Muslim in American Muslim households. As young parents, this group of friends had grown increasingly dissatisfied with the programming, governance structures, and theologies they encountered at local mosques. In 2004, they formally created Webb "to create a space that was comfortable for our families."[2] The founders named their fledgling organization in honor of Mohammed Alexander Russell Webb, the nineteenth-century white Protestant convert to Islam, who was consul to the Philippines under President Grover Cleveland and later served as the official representative of Islam at the 1893 World's Parliament of Religions at the Columbian Exposition held in Chicago.

Malika and others describe the early Webb Foundation as an informal group of "like-minded" friends at similar life stages who were looking to actively strengthen family relationships in an "atmosphere of community love and respect."[3] In the beginning, they organized trips to go bowling, watch movies, and pick apples. They eventually found other families looking to spend time with their young children in "American" ways who had little opportunity to do so with other Muslims. In my conversations with the founding members, all of them stressed that they never intended their organization to replace mosques. Rather, they wanted to host programs to supplement the activities already offered at the masjid.[4] These early Webb families prayed together and occasionally celebrated *ʿīd*s or religious feasts, though they spent other holidays together, such as New Year's Eve, when they gathered for an overnight lock-in. They started to invite other friends to these gatherings, gradually forming a community of several dozen families. During the first three years, the organization grew entirely by word of mouth, through the informal networks of friendship and sometimes extended families. Couples with school-aged children were particularly drawn to Webb events, especially "blended families"—the Webb term for Muslim spouses who each come from different ethnic, national, or racial backgrounds.

Today, Webb's core membership consists of nuclear families who are committed to upper-middle-class norms of intensive parenting, such as supervising homework, shuttling kids between after-school activities, and maintaining an active presence in their social lives. The American Islam they seek to create fits into these constructions of family life, enabling children and adults alike to become American Muslims in ways they believe earlier generations were either unable or unwilling to be. As a result, the Webb community describes itself as a "vanguard" in this commitment to taking up what American culture means and investing it with Muslim significance.

Although Webb is still an emergent community, its efforts have already garnered national media attention and its members have broader influence in key Muslim organizations. In a 2005 article entitled "For U.S. Muslims, It's the American Way," *New York Times* reporter Katrin Bennhold featured one of Webb's founding couples, Humaira Bassith and Edmund Arroyo, alongside two other prominent Chicago Muslims, Eboo Patel, founder and president of Interfaith Youth Corps, and Ahmed Rehab, director of the Chicago office of the Council on American-Islamic Relations. Webb members also regularly appear on the program at the annual conference for the Islamic Society of North America, the largest national organization serving American Muslims. Webb members have spoke on various panels on topics such as Muslim marriages, third spaces, and domestic violence.

Through its connections with prominent American Muslim scholars and intellectuals, Webb members also participate in wider national and transnational networks of Muslim learning, maintaining personal ties with popular, influential American Muslim figures such as Dr. Sherman Jackson, Usama Canon, and Dr. Abd-Allah, all of whom have been featured at Webb events. Through these connections, the organization's leadership marshals the support and participation of many Chicago Muslims who do not count themselves among its regular members. In this way, Webb members maintain wider relationships through online forums, retreats, various forms of writing, formal classes, as well as podcasts. Webb activities range tremendously in attendance, from its smallest groups, such as the book club, to the *mawlid*, which attracts large crowds. For example, when Abd-Allah appears at a Webb event, attendance reaches upwards of three hundred participants. Although many of these attendees do not count themselves as "Webbies," the organization and its mission are both authorized by Abd-Allah's presence and are introduced to a broader audience than at its weekly events. As a result, Webb's reach extends well beyond its core membership to a wide group of Chicago Muslims.

Chicago Islam

Third spaces like the Webb community have helped to make Chicago a key institutional center for US Muslims. Ethnographer Jamillah Karim calls

Chicago the "capital of the American *umma*."[5] With their dizzying array of theological, ritual, and cultural orientations, the city's Muslim communities exemplify the rich diversity of American Islam. Sometimes called "Chicago *Sharif*" ("Noble Chicago"), the city and its suburbs are home to about four hundred thousand Muslims, at least one hundred mosques, and more than one hundred other educational, social, political, and legal institutions with an Islamic mission.[6] These many sites are both grounded in their local neighborhoods and connected by social and religious networks that reach across the city and its suburbs.[7]

Conceptually, Karim envisions Chicago on the north-south axis, tracing the religious and social connections (and exclusions) among Muslims from the African American communities on the south side stretching to the northern communities of Devon Avenue, where many recent working-class South Asian immigrants reside, and to the near north suburb of Morton Grove, a community largely comprised of multiple generations of middle- and upper-middle-class immigrants.[8] Driving along Lake Shore Drive is one way to map out Chicago's Muslim communities, but at least as important, if not more so, is the journey west from the denser urban grid to the sprawling "edge cities" located twenty or more miles outside of city limits.

The Webb community is based in a handful of these "ex-burbs," more than thirty miles from downtown Chicago. Many of Chicago's most prominent Muslim institutions, including many of the large mosques in the metro area, are likewise found in these neighborhoods. These communities are not linked together by sidewalks or the grid of city streets, but rather through a vast network of highways and subdivisions. To my surprise, however, most studies of Islam in the United States—including prior case studies of Chicago—have focused on the city proper.[9] One of this book's main contributions is its attentiveness to the suburbs as a key site for the practice of Islam in the United States.[10]

Formerly small towns surrounded by farms, these far suburbs are now thriving centers of commercial activity, known as the Illinois Technology and Research Corridor, which includes portions of DuPage, Kane, DeKalb, and Cook counties. The Ronald Reagan Highway, the main east-west interstate that traverses the corridor, is dotted by malls, office buildings, and parking structures. Drawn by lower corporate tax rates and construction incentives for office spaces, multinational companies such as McDonald's and Sara Lee established their headquarters here rather than within the city limits. The "village" of Schaumburg alone has a population of 75,000 residents and more than thirty million square feet of office, commercial, and industrial spaces.[11] Contrary to popular images of suburbs as residential enclaves, the communities that comprise the Technology Corridor have rapidly transformed into corporate campuses that visually and numerically dwarf its residential neighborhoods.

During my first drive from Evanston to DuPage County, I was baffled and dejected by the sight of stretches of highway packed with jammed lines of cars. I quickly came to realize that my trips were actually journeys from one type of urban environment to another, one that required me to budget at least two hours to travel just thirty miles. While some residents of these ex-burbs do commute daily to Chicago, most people I spoke with during my fieldwork both lived and worked in the suburbs. Like many of metro Chicago's ten million residents, Webb members occasionally drive to the city for a special dinner or to attend a sporting event. But they seldom travel to the city for more mundane purposes because the ex-burbs have no shortage of excellent schools, vibrant places of worship, retail stores, and entertainment options.[12]

Chicagoland is a microcosm for the astonishing variety of practices among Muslim communities in the United States, including immigrants from eighty different countries spanning South Asia, the Middle East, southeastern Europe, and sub-Saharan Africa, as well as white and Latinx converts, and Black Americans.[13] Yet ethnic and racial markers fail to adequately account for the wide range of theological perspectives and ritual perspectives that are also represented in the Chicago community. During my fieldwork, Chicago was brimming with possibilities, as new Muslim communities and initiatives popped up catering to all kinds of religious, social, and political needs.

Such diversity is predicated on enduring racial and economic inequalities.[14] These racial, economic, and geographic divisions can be traced to migration and immigration patterns in to the early twentieth century. Movements such as the Moorish Science Temple, the Nation of Islam, the Ahmadiyya, and other smaller groups grew their memberships and thrived among African Americans who arrived during the Great Migration, building up what Judith Weisenfeld has termed a "religio-racial identity."[15] Since the 1960s, the Nation of Islam has built and maintained vibrant Muslim communities on the south side of the city. Today, Louis Farrakhan continues to lead Mosque Maryam (formerly the Nation of Islam's "Temple No. 2") on South Stony Island Drive. Until his death in 2008, most black Sunnis in Chicago followed W. D. Mohammed as their religious leader. W. D. Mohammed, the son of Elijah Muhammad, transformed the Nation of Islam into a largely Sunni-based community, which nevertheless has maintained the Nation's emphasis on economic success and racial uplift. Moreover, African Sufi movements, especially the Tijaniyya, also have a large presence in Chicagoland. The Ahmadiyya, still active in Chicago, historically bridged what scholars now understand as the artificial divide between immigrant and black Muslims.[16] As the next chapter explores, Webb participants have complicated relationships to these institutions and movements, shaped by overlapping ideologies of authenticity, race, authority, and competing narratives of the American Muslim past.

In terms of residence, Chicago remains a city segregated by race and socioeconomic status, with poorer communities located west and south of the Loop. Many of the more recent immigrants from India and Pakistan, who are less economically secure than the post-1965 generation, live in the cluster of streets around Devon Avenue that constitutes a vibrant immigrant cultural hub.[17] The Bridgeview neighborhood, located on the city's southwest side, continues to serve Arab immigrants, whose presence in Chicago dates to the early twentieth century.

In contrast to communities located within the city or in the inner suburbs, Muslim institutions in the white-majority ex-burbs serve predominantly, though not exclusively, practitioners of South Asian and Arab descent, as well as converts of varying religious and racial backgrounds.[18] Many immigrants who arrived following the 1965 Hart-Celler Act were professionals or graduate students with some financial resources. Some of these families bypassed the city altogether, departing from earlier patterns of immigration over the last century. Unlike earlier generations, many nuclear and extended families arrived together. While some Arab immigrants settled in older neighborhoods, such as Bridgeview, with its thriving religious and social institutions, many chose to live in the far western suburbs of Downers Grove, Darien, Naperville, and Burr Ridge. Several Webb members were born and raised in these Chicago suburbs, their parents having been doctors, engineers, and other professionals who purposefully sought out these white-majority neighborhoods because of their good schools and low crime rates. Other Muslims already living in Chicago during the 1960s and 1970s likewise flocked to the western suburbs, joining the exodus of many of the city's wealthier residents.

During the childhoods of many Webb participants, the Muslim community was small and scattered, spread out over the diffuse landscape of these outer suburbs. Malika, for example, described the substantive efforts that her parents took to ensure she had a sense of Islamic identity even while living in largely white, Christian, Midwestern suburbia:

> In the summer of sixth grade, we commuted to camp at the Islamic Foundation [a large mosque in Villa Park], and we had to rent eight- or ten-seater vans. The drivers were the younger brothers of the organizers, and they would have these crazy routes, picking up kids anywhere who wanted to go. Our bus would arrive at 5 a.m. and we would go

> from Downers Grove to Dundee and then to Orland Park. I would be in the van for three hours at a time. It was the best time. The driver was really funny, and we would get him to stop for ice cream. It was very loving and very intimate.[19]

As a child, Malika experienced this intimacy and isolation simultaneously. She formed close bonds with her fellow van-mates, while implicitly recognizing the geographic and class differences that separated her from other Muslims.[20] Driving to individual homes made her realize that as a Muslim, she was part of a dispersed yet personally connected minority religious community.

These memories of long van rides demonstrate the great lengths to which many Muslim parents went in order to provide a religious education for their children in the 1960s, 1970s, and 1980s. In contrast to more established neighborhoods like Bridgeview, families in these western suburbs held Friday prayers and Sunday school in their homes because traveling to mosques was costly and time-prohibitive. It took many years for families to raise enough funds and build a large enough community to start their local mosques. The Islamic Foundation was not founded until 1974. Today, the mosque has thousands of members and includes a pre-K–grade 12 school with over 650 students.[21] But in these early years, it counted its membership by the capacity of its van.

In its attempt to build communities out of disparate families, the Webb Foundation is part of an ongoing suburban Muslim effort to create lasting and meaningful communities that overcome physical distances, racial and economic divisions, and a dearth of educational institutions deemed suitable for raising the next generation of American Muslims. Malika wants every single Webb member to feel that their presence is vital to the future of their community.

Like Malika, many Webb members have actively participated in Chicago masjids.[22] Many of their parents helped to start suburban mosques, and many grew up attending their Sunday School classes and social events as children and young adults. As Webb members entered adulthood, however, they experienced disillusionment with their childhood mosques, even as they have continued to volunteer in planning their mosques' educational and youth activities, delivering occasional sermons, and even serving on their mosques' boards of directors. Indeed, many Webb members want to maintain and grow their local mosques, while simultaneously creating an alternative community.

Webb's ongoing engagement with mosques reinforces their status as the most visible American Muslim religious institution and a key site for the enactment of American Islam. Webb partially defines its community in relation to the institutional structures, theological orientations, and ethnic particularism of local mosques, constructing itself as an alternative to the ways that Islam is practiced in those spaces while maintaining that mosques have a vital place in the future of American Islam. Because Webb members are so thoroughly invested in mosques, few imagine that groups like Webb would even replace them altogether, even though for most, Webb's family programming has supplanted mosques as the locus of their social life.

US mosques offer a vital space for the communal performance of salat (ritual prayer), but they also serve as social and educational centers. The term "masjid" derives from the same root as the Arabic term for prostration, "*sajada*." While ritual prayer, obligatory during five daily intervals, is often conducted in homes and workplaces, Sunni Muslim scholars generally consider prayers performed by men in mosques to be more beneficial.[23] Globally, Muslims gather on Fridays for congregational prayers and to hear a *khutbah* (sermon). Historically, some mosques have also served as centers of higher Muslim learning, when they were formally connected to madrasas in which Islamic scholars trained male students in the knowledge and methodologies of the Islamic sciences. In addition to communal prayer, US mosques provide religious education to children and adults, organize holiday celebrations, administer weddings and funerals, offer premarital and divorce counseling, and host recreational activities. In Chicago, some campuses of larger mosques also include elementary and secondary schools, cemeteries, and residences for their imams.

In contrast to smaller Muslim communities in other Midwestern cities, Chicago's suburban Muslims who immigrated after 1965 possessed both the numbers and the financial resources to establish institutions that reflect the cultural norms of particular countries of origin. As such, Webb participants refer to mosques according to those nations or regions of origin: Syrian, Hyderabadi, Egyptian, Bosnian, among others. The actual demographics of west suburban mosques are actually more diverse than these categories suggest, because mosques typically serve diverse constituents from a variety of backgrounds. Regardless of their official demographics, these mosques are perceived as representing a particular ethnic orientation. For Webb members, such an ethnic orientation potentially excludes Muslims who do not claim that identity.

Marital Patterns and the Origins of the Webb Community

Beyond the post-1965 immigration trends I discussed earlier, the shape of Webb should be traced back to wider demographic shifts and particularly marital patterns.[24] The majority of Webb households are made up of spouses who identify as being from different ethnic, racial, or cultural backgrounds. This reflects a generational shift, as increasing numbers of young American Muslims are marrying outside of kin- or geographically based networks of their parents and grandparents. My interviewees frequently declared that it was far more important to marry a practicing American Muslim than it was to marry within one's ethnic or national group. They use "practicing" to mean a person who prays regularly, observes other daily norms, such as dietary restrictions, and who participates in some aspect of Muslim institutional life. Additionally, I heard how important it is for spouses to be culturally American, which Webb members understand broadly in terms of speaking idiomatic English, being educated primarily in North America, participating in American arts, music, and sports, and sharing a commitment to raising children to be "comfortable" as Americans.

Placing a priority on religiosity and American cultural fluency represents a break with past spouse selection processes. Marriage to non-Muslim women was common among many of the earliest, primarily male immigrants to the United States, including enslaved Africans and early twentieth-century Arab, Turkish, and Bosnian immigrants. In the second half of the twentieth century, immigrants tended to marry spouses from their own national or ethnic groups, often bringing wives or husbands to the United States from particular geographic locales where their extended families maintained close ties. This practice remains in place for a smaller set of Webb families I met during my field research. Those who fall into this category often claim to be the "last" ones whose marriages were arranged between extended family members. Although they described being hesitant about marrying a distant cousin or friend of the family, now many of them express gratitude not to have experienced "cultural" clashes with their spouse's parents, like many of their peers at Webb, and they affirm their marriages as loving partnerships.

Among many second- and third-generation immigrants at Webb, however, faith has become a more important factor than familial ties in choosing one's spouse, even though extended families and especially parents remain closely involved in finding a partner. Many Webb couples told me that they were among the first in their extended families to marry outside of their family's broader kin networks. Webb spouses stress the importance of a shared Islamic practice rather than common country of origin.[25] This resonates with wider marriage shifts in the American Muslim community, particularly an emphasis on shared Muslim identification. At the 2009 ISNA conference, to take one example, several marriage panels featured speakers exhorting the audience not to travel abroad to find a spouse, but rather to seek a devout American Muslim. Many of these speakers, asserting their skills as matchmakers, gave advice to their audience for seeking parental approval for these unions, retaining the idea that marriage was between two families, not simply two individuals.

Foreshadowing these spouses' future generational conflicts within their mosques, Webb marriages involved negotiations among families with different marital practices, including questions of guardianship, dowries, living arrangements, and childrearing. Marriages between second- and third-generation immigrants and white or Latinx converts or Black Muslims also raised a host of divergent conflicts over racial hierarchies within Muslim communities and the authenticity of one's extrareligious "culture." Many couples described the lengths they took to seek parental approval and their ongoing efforts to attain acceptance of their spouses within their extended families, both in the United States and abroad. Some Webb spouses also relayed how, upon getting married, they learned that their common Islamic faith was not so easily shared when it came to different traditions of ritual practice.

Webb participants express ambivalence toward the replication of South Asian and Arab practices in mosques and the representation of these practices as normative because they no longer resonate in their most intimate relationships. But without an alternative community, this ambivalence has left many of them without a religious community, feeling isolated and adrift. Couples from differing backgrounds struggle to reconcile their respective "cultural" heritages with what they believe to be the universal aspects of Islam.[26] Within their families, then, husbands and wives often confront differences in religious practice and belief that they must work out on a daily basis. In a public forum on marriage, Malika explained how she had to "become a convert, too" and "re-learn" Islam when she got married.[27] That is, the parsing of religion from culture took on particular urgency, as a way to resolve marital differences in religious practice.

Moreover, many families joined Webb because they no longer believed that their children benefitted from being educated in mosques. For them, extended family networks, not the mosque, are the proper place to preserve and pass on ethnic traditions. Frank, a white convert married to Marwa, who is of Indian descent, put it this way:

> This is not a critique, but when they [immigrants] would come, they experienced a ton of culture shock, an assault from every angle. The masjid can be a retreat. I'm safe here, because my interactions will be somewhat the same as they are back home. And I can focus on my spiritual development. So that's extremely important for them. When

> we started having kids, that's not going to facilitate them growing up in a healthy environment because the mosque isn't going to give them what they need to succeed here.[28]

Frank and Marwa maintain connections to their children's Indian heritage through her family, speaking warmly about extended familial relationships, the emphasis on community over individual desires, and the value of hospitality. But the mosque—with its blurring of the boundaries between "Islam" and "culture"—does not, in their view, properly serve as the site of "healthy" and "successful" raising of American Muslim children.

In their efforts to provide a welcoming environment for these families, Webb leaders seek to embody the ideal of an American *ummah* as a universal community that transcends internal affiliations and differences.[29] And yet mosques continue to function as the touchstone for Webb debates about a wide variety of issues, from Muslim authority, generational difference, assimilation, gender, and civic responsibilities. As an alternative, many of these couples have come to believe that Islam must be properly paired with American culture (as they define it) in order for their children to grow up as lifelong practicing Muslims.

Making American Muslim Spaces in the Western Suburbs

The Webb Foundation is a community without a designated building, making use of multiple locations to host its events and classes. The fact that the organization has no permanent building is both an advantage and a challenge. The portability of Muslim practice helps to facilitate this use of multiple spaces. Prayer, for example, can be performed anywhere.[30] Early on, different families hosted events in their homes. The first classes I attended in the spring of 2011 were located in a small community center, which the foundation had visibly outgrown. In the fall of 2011, Webb rented conference rooms at a local Marriott hotel. And by the spring of 2012, the organization had relocated again to a large public high school.[31] Each week, Webb makes these spaces into Muslim ones, through prayer, study of the Qur'an and other texts, lectures, discussions, and recreational activities.[32] Crucially, none of the spaces that Webb has occupied are overtly religious.

Rather, these buildings blend inconspicuously into the corporate landscape of Chicago's western suburbs. The Marriott conference hotel is a case in point. On Sunday mornings, the Webb community mingled with business travelers arriving for the work week, wedding revelers recovering from the previous night's celebrations, and Christian prayer meetings. This confluence of corporatism, leisure, and religion is a microcosm of twenty-first-century suburban America. Webb moved once again after the hotel closed due to the financial difficulties at the end of 2011, citing a lack of business during the recession.[33] High-school classrooms, community centers, museums, nature preserves, the homes of participants—these many sites have been transformed into gathering places for the Webb community. Participants actively claim these spaces for American Islam.

This constant mobility illustrates the extent to which Webb members have created what I call a third-space alternative to their mosques and homes. Early in my fieldwork, participants celebrated their community's ritual and spatial flexibility, which allowed them to host a variety of programming on an adjustable schedule. Webb plans a variety of programs that change in structure and content somewhat frequently. Members also talked about their ability to participate in controversial and critical discussions.[34] Indeed, the dynamism and fluidity of Webb spaces mirror the free-ranging and less conventional discussions that often take place at the community's events, which, as participants often told me, are rare in other community settings.

As long as Webb did not occupy its own building, I was told, it would remain unencumbered by the constraints and potential routinization that such permanence would potentially produce. Webb even changes its ritual performances on a frequent basis. Such ritual experimentation, as I explain in chapter 4, is particularly evident in the *mawlid*, which in some years hosts hundreds of people, but in other years is a more intimate event. Webb thus moves among different venues not only to accommodate the needs of its core members and to reach a broader network of Chicago Muslims, but also to enhance its critique of mosques and augment its appeal as an alternative.

Even so, as Webb has grown over the past decade, the board, staff, and participants have debated the value of creating a permanent, fixed space for the foundation's regular classes and programming. Visitors and students alike have consistently asked why Webb does not already have a "real" building. Likewise, moving locations each academic year is a monumental logistical task for the volunteers who largely coordinate the day-to-day operations at Webb. Other practical concerns, such as maintaining nonprofit status and financial considerations, have also been cited as reasons to obtain a permanent property to serve as Webb's base of operations.

Ideally, board members envision a physical space that showcases the positive attributes of Islam, but which also evinces the organization's core belief that religious communities necessarily should be visible and welcoming to non-Muslim Americans. Malika articulated this in terms of her desire for

Webb to be a multifaceted community addressing a diverse set of religious and social concerns:

> The space is not the essential thing. It's the community that goes into the space. We've had this idea in the back our minds. It goes back to the 9/11 backlash; we are comfortable with who we are and the greatness of what we believe as a world faith. We said that we needed to put a center or masjid in the mainstream, to just have Mecca on Main Street. We need a reading room. It doesn't have to be big, pretty idealistic. We want a space anyone can walk into, and see what goes on, and that Islam is not scary. Instead of cramming into Sunday, we'd like to have a space where we can do things throughout the week.[35]

Although mosques in the western suburbs are large, visible structures, on several accounts they fall short of Malika's vision for what it means to be Muslim on "Main Street."[36] Suburban mosques occupy large facilities with multiple halls and rooms for prayer, social events, meetings, and recreation. But they lack the "essential thing" for Malika—community. For Malika and others at Webb, relationships must come first and often exist, as their community does, in the absence of a designated building that they exclusively inhabit.

Her vision has also been shaped by her sense of obligation to engage and educate her neighbors about Islam. In the aftermath of 9/11, curiosity about Islam increased tremendously, and Webb board members felt an intense need to inform the public about their faith and to correct misunderstandings. Webb members see themselves as taking on the urgent task of representing the "greatness" of Islam as a "world faith" to their neighbors. In the early days of Webb, its leaders imagined that suburban Americans might want to learn about Islam as they went about running their daily errands at the local strip mall. Rather than being confined to Sunday, the day marked for religious observance, Malika sees the task of religious and civic engagement as requiring continuous effort. She speculated that they might find it intimidating to enter a stand-alone mosque or a building obviously marked as Muslim in search of answers. Here, the storefront reading room facilitates new relationships and the potential for a new community of Muslim and non-Muslim Americans alike.

Moreover, the concept is consonant with secular imaginings of "good" religion as part and parcel of American recreation and consumerism, as well as committed to tolerant coexistence with other faiths.[37] Webb members thus imagine an ideal convergence of Islam with religious pluralism, reasoned debate, and textual engagement. For Malika, she will know when Muslims have succeeded in putting "Mecca on Main Street" when such a convergence occurs. She also hopes that one day, the Webb community will serve just such a purpose.

Barriers to Building Suburban Muslim Communities

Webb members are particularly reflective about community and space because of the roadblocks they have encountered in Chicago's western suburbs. It is difficult for suburban Muslims to build new Islamic institutions. Political and social hostility toward Muslims and other immigrants has manifested itself through suburban communities' opposition to masjid construction, documented in numerous case studies since the 1980s.[38] Various neighborhoods have opposed the building of mosques, citing traffic and zoning concerns. Suburban communities have historically contested the building of churches and synagogues along similar lines.[39] However, the resistance against mosques has been particularly sustained and systemic since 9/11.[40] The board of DuPage County has been especially opposed to new mosque buildings and nearly every mosque construction proposal has prompted objections from local communities. For example, the construction of a Muslim Educational and Cultural Center (MECCA) building in Willowbrook in 2010 led to several zoning and permit disputes with residents and county board members. A combination of a lack of planning and mixed zoning practices contributed to this protracted struggle. Concerns over traffic and parking delayed construction for more than two years. When the construction project was finally approved, a new fight began over the height of the minaret and dome.[41]

Contestations over Muslim spaces took place concurrently on a national stage. The most notable episode was the vitriolic language in public debates over the building of Park 51 in lower Manhattan, now infamously known as the "Ground Zero Mosque." Much like the Webb board members, the project leader, Faisul Abdul Rauf, is a proponent of Muslim civic engagement, interfaith initiatives, service, and "moderate Islam."[42] Much to the Webb board and Imam Feisel's chagrin, their theological and political perspectives did little to diminish public officials' and right-wing media's singular focus on Islam as an existential threat to American security.[43]

In other overt and thinly disguised forms, too, violence and discrimination against Muslim communities occurs with some regularity in DuPage County. Following the mass killing of Sikhs in a Milwaukee suburb in August 2012, the mosque in Lombard was vandalized. Local politicians contributed to a culture of fear surrounding "terrorism" and "radicalism" in the suburbs, drawing on conspiracy-laden narratives of undetected corruption of American values and institutions. Then Congressman Joe Walsh, from the nearby 8th congressional district, declared at a town hall meeting, "There is a radical strain of Islam in this country. . . . It's here. It's in Elk Grove, it's in Addison, it's in Elgin. . . . Islam is not the peaceful, loving religion we hear about."[44] In its insinuation of a hidden radical Muslim presence in America's suburbs, Walsh's rhetoric echoed broader public discourses about "creeping sharia" as an encroaching danger to America's legal institutions and way of life.[45] Walsh's comments implicitly upheld the suburbs as the center of American values and morality. If radical Islam penetrated the suburbs, his logic suggested, then it was indeed everywhere, making it all the more menacing because it had infiltrated white, Christian America.

The Webb community has itself come up against this suspicion of Muslims and Islam, which have limited Webb's efforts to occupy its own building. Initially, the community explored the possibility of renting a storefront in a local strip mall. One board member recalled that a town official told him that Webb would be more likely to secure a lease if they disguised the organization's Muslim affiliation by removing "Mohammed" from their application.[46] But doing so would undermine Webb's broader mission—the public recognition of Islam as a peaceful, pluralistic American religion.

Post-9/11 Networks of Learning and Scholarship

In the aftermath of 9/11, many young, educated, middle-class, second-generation immigrants and converts came to believe that their extant communities and religious authorities were ill-equipped for the urgent tasks that they discerned: remaking the image of Islam, re-engaging traditional Islamic learning, and building a more civically engaged and culturally resonant American Muslim community. The early 2000s produced a range new institutions in the greater Chicago area, of which the Webb community is but one. These fledgling communities often emerged from overlapping networks, even as they built new connections among previously disconnected communities.[47]

These networks augmented the authority of particular scholars and intellectuals to whom members of these networks turned for moral leadership, scholarly expertise, and guidance for building a more robust American Islam. One such scholar is Dr. Umar Faruq Abd-Allah (b. 1942), whose popularity and prominence has grown significantly among young professional Chicago

Muslims. Frequently mentioned in casual conversation, prayer, and classroom contexts, many Webb members refer to Abd-Allah as their "shaykh" or "teacher." Dr. Umar, as his students call him, is a Kansas-born Protestant convert.[48] In the late 1960s, he became a Muslim while enrolled as a doctoral student in comparative literature at Cornell University. After his conversion, Abd-Allah left Cornell to pursue a doctorate in Islamic Studies from the University of Chicago Divinity School, where he completed a dissertation on the formation of the Maliki *madhhab* under the direction of Fazlur Rahman, the Pakistani-American scholar whose work on the Qur'an I explore in chapter 5. During the 1980s and early 1990s, Abd-Allah taught Islamic Studies at a variety of institutions, including Windsor University in Canada, Temple University, and the University of Michigan. In 1994, he joined the faculty at King Abdul Aziz University in Jeddah, Saudi Arabia.[49]

Abd-Allah returned to the United States in 2000 to serve as scholar-in-residence and chairman of the Nawawi Foundation, an educational organization designed to "provide relevant, meaningful Islamic teachings to America's growing first- and second-generation Muslims—teachings firmly rooted in authentic scholarship and taught in a way that is dynamic and applicable to the modern world."[50] Nawawi hosted lectures and conferences, held classes given by Abd-Allah, sponsored small groups of *rihlas* (educational trips) to destinations such as Turkey, China, Russia, and Egypt, and published various papers authored by Abd-Allah on American Muslim history, Islamic law, and theology. He left Nawawi around 2011, and with his departure, the organization became defunct. Despite its short history, many of my interviewees say that Nawawi provided Dr. Umar a platform through which to "save" the Muslim community after 9/11, by infusing them with the confidence to remake American Islam. During the early 2000s, Abd-Allah was also involved with an educational initiative known as the Deen Intensive Program, which hosted weekend conferences featuring speakers similarly invested in reviving classical scholarship and which shared a common audience with Nawawi.[51] Over the past fifteen years, Abd-Allah has built a national and international reputation and regularly appears with Sherman Jackson, Hamza Yusuf, Zaid Shakir, and other intellectuals seen as authorities in both classical Islam and American culture. His growing popularity speaks to the diffuse nature of American Muslim authority, in which students and teachers forge relationships through a variety of institutional locations and contexts, including books, pamphlets, podcasts, websites, films, and social media.

Webb was officially founded four years after Nawawi, and the two communities drew on similar networks of young professional Chicago Muslims. About half of Webb's members also attended Nawawi events as their organization got started informally. Webb participants recalled Nawawi as the first context in which they studied Islam "academically." Abd-Allah's lectures relayed aspects of Muslim history that they had never heard before.[52] As one former student said, "This was not an immigrant approach. It was like studying Shakespeare with the Prophet."[53] This perspective on Muslim history was "exactly what we needed," one board member told me.[54] For example, in his class "Women in Islam," Abd-Allah taught that in the early days of Islam, gender integration and equality were the norm. The first Muslim men and women worked side by side to spread their new faith. Malika recalled how learning that women were visible, public figures in the early Muslim community inspired her to take on additional leadership responsibilities and ritual roles through Webb. As she put it, "Most of what I knew came from my parents' culture. But I really didn't know much about Islam at all until I started attending his classes."[55] For her, Abd-Allah's lectures and writings provided a corrective to "cultural" understandings of Islam by combining authentic Islamic knowledge, historical narratives rooted in academic scholarship, and deep familiarity with American culture. Crucially, Abd-Allah also taught them that prior to modernity, generations of Muslims across the globe embraced local cultures as their own. Conscious that Webb might be seen as something new or experimental, Malika frequently invoked Abd-Allah's dual authority as a Muslim scholar and university professor to claim that Webb was instead recovering the authentic and historically documented practices of the first generations of Muslims. Many Webb members have retained their close relationships with Abd-Allah as he continues to teach at other educational institutions in the Chicago area, including Darul Qasim, another west suburban organization that offers an array of educational and religious programs catering primarily to the South Asian, Deobandi-oriented community, as well as the Ta'leef Collective, which offers religious instruction and support for converts on the north side of the city.

Several future "Webbies" became friends in Nawawi courses, some even meeting their future spouses. When they attended Abd-Allah's classes, Webb founders interacted with other Chicago Muslims who shared a similar religious and cultural outlook and gradually began to believe that it was their responsibility to create a new kind of American Muslim community that embraced American culture.

In the early 2000s, Nawawi's programming and attendance dwarfed that of Webb. But by 2008, the Webb community had grown in leaps and bounds, enrolling kids from across the western suburbs in its Sunday School and bringing entire families together for its recreational activities, rituals, and community service programs. They took to heart Abd-Allah's message that

American Muslims ought to engage in deliberate efforts to build an authentic American Islam.[56] During a time in which many of Chicago's Muslims wanted to take ownership over the direction of their community, Webb provided just such an opening.

Foundational Narratives of American Islam

Although Abd-Allah has no formal connection with the Webb Foundation, he was instrumental in shaping the community's namesake. In the early 2000s, several Webb members helped Abd-Allah in his research and writing of *A Muslim in Victorian America: The Life of Alexander Russell Webb*, published with Oxford University Press in 2006. Many of them helped Abd-Allah to gather materials on research trips, draw maps, and compile the index.[57] The book documents M. A. R. Webb's own complicated journey to Islam and the ways in which Victorian conceptions of progress, race, and science shaped his construction of Islam as a rational, universal faith.[58] In the book's conclusion, Abd-Allah offers M. A. R. Webb up as an exemplary figure for American Islam:

> For [Mohammad] Webb, Islam was not a psychological or cultural impediment, despite the hurdles he and his family confronted because of their espousal of it. Islam did not threaten his self-image as an American but affirmed it, creating a self-confident and optimistic religious vision. Webb refused to surrender his common sense or his own judgment to the authority of others who had no understanding of him or his people. Webb's circles, open to converts and sympathizers, men and women alike, were, in principle, predicated on the same ideal that no one in or outside of Islam should be required to believe what he could not rationally accept. . . . Webb's conversion to Islam did not put him in a bind with himself and his American identity, causing him to forsake his heritage and commit cultural apostasy. On the contrary, Webb found in Islam the very fulfillment of the American ideals he believed in.[59]

Rather than seeing Islam and American culture as mutually exclusive, Abd-Allah argues that M. A. R. Webb embraced them as complementary. He did so despite the constraints and pressures he faced in the nineteenth-century United States, which represented Islam as a foreign "other" to Christianity. Abd-Allah likens these pressures to those facing contemporary American Muslims today.

Webb members found encouragement in Abd-Allah's descriptions of M. A. R. Webb's inclusive vision for American Islam. In Abd-Allah's telling, M. A. R. Webb remained thoroughly Victorian in outlook even as he became an enthusiastic practitioner and proponent of the Muslim faith. Through his study circles and parlor talks, Abd-Allah argues, the "Yankee Mohammadan" created an atmosphere in which no one "should be required to believe what he could not rationally accept." By upholding M. A. R. Webb as a model, Abd-Allah implores American Muslims to build institutions and communities in which "reason" is the basis of religious debate among educated peers. "Reason" here is a fundamental value, fundamental to both American culture and Islam. It was not just that M. A .R. Webb merged his Muslim and American identities, but that he discovered in Islam all of the admirable values of American culture: equality, social justice, tolerance, rationalism, and civic participation. Inspired by M. A. R. Webb's optimism, second-generation and convert participants alike look to combine the "best" of American culture—as they variously define it—with their conceptions of "authentic" Islam.[60] Webb participants have taken on Abd-Allah's charge to claim their authority to serve as arbiters of culture and to contest the authority of Muslim leaders who would have it otherwise.

The board members consciously chose the name "M. A. R. Webb" over other alternatives. This choice was predicated on their awareness of how their religious, political, and social lives have been shaped by a suburban community that is demographically diverse but that has maintained a predominantly Protestant Christian, white, and politically conservative identity. As Malika recalled, "We kept coming back to Alexander Russell Webb, because the reality is we live in a very Caucasian area, a very Republican area. Maybe in the city it would be Malcolm X, but it made sense to refer to this man, a Caucasian, one of the first American Muslims." This choice reflects the local demands and concerns undergirding the Webb project. Malika acknowledged how Malcolm X might serve as an inspiration for American Muslims occupying different cultural, racial, and geographic locations. Moreover, from the start, Webb has sought to make Islam intelligible and recognizable to non-Muslim Americans, by subverting some racialized expectations and norms while reinforcing others. Whatever contributions she recognized that Malcolm X had made to American Islam, Malika also implicitly acknowledged that his politics and affiliation with the Nation of Islam would be unsettling, rather than comforting, to her neighbors.

However, Webb's complicated personal itinerary, idiosyncratic religious proclivities, and Victorian racial ideologies make him a somewhat perplexing figure to serve as a paragon for an organization seeking to appeal to people across racial and ethnic divisions. Born in 1846 in Hudson, New York to a

Presbyterian family, M. A. R. Webb later rejected Protestant Christianity in search of a "more rational and universal faith." He moved to Chicago in 1869 to open a jewelry store, but the Great Fire of 1871 later destroyed the business. Webb's wife, Laura Conger, died in the fire.[61]

Webb relocated to Unionville, Missouri in 1874, where he launched a successful career in journalism and became active in Democratic Party politics. During this period, Webb also began to experiment with his religious identity. In the 1870s, Webb turned to materialism and science, denouncing religion as false, irrational, and superstitious. In 1881, Webb began to experiment with "Eastern" religions by attending theosophist circles, which were increasingly fashionable at the time in greater St. Louis.[62] Through these communities, he explored "Oriental" philosophies and religions by reading hundreds of books. Like other theosophists, Webb was drawn to what he understood as Buddhism's esoteric claims of universal spirituality, and he actively sought to meld Buddhism with philosophical ideals consonant with Victorian notions of individualism, science, and progress. Webb began to find similar attributes in Islam, which he saw as another "Eastern" religion with special access to eternal wisdom, truth, and reason. Webb's interest in Islam grew through his 1886–1887 correspondences with Mirza Ghulam Ahmed, the Indian scholar and founder of the Ahmadiyya. Later, many Muslims rejected Ahmed's claims to be a renewer, messiah, and prophet of God. It is not entirely clear why M. A. R. Webb initially reached out to him, but Ahmed wrote hundreds of letters to European and American intellectuals. These exchanges with Ahmed were likely instrumental in Webb's eventual turn from theosophy to Islam and underscore the broader success of the Ahmadiyya in converting Americans to Islam.[63]

M. A. R. Webb officially converted to Islam sometime around 1888 in Manila, Philippines, where he had been appointed US consul. In 1892, he felt called to convert other Americans to Islam and traveled to India hoping to find and secure financial supporters for his missionary efforts. While in India, Webb observed religious practices that confounded his idealized, philosophical, and theosophical imaginings of Islam. He moved to New York City the following year to start his mission, the first of its kind and a project that would occupy Webb until his death in 1916. To attract others to Islam, he set up formal discussions and reading rooms dedicated to the study of Islam, and he published numerous pamphlets and newsletters, including *The Moslem World* and *The Voice of Islam*.[64] These publications detailed Islam's exceptional status as a faith transcending race and class, as well as truest expression of universal and rational religion. By all accounts, Webb's missionary efforts failed to attract even a small number of converts.[65]

In 1893, the organizers of the World's Parliament of Religions chose M. A. R. Webb to serve as the representative of Islam. He was not their first choice. The organizers originally approached Indian and Ottoman scholars who fit the profile of Muslims as represented in the Bazaar of Nations, which featured replicas of cities such as Cairo and Istanbul. These street scenes depicted Muslims as exotic curiosities of a bygone era, and inferior to Protestant Christianity.[66] Webb attempted to challenge this image in the two speeches he delivered to the Parliament, "The Spirit of Islam" and "The Influence of Islam on Social Conditions." His appearances were preceded by speeches on Islam delivered by George Washburn, who praised some elements of Islam, including its banning of gambling and liquor. Washburn's speech also emphasized Christianity's civilizational superiority and Islam's incompatibility with progress. As a counterpoint, Webb declared that Americans had profoundly misunderstood Islam and its potential to solve urgent social problems, such as urban slums. Referring to his embrace of the "spirit of Islam," Webb tempered his critiques of Christianity and emphasized the universal religious values of Islam.

Through the figure of M. A. R. Webb, the Webb community constructs a recognizable and resonant American Muslim past in which it is possible to find in Islam the fulfillment of American ideals. M. A. R. Webb's biography confirms for Webb members that Islam and Muslims have always been a part of the United States, a historical reality rarely acknowledged in media and political discourses that cast Islam as a foreign, unfamiliar faith. They identify with M. A. R. Webb's struggles to represent Islam as a viable faith to other Americans and share his conviction in the power of reading, peer discussion, dialogue between Muslims and non-Muslims, and the profound spirituality of Muslim ritual. Through Webb, they imagine a different narrative of American Islam, one in which Islam could be an indigenous faith appealing to a wide swath of Americans.

Conclusion

As a third-space community, the Webb Foundation was created to meet the multiple religious and social needs of its educated, middle-class, multiracial families. Webb emerged out of broader demographic and generational shifts in the Chicago ex-burbs. The mosques built by post-1965 immigrants grew out of informal groups of families not unlike those at Webb, who created

Muslim communities amid the maze of west suburban highways. By the 2000s, however, these mosques had grown in membership, financial standing, and visibility, functioning as powerful ritual and educational centers and as visible representatives of American Islam. As the next chapter explores in greater detail, Webb members often feel like they do not "fit" into their area mosques. Nor do many of them feel comfortable in many of the other educational institutions built around particular theological orientations.

Webb members desire a more flexible, malleable kind of space, suited toward its members' dual desire for an American Islam that is responsive to the representational demands of "Main Street" and that facilitates their belonging as Muslims and as Americans. As Malika put it, what these families wanted—and continue to want—is a "virtual space, an atmosphere, an environment" in which to belong as Muslims and as Americans.[67] From the beginning, Webb's focus has been on building an "indigenous" American Islam through relationships. In the immediate aftermath of the 9/11 attacks, this growing segment of American Muslims found themselves further marginalized in American society, and it was this sense of insecurity and alienation that provided the impetus to plan and execute the leisure and educational programs that later became more formalized as Webb's bread and butter. The next two chapters examine the role of critique in the construction of Webb's third-space community and the rituals through which they enact this "indigenous" American Islam.

2

Imagining Religion and Culture at Webb

AT THE CRUX of the Webb community is a shared vision of being fully Muslim and fully American. Yet because of this very effort to be both, Webb members often find themselves on the margins. Ambivalent toward the ethnic orientations that dominate Chicago's mosques, excluded from full participation in civic life, and feared by many Americans, Webb members correctly perceive themselves as both defying Muslim institutional norms and yet still living on the edges of American society. The Webb critique of mosques centers on this dissonance, created by the gap that they experience between who they are and are expected to be in mosques and who they are in their workplaces, at home, in schools, and in their neighborhoods. Many Webb participants share profound experiences of exclusion that have left them feeling that they do not belong in mosques, institutions they consider to be vital for the future of American Islam. Compounding these experiences of religious exclusion, they believe that mosques have also contributed to the marginalization of Muslims generally from the American "mainstream."

Here I am concerned primarily with the internal discourse through which Webb members articulate their marginalization and the strong sense of belonging that this sense of being on the margins solidifies. In particular, the community offers a third space for participants to challenge extant visions of American Islam. Webb members reimagine the United States as an ideal site of religious practice, carrying the hope of its participants that American Islam could someday be "seamless." The United States, they believe, holds the promise of an Islam free of racial and ethnic divisions, if only they can disencumber American Islam of its immigrant ethos and show other Muslims the value of embracing cultural norms of American society.

This chapter examines grievances against mosques and how they reveal the overlapping networks and contested boundaries that constitute Chicago Muslim communities, as individuals and families seek to navigate complex intergenerational, spatial, racial, class, and gender dynamics. As Webb members seek to render Islam an acceptable faith within the US political and religious landscape, such critiques become all the more urgent. To do so, I focus on the stories of seven Webb members: Zaid, Fatima, Frank, Marwa, Lisa, Fauzia, and Patricia, who, in the course of their interviews, shared their varied experiences and described how Webb provides their families with a different kind of religious and social community.

My conversation partners constantly attended to moral distinctions between "religion" and "culture," which they implicitly conceive of as autonomous domains, to imagine a different future for American Islam. These distinctions are inflected by Webb members' particular social locations and life histories.[1] Rogers Brubaker calls this "a world in which Islam is a chronic *object* of discussion and debate, a world that is thick with self-conscious and explicit discussions *about* Islam."[2] These reifications are the product of a global political economy in which the category "Muslim" has become racialized through its inextricable connection to the term "terrorist."[3] The interview setting potentially amplifies these objectifications, as participants reflect consciously on their experiences within American Muslim communities, and the differences between Webb and other institutions.[4]

In order to properly attune Islam to culture, Webb participants believe that American Muslims must recover an Islam that embraces the norms of each culture to which it spreads. Islam is not simply compatible with American culture, they argue; rather, all American Muslims have a moral obligation to reconstruct Islam, just as prior generations of Muslims have always done in their own times and places. In this way, Islam's diversity is proof of its universality.

As categories, religion and culture do important boundary work at Webb, carving it out as a more inclusive community than mosques. These conversations are more than simply talk; rather, they help to constitute what Brubaker describes as "identifications."[5] The concept of "identification" is more precise than "identity" to describe the ways that Webb participants articulate and embody their individual and collective locations in different social and religious spaces and within overlapping sets of relationships. The term "self-identification" denotes meaning-making action on the part of the individual or community. Webb members do not just pick and choose from available, static identities. Instead, working out what it means to be an American Muslim is an ongoing, dynamic process involving conversation and practice. Moreover, these identifications are highly contingent on the spaces in which they are constructed, whether in mosques, private homes, schools, the workplace, or in third spaces such as Webb. These discussions of religion and culture also mark the efforts of Webb participants to contend with, challenge, and sometimes appropriate representations of Islam and Muslims that they encounter in the media, governmental programs of surveillance, and everyday encounters with Muslims and non-Muslims.

Zaid: Challenging Ethnic Particularism

The son of Syrian and Mexican immigrants, Zaid is a longtime Webb member who grew up in Chicago. He attended college and medical school in the city and now runs a successful practice in the suburbs with his wife, Noor. She is also a Chicago native, the daughter of Pakistani immigrants. When I met with Zaid in his home, he and Noor were in the midst of a typically hectic weeknight, shuttling their three kids among various activities, making dinner, and divvying up household tasks. Amid these comings and goings, Zaid reflected on the challenges facing second-generation American Muslims:

> Generations don't maintain themselves as an isolated community. If you don't allow a generation to become comfortable in their own skin, eventually they're not going to integrate. They're going to assimilate. Then you risk losing the religious tie. Not that I think it's [American culture] is superior but it's ours. Clothing—it's a big thing in South Asian community to wear *shalwar kamiz*. There's nothing wrong with that but you don't have to wear it. The point is, you can wear a suit and tie.[6]

While South Asian or Arab cultures might be dominant in their countries of origin, Webb members feel that American Muslims need to claim "American culture" as their own. Zaid wants American Muslims to reclaim the sense of belonging they lost after 9/11 and to ensure that future generations remain Muslim. For him, this requires deliberate choices about what is American and what is not, in order to ensure that his kids are fully enmeshed in the American cultural mainstream. This is what he means by a culture that is *ours*.[7]

Signs of ethnic heritage carry ambivalence in Webb participants' assessment of mosques.[8] I use Sylvia Chan-Malik's term "ethnic particularism" to describe this orientation against which the Webb community largely defines itself.[9] In Chicago's mosques, markers of ethnic particularism include the hiring of imams from the countries of origin, conducting classes and sermons in languages other than English, retaining gender separation in social activities, serving foods like biryani and samosas, and sartorial choices such as the wearing of the *shalwar kamiz*. In mosque spaces, such practices came to acquire religious authority as markers of an authentic Islam.

Diasporic practices no longer confer religious authenticity for Zaid and other Webb members. For Zaid, the *shalwar kamiz* does signify one's participation in multicultural America. Zaid acknowledges that ethnic practices fostered belonging and community for first-generation immigrants. But for Zaid, this sartorial choice potentially signals alienation from "mainstream" American culture when imposed as a religious norm on individuals who do not share that ethnic identification. He challenges the way these "shards of memory" have come to be imposed as on mosque attendees like himself, for whom these practices have little resonance with his educational, professional, and other social experiences, not to mention his multiethnic identifications.[10] Moreover, Webb families like Zaid's struggle to reconcile the ethnic particularism of local mosques with the racial and ethnic diversity within their nuclear families. Their empathy for earlier generations often gives way to frustration over what they perceive as the prevalence of "cultural Islam."

Zaid began to notice distinctions between religion and culture when he traveled to Damascus as a college student. He had yearned to see the Syria his father had so effusively described. The experience left Zaid more committed to being a Muslim than when he left, but he also became disillusioned with Syrian politics:

> I got a much fuller understanding of my dad within a week and a fuller understanding of a Muslim city as an organic place and not some kind of construct. Where people actually felt comfortable. It was not big deal to pray. Praying here is hard when you have to explain to others what that means. Once I saw it in action, I realized that Syria was a whacked out political mess. It was not a dreamland. My dad had a lot of romantic imagery that did not exist. I saw that it was a way of life. When I came back I started claiming that identity.[11]

Zaid envisions an American Islam fully integrated with American culture and politics. Going abroad provided him the opportunity to see such an "organic" ideal in action. Damascus represents the possibility of a "seamless" identity, where prayer is a matter of fact and practitioners feel "comfortable." For Zaid, the United States falls well short of this ideal. Though he admires the integration of religion and culture in Syria, Zaid does not want to replicate Syrian norms in the United States. Instead, he wants to make that kind of environment a daily reality for his children in an "American" way. The third space at Webb offers him the opportunity to work toward this vision in which his kids belong as American Muslims.

Webb families, comprised of members with multiple ethnic and racial identifications, are enmeshed in a complex field of racial and religious politics that have elevated particular forms of culture over others. In the late twentieth century, multicultural ideologies helped to foster ethnic particularism among immigrant communities. Moreover, wealthier immigrants have benefitted from the "model minority" discourse that lauds certain groups (especially Asian Americans) as inherently hard-working and productive members of American society. South Asian Muslims, and to a lesser extent Arab Americans, buttressed by their higher socioeconomic status, thus appropriated "signs of ethnicity" recognizable to other Americans.[12] These representations, tied to diasporic homelands, place them in the company of white Catholic and Jewish immigrants whose cultural differences came to be seen as more of a virtue than a threat to the social and economic fabric of the United States.[13] For these groups, ethnic heritage has become another contribution of white immigrants to American culture.

By contrast, Black Muslims' cultural claims have been perceived as less authentically Muslim and less assimiliable to "mainstream" society. For much of the twentieth century, African Americans were assumed to lack an ethnicity and thus a distinctive cultural "heritage."[14] Black Muslims have challenged their exclusion from an ethnic heritage. For example, in the early twentieth century, the Moorish Science Temple engaged in practices of ethnic heritage that Sylvester Johnson argues "redeemed converts from social death, a condition marking them as a people without peoplehood, relegated as nonmembers of the American nation."[15] Discourses of multiculturalism have continued to enable immigrant communities to claim a less threatening cultural, "ethnic" identity, but these same discourses render Black practices as less authentic expressions of Islam.[16] That is, the claim of ethnic mosques to represent American Islam writ large is made possible, in part, by the marginalization of African American Muslims from some mosque spaces and their obviation from broader imaginings and practices of "authentic" Islam. As we have seen, racial segregation patterns in Chicago, reinforced by geographic and often class divisions, also helped to facilitate the rise of "ethnic Muslim spaces," whose boundaries are distinct yet permeable. Junaid Rana has argued that while the "racialization of Islam" dehumanizes all American Muslims, Black Muslims are "racially assigned" to blackness. Immigrant Muslims can "aspire" to full citizenship and socioeconomic status through partial access to markers of whiteness.[17]

At the same time, all Muslims are subject to racialization practices that have rendered them suspect, "less-than" Americans. The history of immigration policies and the shifting racial hierarchies upon which they are based have made it so that Arab and Asian Muslims fit uneasily into existing categories.[18] Over the course of the twentieth century, this ambivalent status has made it more difficult for them to gain political recognition as minorities, to access social services, and to apply for legal citizenship.[19] The construction of Muslim-as-terrorist subsumes the astonishing diversity of American Muslims into a single category that signifies danger. This racial construction of Muslims as "other" is connected to other discourses that have rendered immigrants as foreign and potential threats to American democracy. Being identified as a Muslim, or mistaken for one as in the case of Sikhs, has resulted in acts of discrimination, surveillance, and violence. These fluid modes of external and self-identifications demonstrate how the structural logics of race undergird American Muslim attempts to overcome them.

Comparing the efforts of South Asian Hindus and Muslims to make their respective faiths recognizable as American after 9/11 helps to illuminate these intersections of ethnicity, race, and religion. Identification with a religious faith helps to confer recognition in the US context, but different religious communities are subject to different constraints even when they share ethnic identifications. In the wake of the World Trade Center and Pentagon attacks, some American Hindu organizations drew on "model minority" language to extol the contributions of American Hindus to US society and to claim the inherently peaceful nature of Hinduism over and against the violent propensities of Muslims. Speakers for groups like the Infinity Foundation sought to exclude Muslims from the "South Asian" identification by casting Pakistan and Bangladesh as hotbeds of terrorism and India, defined as a Hindu nation, as a bastion of universal, tolerant religion.[20] These Hindu organizations do not necessarily represent American Hindus broadly speaking. And American Hindus have themselves repeatedly experienced racism and ongoing exclusion from the Abrahamic religious ideal. But such discourses suggest how the affirmation of ethnic and religious identity, couched in the language of peace, tolerance, and religious pluralism, can also contribute to the replication of racialized categories. In the post-9/11 era, efforts to increase public visibility in the American public square were more readily accomplished through the available anti-Muslim representations circulating widely in the media and political discourse.

Fatima: Governance and Generational Conflict

Fatima is the mother of four young children and the daughter of Arab-American parents. Like Zaid, she grew up in Chicago. She explained her choice to join Webb in generational terms:

> It's like they're going to have to die or something. Or they're grooming particular people to take over. But look, we are just trying to do what our parents did. We are trying to build an American Muslim community to the best of our abilities. We just can't do that in mosques right now.[21]

Fatima's comments about boards of directors reveal broader struggles over governance in suburban mosques. The lack of changeover in leadership that she perceives suggests that change, when it does occur, tends to happen slowly. Although elections for new board members may happen regularly, in reality many of my interviewees noted that some board members seem to hold their positions for life. The emergence of generational conflicts between an aging first-generation group and their adult children, now approaching middle-age, partially explains the development of institutions such as Webb. Prevented from assuming leadership positions, Webb founding members started a new community in order to take on the roles that have been denied to them and to enact a vision of American Islam that resonated with their own experiences.

When Webb participants' parents founded local mosques, they created boards of directors responsible for finances, making prayer calendars, and planning religious and social activities. The professional status of these board members, as primarily engineers and doctors, conferred on them authority within their communities.[22] Many of these board members were steeped in modes of learning and practice common among Muslims who came of age during the Islamic Revival. Educated in secular institutions, they acquired Islamic knowledge and authority through the activist and *da'wa* organizations that gained prominence in the latter half of the twentieth century. When mosques had designated imams, they were typically hired part-time or served on a volunteer basis. A 2011 survey conducted by the Council on American-Islamic Relations shows how the office of imam has been gradually becoming professionalized in the United States, as more mosques have appointed imams to permanent positions, which include direct administrative functions.[23] As the second generation entered their thirties and forties, they sought to assume greater responsibilities in their masjids.

Webb men and women also object to the exclusion of women from mosque leadership roles. They affirm the importance of female presence in mosques, a view that reflects global shifts in space and gender among Muslims. Historically, women's presence in mosques was not required, much less expected.[24] This is beginning to change, however. In a wide array of Muslim contexts, from China to Morocco, women have increasingly assumed official roles in mosques. As instructors and sometimes prayer leaders (usually for women) in mosques, Muslim women have attained their authority through religious learning, their commitment to Islamic activism and volunteer work, their successes in teaching, and their family networks.[25] Some of these programs, like those in Turkey and Morocco, have created leadership positions for women under the auspices of the state bureaucracy. These roles, while suggesting new avenues of authority for women, largely do not disrupt the largely male structures of authority through which their positions are defined.[26] But they have created an opening, across a range of Muslim societies, for women to claim new forms of authority, the consequences of which will unfold in the next several decades.

In the United States, American Muslim women have always been active participants in mosques, though not in the roles that Webb participants want for themselves. Because board positions have traditionally been occupied by men, women remain underrepresented. Fatima remembered the aroma of biryani in the mosque, which women prepared and served after Friday prayers. But presence is not enough for many women in the Webb community. Furthermore, many Webb members, men and women alike, have come to perceive mosques as spaces of female exclusion. Their focus on two areas in particular—gender separation and the lack of women authority figures—reflects a broader critique of mosques as gendered spaces of inequality.[27] Such practices include separating men and women for prayer, often with women in the basement, a balcony, or behind a partition. Webb women's experiences of gender separation and lack of women's representation on mosque boards are key sources of discontent, marginalization, and even despair.

For members with immigrant backgrounds, mosques simultaneously evoke reverence for the prior generation's struggles to make a Muslim community from scratch in the 1960s and 1970s. Fatima described her childhood as a "warm, supportive time" in which all the members volunteered to create a close-knit community, mostly centered around educating kids like her. She spoke fondly of her parents' financial sacrifices and hard work, which helped to build their mosque from just a few families to a thriving institution serving hundreds of practitioners. She sees the Webb Foundation as arising from similar motivations and circumstances, as a group of friends and family gathering for prayer and religious lessons in basements and living rooms. The intimacy of Webb spaces emulates the masjid of Fatima's childhood.

But when it came time to find a Sunday School for their children, Fatima and her husband were troubled by what they discovered at their local mosque:

> The Sunday school curriculum, it was the same photocopies that my mother-in-law used thirty years ago! You kind of have to de-program the kids who attend mosque Sunday schools, because there are a lot of cultural opinions that creep in. Like, no, it's ok to celebrate Thanksgiving. At Webb, you don't feel judged. There are older girls who don't cover, for example. It is welcoming and supportive. In the classroom, kids are encouraged to ask questions about really core things, like belief in God. At other Sunday schools this would be called blasphemous. For many kids, it gives them a comfort level to explore their faith. We have pretty high standards, we have high standards for ourselves and where we find Islamic knowledge, and we won't take anything less for our kids. Dr. Umar [Faruq Abd-Allah] sets the bar pretty high. We want academic rigor for our kids.[28]

Despite her fondness for her parents, Fatima's narrative connotes stagnation and conformity. The robust and vibrant leadership of the 1970s, she said, now offers only a stale curriculum based on "cultural opinions" rather than religious truth. She inverted the privileging of Islamic authenticity based on Arab or South Asian origins, arguing instead that allowing for children to celebrate American holidays or to question aspects of their faith was in fact a marker of authentic (and academically rigorous) Islam. From her perspective, the teaching of culture as religion not only prevents her children from embracing American values, but also excludes traditions of scholarship that the Webb parents now seek to impart to the next generation. This two-pronged appraisal, rooted in hierarchies of culture and knowledge, formed the starting point for the foundation's programming.

Fatima's narrative also reveals competing constructions of authority across generations. Fatima claims access to authentic religious knowledge that she believes is unavailable to earlier generations because they remain steeped in culture. She has gained this knowledge by enrolling in courses on theology, law, and Islamic history, taught by Abd-Allah and other scholars as the recuperation of classical sources. These sources constitute a robust, original, and "rigorous" Islam unmoored to cultural constraints and capable of contesting extant visions for American Islam at mosques. Animated by an urgent sense that she and other second-generation parents needed to take charge of their children's educations, Fatima enrolled her kids at the Webb Foundation Sunday School.

At Webb, the objectification of Islam and culture emerges in relation to broader contemporary and especially American conceptions of "true" religion as the moralistic framework for social good. Sociologists of "new immigrants" in the United States have shown that many religious communities respond to internal diversity by seeking to extract culture from the universal aspects of their religious traditions. At Webb, participants seek to recover Islam from perceived "foreign" cultures and then to pair Islam with the "best of American culture."[29] In Webb imaginings, only cultures perceived as foreign to America are considered parochial or limiting, and as such interfere with the development of a robust American Islam.

But what is "culture" in this context? Usually, participants use the term to describe the beliefs and practices that immigrants present as normatively Islamic, but that Webb members understand to be parochially cultural. Webb participants take special care to distance themselves from first-generation immigrants. Even though many arrived in the United States during early childhood, they commonly refer to themselves as "second-generation" immigrants, reserving the category "first-generation" for groups of Muslims they see as resistant to adopting the practices that they deemed American. Like many second-generation immigrants, they differentiate between immigrants who have spent considerable time in the United States and those who are "fresh off the boat," aka "FOBs" or "boaters."[30] FOBs are marked by their accents, dress, and food. These categories confer religious and social authority on immigrants who have more readily assimilated. Webb participants deploy these categories selectively as they are, though they are far more charitable in describing their own families, light-heartedly referring to the time when their parents refused to let them drink Coca-Cola because it was too "Amrikeen."[31]

When Webb members voice unrelenting criticism of "cultural Islam" in their mosques, they flag a range of practices: foreign-born imams, gender segregation, events starting later than their published start time (according to what informants refer to as "Desi" time[32]), and ill-conceived interfaith efforts. The fact that my interviewees previously entrusted mosque leaders with the authority to represent Islam to the broader American public only made their critiques more impassioned. After 9/11, they found mosque attempts to represent American Islam not only be dissatisfying but potentially harmful to the Muslim community writ large. In other words, the term indexes those beliefs and practices that were imposed on American Muslims as religious and universal, but that Webb participants believe are either not original to Islam or are particular to a specific non-US culture. "Cultural Islam" is thus foreign, parochial, and potentially damaging to American Muslims on the whole.

Representing American Islam

These criticisms are inextricably bound to anxieties over the representation of Islam. For example, almost all of my interviewees remembered how they dreaded local news interviews of imams, who were sometimes called upon to explain Islam to the public. They were horrified that the very authority figures whom they held responsible for the marginalization of the Muslim community now served as spokespersons to the broader American public. The idea of Islam as "scary" marks the claim among a range of many recent Muslim activists and authors that "true" Islam—understood as rational, tolerant, and peaceful—was inadequately represented in US Muslim institutions. From this point of view, the most visible institutions were the least suited to represent Islam.

In addition to ethnic particularism, Webb members also shared their opposition to what they labeled as "Wahhabi" practices that they observed. The genealogy of Wahhabism is the subject of extensive scholarly and political debate, and I highlight only the relevant features here.[33] Adherents to this perspective rarely identify as "Wahhabis," preferring the term "*ahl al-Sunna*" or "people of tradition" to assert their view as representing the authentic practice of Islam.[34] The terms "Wahhabi" and "Wahhabism" refer to the eighteenth-century Saudi reformer Muhammad Ibn Abd al-Wahhab (d. 1792), who advanced a set of theological views designed to purify the faith of what he saw as dangerous, "superstitious" elements: vigorous adherence to *tawhīd* (oneness of God); prioritizing the content (as opposed to the chain of transmission) of hadith; and the eradication of *bid'a*, or harmful innovations. In particular, Sufi practices fell under this rubric of *bid'a*, including visitation to saints' tombs, *mawlids* (celebrations of the Prophet Mohammed's birthday), and *dhikr* (remembrance of God through ritual chanting of the names of God other litanies). Al-Wahhab's approach became a much more visible and important ideological force as the state religion of Saudi Arabia. In the twentieth century, Saudi publication houses, scholarly networks, and financial support for mosques have amounted to a global effort to distribute religious literature across disperse geographical areas. Especially after 9/11, "Wahhabism" has become synonymous with terrorism. Al-Wahhab himself did not support violence or destruction of sacred sites.[35] At the same time, he referred to Muslims who practiced *bid'a* or contested his vision as unbelievers and apostates, which opened up the possibility of engaging in violence against them.[36]

Although Webb members use the term "Wahhabi," they are often taking aim at a broad range of practices that signal the more general influence of Salafism (*al-Salafiyya*). The name derives from the *Salaf*, or first generations of Muslims, who serve as the standard for normative and authentic practice. Unlike Saudi intellectuals who tend to follow Hanafi theology and law, Salafis reject *madhhab*-based legal reasoning and instead rely on literal interpretations of the original sources of Islam (the Qur'an and Sunna). They also seek to purify Islam of *bid'a* and devotional forms of piety associated with Sufism. In the twentieth century, Salafism shifted from what Henri Lauziere describes as a "theological doctrine and approach to Islamic law" to a "worldview that encompassed the whole of existence, from knowledge to practice, from morality to etiquette, and even from religion to politics."[37] Salafism is an internally diverse movement, the contours of which are only beginning to be understood in global contexts. The extent of Salafi influence in the United States is difficult to assess, but it is clear that its theological stances had an impact on American Muslim institutions and communities in the twentieth century. The financial resources of the Saudi state have supported global missionary efforts that have helped to circulate literature, religious authorities, and ideology. The Muslim World League, a Saudi missionary organization founded in 1962, and now with networks around the world, reached out to Muslim minority communities around the world, including in the United States. The League brought together a variety of groups looking to Islamicize society, including Wahhabis, Salafis, the Jam'at-i Islami, and the Muslim Brotherhood.[38] There is also evidence to support the claim that various foreign governments, including Saudi Arabia, have contributed to the financing of some mosques. Locally, a story in the *Chicago Tribune* documented Saudi contributions to the Mosque Foundation, located in the Bridgeview neighborhood on the southwest side. Many mosques carry pamphlets, books, and other religious material published in Saudi Arabia. But most mosques in Chicago, as elsewhere in the United States, were established and funded locally, as families sought a place of worship and community.[39] Moreover, accepting funding does not entail that a community accepted or implemented Salafi ideology. The actual content of Salafi thought and practice in the United States deserve more careful attention, not least because of the political stakes undergirding this form of inquiry.

Rather than "Wahhabism," which carries ideologically negative implications, or "Salafism," I use the term "revivalism" to more accurately encompass the widespread postcolonial resurgence of Muslim identity that was supported by a range of organizations, intellectuals, and activists beyond those formally associated with the Saudi state's missionary program or with Salafism per se. Generally, revivalists wanted to elevate Muslim identity publically and sought to infuse society with Muslim principles by promoting ritual observance, displaying visible signs of Islam such as the hijab, and inculcating political institutions with religious ideologies. In part, this revivalist orientation developed as a response to authoritarian, secular regimes in the Arab world and to express criticism toward ongoing Western (neo)-imperial projects.[40] It also reflected shifting conceptions of textual interpretation, piety, and religious authority.[41]

During the 1960s and 1970s, many revivalists, energized in their efforts to do *da'wa* (call to the faith), sought to make the United States into a place to implement their utopian vision for Islam.[42] Some of these students came to the United States as part of the post-1965 influx of immigrants.[43] As their numbers grew in places like Chicago, it became possible to create their brand of a distinctly Muslim set of behavioral and ethical norms, regulated by official institutions, in a manner that was impossible when Muslim communities were small, informal, and impermanent. Activist in outlook, other revivalists, who were not always affiliated with Salafism, had a broad impact, even as they modified contingencies of the US context and their lived realities molded their theological, social, and political expectations. Organizations founded in the 1960s and 1970s, such as the Islamic Society of North America and the Islamic Circle of North America both originally promoted gender separation and modesty norms that many at Webb find objectionable. Global in scope, the influence of revivalists normalized new performances of piety in a relatively short period, changes that proved significant for Webb participants' perception that mosques had grown increasingly rigid in the areas of ritual performance and gendered practice.[44]

Webb members came of age during the 1980s, and they encountered this orientation as a dominant, vision for Islam, one that they have come to reject. The term "Wahhabi" usually emerged in my interviewees' memories of their adolescence, in which they claimed that American mosques changed to be more restrictive, especially with respect to women. Recalling the 1970s and 1980s, many interviewees reminisced about a more flexible childhood, a time in which girls wore short-sleeved shirts to the social events at the mosque, though not to pray. By the 1990s, they remembered that the expectations had changed and that "Wahhabis" made them "afraid" to challenge such norms.[45] Women were expected to dress more modestly, by wearing long sleeves and skirts, and the hijab.[46] They also noted staunch resistance to American cultural forms, like music, and the marginalization of devotional practices, like the *mawlid*.

At Webb, then, culture is at once the problem and the solution to the crisis facing American Muslims. Participants described at length the ill effects of the improper attunement of culture in American Islam, that is, practices marked as foreign that do not resonate with their experiences as *American* Muslims or theological perspectives that seek to exise cultural influence from a pure Islam. These discourses bear the mark of what Mahmood Mamdani has deemed the "good/bad" Muslim paradigm, which has its roots in the Cold War, but has enduring discursive power in the post-9/11 era.[47] From this perspective, "cultural Islam" or "Wahhabism" are not merely outdated or dissonant, but rather an obstacle to the integration of Muslims into American society.

Although Webb members' grievances preceded 9/11, the attacks and their aftermath provided the urgency for this group to act on their criticisms. As many observers have argued, the 2000s instigated a swift and harsh ideological turn in America's racial and religious politics.[48] Whereas Muslims of South Asian and Arab descent garnered little attention before 9/11 as Muslims per se, they now found themselves as objects of intense US governmental and public scrutiny.[49] Arab Muslims in particular were subject to global efforts on the part of many governments to root out terrorist threats.[50] The Webb project of constructing a seamless Muslim American identity is in part an effort to contest the racialization of Muslims in the contemporary United States.[51] In the context of US debates about the compatibility of Islam and liberal democracy, "culture" becomes the lens through which Webb members evaluate past and present efforts of other American Muslims to create an American Islam.

The rhetoric of religion and culture thus reflects an ongoing concern for the representation of Muslims in broader settings, especially the media, and the question of who speaks on behalf of and for American Muslims. The inclusive rhetoric of "American culture" at Webb is itself laden with appeals to American superiority. While Webb members reject the idea that Islam can or should be free of culture, their valorizations of American culture imply that it does not have the same limiting constraints as other cultures. This series of reifications implies that those practices labeled as "immigrant" or "cultural" are in fact less American than those practices coded as uniquely or quintessentially American. Although US mosques and national Muslim institutions have been, from their inception, concerned with how to best situate American Muslims in the United States, Webb members largely do not recognize these efforts as legitimate resources upon which to draw. To adapt Mamdani's formulation of this construct, earlier generations *are* a culture, whereas Webb aspires to *have* American culture. As they define it, American culture is free from the parochial limitations of immigrant culture because, as Zaid put it, American culture is *ours*.[52]

Powerful forms of self-identification and external categorization are at work in this delineation between religion and culture. Webb members contest normative forms of Muslim practice and belief that they perceive as rooted in ethnic particularism. They resent it when these practices are represented as legitimate, authentic, and universal Islam. As an alternative, Webb members want to practice Islam in a way that validates their experiences as American Muslims, resonates with their education in Muslim and non-Muslim settings, and that is inclusive of the practices they and their spouses bring to their nuclear families. Having endured painful experiences of marginalization and exclusion in ethnically based mosques, Webb mothers and fathers want to provide alternative associations between Islam and American culture, in which "America" serves as the locus for the practice of an authentic Islam.

Frank and Marwa: Religion and Culture at Home

Although Webb members voice strong critiques of cultural Islam, they are far less concerned with blurred distinctions between cultural and religious practices in their childhood homes. This tension reflects a kind of conceptual division that emerged in my interviews between domestic spaces, the mosque, and third spaces such as Webb. Webb members mainly recalled domestic religious practice with affection and admiration. The politics of representing Islam are still present in these spaces but have less urgency and are mitigated by the emotional bonds that Webb members have with their family members.

These different meanings became apparent during my conversation with Frank and Marwa, who have four young children. Raised in a Midwestern Protestant family, Frank became a Muslim in college, finding the faith after being a "hard-core atheist."[53] Marwa grew up in Chicago among a large South Asian extended family:

MARWA: You grow up [as a Muslim] with this sense of obligation to not just yourself, but to the community. You're Muslim, but you're not individually Muslim. Being hospitable hosts, and opening your home and inviting everyone. Your actions are always on display because you look different and you stick out. I felt that even more because I wore hijab at a young age. Does your dad make you wear that thing on your head? And the answer was no. He thought I was way too young. My mom started in early 2000s after I started college. They were not very religious in India. They fasted, gave to charity, but it was never an active, "I'm going to seek knowledge." That's what happens in a predominantly Muslim country. You're not forced to think about these issues.

FRANK: You establish your connections with people, your family, your extended family, people in your community. Like respecting elders, and that gets manifested in different ways. In Indian culture, like the title, you never call elders by their names, rather their title, and that flows throughout. The emphasis on hospitality, that was shocking to me. Things like the use of resources, like not wasting food. When I was in college, it would drive people [Muslims] from all backgrounds crazy because I would not finish the food on my plate. After a little while, that became my attitude too, but whenever people come over they always finish. The non-Muslims always leave a ton of food on their plate. It's very rare for them to finish. There are a lot of little things like that in Islam. It's not about a list of rules. It's about your relationships and living your life appropriate to that reality and your relationship to the creator.[54]

Both Frank and Marwa see her extended family as a vital site of ethical instruction for their children. So many of the embodied practices this couple find foundational to being a good Muslim fall under common-sense notions of "culture." What is more, Frank and Marwa connect South Asian practices associated with dress, food, hygiene, and honorific titles to "universal" Islamic principles.

Tellingly, in this context they do not see cultural practices as problematic. In fact, practices around hospitality and food constitute a superior alternative to the individualism and waste that they encounter among non-Muslim friends and family. Marwa's family provides a network of relationships, a space in which Frank and Marwa understand culture and religion to be mutually constitutive. As a convert, Frank emphasized many times that Islam is more than the "rules," citing the Quranic idea that Islam is a religion of ease, rather than hardship. Marwa was more ambivalent. She noted her personal autonomy to wear a hijab, because her mother does not. She also lamented the restrictions that her parents enforced in her youth, especially as a girl. But Marwa's and Frank's complaints about family obligations are far more muted than those they articulate against mosque leadership. Instead, practices of hospitality and charity are enmeshed in intimate relationships that the couple finds meaningful. The couple makes ample time for their four children to be with their maternal extended family, where they fulfill important religious obligations and develop ethical dispositions they would not find elsewhere: respect for elders, cleanliness, dietary norms, and generosity.

In these discussions of domestic spaces for religiosity, Webb participants reveal how the critique of "cultural Islam" is deployed in certain contexts, such as the mosque, but largely absent from others, such as the home. That is, it is unnecessary to separate religion and culture in all contexts; those boundaries remain permeable and contingent in domestic spaces. Unlike the mosque, among extended family, the demands of representing Islam are less viscerally present, and therefore critique is not appropriate. Instead, extended kinship practices offer much in the way of ethical instruction and ethnic heritage, but Webb members invest less significance in their import for broader representational politics. As we will see in the next chapter, it is the nuclear family that serves as the focal point in the public-facing aspects of Webb's project.

Lisa: The Politics of Belonging among Converts

Converts experience exclusion less in generational terms and instead frame their discontent through the multiple life changes that accompanied becoming a Muslim. Some converts at Webb reported instances when they felt they were upheld as standard-bearers of true Islamic belief and practice. As one convert put it, "You're expected to be a super Muslim who does everything right. I'm always on a pedestal."[55] But the more common experience among converts at Webb was that they received chilly receptions at local masjids when they tried to take an active role in the community because they were perceived to be "too" American.

In June 2012, Lisa and I sat together in Grant Park in downtown Chicago, squinting at each other against the noonday sun and pausing on occasion to admire the bright pink and pale yellow rose bushes that framed our bench. In her thirties, Lisa is a white convert and native Midwesterner married to a first-generation Arab immigrant. They have two school-aged children. Her eyes filled with tears as she recalled her first attempts to volunteer through her local mosque.

> I had this terrible experience when my husband and I decided that we wanted to volunteer in our community. We turned to the masjid first. There is a huge refugee population in the western suburbs, and we tried to help with the assistance program at the mosque. We got into a dispute about who is worthy of help. Certain funds collected during Ramadan could be used to help some people of some faiths but not others. I disagreed with this. It turned into a really nasty situation that ended with the *shaykh* who gives all of the *khutbahs* [sermons] telling me that he didn't appreciate an outsider coming in and telling him what to do. And I said, "What exactly do you mean by outsider?"

> He said, "We didn't ask for your help." And then he listed a bunch of Christian organizations that he thought would be a better fit. I was deeply offended. I had a spiritual crisis after that. I didn't want to go back there. I didn't want to hear that guy's voice anymore. At the masjid, I felt like I was an outsider because I was American and because I was a convert. At Webb, it doesn't matter what you are. If you're a convert you're still a Muslim.[56]

I heard similar stories from many other converts I spoke with at Webb, for whom the experience of exclusion from the local masjid was jarring because they felt that as new Muslims, they were obligated to devote religious energies to mosque initiatives. Many female converts in the United States, who grew up going to church regularly, see going to the masjid as a primary religious duty and an obvious place to form relationships with their new coreligionists. But the "spiritual crisis" that many female converts experienced as a result of their time in mosques led some of them to avoid masjids altogether and to seek out alternative religious spaces such as Webb.[57]

Lisa's experiences demonstrate how contestations of religious authenticity reflect competing idioms of race and national identity. The shaykh's labeling of Lisa as an outsider reflected a conflation of religious identity, nationality, and race.[58] Just as many immigrants view Islam as inextricable from their cultural and national identities, the imam pointed Lisa toward the Christian service organizations that he deemed more appropriate for her as an American-born white woman.

Her struggles thus hinge on her concurrent exclusions from multiple communities. Alongside this encounter, she remembered the loss of friendships and her church community when she converted, not to mention the stares of suspicion she continues to endure when out and about with her husband and children in their suburban community. Her efforts to build relationships within Muslim institutions left her frustrated and angry because they made her American identity explicit, problematic, and conscious in ways that she had never experienced before. Expecting for Islam to transcend national and gendered identities, she found instead that the imam construed them as barriers to her full inclusion.

I do not mean to imply that American women rarely experience exclusion or discrimination, nor do I wish to diminish the daily acts of discrimination and sexism in US workplaces and other social spaces. But the converts I interviewed experienced these encounters as uniquely insulting because they had rarely perceived their presence to be threatening or problematic in their prior religious communities. Moreover, because she had volunteered in programs that provided social services to refugees and immigrants, Lisa understood her rejection on account of her citizenship and gender to be particularly unjust. Coupled with the new stigma attached to becoming Muslim in non-Muslim settings, Lisa resented her inability to establish relationships with other Muslims for whom religious identity did not automatically confer acceptance. For her, becoming Muslim was her deliberate choice, one that she expected to be affirmed by other Muslims. She then turned to Webb to find friends who would support the choice that she had made.

Fauzia: Recovering Cultural Diversity

In part, Webb's vision of culture and Islam has been shaped through its members' opportunities to encounter Muslim communities abroad. A product of their mobility and access to "other" places, these experiences have led them to celebrate Islam's diversity. Many Webb members have made *rihlas* (religious journeys) with scholars such as Abd-Allah to distant places in order to witness how Muslims practice in accordance to their "indigenous" cultures. Usually just a month or so in length, these trips have inspired the Webb leadership in their construction of American Islam and have shaped how they imagine the spiritual topography of global Islam.[59]

I spoke at length with Fauzia, who, at the time of our conversation, was serving as Webb's first executive director. In her early thirties, Fauzia was born in Chicago to Pakistani parents. A successful event planner and consultant, she became an avid participant in Deen Intensive and Nawawi programs, experiences that influenced her decision to change career paths and devote her time to serving the Chicago Muslim community. A few years ago, she traveled to China on one of Nawawi's *rihlas*. She explained how she realized that American Muslims could draw on the examples of distant Muslim communities in their efforts to create a more authentic American Islam:

> In China, we saw mosques that were historic and those funded from outside sources. They took these colors and concepts known by the Chinese and then as Chinese Muslims, they incorporated them into mosque architecture. It's actually not unfamiliar to Islam; it's actually very familiar to Chinese Muslims and to the Chinese.[60]

For Fauzia, the Niujie mosque offered a powerful counterexample to American mosques for how culture and Islam could relate to one another. She saw the building as timeless evidence of Chinese Islam's cultural flourishing and authenticity against the influence of culturally deficient "outside" sources and a sign of its historical success as a minority faith.[61] What Fauzia saw when she admired the Niuijie mosque was its recognizable Chinese architecture and colors, elements that she saw as authentic markers of a distinct, singular Chinese culture. Distilled to these essential features, the Niujie mosque seems to be impervious to political and cultural change.

These architectural elements captured Fauzia's imagination because she did not immediately recognize them as markers of Islam, as she would the color green or the symbol of the crescent. Yet in China, the pagoda roof and the color red are all the more *Islamic* because they reflect an indigenous Chinese culture. Niujie functions as a powerful exemplar of cultural and religious integration, attesting to Islam's ability to adapt to cultures far from the land of its origin, appropriating their forms for its purposes, across time and space. The Niujie mosque enabled Fauzia to imagine a similar cultural achievement for American Muslims, one that she believes has so far eluded her American community. Such an achievement depends on the capacity of American Muslims to integrate recognizable elements of "America" with their faith.

Fauzia drew comparisons between American Muslims' struggles to combine religion and culture with those of Muslims in distant times and places whom she imagines have had to do the same. In fact, by combining American culture with Islam, Webb participants believe they are fulfilling a central religious duty by following a long, learned tradition of religious adaptation and flexibility. In their attempt to distinguish between these categories, they in turn contribute to broader Islamic discourses about the proper relationship between Islam and custom (*'urf*), and the internal cultural diversity of Muslims that date to the beginning of Islam.[62] Fauzia has looked to Abd-Allah for guidance in navigating what she sees as competing expectations of religion and culture:

> A lot of times other immigrant imams would impose the cultural values of their ethnicity or where they're from. Dr. Umar is there to tell us that it's ok if your pants aren't above your ankles and it's ok that you shake hands. It's the cultural norm here; it's actually inappropriate if you don't. He made people feel like they were good Muslims. Those things have a different weight here. Our faith can have these nuances and still be valid.[63]

When properly practiced, I was often told, Muslim communities ought to reflect the specific culture of where they reside. In this way, Fauzia attempts to embody universal Islamic norms through the particularities of American culture. The Niujie mosque is just one example, among many, of how Muslims have historically integrated religion and culture. In this way, by embracing cultural norms of American society, Webb participants fulfill what they consider to be a religious obligation incumbent on *all* Muslims.

Patricia: Searching for Authenticity and Belonging

Patricia's story demonstrates how daily negotiations of authenticity within religion and culture undergird the community's engagement with visions of American Islam in local mosques. Patricia, a mother of three in her forties, relocated from Michigan to the Chicago area in the early 2000s. We sat under the buzzing fluorescent lights in her company's conference room. She drew the blinds against the oppressive summer sun, obscuring the view of the Ronald Reagan highway. She and her husband, Anthony, both African American, live in an upscale western suburb. Though his father was a member of the Nation of Islam, Anthony embraced Islam as an adult in the late 1990s. Patricia was raised Catholic. She attended parochial schools and a Catholic university. Her extended family belonged to different Christian denominations, so she grew up believing that "everyone gets to heaven in their own way."[64] In 2003, a couple years into their marriage, Patricia converted to Islam.

Sharing a faith has brought her and Anthony closer together, but Patricia has had trouble making female friends in mosques and felt that her family was also not particularly welcome. She spoke openly about her family's sense of isolation:

> I could go to the mosque for *jumaʿa* [congregational prayers] on Friday, but I don't normally. To be honest, I never felt comfortable at any mosque. None of them are welcoming to me as an African American woman. The women are really cliquey. They're not rude, but I don't feel a sense of inclusion. I don't feel inspired to go. The other thing is that the friends we do have are from very large families. They are Indian, Pakistani, and Syrian, and have large families in the area. How did you all end up in Northbrook or Schaumburg? And come time for *ʿīd* [an Islamic holiday] they are with their families. My kids don't have cousins to play with on the weekends. It's just us. Even now, it's still just us.[65]

Patricia has encountered the contours of ethnic particularism in suburban masjids, where she perceived that her racial identity marked her as an outsider. By contrast, at Webb, Patricia found a welcoming environment where other women "think and feel like me."[66] She began to take her kids to early Webb events hosted in families' homes, like movie nights and "lock-ins" on New Year's Eve. She smiled enthusiastically as she began to speak about fellow Webb women, who invited her and her kids to movie nights and other activities before she decided to convert. She met other mothers who made her feel comfortable asking questions about being Muslim, such as whether she needed to wear hijab (they said she did not) or what the Muslim conceptions of Jesus were (that he was a prophet, not the son of God).

However, these dynamics of exclusion and belonging, refracted through intersecting frames of culture, race and religion, remain salient for Patricia. Webb only partially alleviates her isolation. Patricia's extended family has since moved away from Chicago, and she and Anthony, although native Chicagoans, sometimes find themselves celebrating holidays alone, while their Muslim friends seem to have scores of extended family with whom to share meals and prayers. Even though Webb provides community to families such as the Johnsons, the organization is not a substitute for the extended family relationships that form the backbone of many Webb families' religious and social ties. As I discussed earlier in this chapter, these networks are intimately connected to mosques, where Patricia and other converts often feel unwelcome. Like many converts who anticipated that becoming Muslim would provide her with a social network, Patricia and her family's search for Muslim community has been a difficult one, marked by uncertainty and isolation. Unlike some Webb families, who participate in multiple communities, Webb is the center of the Johnson's religious life. Patricia wishes they had broader familial and social connections, like Frank and Marwa do.

Despite the optimistic rhetoric of Webb literature, delineating religion from culture requires ongoing, daily negotiations that are never fully resolved. Within Webb families, husbands and wives sometimes disagree about the proper relationship between American culture and Islam, and the authentic sources of each. I asked Patricia to tell me about how she and her husband approach raising their children. She responded by recounting a recent argument surrounding her daughter's senior prom. Patricia initially told her daughter that she could attend, but her husband emphatically disagreed, stating that dating was forbidden in Islam.[67] In the second-generation social circles that the Johnsons inhabit, the senior prom often sparks disagreements among parents and their teenage children, as it did in the Johnson household. Patricia grew frustrated with her husband's opposition. "It's like my husband grew up the Middle East. I have to remind him, this is *our* culture. I swear he gets more conservative every year."[68] Patricia recognized that her husband imagines the "Middle East" as the locus of authentic Sunni Islam.[69] In Patricia's view, her husband mistakenly relies on their Arab and South Asian friends to adjudicate the boundaries of tradition and culture.

By contrast, Patricia sees her friends' opinions as rooted in their ethnic particularism and not necessarily as a source of Islamic knowledge. As such, Patricia had a different take on the prom, which she embraced as an essential American rite of passage. She delineated "our culture" as distinct from the culture of her immigrant friends, despite the fact that most of her friends are also American born. For Patricia, restrictions on dating render Muslims outside the normative fold of American culture as she defined it. Her daughter's attendance at prom presented an opportunity to enact her American Muslim identity at a formative moment in her adolescence, even though Patricia acknowledged that the prom posed potential religious risks:

> I want her to be a good Muslim and I want her to eventually attract the right husband. I want him to be a good Muslim, and so he'll be looking for a good Muslim woman. If he doesn't see that in her because of the way she looks, because she's assimilated to the way that American women look or acts the way American women act, then that would be bad. But it's a fine line because I don't want her to change for any man. I want her to find someone just like her dad. He's perfect except for that whole Middle Eastern mentality.[70]

The careful parsing of religion and culture allows Patricia to assert the Muslim legitimacy of her actions. Within the realm of culture, women at Webb maintain their ability to mark out the boundaries of American Muslim behavior. When Patricia claimed "our culture" as American, she upheld her ability to determine what is Islamic. As such, women—by virtue of experiencing American culture in their daily lives—gained the ability to negotiate ethical norms not just as Americans, but as Muslims as well. This authority is contested and marked by persistent anxiety over the correct path for their families. In the end, her daughter attended the prom with Patricia as the reluctant chaperone.

For Patricia, Islam is defined by its flexibility and accommodation to cultural norms. She struggled to understand why her husband took what she perceived as external cultural standards as religious norms. Foreign cultures represent restriction, depriving her daughter of quintessentially American experiences that Patricia remembers fondly from her own youth. The prohibition against dating is "cultural" because Islam—a flexible and egalitarian faith—does not set arbitrary limits on human behavior. As an African American woman, born and raised in the United States, and once a Christian, Patricia is confident she *knows* American culture because she has lived it her entire life. Not all Webb members agree with Patricia that their daughters should attend school dances. But all of them express similar confidence in their experiential knowledge of American culture.

Patricia's account underscores the contingencies of categories such as "culture," which are produced in real time, in everyday negotiations of unpredictable situations. The different moral valences undergirding Patricia's and Anthony's divergent understandings of "culture" and "Islam" return us to the contingency of these categories. They are not simply out there, waiting to be claimed by individuals and communities. Rather, they must be negotiated, created, and altered in historically situated moments. Culture, like ethnicity, race, and even "Islam," functions as a highly malleable discursive concept that marks important boundaries of authenticity and confers authority on particular practices and texts, while excluding others. Patricia marks out the difference between her and Anthony along the lines of "culture"—she promotes "American" culture, while he advocates for "Middle Eastern" norms. She is fairly confident, but by no means certain, that embracing "American culture," as she defines it, is also authentically Muslim.

Conclusion

Through shared experiences on the margins, members of the Webb community come together to imagine a more inclusive American Islam. Greater inclusion and belonging is the only way for American Muslims to move in from the margins of cultural citizenship. For all of the grievances articulated against mosques, through their ongoing critiques Webb members reinforce the idea that the mosque is a key institutional center for American Muslims. That is, mosques should not be abandoned; they need to be reformed to reflect what Webb members believe to be the proper relationship between religion and culture. But in order for such reform to occur, the voices of those Muslims unwilling or unable to conform to this vision must be diminished.

In their third space, Webb members seek to create an alternative community that facilitates religious and social belonging among disaffected Muslims, in order to help navigate the gap between dominant representations of Islam and their daily, lived experiences. While Webb members feel themselves to be on the margins of their religious communities, they have little doubt that they possess the cultural fluency to bring Chicago's Muslims closer into the

American cultural “mainstream.” This cultural knowledge makes their exclusion from leadership positions within mosques all the more unjust. These efforts center on a range of practices—*mawlid* and other devotional rituals, leisure activities, service, reading, and peer discussion—designed to produce a more relevant, authentic, egalitarian, and politically viable American Islam.

Although the Webb Foundation imagines itself as a kind of postethnic or postracial organization, its members rely (often unwittingly) on familiar teleological narratives that depend on the continuation of structural racial inequalities. These elisions are particularly vital to the construction of an American Islam in which they and their children unequivocally belong as authentic Muslims and patriotic Americans. The bifurcation between religion and culture marks certain Muslim practices as potentially contrary to broader “American” values. As the Webb community seeks a new foundation for an “indigenous” American Islam, in practice they unwittingly reinforce some of the same exclusions they seek to undermine.

3

All-American Islam

THIS CHAPTER SHIFTS our attention to Webb members' efforts to enact an alternative, "indigenous" American Islam through two areas of practice: leisure and service. As we have seen, Webb members define their community in opposition to two orientations in their mosques: diasporic practices imposed as religiously normative and revivalist theologies they conceive of as unduly restrictive and spiritually impoverished. As an alternative, they embrace American culture as the fullest expression of their Muslim identity. Webb members situate these efforts in two foundational narratives: that of premodern generations of Muslims, who embraced local cultures as their own, and that of white ethnic immigrants, who successfully made previously suspect religious traditions into mainstream ones.

The practices I explore here demonstrate both the possibilities and constraints of Webb's mission to rehabilitate American representations of Islam. Because of Webb's relatively open system for proposing new social events, the organization features a wide range of activities centered on attempts to construct American Muslim culture. This initiative includes activities such as apple picking, skiing, movie nights, canoeing, football games, and camping. All of these events center on the nuclear family unit, especially building relationships among parents and their children, as well as among peers, both parents and children alike. In addition to leisure activities, Webb youth and parents participate regularly in community service, partnering with various local organizations to provide assistance to less privileged communities. Service is an integral feature of Webb programming, as a regular part of the youth curricula and projects involving adults, such as fundraisers, walks for different causes, and an annual turkey drive. My interviewees understand these leisure and service activities to be the pillars of Webb's mission, both in filling a need for programming for Chicago's diverse Muslim community and in offering a positive, affirming representation of American Muslims as good citizens and the right kind of religious practitioners.

While Webb members would likely acknowledge that many different expressions of American culture exist, they largely discuss and perform "American culture" in the singular, through a constellation of practices that they deem to be unequivocally and authentically American. As we have seen, this project is born of the post-9/11 political and religious terrain, in which "Islam" and "American culture" have been represented as monolithic, oppositional entities. Within this binary, "America" signifies modernity, liberal democracy, and religious pluralism, while "Islam" represents violence, oppression, and exclusivism. At Webb, embracing and performing American culture represents their creative effort to contest this entrenched opposition. Moreover, this project works against the assumption that Muslims are innately bound to unchanging religious dictates.

These appeals to an overarching American culture reflect the organization's attempt to produce new practices of belonging and community. Its members attest to the ways that these rituals of American culture generate feelings of comfort, enabling them to "be themselves" in ways that they cannot in other Muslim spaces. Through leisure and service, Webb constructs possibilities for the inclusion of Muslims in America as well as a more inclusive, "indigenous" American Islam.

This double-edged use of "culture" rests on a broader ideology that uplifts the nuclear, heteronormative family. Although members maintain their ties to extended kinship networks, Webb activities center on the moral project of parenting within a companionate marriage in which spouses actively contribute to raising their children. Through leisure and service practices involving fathers and their children, the community contests representations of Muslim men as patriarchal and oppressive.[1] In its place, Webb shows Muslim fathers as loving, active parents equally committed to the well-being of their sons and daughters. Leisure and service activities in this third space, practices that are themselves shot through with gendered, classed, and racial hierarchies, help members to navigate the fraught cultural location of American Muslims, while aligning the representation of Islam more closely with their everyday lives.

Imagining America through Culture

Consumer practices are foundational to the construction of selfhood in the contemporary neoliberal marketplace. Webb participants enact American culture through a specific consumer practice—leisure—which they invest with particular importance in their construction of an American Islam. In this way, leisure is just as important as studying the Qur'an or performing the *mawlid*. But such practices have been nearly absent in the study of American Islam. Their exclusion from religious studies is the result of the pervasive tendency of scholars to cordon off what they consider "religion" (interior, individual belief oriented toward the transcendent) from practices that they deem as base, profane, and worldly.[2] It is tempting to see apple picking or football games as trivial activities that have nothing to do with the "real" work of religion, or as superficial and shallow constructions of "America."[3] To do so would obviate the meanings these rituals have for Webb members, who see them as profoundly serious acts linking them to other religious communities in the United States and to prior generations of Muslims. As cultural geographer Justin Wilford has argued with respect to evangelical Christians in the analogous suburban communities of southern California, "the mundane spaces of recreation, consumption, and labor become stages for spiritual self-transformation."[4] Webb members recognize the potential of these "stages" for achieving their vision of American Islam.

Consumerism is also foundational to the institutions, relations of power, representations, materiality, and embodied practices that constitute contemporary imaginings of "America."[5] During the Cold War, American household consumerism was celebrated as a marker of America's superior wealth creation, technological prowess, and moral ascendancy over the Soviet Union. At mid-century, the suburbs represented the locus of US middle-class prosperity and security, while cities became synonymous with danger, moral degradation, and fear. During the Great Recession of 2008 and in the years following, consumers have frequently been called upon to revive America's economy and its national spirit through household spending. These deep associations between consumerism and being American have enduring resonance for religious minorities who must deliberately prove their Americanness.

In the twenty-first century, "American culture" or "way of life" has emerged from transnational political and economic flows generated by global capitalist economies, governmental interventions, labor and migration patterns, travel, and military conflict. As such, immigrants do not encounter "American culture" for the first time when they arrive in the territorial United States. Instead, actors and communities in a variety of global contexts negotiate and shape ideologies and practices of "America" through their labor, what they consume, and what they do for fun.[6] "America" is a transnational commodity that is exported through multinational corporations, linking consumers across nation-state borders. That is, material goods and advertising have produced a "dominant white lifestyle of power and plenty as well as a multicultural and 'global' one."[7] Second-generation immigrants at Webb remember their parents having an ambivalent attitude toward consumer goods. As parents, Webb members limit their kids' access to television and restrict their amount of time on electronic devices. By and large, however, they do not see such material goods as morally questionable. Instead, consumer culture is a crucial mechanism through which Webb works to overcome differences of ethnicity and race. These activities also require disposable income that many immigrant families lacked or were hesitant to devote family resources toward.[8] They also require available time on weekends to spend with family and friends, largely free from the constraints of working-class employment that often requires unpredictable shifts. Many interviewees recall how their parents lacked the time on the weekends to play sports or socialize. This was a common observation among the children of students, factory workers, or parents who worked a combination of jobs to make ends meet.

Here, I take "class" to designate more than the material wealth of Webb participants. Instead, class is a dynamic form of identification that includes multiple markers, such as education, geographic location, income level, and social capital. Not all Webb families have high levels of income. The community offers financial aid for participants who cannot afford classes or activities. This self-understanding frames the construction of religious authority and the kinds of religious practices, such as leisure, service, and reading, that the organization promotes as enactments of American Islam.[9]

Class identification confers an important kind of authority on Webb participants themselves. In a crucial sense, it makes possible the Webb imagining of the end of ethnic particularism and to mark their generation as distinct from earlier ones. Webb members often alluded to their obligations as wealthier Muslims—those who have "made it"—to become a "vanguard of Islam in the West."[10] That is, they understand—as in many mosques—those people with financial resources, professional success, and educational attainment to have a special obligation to act as leaders in the American Muslim community. These class markers reflect Webb members' access to education opportunities, trips abroad, and consumer practices that foster both knowledge of Islamic diversity *and* experience with mainstream American culture. Many Webb members explicitly acknowledge that the privileged class position they now occupy undergirds their vision for American Islam. Many parents say that it is essential for their children to perform community service because they are wealthier than 99 percent of the world's population. That is, they recognize that their capacity to perform service is itself a product of class position. According to their logic, this group of American Muslims, with their breadth of experience and exposure to authentic sources of Islamic knowledge and American culture, are better positioned to speak on behalf of American Islam and to construct its vision for the future.

At the same time, Webb members admit that expectations of professional success have contributed to the lack of acceptable religious authorities in the United States. For Webb members, the ideal imam or scholar is an American-born Muslim who has obtained degrees from both a secular American university and a venerable Muslim institution abroad. Imams with such qualifications are hard to find because, as one participant said during a Webb conversation, "no Desi [immigrant of South Asian descent] wants their kid to grow up to be an imam. We all know the acceptable professions, and that's not one of them."[11] Several students, who by and large occupy such acceptable professions, mainly doctors and engineers, laughed in agreement.[12] At the same time that participants lamented the dearth of trained Muslim scholars, they recognized that it was unlikely they would support a path of Islamic scholarship for their own children. So long as Muslim scholars cannot come up through their networks of educational and financial elite, then this dearth of authority would persist.

At Webb, recreational and leisure practices generate a "comfortable" cultural atmosphere. Many of my interviewees indicated that Webb is a place they "can be themselves," much like their grandparents and parents who created places of worship where they could speak in their native tongue, dress the way they wished, and pass on essential practices and values to their children. In this respect, many of my interviewees believe they are following in the footsteps of earlier generations of Muslims. At Webb, its members' true and authentic American Muslim selves emerge in powerful and cathartic ways, but only, as I was repeatedly told, because they feel "comfortable" in the Webb environment. This feeling of comfort is achieved through practices that resonate with the choices and experiences of members' everyday lives. As I neared the end of my interview with Frank and Marwa, we had become somewhat distracted by the sounds of their kids running around our chairs at the dining room table. Even in the midst of all the commotion, Frank reflected at length on the benefits of Webb's leisure program:

> It's not just the formal program. That's important, but it's being in a community with lots of other people that are normal. They're not crazy in that they don't view Islam as *haram, haram, haram*. All these things are forbidden and try to carve out a little place that's different from America. Everyone is part of the society and professionals who are successful and engaged. Their kids are culturally American and very Muslim. That's one of the main benefits. It's very hard to be an individual Muslim in

> this society. You have to have a family and a broader community. That's one of the main benefits of Webb. It gives people the context. If someone comes from the angle that you can't be Muslim and be successful, you can say that's not even true. The kids look at the aunties and uncles. They're extremely successful people who are completely normal. And involved in all the aspects of society. And then there are the extremists—people who say society is evil and you have to reject it. You can easily deflect that too. You can say, "I grew up in a very healthy community invested in society." Our daily lives show them it's a false dichotomy. It's a lie because our whole lives show that it's a lie.[13]

Frank's description of Webb underscores how relationships construct this community, rather than any formal doctrine or program. That is, for its members, Webb offers the "context" through which they challenge dominant orientations within Muslim institutions and representations of Islam in broader cultural discourses. Parents offer their children models of being American Muslim, as "successful" exemplars who are "completely normal" Americans and devoted Muslims.[14] A variety of events, activities, rituals, and conversations contribute to this overarching goal of affirming the everyday experiences of Webb members and providing kids and parents alike with the resources to meet the representational demands on American Muslims.

The Webb community connects comfort with "spirituality," treating both as markers of cultural fluency and religious authenticity. In the foundation's self-description, creating a comfortable space facilitates the development of "spirituality":

> We seek to create a comfortable and inviting space for Americans to experience Islam through spirituality, and an atmosphere of community love and respect. We stress authentic relationships in an environment that offers opportunities for small groups of people to develop spiritually while building life-long friendships.[15]

The website presents Webb as a community of friends, united in their goal to develop authentic spiritual selves and to build a more inclusive, welcoming, "authentic" religious community for Muslims and non-Muslim alike. Through overlapping sets of relationships—among spouses, friends, and children—Webb offers the possibility of connecting with and exploring faith, broadly conceived, with the hope of generating more profound connections with God, the Prophet Muhammad, and other members of the

Webb community. In this self-description, Webb is a community embracing individual exploration within the context of supportive relationships. These relationships generate the possibilities for spirituality.

In this vein, Webb's mission statement affirms Islam as a source of "spirituality," an association that places the community in a longer tradition of American imaginings of the demarcation between "religion" and "spirituality." As a term that came into use during the nineteenth century among religious liberals, spirituality has long been associated with individual mystical experience, conceived of as unmoored from the constraints and conformist demands of religious institutions. Despite its common-sense association with liberation from the past, "spirituality" has a history, enmeshed in institutions, communal practices, and discourses, or what Courtney Bender refers to as multiple "historical entanglements" that have shaped not just contemporary conceptions of religion but also citizenship.[16] Spirituality here places the Webb community in the company of American religious practitioners and seekers who have sought out, among other things, a deeper affinity with other faiths, a commitment to progress, and optimism in ever-expanding human freedom.[17]

M. A. R. Webb emphasized the universal potential of Islam, as the fullest expression of the truths underlying all religious traditions. Although the consummate seeker for most of his life, trying out a range of religious identities, M. A. R. Webb ended up finding spirituality in the specific practices of Islam, such as prayer, fasting, and pilgrimage. To be sure, he celebrated the rational, universal aspects of Islam that resonated with his Victorian outlook over and against Islamic practices that he encountered in India as too ritualistic and backward.[18] In his final years, M. A. R. Webb anchored his formerly wayward spirituality in recognizably Muslim rituals.[19]

Even as spirituality helps to construct the Webb community as inclusive, it is also a term of exclusion. To be "spiritual, not religious" means to be liberated from "bad religion," or practices that are too material, too ritualistic, and too embodied.[20] "Spirituality" situates Webb as an alternative community to mosques and other established Muslim institutions that are seen as neglecting the spiritual development of its members. Instead, mosques have promoted stale ritual practices, rooted in either too much culture (ethnic particularism) or a lack of cultural resonance altogether (revivalist orientations). As we have seen, neither perspective resonates with the contemporary lived experiences of Webb members. Moreover, these perspectives, according to Webb members, foreclose American Muslims' relationships with non-Muslims, who possess valuable religious truths of their own. Spirituality marks Webb's opposition to the exclusive claims to salvation that they encounter in other institutions.

I explore discussions of the salvific potential of other religions more fully in chapter 5.

Here, I want to stress that discourses of spirituality also implicitly mark Muslims who retain these orientations as disruptive to the demands of "good" religion in the United States.[21] At Webb, spirituality is juxtaposed against certain kinds of Muslim institutions and practices, but not against Islam per se. Members find spiritual fulfillment in prescribed ritual practices such as prayer, though as we will see in chapter 6, the goals and meanings of prayer are open to debate. This emphasis on spirituality affirms individual choice of religion and culture rather than being subject to their dominance and power. Just as Webb participants choose American culture against diasporic forms of belonging, they also affirm their spiritual development through Muslim practice, which they align with a more authentic, personal, and culturally resonant expression of their faith.[22] Spirituality elevates the Webb vision of American Islam as superior to religious practices in mosques that Webb casts as narrow, overly ritualistic, and exclusionary. The possibility that "American culture" could itself be a source of oppression, exclusion, or marginalization is mitigated through this emphasis that members place on individual agency and choice.

This equation of culture with comfort is not unique to the US context, but rather indicative of broader trends in the global neoliberal economy. In their study of the youth café culture in Beirut's suburbs, Lara Deeb and Mona Harb document how negotiations over class status, ethical norms, and "fun" are inflected by subjective understandings of "comfort" and like-minded sensibilities among café patrons:

> Above all people go out where they feel comfortable. And indeed, "comfort" and the ability to feel at ease were among the most cited reasons for patronizing businesses. People often described feeling most comfortable around others who seemed to be like them—a feeling related to shared sensibilities about appropriate morals and social behavior, perceptions of class congruity, a sense of security linked to safety from physical or verbal harassment, and territorial belonging.[23]

Here, comfort indexes the complex construction of belonging, which cannot be adequately theorized through the framework of piety or through the material concerns of class. Rather, comfort suggests the multiplicity of desires, emotions, and goals that structure the moral, social, and economic practices of individuals and communities. Consuming experiences are vital to the construction and negotiation of class position, ethical practices, political stances, and social expectations.

In this way, performing American culture shapes pious selves. Webb participants maintain that these activities preserve the next generation's attachment to the faith that would otherwise be lost. Zaid puts it this way:

> You need things that make you feel culturally at home. I didn't have that. I didn't fit in. I had a funny name. I got picked on. I want the next generation of kids to feel comfortable in their own skins. It might sound superficial, but they're important if you want to develop an indigenous Muslim community and feel comfortable and be Muslim.[24]

Zaid longs to give his children this elusive feeling of belonging and comfort in which the boundaries between being Muslim and being American are no longer so evident and in which American Muslims will no longer have to explicitly name and claim American culture as their own. But in the meantime, he and other parents have to consciously select and emphasize certain practices as "very" American and distance themselves from practices that do not carry the same potential.

Through leisure and recreation, converts and immigrants alike at Webb affirm their American identity in the wake of their exclusion from mosques and from a wider culture that posits Islam and American culture as antithetical. Lisa, whom we met in the previous chapter, brimmed with enthusiasm as she recalled a Webb trip to take Iraqi refugees to a local apple orchard:

> I was really attracted to Webb because they don't care who you are and they say, "Let's go do something really American. Let's go apple picking! Let's go hiking!" What a great idea. There was no difference of being American and being Muslim. I sensed that at mosques, I was an outsider because I was American.[25]

She no longer takes her Americanness for granted and now deliberately seeks out experiences and institutions that celebrate American culture as positive, distinctive, and affirmative. This narrative occludes the possibility that American culture is itself a potential source of marginalization and exclusion for other American Muslims such as the immigrant imam. Instead, Webb offers the opportunity to participate in "really" American activities, things that are unmistakably, irrefutably American.[26]

However, proving one's American credentials is a continuous, urgent, and exhausting endeavor. Rahma, a second-generation Egyptian-American also in her thirties, has a sharp sense of humor and a self-awareness cultivated through more than a decade of activism in a variety of Muslim organizations in Chicago. Webb is just one of her many entrepreneurial, religious, and social commitments. Despite her seemingly boundless energy, Rahma lamented the emotional toll of these efforts:

> Usually the word American, when first generation immigrants speak about Americans, it's in a negative way. It means they don't have a connection to religion, they don't have a connection to character, *adab*. I'm hell-bent on changing that. I'm American before I'm an Egyptian. Even calling myself not a Muslim American, but American Muslim. I have to constantly prove myself as being American as everyone else. When people ask where I'm from, I say my parents are Egyptian, but I was born and raised here. So my language is very concise and precise. It's very deliberate. Its annoying and exhausting that I always have to go above and beyond. My goal ultimately is for my Islamic identity to take a back seat. I don't think I can do that with hijab, but I can't take off hijab. My religion can never take a backseat to who I am. I would have to go to a Muslim majority country. Then my nationality would take a front seat, and that might become annoying. So that's been my biggest struggle now and because of the media frenzy, which is so anti-Islamic. I try not to worry about it, but then I think, ugh, just more work, to overassert my Americanness, overemphasize my accent, and point out how much I like America.[27]

Rahma's exasperation demonstrates the active work and constant attention it takes for Webb participants to be American Muslims as they respond to multiple expectations of different communities. Among her Egyptian in-laws, she is too American; among non-Muslim Americans, she is too Muslim. Crucially, though Rahma experiences the bifurcation of her identities as externally imposed by her extended family, her coworkers and friends, and broader cultural discourses about American Muslims, Rahma herself does not see an inherent contradiction between being Muslim and American, but she does need to parse her enactment and representation of these identities carefully. In fact, she feels it is her obligation to do so, but this does not make her any less discouraged. Affirming her Americanness is both a choice and a burden. She cannot simply *be* Muslim American, or, as she deliberately put it, American Muslim.[28]

This affirmation of a singular American culture reflects the political constraints and possibilities facing American Muslims in the twenty-first century. Leisure and service at Webb aim to transform the public image of Islam from that of violent radicals to innocuous suburbanites. Lisa's insistence that Webb activities are "really" American highlights the need to amplify, and make indisputable, the political loyalties of American Muslims. It is undesirable, even dangerous, to contest these normative imaginings. Further, Rahma's remarks reflect what Zareena Grewal calls the "mediatization" of Muslim debates in the contemporary era of surveillance and scrutiny of Islamic institutions. Public discourse on Islam, which, as we have seen, relies on tropes such as "infiltration" and "creeping" into the suburbs, implies that "bad" Muslims are difficult, if not impossible, to detect and root out. These discourses and practices surrounding American culture are part of larger shifts in Muslim self-representation in which, as Grewal argues, "each is calibrated as a way to make Muslim Americans recognizable as (social) citizens who could 'stand for' the nation. . . . By identifying themselves against an incommensurable (anti-intellectual, sexist, racist, fundamentalist, and backward) bad Muslim immigrant, they reinscribe the exclusion of (some) Muslims from American social citizenship."[29] Performing American culture deliberately foregrounds Webb participants as "good" American and as "good" Muslims, but it also potentially calls into question the citizenship of other American Muslims who are unwilling or unable to do so. That is to say, the representational demands on American Muslims, especially those of the Webb community's social location, make certain avenues of practice—those perceived as producing spirituality and cultural comfort—especially urgent.

Football as Metonym of American Culture

In 2013, Webb hosted its inaugural father-son football game, an event that was a resounding success, generating a lot of enthusiasm from fathers and sons alike. Shortly after, the foundation posted a promotional video on its website to highlight the event. The video begins with a shot of Webb fathers and sons clad in matching orange and black shirts, with the phrase "a family that prays and plays together stays together" emblazoned on the back. The players warm up on the local high-school football field, jogging, doing jumping-jacks and push-ups, and applying "eye black" to their cheeks. Before the game, the teams perform *takbīr*, first shouting "*bismillah*!" followed by the requisite "*Allahu akbar*!" Set to upbeat music, the video depicts smiling fathers and sons, making long passes, running upfield to score touchdowns, and warmly touch-tackling and hugging each other. As a father takes a portable microphone for the call to prayer, the music dies down. The two teams line up on the field, shoulder to shoulder, facing east, performing the required prostrations, postures, and recitation of salat. The music resumes, along with the passing and tackling, until the video pans to the team of fathers clutching their victory trophy and a final shot of the two generations posing for the camera.

In terms of television ratings, revenue, merchandise sales, advertising, gambling, and its reach in both the National College Athletic Association (NCAA) and the National Football League (NFL), football is the most popular sport in the United States. What is more, football games are collective rituals that evoke patriotic sentiment, foster intense interregional rivalries, support a vibrant material culture, and celebrate aggressive, masculine strength. This is what David Chidester refers to as the "serious" side of popular culture in which transcendent concerns are addressed in spaces seemingly marked as separate from "real" life.[30] Football accomplishes just this kind of work, producing powerful communal effects of belonging and exclusion among and between fans.[31]

The choice of football is heavily symbolic as well as resonant with mundane realities. The Webb film shows American Muslims playing football, just like thousands of other men and boys in the Midwest. On weekends, Muslim boys toss footballs with their friends (of all religious faiths) and their dads. This is what Frank understands as combatting the "lie" that American Muslims cannot lead "normal" lives. Zaid invests sports with a similar potential to create integrated American Muslim selves:

> Basically, we need things that help bind us to the greater community—sports. We started doing father-son football; that was a big hit. We don't have to play cricket or soccer. . . . It was fathers on one team and sons on the other and they loved it. It's like any father-son event. The boys really liked roughhousing in a way that football is understood by everybody, your friends at school; they play it in the schoolyard. That translates very easily.[32]

For Zaid, football has the kind of overarching cultural appeal to transcend ethnic differences and tie Muslim boys to other American kids. The message here is that far from subverting American society, Muslim fathers and sons love this quintessentially American sport. In addition to playing football at school, it is also important for boys to play football with other Muslims because doing so removes any doubt of the sport's permissibility or legitimacy. In this way, Webb fathers help their sons feel comfortable as American Muslims, that feeling of belonging that eluded many of them in their youth. Zaid described football as a deliberate choice made over and against other options like soccer or cricket, or other sports that are potentially marked as foreign. Although soccer has become increasingly popular among

American youth, football is an American game. For Webb, football functions as a metonym for a distinctive and exceptional America.

These representations play on similar images as the 2013 documentary *Fordson*, directed and produced by the Chicago-based director and ESPN producer Rashid Ghazi. *Fordson* follows the football team at the Dearborn High School during its 2012 season, during which the players were also fasting for Ramadan. The film underscores the Americanness of Dearborn residents, interspersing scenes of American flags flying outside of Muslim homes, the Fordson team praying before games, and interviews with players and their families focusing on their patriotism. Like Christian players who form prayer circles prior to football games, American Muslims perform their own prayers, transforming the field into a devotional space. Salat can be performed anywhere; observing the prayers on the field at the required time is an act of asserting Muslim claims to use this field as Christians do, for prayer as well as for competition.

Beyond reworking associations between football, religion, and America, the ritual of the father-son game constructs overlapping layers of meaning that fulfill a set of broader purposes. At Webb, football, nature walks, ski trips, and going to the movies are meaningful performances because of their generative potential to create a new kind of American Islam. They are just as important as the *mawlid* and Sunday School, perhaps more so, because they engender religious and social belonging for the next generation. In this way, the American culture imagined at Webb is one in which religion pervades social life, rather than being limited to the boundaries of the mosque or the church. At Webb, using leisure practices to become better American Muslims is a deliberate and creative process. They remake football games, ski trips, and farm visits into morally laden, politically efficacious rituals. Combining quintessentially American activities into Muslim rituals claims these practices as sites of normative significance for Muslims, destabilizing representations of Muslim ritual as incompatible with an American "way of life."

The father-son football game further highlights the sophisticated ways that Webb members construct categories such as "religion," "spiritual," and "secular." These labels undergird the moral investments that they make in leisure practices and community service. As we recall from chapter 1, Malika called recreational activities at Webb "spiritual events in disguise." That is, for Malika, Webb activities such as apple picking and nature walks do not immediately strike one as "spiritual" because they are recreational activities that parents and their children do for fun. There are no sacred texts, no obvious set of beliefs, and no immediate religious benefits. But this is precisely where the generative power of these activities lies. Malika recognizes Webb's transformative potential to enact a new kind of American Islam, where "spirituality" is cultivated through an expansive range of practices that go beyond the rituals performed in mosques. Such practices offer the potential for Webb members to work out what it means to be an American Muslim through practices that exceed conventional boundaries of "religion." As a Webb leader, Malika sees tremendous possibilities in practices that at first glance seem to hold little religious power. In fact, their "secular disguise" is their greatest asset, as they are performed by participants who unwittingly engage in authentic enactments of American Islam, without recognizing or acknowledging that is what they are doing.

Model American Muslims

These links between race, culture, and religion are nowhere more visible than in the exemplary American Muslims who serve as models for the Webb community. As we have already seen, Webb founders are well aware of the political and religious elisions in their choice of M. A. R. Webb as their namesake, over a figure like Malcolm X. Malika identified Malcolm X as a key figure in the genealogy of American Islam. During a time in which American Muslims face discrimination and other obstacles to securing community spaces, it is easy to see why the community did not want to be immediately marked as Muslim, nor associated with an intellectual and activist known for his critiques of American structural racism. Moreover, as the majority of members grew up in communities where the Nation of Islam had questionable normative status, Malcolm X was a less appealing representative for the American Islam they wanted to build.

Instead, Webb publicly situates itself as a community in a genealogy of Anglo-American male converts.[33] The Webb Foundation's mission statement celebrates the "legacy" of two British converts, Abdullah Quilliam (1856–1932) and Marmaduke Pickthall (1875–1932), who produced a well-known translation of the Qur'an into English in 1930. The organization is not alone in its valorization of white male converts as models of American Muslim authority.[34] As Marcia Hermansen and Mahdi Tourage have theorized, in the North American context, white male converts offer the possibility of an idealized Muslim subjectivity that hinges on the "hyper-performance" of authentic belief.[35] For example, both Abd-Allah and Hamza Yusuf perform these signs of authenticity, and their biographies contain similar narrative elements. Like Abd-Allah, Yusuf exudes both religious expertise and cultural fluency. Abd-Allah and Yusuf share many overlapping Sufi connections in Africa and have hosted many conferences, retreats, and trips together both in the United States and abroad. Abd-Allah and Yusuf, along with M. A. R. Webb, are more than model Muslims; they are model *American* Muslims. Through their unmarked racial identity, Abd-Allah and M. A. R. Webb represent a universal American culture free from the constraints of race and ethnicity.[36] Here, whiteness is not a static racial identity. Rather, it functions as an ideological marker or "absence" that can stand in for American culture writ large. By contrast, as Malika conveyed, a figure like Malcolm X does not hold that universalizing potential in the religious and political context of west suburban Chicago. Black Muslim intellectuals and institutions potentially signify particularity and ambivalence toward the American nation-state.[37] M. A. R. Webb and Abd-Allah offer the possibility of an American Islam that transcends ethnic and racial particularity that members see as limiting and divisive. Conversely, whiteness functions as a signifier of moral and cultural superiority.

However, the crucial role of Black Muslim intellectuals in Abd-Allah's own conversion narrative highlights their influence on his development as a scholar and by extension, on the Webb community's understanding of their project.[38] The specific details of the narratives are less important than their structural features and the meanings that others derive from them. Webb participants find multiple compelling threads in Abd-Allah's account: the validation of convert experiences; the importance of activism and service; the critique of ethnic particularism; and the dual foundations of American Islam in Sunni traditionalism and American culture. Abd-Allah's journey to Islam centers on a crystallizing moment, shortly after he read *The Autobiography of Malcolm X*:

> I had no doubts about it. But I didn't know that you had to embrace the faith, and I didn't know any Muslims. I was believing it. I memorized *al-fatiha* [the first chapter of the Qur'an] in English. I remember standing on those beautiful hills of Cornell and reciting it facing toward the West, which is not the *qibla* [the direction of Mecca]. But I was having these incredible spiritual experiences as I recited *al-fatiha* in English. . . . We do get something out of the English translation. Do you understand that? It's not some kind of marginal thing. You can get some guidance out of that.

While Abd-Allah emphasizes the transformational gravity of this moment, he goes on to describe the gradual process through which his Muslim identity took shape, largely through his participation in the Civil Rights and anti-Vietnam War movements of the late 1960s and 1970s. During this period, Abd-Allah was drafted to serve in the Vietnam War, a cause that he strongly opposed. Like other Muslims, most notably boxer Muhammad Ali, who was at the time a member of the Nation of Islam, Abd-Allah began to build a case for conscientious objection. Alongside this legal effort he began to seek out other Muslims at Cornell and initiated a lifelong immersion in religious learning. At the same time, Abd-Allah found inspiration in the Black Power movement, discovering that it was "therapeutic" and that "the emphasis on the duty of black people, the integrity and the assertion of their humanity was really good."[39] He has also noted his admiration for leftist West African students on campus, especially their commitment to racial and economic justice.

Abd-Allah's account appeals to both converts and immigrants. On the one hand, he affirms American converts' experiences of marginalization, as he recounts his own struggles to learn Arabic, pray properly, and adopt other norms such as giving up pork and alcohol. Like many converts, Abd-Allah locates the beginnings of his conversion in his undergraduate and graduate coursework, where he began to question aspects of Protestant Christianity such as the Trinity. His firsthand experiences as a kid growing up in Kansas lend him a cultural authenticity enmeshed in Midwestern imaginaries of humble origins, hard work, and solid morals. On the other hand, Abd-Allah embodies a religious authenticity that resonates with second- and third-generation immigrants. Such signs of authenticity include his extensive links to foreign Muslim scholars, his impeccable knowledge of Arabic and classical sources, especially theology and jurisprudence, and traditional modes of dress. In my fieldwork, I sometimes heard the story of Abd-Allah's conversion following his encounter with the *Autobiography of Malcolm X*. But his involvement in racial justice movements, antiwar protests, and pan-African networks rarely, if ever, came up. Abd-Allah has in fact maintained links to African thinkers through his ongoing participation in African scholarly and Sufi networks, which take him to the Gambia for several months each year. These elements of Abd-Allah's past, especially his opposition toward American military power and the racist legacies of colonialism, are harder to detect in his more recent writings and speeches that emphasize the religious obligation of Muslims to embrace American culture. Instead, Abd-Allah's conversion narrative complements enduring narratives of progress and acceptance that have potent sway on the religious and political imaginings at Webb.

Consumerism and National Belonging

In their leisure practices, Webb members follow in the footsteps of other religious communities who have confronted the challenges of exclusion and marginalization of being outsiders to the Protestant mainstream.[40] In Chicago in particular, such ongoing dynamics of inclusion and exclusion have played out among white Catholic and Jewish communities in the suburbs throughout the twentieth century. Numerically speaking, the Jewish comparison is more appropriate. In the 1950s and 1960s, middle-class Jews settled in northern suburbs such as Lake Forest and Skokie. Consumerism facilitated the creation of an American Orthodox Judaism through a "kosher lifestyle." With its foundations in dietary regulations, "kosher" came to include a broad range of recreational and entertainment options.[41] The mass production of kosher products and the labeling of many popular American food products as "kosher" facilitated an American Jewish culture that embraced traditionalism while fitting into the expectations for American consumers in the twentieth century. Catholics have also historically engaged American culture deliberately and intentionally in order to prove their loyalty. Demographic shifts facilitated their entrance into the American "mainstream" as the children and grandchildren of European immigrants left urban parishes for the suburbs. By the late 1960s, white Catholics largely resembled their Protestant counterparts in terms of income and education level. Many also took up residence in the suburbs, where it became increasingly common to socialize with non-Catholics and to embrace cultural markers of Americanness such as food, dress, and language.

The teleological progression from exclusion to inclusion, marginalization to acceptance, erases the role of broader geopolitical developments, governmental intervention, and the reconfiguration of racial ideologies that facilitated the recasting of Judaism and Catholicism as American faiths. In Chicago, for example, housing discrimination practices and the lack of access to mortgage loans denied African American families housing options in suburban neighborhoods, while barriers to Jewish and Catholic residence were lifted.[42] As historians of "white ethnics" have argued, some Catholics, such as those of Irish, German, and Italian descent, have indeed benefitted from their designation as white, though this was only "achieved" in the latter half of the twentieth century. At the same time, the eventual, though partial, inclusion of Catholics and Jews in "tri-faith America" also depended on wider political developments.[43] With the Allied victory after World War II and the dawn of the Cold War, Catholics and Jews became willing partners with Protestants as fellow religionists fighting against godless communism. The American military became a more religiously diverse institution and promoted the three faiths as equal partners in the fight for freedom. Moreover, these narratives are predicated on the notion that the United States became a "Judeo-Christian" nation through the hard-working efforts of ordinary Jews and Catholics. To be sure, Jews and Catholics worked for decades, through a variety of institutions and initiatives, to be considered fully American. Historian Kevin Schultz how Catholics and Jews negotiated religious differences in post-war suburban neighborhoods, ensuring that the United States kept its "Protestant promise" to become a Judeo-Christian nation. That is, ordinary Catholics and Jews facilitated their entry in everyday negotiations of space and belonging and had agency in working out what religious pluralism meant in the mid-twentieth century.[44] Such processes are far from settled, even for Catholics and Jews. Anti-Catholicism and anti-Semitism remain powerful discourses in American society. What is more, this success story excludes Latinx and Asian American Catholics, who, like Muslims, remain under suspicion as foreigners who potentially undermine American democratic capitalism, security, and social integration.

These narratives of Americanization also obviate the contributions of Black Muslims who have creatively drawn upon racial and religious signifiers to refashion markers of Protestant, middle-class identity into signs of authentic Islam. In the twentieth century, the Nation of Islam built mosques in Chicago, Detroit, Los Angeles, Cleveland, and other industrial cities, gathering thousands of recent Black migrants to its message of racial liberation, moral critique of Christianity, and alternative narratives of Black origins. Edward Curtis IV argues that "rather than negating traditional Black Christian middle-class ideals, members appropriated them within a new Islamic matrix. Likening the liberation of Black people to the purification, strengthening, and protection of the Black body, Elijah Muhammad incorporated many middle-class Protestant values into a new Islamic framework."[45] In this way, Black Muslims have sought to challenge their racial and religious exclusions through an alternative Muslim imaginary or what Grewal calls a "utopic moral countercategory."[46] Through their critiques of American racism, Black Muslims belonging to various groups have sought both distinctiveness and recognition through their different claims to nation and peoplehood.[47] Though largely unrecognized by participants, Webb enactments of American culture build on these efforts to claim Muslim spaces and locations, but to different political and religious ends, namely, to confront the moral and political problems associated with racial divisions and offer alternative models of belonging and inclusion.

In the latter half of the twentieth century, Warith Deen Mohammed, perhaps more than any other leader, shifted American Muslim rhetoric and practice surrounding the American state. W. D. Mohammed called on American Muslims to celebrate their national citizenship and to turn their attention to the US context rather than a transnational one.[48] Rather than emphasize the exclusion of African Americans from the nation, Mohammed wanted Muslims to consider the United States their "home."[49] Moreover, he emphasized core values of the American nation—individualism, democracy, and freedom—as foundational to a universal Islam.[50]

The Webb community's models of American Islam suggest familiar narratives of assimilation and pluralism. Together with their corresponding occlusions, these narratives have enduring power and utility. Such histories offer appealing models for pluralistic inclusion for Muslims, in the form of the hope that Islam could one day be an American religion like Judaism and Catholicism. These narratives provide Webb participants with an essential historical orientation that animates their efforts to build inclusion and belonging during a time of profound anxiety. As Webb constructs its history through model white American Muslims like Webb and Abd-Allah, they unwittingly reproduce hierarchies that exclude racial minorities while replicating teleological narratives of American progress that also overlook Catholic and Jewish efforts to offer critiques of dominant religious discourses in the United States.

Yet these racial and religious dynamics are more complex than the mere replication of exclusionary practices. In fact, Webb members look to Sunni black intellectuals for inspiring their work toward an "indigenous" American Islam, most notably Sherman Jackson, the King Faisal Chair of Islamic Thought at the University of Southern California.[51] Jackson was the keynote speaker at Webb's tenth-anniversary fundraising dinner in 2014. A convert like Abd-Allah, Jackson's authority is constructed through his expertise in classical Muslim learning and his university credentials. In addition to the extensive scholarly impact of his ideas, Jackson's work has become more widely influential among younger Muslims.[52] In his academic and public intellectual work, he has argued that the development of a robust American Muslim community has been hampered by the privileging of "immigrant Islam" as inherently more authentic, to the effect of excluding black Muslims.[53] Here, the label "immigrant" refers to an ideology, not to immigrants per se.[54] This means that one need not be Arab or South Asian to privilege "immigrant" practices at the expense of African American perspectives, a dynamic we saw with Patricia and Anthony. Rather than representing universal Islam, Jackson argues that this ideology is instead the historical product of the political and religious traumas of colonialism and postcolonialism.[55] In place of immigrant Islam, Jackson seeks a "third resurrection" for black Muslim Americans through a renewed engagement with the classical sources of Sunni Islam and a conscious effort to enrich Muslim practice with the distinctive cultural and historical experiences of African American Muslims. That is, the cultural contributions of black Americans enhance, rather than detract from, Islamic claims to universality. On this point, Jackson and Abd-Allah find much agreement.

This robust critique of how religious authenticity is conferred through culture in American mosques is deeply appealing to Webb members. Like Jackson, Webb participants understand "indigenous" to signal a process of inhabiting Islam as Americans. For them, an indigenous American Islam must be brought into existence through third-space initiatives like theirs, where cultural and religious experimentation are allowed to flourish. Moreover, Jackson questions the indigenous/immigrant binary in a way that Webb members find resonant within their own families. Webb uses Jackson's language, calling for the creation of an "indigenous" American Islam in its print materials and at public events. This appeal to a new basis for normativity, enmeshed in authentic religious knowledge and cultural fluency, animates Webb constructions of American Islam. They use the term as a way of promoting a recovery of the Sunni tradition, as a means to create an American Islam that is inclusive of Muslims of all ethnic and racial backgrounds. Jackson's work points us to the ways that Black Muslim thinkers and communities serve as an important, though less acknowledged, foundation for the Webb project. Jackson himself serves as an example of Webb's embrace of black Sunni leaders who provide guidance into how classical religious knowledge offers a path to a more inclusive, dynamic American Islam. At Webb, playing football and doing community service are more than exercises in proving loyalty to the American state. Instead, Webb members take up Jackson's vision that to be American in this way is to fulfill their obligations *as Muslims*. That is, embracing American culture is not just a patriotic duty. It is an Islamic one.

Parenting, Masculinity, and the Moral Valences of Recreation

Webb participants draw from the intellectual and religious projects of Abd-Allah and Jackson, but the enactment of American Islam is decidedly a creative and sometimes unpredictable endeavor built on their localized, particular experiences. This is especially evident in the moral weight that the Webb community attaches to parenting, which has more to do with broader social constructions of childrearing and the nuclear family than any particular claims of the American Muslim intellectuals that they admire. In other words, the pivotal role that recreational practices play at Webb reveal how American Muslims are enmeshed in broader normative discourses that transcend any particular religious tradition.

Leisure activities at Webb center on fostering spiritual development through the nuclear family. This is not to say that Webb participants eschew extended family ties. In fact, as we have seen, many members live with and support their parents, participate regularly in extended family gatherings, and travel regularly to see family in other parts of the world. But Webb emphasizes nuclear family relationships, which it elevates as the locus of indigenous American Islam. One of the most popular parent-child events is father-daughter camping. Each year a group of fathers and daughters pitch their tents at a local campsite. They sing songs, make a campfire, go hiking, and stargaze. Frank, who likes to take his daughter on the trip, sees camping as something important that Muslims do together:

> Part of the value is having a bunch of people that are doing normal American things. The Muslims are doing it, so everyone prays. We have hot dogs and hamburgers, but they're all beef. We wake up and pray *fajr*. You can do everything that other people do. But we do it a slightly different way. It's a Muslim way of doing it.[56]

As with football games, Frank describes camping as an opportunity for Webb fathers and their children to claim American Muslim space. They make such a space through a variety of practices: eating according to Muslim dietary laws, praying at the customary times, and following the rituals of American camping such as lighting a campfire and singing songs around it. For Frank, these practices affirm his religious and social location; they produce comfort and belonging for him, and, he hopes, for his daughter. The camping trip allows them to be distinctive and "normal" at the same time.

Although Frank refer to the group as just a "bunch of people," in reality leisure activities highlight the intentional focus on parent-child relationships. In particular, Webb emphasizes the companionate marriage, dual-parent household that serves as the primary center for developing the proper relationship between religion and culture in the United States.[57] While extended family members participate in larger events such as the *mawlid*, by and large, Webb classes and other events revolve around the nuclear family unit. Companionate marriages that emerged in the twentieth century were largely without precedent, beginning with the husband-as-breadwinner marriage in the 1950s. However, this ideal was the product of multiple changes in attitudes and economics that began in the eighteenth century. These socioeconomic changes, coupled with the ideological shift toward emphasizing love as the basis for marriage, have created new possibilities as well as constraints within spousal relationships.[58] Whereas in centuries past, people married to extend kinship groups, for financial benefit, and to cement relationships between two families, in the twentieth century, marriages largely became about two individuals who were meant to seek and find their emotional fulfillment through each other.[59] This shift toward companionate ideologies was precipitated by broader, structural changes, but also resulted from the preferences and actions of spouses themselves.[60]

Webb members largely embrace this ideal, regardless of the various courtship practices through which they found their spouses. Fatima, whom we met in the previous chapter, explained that she met her husband through her extended family's social networks. Although they corresponded by e-mail extensively, prior to getting married they had spent only a few hours together in person. "You must not hear this kind of story very often," she said.[61] I laughed in response, telling her that she was at least the third person that month to offer a similar account. Other Webb participants met their spouses through mutual friends or siblings, at Muslim Students Association (MSA) events, or after graduation in settings like the Nawawi Foundation. However these relationships began, everyone I spoke with discussed the emotional bond they shared with their spouses and, most importantly, their shared commitment to raising their children as culturally fluent American Muslims.

The gap between marital ideals and lived realities often came up often in my conversations about families at Webb. For example, my female interviewees, whether their spouses were Arab, South Asian, or white, often complained that men rarely do their fair share of cooking and cleaning. Current surveys of contemporary American families show that although men spend increasing amounts of time with their children, women still do the bulk of the domestic labor, even when both spouses are employed full-time. That is, men and women actively construct and implement this ideal of spouses as companionate partners and parents, even as they are subject to its constraints and inequities.[62]

Many Webb parents believe that mosques impede their ability to fulfill their moral obligations to their children. amina is a white convert and mother of three who is married to a Pakistani immigrant. She had many grievances to share about the gendered dynamics of mosques, but she was particularly frustrated by the ways that gender separation impeded her ability to fulfill her parenting obligations:

> I can't pray with my boys, so it's scary because I can't even see them. I can't see them, and they can't see me. What if there's a problem, what if something happened? If they would let the small kids sit between the men and women, that would solve the problem. There are many ways to have separation that is family friendly and equitable, and they just don't do it.[63]

amina struggles to reconcile what she sees as an important task—to teach her children to pray in the mosque environment—with her desire to protect her kids and be a source of comfort for them. She could teach the rituals to her children at home, but she believes that the mosque affords a type of Muslim socialization that is difficult to replicate in other contexts. The mosque's spatial configuration does more than limit her mobility as a woman; it also raises amina's anxieties over the safety and security of her children in what continues to be a deeply unsettling environment for her.

In order to elicit these elusive feelings of "comfort," Webb's leisure practices elevate the role of nuclear families, parents, and especially fathers in generating new possibilities for American Islam. In particular, recreational activities enable parents to create a "comfortable" environment for their kids as American Muslims. For the Webb group, many of whom became disillusioned with mosques, the nuclear family has become even more important. This moral investment in the companionate, heterosexual family unit also reflects broader twentieth-century ideologies of familyhood and domesticity produced in suburban milieus. During the Cold War, the suburban home became the site of "domestic containment" against the Soviet threat, providing men and women the promise of security through prescribed gender roles, access to consumer comforts, personal fulfillment, and a refuge from new institutional and bureaucratic demands.[64] In the 1990s, as increasing numbers of Americans became "spiritual, not religious," parenting literature and consumer products began promoting the nuclear family as the site for "sacred" practices and values that did not belong to any one particular faith. Rather, as Kathryn Lofton puts it, parents were responsible for imparting values that were the "generally agreed upon moral middle of the presumptively plural society."[65] This period of growing wealth among middle- and upper-middle class families enhanced the expectations of parents to provide increasing opportunities for personal enrichment and growth for their children, and to measure their own moral value in terms of their kids' successes.

This intensive mode of parenting became ever more demanding for Webb parents in the years following 9/11. The uncertainty and marginalization of American Muslims amplified the nuclear family as moral center. As we have seen, Webb members did not trust local Muslim leaders to navigate the political and religious uncertainty of this period. They wanted a refuge during these trying times; Webb began as a group of nuclear families doing activities that would make disorienting times more inhabitable. The popularity and prominence of Webb leisure events represent the extension of these parental obligations beyond the immediate aftermath of the attacks. More importantly, they reveal how third-space practices provide the context through which everyday tactics become more regularized in an institutional context.

In addition to creating belonging and comfort, this project is inextricably tied to challenging prevailing discourses that conceive of Muslim men and fathers, in particular, as existential threats to liberal democracy. As a space in which members challenge overwhelmingly negative representations of Islam, leisure addresses the specific dissonance between Webb members' experiences as Muslim men and women, and the broader discourses that construct Muslim masculinity. In familiar historical Orientalist tropes as well as contemporary discourse, Muslim men are reduced to what anthropologist Marcia Inhorn identifies as "toxic traits": patriarchal, fanatical, hypervirulent, and violent, among other negative tropes.[66] According to this set of representations, Muslim men generally rule their wives and children by fear and use physical force to compel obedience to strict Islamic norms that deny women individual freedom and agency.[67] In these hegemonic imaginings, Islam serves as the unchanging religious dictates that ensure continuity and conformity.[68]

These representations have negative implications for Muslim men, who are subject to both formal and informal suspicion in European and US society. Such tropes are endemic to Western popular culture, political discourses, and religious traditions, which have helped to justify violence and surveillance against contemporary Muslims in the United States and in Europe.[69] They take on particular local effects, depending on the ways that religious commitments, national identities, gendered politics, and global geopolitical events intersect. For example, Katherine Ewing explores how Muslim masculinity has come to be stigmatized in Germany, occupying the position of "abject" other who is excluded from, and rendered invisible within, the modern national imaginary.[70] Highly publicized reports of "honor killings" recurred during my fieldwork in Chicago, playing into tropes of angry Muslim men who oppress women in the name of patriarchy and religious extremism. These representations have served a variety of ideological purposes, including various military interventions in Muslim-majority societies under the auspices of the "War on Terror," which served to "save" Muslim women from the oppression of their fathers and husbands.[71] Damaging to both Muslim men and women, these tropes portray Muslim men as domineering aggressors and women as their passive victims.

This list of toxic traits bears little resemblance to the complex and vibrant family dynamics that I observed during my fieldwork. As we have seen, Webb members—both men and women—are themselves critical of patriarchal norms and practices of gender inequality and exclusion. Ethnographies of "emerging masculinities" confirm that such Orientalist imaginings of Muslim men do not conform to empirical realities, nor do they account for the ways that marriage and family norms have changed over time. This is not to deny the existence of unhappy marriages, domestic violence, bitter divorces, or unequal shares of labor in contemporary American Muslim marriages. But in my fieldwork, I rarely heard about them in the context of nuclear familial relationships. Instead, I listened to stories about the shared spousal labor of raising children. In her recent study of Lebanese couples, Inhorn finds that "romantically companionate marriage" has become an important marital ideal, one in which (theoretically) heterosexual spouses share in the responsibilities of parenthood.[72] The men she interviewed for the project expressed devotion and love for their wives, seeing them as supportive life partners. Many of her interviewees took on the blame for their inability to have children.[73] Similar marital ideologies came through in my interviewees. Male and female Webb participants talked fondly about the efforts of both parents—fathers and mothers alike—to teach them to recite the Qur'an, to learn to pray, and to live an ethical life. Alongside critiques of gender inequities in mosque governance, I also heard about fathers who are ongoing "advocates" and "supporters" of their daughters' education and careers. Webb women largely affirmed that their husbands and fathers are nurturing mentors and companions, respectively.

Female Webb members also described how men at Webb promoted gender equality and female authority. Marwa, Frank's wife, told me that from the outset she felt a part of the Webb community because of how male members interacted with her:

> The first time I visited Webb, one of the male board members came to talk with me, looking directly at me, looking me in the eye, treating me as his equal, wanting to introduce me to other people and other board members. It didn't matter if I was male or female. That felt really good. Those things matter. Usually it would be a woman taking you around. I don't want to raise my kids, especially my daughter; to think that being a woman is a limitation.[74]

Marwa interacts with men in the Webb community in a variety of contexts, including the classroom, in board meetings, and during informal conversations. These interactions help to provide her with that elusive feeling of comfort that she has found lacking in other Muslim spaces. She interprets these multiple interactions with men as signs that they respect her as an individual and an equal contributor in this shared project of constructing

American Islam. Most importantly, Marwa reveled in the convergence of American Islam as an ideal and a reality, and the future it promised for her young daughters.

Serving Chicago

"Community service" is the other major piece in Webb's enactment of American culture. Service projects are a regular feature of its youth Sunday school program, in which children engage in volunteer activities. The largest-scale community service initiative associated with the Webb Foundation is the Muslim Community Turkey Drive, a collaborative project involving the Innercity Muslim Action Network (IMAN), the Sabeel food pantry, and the Webb Foundation. Zaid organizes the drive with his wife, Noor. Under his leadership, the 2014 drive distributed 1,400 turkeys to families in three schools located in predominantly African American communities on Chicago's south and west sides, Emmett Till Academy, Fairfield Academy, and Fisk Elementary Schools. Zaid told me that the drive began as a direct response to 9/11, at the initiative of a Hyde Park lawyer and his wife, who were active in local schools. They began reaching out to their friends and broader social networks requesting money to buy turkeys for needy families on Thanksgiving "as an expression of goodwill."[75] From its inception, then, the Muslim Community Turkey Drive, carried out during one of the most recognizably American holidays, aimed to promote Muslim inclusion and belonging.

This is when Zaid and his wife got involved, first by sending money and then serving as volunteers. As it expanded, Zaid and Noor took over the drive and partnered with the Islamic Food and Nutrition Council of America (IFNCA), the largest organization that certifies halal food in the United States. IFNCA is a 501(c)(3) nonprofit organization with access to wholesale pricing and inventory, and it runs the Sabeel Food pantry as well. As a result, the distribution of turkeys became far more efficient, and donations could then be tax-deductible. Within a couple years, Zaid and Noor were managing orders of more than a thousand turkeys, which they distributed entirely to families of children who attend Emmitt Till academy, an elementary school located at 63rd Street and Cottage Grove Avenue. Ninety-nine percent of the families at the school live below the poverty line.[76]

In order to distribute an increasingly large amount of food more effectively, Zaid turned to his longtime contacts at IMAN, the organization central that he identifies as pivotal to his religious development, especially his dedication to community-based activism. Zaid links his religious commitment to service to his particular itinerary:

> It's not that I'm a convert, but I learned everything a lot later. In college, I learned you can't trust anyone. The only thing I had, and still have, is that I grew up with most of my relatives being American, not Muslim. When I traveled to Pakistan, and then served for a month as a medical volunteer in Bosnia, I saw Islam being practiced many ways, every one organic and culturally appropriate. I focused more professionally and personally on community activism and charity. I was part of a medical school clinic that was part of a church. And then IMAN was founded shortly after. Me and Noor were part of the founding group of that clinic. I remember exactly where we were, working the blood pressure and glucose check. It was easier because I don't have the ability to recite all these suras. I didn't learn them as a kid. I just don't have the rote memorization to reel off this or that. I don't do a lot of stuff on that angle. The stuff I do is oriented toward public service. I don't have the time to do that. There is work to be done. And I would much rather do that work.[77]

Zaid sees his primary religious obligation—as a financially secure, educated, professional American Muslim—is to serve disadvantaged communities in Chicago who often lack access to affordable and high-quality food and healthcare. This is the "work" he believes is incumbent on him as a Muslim, much more so than embracing a particular theological or legal orientation, or knowing the ins and outs of Quranic interpretation. As an undergraduate and then a medical student at the University of Chicago, Zaid found himself increasingly impatient with fellow students who spent time debating the merits of particular movements or ideologies. He cultivated a deep skepticism of religious authority. Like many other Webb members, he began attending Abd-Allah's classes at the Nawawi Foundation in the early 2000s. But unlike the effusive praise I heard from other interviewees, Zaid was more sanguine. Similar to other Webb members, he says that Abd-Allah "saved" the Chicago community after 9/11, but Zaid also maintains that Abd-Allah is merely the scholar he "mistrusts the least."[78]

Zaid's impatience with what he views as theological and legal minutiae led him to seek out communities that would most benefit from his medical expertise and financial resources. He found like-minded advocates at IMAN, founded in 1997 by a group of DePaul University students. Palestinian-American Rami Nashashibi, who holds a sociology doctorate from the

University of Chicago, serves as its executive director.[79] Nashashibi was recognized as a White House "Champion of Change" in 2011 and serves on the State of Illinois's Commission for the Elimination of Poverty and the Governor's Muslim Advisory Council.[80]

In addition to volunteering in its medical clinic, Zaid and Noor attended IMAN's "Community Café," a regular social gathering featuring "socially-conscious" artists and performers.[81] Su'ad Abdul Khabeer shows how IMAN became a generative ground for "Muslim Cool," a way of being American Muslim rooted in social activism, especially the commitment to racial justice, and cultural innovation, through artistic expression, such as Islamic hip-hop.[82] As a site of dissent and protest against racial and religious inequality, IMAN has also been subject to constraints of state power that depend on nonprofit organizations to provide social services and are rooted in rights-based discourses.[83] The organization's mission extends to ending racism and promoting racial justice, improving the economic conditions of Chicago's urban communities, reducing recidivism among recently incarcerated men, and making educational and social improvements in the city. IMAN works toward these goals through job training programs, assistance in finding affordable housing, supporting grocery stores that sell fresh fruits and vegetables, offering medical care, and promoting arts and culture. Although a Muslim organization run by a Muslim staff, IMAN serves non-Muslims living in the immediate vicinity of their location. In the aftermath of the Great Recession of 2008 and the decline in federal funding for social services, IMAN, along with other nonprofit organizations, has provided increased support for marginalized and poorer communities.[84]

While at IMAN, Zaid developed his conviction that serving Chicagoans of different socioeconomic and racial backgrounds is an Islamic obligation:

> I give Webb a lot of credit. We used to go to the mosque and say can you donate and put a sign up on your wall. Some would give, and I respected those who did. Even before I was involved, Webb promoted the event. So many donations come from the Webb community. Because we have three sites, we asked for volunteers and got twenty volunteers from the Webb community who took a day off. It's another example of how they are different. What I used to get from people was, "Are you going to give this to Muslims? Are these turkeys halal?" And I said, "No, of course not. Halal doubles the price and the vast majority of the families are not Muslim, even at IMAN." I don't get that response anymore, but Webb never asked those questions. They just gave.[85]

Zaid believes that Muslims are at their best when serving the less fortunate, whether they are Muslim or non-Muslim. Keeping with his orientation toward action, he expresses exasperation at fellow Muslims who subordinate service to what he sees as secondary ethical technicalities or because they privilege foreign causes over local ones.[86] The closing of many Chicago public schools has threatened the existence of the turkey drive altogether. In 2013, Chicago carried out the largest single school closing in the nation's history, displacing over twelve thousand Chicago schoolchildren, predominantly in neighborhoods with primarily black and Latino residents.[87] Emmitt Till Academy was initially slated for closure. Zaid joined parents, community members, and activists to protest the closing; ultimately their efforts were successful, though many similar efforts fell short.

Noting that mosques no longer ask whether the turkey drive will benefit Muslims, Zaid identified a shift in broader Muslim organizations and communities to emphasizing the importance of community service carried out domestically and of highlighting these contributions publically. His family did not have the capacity to do community service. Zaid's father, who ran a struggling business during his childhood, had neither the time nor the resources to engage in community service in this way. Other conversation partners described how their parents and grandparents contributed to hospitals, schools, and other community organizations. Rahma attributed her activism and service to her grandfather and mother:

> My mom raised us on this service-oriented life. My grandfather was a great man, and he gets romanticized. My mother said that my grandfather used to say, "The leader of his community is its servant." Actually, the Prophet said that. Its not your dad's saying. But he was quoting the Prophet. The leader is one who serves it. Every Friday my mother makes rice pudding for the local mosque. And we haven't had ties to that mosque for ten years . . . so that's why I started working and volunteering in service.[88]

Rahma shares this commitment to serving the community with her mother and grandfather. What separates Rahma from her mother is that she felt compelled to represent these activities as markers of American citizenship.

This connection to American citizenship also shapes the types of activities that "count" as service. Many American Muslims also financially contribute to causes in their countries of origin, especially communities facing political, religious, and economic oppression. As an undergraduate student in the early 1990s, Zaid was drawn to these causes, protesting the first Iraq war and later spending a month as a medical volunteer in Bosnia. Despite investigations into potential terrorist connections of Muslim charity organizations, this has not prevented some American Muslims like Zaid from continuing to contribute to improve the conditions of Muslims abroad, especially since the outbreak of the Syrian civil war in 2011, which has contributed to the largest displacement of human populations since World War II, exceeding several million refugees. In 2016, Zaid and other Webb volunteers traveled to Syria, once again to provide medical assistance to refugees fleeing violence, famine, and political oppression. Other Webb members have provided financial support for organizations benefitting Syrians who remain in the country under horrific material conditions. Yet despite the long (and not unproblematic) tradition of American relief efforts in war zones, these activities are not necessarily understood as acts of benevolence or patriotism. As investigations into alleged links between Muslim charities and terrorist organizations continue, such relief efforts carry no small amount of risk. For Zaid and other American Muslims committed to fulfilling what they see as a fundamental religious obligation, the risk is worth taking. Zaid sees these efforts as part of the same category of ethical obligation as coordinating the turkey drive. But they have very different implications for his position as an American Muslim. Service abroad potentially calls his American loyalties into question; his service in underprivileged neighborhoods is a gesture of "goodwill" toward the American state.

The turkey drive initiative was also part of a broader turn toward community service in the wake of 9/11. In subsequent years but especially in the 2010s, mosques and other national organizations, such as the Islamic Society of North America, as well as key American Muslim intellectuals, began calling for American Muslims to be less insular and to integrate themselves more deliberately into local communities to demonstrate their Americanness. In Chicago, the Mosque Foundation, which serves the historic Arab American community on the city's south side, installed solar panels on its roof and received LEED certification for its recently renovated building in 2008.[89] By caring for the environment, the mosque sought to demonstrate that it was a good neighbor and attuned to the broad ethical concerns of other Americans.[90] This was part of an explicit attempt to bolster the mosque's American credentials after one of the masjid's imams had been accused of promoting Islamic extremism after 9/11. When I met with the wife of the mosque director who led the environmental project, she conveyed that these efforts took place as part of a broader phasing out of the "immigrant" leadership. Although Webb members like to say that such community service initiatives are "unheard of" among Muslims in Chicago, in fact many other Muslim institutions in

Chicago are working along similar lines to prove their American credentials through community service.

By using service to make the case for national belonging, the Webb Foundation and other institutions follow in the footsteps of other US religious minorities who have made service integral to their efforts to gain public recognition. Such efforts have produced ambiguous results.[91] During World War I, community service first emerged as an alternative to military service for conscientious objectors. Groups such as the Quakers and Anabaptists formed service programs for humanitarian assistance abroad. After World War II, community service came to denote the shared ethical aims of patriotic "Judeo-Christian" American citizens. In this capacity, Catholics and Jews created organizations that provided community services to immigrants and other marginalized communities, filling in gaps where the government was unwilling or did not wish to provide assistance.[92] While white ethnic minorities have gradually gained acceptance (though not without ongoing contestations and ambivalence on the part of Protestant religious and political authorities), American Muslims, who have been serving their communities throughout the twentieth century, have not earned similar recognition. Zaid and others hope to change that by highlighting the service contributions of American Muslims to their communities, as proof of their integration and loyalty to American society.

As with leisure, the ability to do community service depends on access to financial resources and the time to do this kind of work. The turkey drive draws donations from hundreds of primarily suburban Muslim families who give money, and often time, to this initiative. These laudable service endeavors potentially replicate the bifurcation between hardworking, successful "model minorities" who have succeeded under democratic capitalism and the less deserving, marginalized poor who require the charity of others.[93] Such initiatives also underscore that the needs of many urban communities remain unmet by the government.

While community service may have begun as a way to serve "others," over the years some Webb members have built longstanding partnerships through which they work to address structural problems that have compounded racial and economic inequality. Members like Zaid are part of broader networks of social activists in Chicago, who work in a variety of institutional settings to combat poverty and racism. For Zaid, serving others is the most important action he takes to serve God. In this way, acts of service do more than meet the representational demands that American Muslims be "good" or "moderate." Zaid's quest for social justice, whether on the south side of Chicago or in Syrian refugee camps, is perhaps exceptional. But it is also emblematic of the multiple spaces and practices through which he and other Muslim activists seek to bring about a socially engaged, justice-oriented American Islam attuned to the needs of all American citizens.

Conclusion

The previous two chapters have explored how Webb participants conceive of and enact American Muslim culture. Through rituals of leisure and service, Webb members publicly display a portrait of how American Muslims are already leading a quintessential suburban lifestyle. These efforts demonstrate the interplay between external pressures to prove Muslims' Americanness and Webb's internal conviction that American Muslim identity ought to be rooted in practices of marriage, parenting, and recreation. At the same time, leisure and service also reveal Webb members' intentions for these activities to have effects, namely to claim American Muslim space in a particular suburban social, cultural, and political location, and to generate belonging and individual spiritual development.

The practices discussed in this chapter are not unique to Webb. Rather they pertain to how American Muslim individuals and communities concurrently construct spaces and boundaries of belonging, making creative use of consumer culture and experimenting with real alternatives to the inequalities that shape their lives. Events such as the father-son football game depend on the available time and energy of individual Webb members. It remains to be seen whether these events will actually shift broader perceptions of American Muslims in a more positive direction. As we have seen, third spaces do not provide an ever-advancing path to liberation from gendered, racial, and classed hierarchies. These discourses partially determine the religious and social possibilities available to Webb participants as they construct an alternative American Islam, even as they seek to contest the marginalization of Muslims along gendered and racialized lines. In these practices of leisure and service, it is possible to observe the ways that marginal religious communities imagine and sometimes enact a more inclusive future.

4

Honoring the Prophet, Performing American Islam

THE WEBB *MAWLID*

THE *MAWLID* IS the Webb Foundation's most important public ritual. The celebration attracts large audiences and reflects Webb's growing confidence to promote American Islam beyond its core group of regular participants. The term "*mawlid*," also known as *milad* and *mawlud*, refers to a range of practices honoring the Prophet Muhammad, often conducted during the month Rabiʿa al-Awwal, the third month of the Islamic calendar and the month of the Prophet's birthday. Although historically connected to Sufi ritual and theology, *mawlids* are often performed outside the auspices of formal Sufi organizations in the United States. *Mawlids* in domestic spaces typically involve recitations of Urdu or Arabic hymns praising the Prophet Muhammad, recitations of the Qur'an, prayers and poems for God, and litanies recited in Arabic and Urdu.[1] Webb members grew up going to *mawlids* on a variety of occasions, including during the month of the Prophet's birth, as well as those conducted for other special events such as housewarmings and weddings. They remembered sitting on cushions in the company of family and friends, with recitations and songs stretching into the evening, punctuated by the sharing of copious food and animated conversation.[2] Many Webb members had performed *mawlids* in their homes; now, they seek to transform this domestic practice into a public claiming of American Muslim space.

The first half of this chapter focuses on *mawlids* performed at Webb in 2011 and 2014. These rituals highlight Webb's appeal to a broader network of Chicago's Muslims across multiple generations. Webb *mawlids* build on traditions of female authority in domestic performance to elevate women's participation and leadership in a public space. Women at Webb have been at the forefront of making the *mawlid* one of Webb's signature events, by leading in all aspects of planning, such as selecting the performers, choosing the texts for recitation, serving as emcees, delivering sermons, and leading the audience in poetry and song.

Mawlids at Webb are dynamic and improvisational in other ways as well. From year to year, various elements change, combining devotional, pedagogical, and cultural elements to produce individual and communal connections with the Prophet Muhammad. Shifts in ritual elements, namely music, language, and texts, reflect the conscious efforts of Webb members to cultivate American Muslim "spirituality" and produce an authentic American Muslim culture. For example, the 2014 *mawlid* was notable for both its exclusive use of English and its incorporation of spoken word poetry.

I also attend to the limits of such ritual experimentations in this third space. Not every *mawlid* is perceived as successful or efficacious. But these contestations over what constitutes a successful *mawlid* shows how the construction of American Islam at Webb is a process rather than its culmination. These missteps produce less anxiety and consternation than one might expect for a practice invested with such significance. Rather, participants are confident in the *mawlid*'s import as an inclusive practice that brings disillusioned Muslims back to a communal devotional setting. This is precisely what makes Webb so appealing to its members, who have found religious and social experiences at other Muslim institutions to be too static.

The second part of the chapter examines the broader ideological implications of Webb's efforts to revive devotional practices like the *mawlid*, which its members believe have been unduly and unjustly marginalized by what they refer to as the "Wahhabi" influence in Chicago. In response to these efforts to stamp out *mawlids*, Webb members present the ritual as an authentic, foundational Islamic practice that has been continuously legitimated by Sunni scholars. By engaging in these broader debates over *mawlid*'s permissibility, Webb members seek to carve out their community as an alternative for Chicago Muslims, filling a religious and social void that they have identified in mosques. Since 2008, Webb has hosted *mawlids* with audiences of up to four hundred attendees, well in excess of its one hundred or so regular participants on Sunday mornings. Participants bring multiple concerns and motivations to the practice, as a way to facilitate their individual relationships to the Prophet Muhammad and to God, and to represent Islam as a "good" religious faith in the United States. In response to a political context that depicts Islam as monolithic and incapable of change, Webb offers up the *mawlid* as an adaptive practice fully consonant not only with centuries of authentic Muslim practice but also with American liberal democracy.

The 2011 *Mawlid*: Performing Intergenerational Piety

The 2011 *mawlid* took place in a memorable location—remarkable not because of picturesque vistas, but rather because it blended itself so thoroughly into the suburban landscape of Chicago's ex-burbs. To get there, I drove to a large corporate park in Downers Grove, my Rav4 weaving through a maze of parking lots dotted with small shrubs and trees. I eventually reached my destination, a Doubletree hotel with a dark brown exterior and tinted windows, joining a stream of other attendees slamming car doors and calling on children to hurry up. I entered and joined the meandering crowd of several hundred already inside the lobby, all of us waiting for a signal to enter through the ballroom doors. I soon found Malika, who guided me to a table covered with a variety of objects. "If you want to know about what we are doing here, you should take a look at these things. We honor everything about the Prophet, including his favorite foods, such as dates, figs, olives, as well as things that he valued, such as a sword and a *miswak*, a brush used to clean teeth. Everything about his example is important."[3]

The ballroom doors opened, and members of the crowd took their seats around the small, elevated stage. I counted at least three hundred people in attendance, a crowd size Webb board members later attributed to Dr. Abd-Allah, who headlined the event along with a well-known *nasheed* act flown in from the United Kingdom. The emcee, Tahera Ahmad, chaplain at Northwestern University, began by instructing the audience on proper *adab* or etiquette. She told parents to keep their children quiet to allow for people to focus on the recitation and to ensure that everyone would receive *baraka*, or blessings, from the performance. As the main portion of the program began, Dr. Abd-Allah took the stage, leading the group in *dhikr*.

The musical group Shaam performed in three languages: Arabic, English, and Urdu. "We know all of you will be fine with English, some of you may struggle with Urdu, and that's OK because Malika told us there are a lot of Syrians here. But you have no excuse with Arabic."[4] The audience laughed, then followed along the trilingual lyrics printed on the programs, punctuated by the percussive beat of Shaam's performers and the sound of their poetic, soothing vocals. But singing was not the only sound coming from the crowd. Young children ran through the aisles, whispering to their parents, and calling to their friends. Adults carried on their own conversations as well, earning another rebuke from Ahmad, who again reminded them of the need for a quiet, reflective atmosphere to ensure the efficacy of the ritual performance. She encouraged parents to sit with their children in the front of the room. After repositioning themselves accordingly with children on their laps, the audience grew noticeably quieter, and Dr. Umar's voice seemed to float above the crowd. Participants began to close their eyes, swayed in their chairs, and began to recite, "*lā ilāha illā-llāh.*" The event concluded with men and women going to separate rooms to conduct evening prayer.

The *mawlid* had brought together a large, multigenerational audience. Arabic and Urdu were the preferred languages, reflecting the repertoire of the performers, Shaam, who had made a name for themselves performing for a largely South Asian audience. Indeed, Webb members of South Asian descent grew up performing *mawlid*s in their homes, where *dhikr*, poetry, and song were recited and sung in multiple languages. *Dhikr* centers on the remembrance and invocation of God through recitation and chanting of litanies, names of God, poems, and songs. *Mawlid*s appear to be less common among Arab families, though I spoke to several Webb members of Arab descent who also performed *mawlid*s in their youth. Some Chicago families participate formally in Sufi networks, while others retain connections to particular saints who are based on the Indian subcontinent, Africa, or the Middle East. Sufism, which derives from the Arabic term "*tasawwuf*," refers to Islamic mystical practices. Carl Ernst defines Sufism as "a teaching of ethical and spiritual ideals, which has historically been embodied in the lineages of teachers who held prominent positions in Muslim societies."[5] Some families of Webb members followed particular liturgies that linked them explicitly to transnational networks of Sufi devotees. But for most Webb attendees, *mawlid*s were part of a broader nexus of devotional practices centered on cultivating attentiveness to God and the emulation of the Prophet Muhammad.

Praising the Prophet

Webb's efforts to make the *mawlid* a foundational ritual for American Muslims is rooted in a particular theology of the Prophet Muhammad that celebrates him as an exemplary figure worthy of emulation. Indeed, following the Prophet's words and deeds has formed an important foundation for ethical action since the first decades of Islam, when early Muslims sought to follow the model for behavior established by Muhammad, his family, and his companions. For Muslims, the Prophet is the perfect human. As God's chosen vessel for revelation, preordained well before his birth, Mohammed was uniquely capable of bringing and enacting the final and complete revelation, the Qur'an. His wife Aisha is said to have referred to the Prophet as the "Walking Qur'an." Many Muslims also learn about the example of the Prophet through the corpus of hadith, or collection of prophetic words and actions. The table of his favorite foods and the objects he used demonstrates the material and embodied ways that the Prophet serves as an exemplary model. These objects signify the Prophet's humanity while also imbuing his daily acts of human existence (eating, dress, and hygiene) with devotional significance. Of course, Muslims disagree about the specific ways that they should emulate the prophetic example. At Webb *mawlids*, for example, these objects are on "display," in a glass showcase that could be shown to the outside ethnographer and observed by the *mawlid* attendees. The material objects are intended to connect contemporary Muslims to Muhammad as both an exceptional and fully human being.[6]

The *mawlid* is also linked to Islamic conceptions of the Prophet's intercessory powers, which depend on important relationships of ritual exchange. For all of his humanity, the birth of the Prophet Muhammad holds divine significance, since many Muslims view the Prophet as an intercessor between humans and God. One of the most tangible benefits of this role is the production of *baraka*, which refers to the blessings that are created through proximity to the Prophet Muhammad and other exemplary religious figures (including *shaykhs*, scholars, and saints). *Baraka* can also inhabit devotional spaces and objects, such as shrines and tombs. Recitation, listening to pious poetry or hymns, and prayers generate and confer blessings on those who perform them. Premodern *mawlid* texts emphasize the importance of rejoicing in order to express gratitude for God's blessings and to cultivate love of the Prophet. Prayers and remembrance offered up during the *mawlid* are a means to both express and to engender love of the Prophet as well as to express gratitude toward God for sending the revelation of the Qur'an to Muhammad.

For participants, the *mawlid* affords an opportunity to connect with the Prophet in an embodied, experiential way. Rahma, who helped to organize the mawlid, put it this way:

> It's not about the frills. It's about expressing the hadith that you have to love the Prophet more than your own self. It's a physical manifestation to me. And that's what sometimes gets lost. I've been really interested in *sīra* literature in general. If I were to study something, that's what I would focus on. I've always loved it; I love hearing about it. I can study it over and over again. But I still never felt a connection to the Prophet. I have a connection to his story, to his life, but not to *him*. And that I feel like is a result of years and years that people said you can't venerate the Prophet; it's akin to worship. So to be able to go to a *mawlid*, it's experiencing the physical manifestation.[7]

Rahma's description indexes the many benefits that she receives from the *mawlid*. For those Muslims who choose to perform it, the *mawlid* has its roots in the foundational traditions of the Prophet himself. Here, love is both the emotion that motivates Muslims to practice the *mawlid* and the emotion cultivated in the performance. An earnest student of *sīra* and other Islamic texts, Rahma knows the events of the prophet's life and the ethical lessons to be drawn from them. Her knowledge of hadith and *sīra* taught her that she comes from a "rich tradition," which gives her the confidence to embrace her identity as a Muslim during a time it is much easier not to be a Muslim. From the *mawlid*, however, she seeks something different—a direct, experiential relationship with the Prophet Muhammad that complements her religious study of the prophetic example and legacy. Rahma was one of the few participants I spoke to whose family has maintained connections to formal Sufi brotherhoods. In this case, her Egyptian family members are part of the Shadhiliyya, a brotherhood that has branches across several continents.

Accordingly, Rahma had a very specific epistemological distinction she wanted me to understand between the *mawlid* as a ritual and the story of the Prophet Muhammad as told in the *sīra*. For her, the pursuit of Islamic knowledge in academic and devotional contexts cannot produce access to "him," that is, the Prophet, as an embodied presence in her life. In our interview, she differentiated between the realm of religious knowledge derived through reason, study, and intellect, and the realm of "physical manifestation," the one that has remained elusive in her religious practice. Rahma's delineation between the *sīra* suggests her desire for an experiential relationship to the Prophet, rather than a discursive one. Rahma and many at Webb believe that these kinds of relationships have been marginalized in their religious communities and need to be restored through the revival of the *mawlid*.[8]

Building Community Bonds

In addition to their relationships with the Prophet, Webb members also seek out and build relationships with each other, pointing to the ritual's potential to create community and belonging. Webb's first executive director, Fauzia, spent her childhood going to *mawlid*s in her parents' and relatives' homes. She recalled how her mother led family members and friends in reciting the *Qasīdat al-Burda* (The Ode of the Cloak), a poem honoring the miracles of the Prophet Muhammad composed by the Egyptian scholar al-Būsīrī (d. 1298).

Like Rahma, Fauzia struggled to find the words to capture the *mawlid*'s profound individual and communal effects:

> How do I explain it? I feel spiritually moved, rejuvenated, and refreshed. You can't just come together once a year and expect it to feel it because it's not just about what you are saying. It's the people you're with. We say, "The souls steal from each other." It's the energy in the room. It's the vibe. One of the places I felt it best was in 2005 at the University of Chicago. There was a woman who was a student and she had a beautiful voice. She could lead the *Burda Sharīf*. She would lead, and we would sing together. All the chapters have a different rhythm, and every other one you read. We did it once a month. I would go religiously once a month. I had done hajj this year, and it carried my spirituality for months afterwards.[9]

For Fauzia, the *Burda* embodies the depth of the connection to the blessings of the Prophet Muhammad, connecting her to childhood recitation practices led by her grandmother, to prior generations of Muslims, to her own hajj experience, and to the other female participants. Many Webb participants discussed all-female *mawlids*, gathering women and girls from different generations. Webb members talk about *mawlids* as one of the ways that their mothers, grandmothers, and aunts instilled Muslim piety in them as children, whether teaching them to recite the Qur'an, sharing *du'as* (superogatory prayers) for various daily situations, instructing them on the mechanics and meaning of salat (daily ritual prayer), and serving as a model of *adab* (moral etiquette) through their hospitality and generosity to others. Malika described the "sisterhood" created by *mawlids*:

> In Schaumberg, my family, we used to have a *mawlid an-nabī*, once a year, for women only, and get together and sing. It was a lot of sisterhood and felt good. I had that memory. I knew from what I learned that people all over the Muslim world did *mawlids*, in different languages. There is a huge array of songs in languages praising the Prophet and talking about his characteristics and attributes. When did that become wrong?[10]

Other interviewees recalled *mawlids* in which male relatives also participated, often to mark various occasions. Women frequently led these mixed-gender gatherings as well, with *mawlids* being one example of "networks of connectedness among women and among men."[11] In this way, *mawlids* counter expectations of gender separation, female seclusion, and assumed male dominance in Muslim homes.[12] These and other domestic rituals function as sites of female authority that are often overlooked when scholars focus on mosques as the locus of Muslim practice.

Cultivating Female Religious Authority

Webb seeks to make these domestic ritual roles into public ones, and in the process, promote women's authority through what they conceive of as a foundational Muslim practice. Although Webb offers an alternative devotional environment to mosques, its members rarely advocate for women to take on functions usually reserved for men in these spaces, such as leading congregational prayers and delivering sermons. In the context of the United States, Juliane Hammer has argued for the interdependence of space, leadership, and voice in the construction of female authority in the United States.[13] Like the *mawlid,* many opportunities for female religious authority in the United States occur outside the mosque.[14] For example, Ingrid Mattson, the first female director of the Islamic Society of North America, has encouraged women to become chaplains and teachers. Mattson has argued that in these capacities American Muslims are not claiming some "new" role but rather recovering the continuous "spirit" of the early community.[15] The Webb Foundation cultivates ritual and governance roles for women in this same vein, grounding its emphasis on female authority through the recovery of tradition and a particular understanding of early Muslim history.

Webb also constructs female authority by elevating women's voices, to use Hammer's term, through poetry, lectures, Qur'anic recitation, and song. Hammer calls our attention to debates that link woman's voice to her sexuality and her subsequent representation of sexual temptation and danger.[16] In this way, women leading men in prayer or reciting the Qur'an poses a potential problem for ritual efficacy. The *mawlid,* as historian Marion Katz has argued, "sidesteps issues of ritual purity and mosque access" and thus does not hold the same potential to disrupt models of authoritative practice.[17] In all aspects of the *mawlid*—performative and pedagogical—Webb women occupy a visible and central position, alongside various male leaders—scholars, performers, reciters, and chaplains.

At Webb, these links between gender, space, and ritual efficacy never came up explicitly. But participants implicitly acknowledge the ritual advantages of their third-space community, especially its flexibility. From their religious and cultural location, which affords the possibility of generative ritual practice (but always cast as a recovery of original Islam), Webb *mawlid* organizers represent the practice as not just acceptable or permissible, but as foundational for American Islam. In this context, women's voices augment the devotional practice rather than threaten or undermine its power. By carving out an alternative third space, Webb women contest the relegated position of the *mawlid*, seeking to move it from the margins to the center of American Muslim practice.

Many participants praise the event for incorporating and building leadership opportunities for women. Rahma told me that she gained valuable skills in proposing, planning, and executing a major event. For her, *mawlid* has other benefits beyond those that she recognizes as spiritual. Planning the *mawlid* gives female volunteers the opportunity to cultivate necessary leadership skills. She described the multiple logistical tasks that she took on, from making the program, to setting up the stage, deciding where the potluck dinner should be held, advertising, and coordinating the various participants. All of these actions made it so that she was unable to participate in the singing and recitation portions of the evening. Rahma was proud of her contributions that made the event possible and that helped to facilitate participants' devotional practice.

Moreover, Webb women took on the responsibility of articulating the *mawlid*'s legitimacy and importance. Malika assumed this task, opening the 2014 event with this explanation of the practice's importance:

> The *mawlid* is a word that needs to enter the English language. We can have *mawlid*s any day, and we honor the Prophet daily. I want to emphasize two aspects of the *mawlid*, its continuity and its relevance. We perform the *mawlid* as an authentic, sound practice, and we do it in a way that is relevant to our neighbors, our community, and our time. If it was good enough for the *sahāba* [companions of the Prophet Muhammad], it is good enough for us.[18]

Her talk included many of the essential elements of Webb's overarching vision for American Islam: the call for culturally resonant practice, the need for spaces of religious belonging, and the continuity of American Muslims with other Muslims, past and present. Malika was one of many speakers and performers at that *mawlid*. Her talk laid out the legitimacy of the *mawlid* as an authentic, original Muslim practice that has particular relevance for American Muslims. As a public performance, it lays claim to the Islamic tradition while it is also invested with cultural forms recognizable to non-Muslims as

American. Like other religious terms such kosher or karma, Malika envisions a time in which the word "*mawlid*" stands in not only for Islam's distinctiveness but also its acceptance as an American religion.

Permissibility and Authenticity in *Mawlid* Debates

Rahma's comments regarding the charge that the *mawlid* is worship, rather than veneration, underscores the contested climate in which the ritual is performed in contemporary Chicago. At Webb, practices of the *mawlid* revolve around connecting this localized performance to broader Muslim debates over worship, permissibility, and authority. For Rahma, American Muslims lack an essential connection to the Prophet because they have been discouraged or prohibited from performing *mawlids* and similar devotional practices. As a result, *mawlids* assume a special purpose, both to build a more robust devotional life and to contest theologies and legal perspective that condemn the ritual as un-Islamic.

Mawlids have been variously practiced in Muslim communities since at least the eleventh century.[19] Scholars dispute the origins and dating of these celebrations, though there is evidence that large-scale celebrations took place in Fatimid Egypt starting in the eleventh century. These festivals were linked to the rich tradition of Imami Shiite devotional narratives and practices surrounding the Prophet and his family (*ahl al-bayt*). By the fourteenth and fifteenth centuries, large- and small-scale *mawlids* in Sunni contexts were a regular feature of piety in a range of Muslim societies in North Africa and Asia. They were often multiple-day festivals, blending a variety of activities such as poetic and musical performances, *dhikr*, eating, commerce, pilgrimage, and socializing.[20] The festive atmosphere of *mawlids* created opportunities for participants to build relationships among individuals, the Prophet, and God, as well as among the practitioners themselves. The *mawlid* thus served many collective and individual purposes, including the cultivation of the community, remembrance of God, giving thanks for divine gifts to humanity, and the attainment of *baraka*. As superogatory practices, *mawlids* have never been required. Rather, their performance shows how premodern rituals were infused with Sufi piety, especially its emphasis on the cultivation of particular emotions such as joy, the acquisition of *baraka*, and the veneration of saints.

As a practice that emerged after the first generations of Muslims, the *mawlid* has always been understood as an innovation. As a result, it has occupied a somewhat ambivalent position in Muslim scholarly discourse and in various contexts has been subject to debates over its permissibility. Katz has usefully outlined the variety of positions taken by Sunni thinkers on the *mawlid.* Some scholars, it was a beneficial innovation, providing the ritual context to give thanks to God, as in other worship practices such as fasting and prayer.[21] *Mawlid* supporters argued that the practice enabled Muslims to thank God for his greatest gift to humanity—the Prophet Muhammad. In this way, the *mawlid* constituted a nexus of practices rooted in exchange, reciprocity, and reward among Muslim communities, the Prophet Muhammad, and God. The Prophet-as-gift further linked *mawlids* to other forms of reciprocal exchange, such as charity.[22] The *mawlid* thus facilitated various kinds of social and pious relationships, which its intellectual supporters and practitioners saw as having benefits in this world and rewards in the next. Such relationships were embedded in "non-homogenous" and auspicious times that structured Islamic piety so that participants could most fully access divine blessings and rewards.[23] Within these interconnected relationships, scholars writing on the *mawlid* also focused on the cultivation of emotions, especially love and joy. These emotions were connected to the particular attributes and characteristics attributed to the Prophet Muhammad, as the perfect example of humanity, a patron and benefactor, and a potential intercessor with God.[24] Certain ritual elements, namely *qiyām*, or standing, at the moment when the Prophet's birth is spoken, embodied joy and reverence.[25]

Other Muslim scholars have seen the *mawlid* as a harmful practice. Such opponents worried that it crossed the line from the expression of joy and thanks into worship of the Prophet Muhammad. Others objected to specific elements they deemed excessive, such as banquets and music, and argued against the forms of reciprocity and conceptions of time described above. These scholars also reported ecstatic mystical practices in *mawlid* contexts, which they cited as dangerous and outside of the scope of the sharia. Scholars such as Ahmed ibn Taymiyya (d. 728/1328) (to whom we will return later in this chapter) saw the *mawlid* as one among many inauthentic Sufi rituals that ought to be eliminated in order to purify Islam. Despite ongoing scholarly debates concerning their permissibility and efficacy, these views represented a small slice of Sunni assessments of the practice. Although the *mawlid* has always had its detractors, the majority of Sunni scholars supported the practice for having immense spiritual benefits for participants so long as it stayed within the limits of the sharia.

With the onset of modernity, new opponents launched critiques against *mawlids*. Among them was Muhammad ibn 'Abd al-Wahhab (d. 1792), who argued that *mawlids* infringed on *tawhīd* (monotheism). In an effort to purify the faith, al-Wahhab wanted to eliminate all practices that fell under the rubric of *bid'a*.[26] Other scholars objected to specific elements of the *mawlid*, such as the *qiyām*. Critics often pointed to the practice as a sign of moral decay and decadence, particularly the festival-like atmosphere of some *mawlids*. From this standpoint, Muslim practice ought to be purified of elements that deviated from the original practices of the Salaf, especially those surrounding the veneration of saints, visitations to their tombs, forms of ecstatic practice, and various forms of recitation.

Modern Critiques of the *Mawlid*

Modern scholars also came out against the *mawlid*, casting doubt on the legitimacy of practices that developed after the time of the Salaf and questioning their compatibility with the cultural, religious, and political demands of modernity. Among them were the jurist Muhammad 'Abduh (d. 1905) and his protégé Rashid Rida (d. 1935). 'Abduh saw the practice as antithetical to modernization and its concomitant requirement to purge society of backward, "superstitious," and primitive practices. 'Abduh believed that *mawlids* and similar devotional practices weakened Muslim societies' capacity to challenge European colonialism. Other critics argued that the ritual led to emotional, sensual excesses among the masses who became beholden to religious imposters. These appraisals separated "true" and "authentic" Islam from "false" or "backward" superstition in order to facilitate social progress in the face of the European colonial threat.[27] Unlike other rituals, such as salat or *wudu'*, which fit more easily into recognizably "modern" values of order and cleanliness, respectively, the *mawlid* lacked such obvious functionality. Instead, the practice was relegated to the dustbin of "culture" or "folklore" as antithetical to rational and civilized religion. For his part, Rida sought to reframe the *mawlid* as an opportunity for pedagogical advancement, rather than a celebration of the cosmic importance of the Prophet's birth. In a *mawlid* text published in his journal *al-Manar* in 1916, Rida tried to eliminate all forms of *bid'a* from the ritual by crafting a *mawlid risāla* (expository essay), designed to teach lessons from the Prophet's life. By 1931, Rida had participated in efforts to recast the *mawlid* as an educational practice, and in the process, to distance it from its festival-like practices.[28] But he also maintained certain recognizable prayers and standard ritual elements of established *mawlid* texts.[29]

These critiques of *mawlids* as regressive or backward drew on similar categories as late nineteenth- and early twentieth-century European scholarship, which also characterized the ritual as "popular" (as opposed to "orthodox") forms of religious practice that deviated from what these scholars took to be the essential characteristics of Islam, namely its rigid legalism. As we have already seen, *mawlids* also have important gendered dimensions centered on female participation and authority in Muslim ritual life. This connection has contributed to their designation (and denigration) as "folk" or "popular" practice, a scheme that differentiated between "true" religion (that is, practices centered on belief and inward individual religious experience) and "folk" or "cultural" or "popular" rituals often designated as female.[30]

These classification schemes obviate the historical evidence that suggests the *mawlid* had broad social appeal. Wealthy patrons, Sufi shaykhs, religious scholars, and laypeople all participated in these events. Professional chanters and reciters came from across the socioeconomic spectrum.[31] As opportunities for more "open-ended" expressions of mystical piety, the *mawlids* became contexts for practitioners to sometimes exceed the constraints of conventional morality and worship. But this does not mean they were part of a devalued embodied "lay" practice that only appealed to Muslims on the margins of "orthodoxy." On the contrary, by the eighteenth and nineteenth centuries, *mawlids* ranged from state-sponsored affairs to performances hosted by Sufi brotherhoods to domestic practices.[32] In Egypt, for example, Samuli Schielke points to the close ties between legal scholars of al-Azhar and Sufi brotherhoods, suggesting the inadequacy of the popular/official binary for analyzing contemporary *mawlid* practices.[33] In parts of South and Southeast Asia, the term refers to large-scale festivals honoring saints or other holy figures, which can last for many days and involve a variety of activities including *dhikr*, dancing, socializing, and eating.[34] That is, *mawlids* often appeal to a range of religious and social actors who participate for different reasons. At Webb, too, *mawlid* performance reflects the multiple concerns of its organizers and participants, who similarly hail from broad social groups.

Improvisation and Experimentation

Webb's eighth-annual *mawlid* was held at the suburban community center where many of the community's classes and events took place. The atmosphere was more intimate than the *mawlids* held in large hotels. I recognized most of the participants as Webb regulars who attended with their extended families. The table displaying the objects associated with the Prophet was in its usual spot next to the registration desk. Participants milled around waiting for the event to begin. We entered the community room, its familiar cinderblock walls adorned with colorful tapestries. A small stage with large pillows, candles, and a couple of microphones sat ready for the performers and speakers to take their places.

This *mawlid* clearly had a different purpose and tenor than in years past. The emcee, Tasleem Jamila, an African American poet, musical performer, and producer, led the ceremony and read her poems honoring the Prophet Muhammad. Webb's intention to try out new forms, while remaining true to historical continuity, was then reiterated by the next speaker, Aria Razfar, a professor of linguistics at the University of Illinois, Chicago. Razfar noted that the idea for an English-only *mawlid* came to him and other Webb members while watching the Super Bowl. They observed that all-English celebrations were uncommon and wondered why that would be the case. Razfar went on to say that God sent the Qur'an in the "*lisān* [tongue] of the people," and by performing the *mawlid* in English, they too could access this original miracle of language.

The speeches ended so that the performance could begin, led this time by two Chicago-based musicians, Zain Lodhia and Aasim Chowdhry, known as the Green Conservatory. The two musicians played guitar while singing original compositions:

I'm racing around in all this clutter
Trying to prove I believe what you've said.
Sometimes the darkness in my soul feels so much better
Than any of the hope left in my head.
So tell me why, why should I believe in you?
Why, why should I believe?
Sometimes I close my eyes and wonder why.
Sometimes I just don't care.
But I know that we were born to rise before we fall, but I
Can't seem to figure out why I'm here.[35]

Following the poetic and musical performances, the program concluded with a talk, "The Remedy That Is the Messenger of God," delivered by Ustadh Usama Canon, a well-known scholar affiliated with Zaytuna College. Canon had recently relocated to Chicago and at the time was teaching at the Ta'leef Collective, an educational foundation that caters to converts. He began by naming the ways that this particular *mawlid* departed from the "expected" forms of worship:

> We feel unease about calling this a *mawlid*, but it is a productive unease. We have a female emcee. Performers are playing guitars. We are honoring the Prophet in English. We have a profound love of Arabic because the Prophet was connected to the context of the Arabian Peninsula and

> revealed the Arabic Qur'an. But I want to tell you a hadith from Umar ibn Talib, who heard the Prophet speak to different tribes in a dialogue not spoken by the Quraysh. The Prophet used that dialogue to respond to tribes regarding a dispensation from fasting during travel. This was the *adab* of the prophet. . . . Similarly, English doesn't work for all portions of our society, and there are many distinctions within English, many tongues. The Prophet embraced this complexity.[36]

Canon's remarks anticipated the mixed responses of many participants who remained unsure about some of the ritual elements in the 2014 event. Is it a *mawlid* if it is only performed in English? The linguistic choice generated ambivalence for Canon. Punctuated by multiple Arabic recitations of the Qur'an and hadith, his talk suggested that Arabic retain its prominent place in ritual life. Deployed in this way, the multiple Arabic references reinforce the ongoing authenticity and authority of Arabic, marking the doubts that Canon expressed with the music and language of the *mawlid*. As an authoritative figure who is part of the network of male scholars who inspired Webb to revitalize the *mawlid*, Canon's mention of the female emcee potentially unsettled and perhaps even undermined the organizers' intent to uplift female voices, incorporate musical forms usually associated with African Americans, and promote the use of instruments recognizable to other Americans, such as the guitar.

Noting the change in language and musical elements, planners of the *mawlid* were also not entirely sure the ritual had achieved its goals. Sharing Canon's conviction that the *mawlid* was "productive" nonetheless, Rahma put it this way:

> A few people were weirded out, and the crowd was not prepared. The linguist did not end up conveying the message that we wanted about why its important. . . . That message didn't really get across at the end of the day. This was a first effort. This is going to take time. Just to tell people that there is an American Islam or to be American and Muslim. Still a lot of people can't accept that.[37]

The all-English *mawlid* highlights the significance of Webb as a third-space community in which experimentation emerges, but to unpredictable effects. *Mawlid* practices are highly contingent on the particular motivations and resources of the members who plan them. In the case of the 2014 event, the idea came to a group of friends during a football game, and they worked to make the all-English *mawlid*, centered on spoken word poetry and guitar performance, a reality. They had no established ritual text on which to base their program, as with previous *mawlids*; rather, they drew together the artists and scholars with whom they were familiar and knew would support such an endeavor. They envisioned a more expansive conception of *dhikr*, in which remembrance and reverence could be expressed in language and genres outside of known songs, poems, and litanies. The program celebrated the contributions of African American culture to American Islam, gave ample space for female participation, and made English the language of ritual performance. These changes raise questions about what exactly connects individual Muslims to the Prophet. For example, is the connection forged through historically established recitations in Arabic, or through a culturally resonant expression that is familiar to the audience? The two are not mutually exclusive, but at Webb such tensions endure.

After the event, many of my conversation partners remarked that the event did not "feel" like a *mawlid*. *Mawlid* planners did not see ritual missteps as a problem for their community. In fact, participants described these changes part of a "process" of enacting American Islam. The only inevitability of this process is that new disagreements will emerge. These lived religious practices create new uncertainties (what makes a *mawlid*?). But participants saw all of them as essential opportunities for them to work out what it means to be an American Muslim. From this perspective, *mawlid* performance requires a pedagogical element. Its efficacy cannot be taken for granted.

Language and Belonging

The Webb *mawlid* points to the insufficiency of teleological frameworks that assume a linear process of assimilation. The absence of familiar Arabic and Urdu songs and the inclusion of unfamiliar forms of poetry and song in English made the event less resonant. Moreover, the organizers' inclusion of "American" poetry and song were not immediately compelling or moving to the audience as such. In other words, Rahma argued that it was less the inclusion of these elements and more that the audience lacked a framework to understand why these elements had been included. These efforts underscore the challenges of selecting "indigenous" American cultural forms for a diverse audience with different expectations of what this entails.

These internal debates reflect broader linguistic shifts around the use of English in Muslim spaces. Recently, scholars have observed the increased use of English in mosques. Mucahit Bilici has argued that American Muslims are undergoing a sea change with respect to English, from "diasporic suspicion" to "appropriative embrace."[38] This embrace is bound up in changing foundations of leadership and authority that recall the experiences of other American immigrants such as those in Catholic parishes. Whereas imams were once expected to preserve the languages, social customs, and ritual forms of their homelands, they are now increasingly expected to be fluent in English and possess facility in American culture more broadly. According to Bilici, American Muslims have retained Arabic as the "language of ritual," while they have made English into the "language of communication" and "communal unity."[39] Indeed, English has become the everyday mode of communication and has facilitated, among other effects, a common language for American Muslims. In the case of its immigrant members, the Webb Foundation is an outgrowth of these transitional linguistic and spatial processes that for immigrants help to transform America from a diasporic stopping point to a permanent home.[40] The overarching goal of making the American Muslim identity "seamless" reflects this sense of permanence, of the wholeness that many second- and third-generation immigrants want for their children.

As an organization that appeals to an ethnically diverse membership of mostly native English speakers and a sizeable group of converts, the diasporic framework only partially explains internal contestations over language at Webb. Moreover, we must be cautious about equating the category of "ritual" to mosque practices. This conflation ignores the rich devotional life of Muslims outside the mosque and the multiple languages that have always been a part of these practices. In Webb *mawlid*s, Arabic, Urdu, and English are used differently and variously. And as their childhood experiences have borne out, *mawlid*s have been performed in many languages over the course of generations.

Indeed, the use of the vernacular in *mawlid*s or other devotional practices is not a new phenomenon nor unique to the generational struggles of second- or third-generation and convert American Muslims. Fauzia told me about the time she invited her Pakistani grandmother to a Webb *mawlid*. Her grandmother asked if the ritual would be conducted in Urdu, her native tongue. Fauzia responded that they would be using mostly Arabic and some English *mawlid* texts. Her grandmother asked, "If the *mawlid* was in Urdu, I would go, but why would you go if you don't understand?" She had grown up leading others in Urdu translations of the *Burda* and celebrated *mawlid*s during life-stage occasions in her home. But in the absence of such familiar texts, the *mawlid* lost its appeal.

Agreeing with her grandmother that vernacular languages promote connectedness to the Prophet and to her Webb community, Fauzia told me that she would like *mawlid*s to be conducted entirely in English. Yet she identified the practical obstacles to achieving this goal. Unlike Urdu poems and songs, which have been in widespread use for generations, English texts honoring the Prophet Muhammad lack this deeper history and links to the classical traditions of Islam in which Fauzia invests authority. They tap into a familiar language but fail to produce the emotional depth that Fauzia finds in the poems and songs she grew up reciting in Arabic and Urdu. Fauzia could not really put a finger on why the singer at the University of Chicago moved her so much. But she did say that the power of the *Burda* is connected to al-Būsīrī classical Islamic knowledge, especially his expertise in hadith and *sīra*. Fauzia hopes that American artists can be similarly trained in these disciplines to ensure that their work reflects the wisdom of what Fauzia sees as the authentic Islamic tradition, the ultimate source of the *Burda*'s power. Although she sees English *mawlids* as a laudable project, this effort must be invested in the recognition and recovery of classical scholarship.

Between 2011 and 2014, the Arabic language became a contested issue at Webb as parents debated whether knowledge of Arabic was essential to being a good American Muslim. On the one hand, many parents called for more rigorous Arabic instruction for children that would augment the various other aspects of the program. For these parents, Arabic was necessary to the formation of their children as Muslims, not just for the recitation of the Qur'an and the performance of salat, but also as a foundation in Islamic literacy and access. A certain level of Arabic fluency would facilitate their children's entrance into a wide variety of Muslim communities, even though their primary language was English. Arabic would make their children recognizable *as Muslims* in the global *ummah*, providing them with the ability to participate in Muslim institutions where English is not widely used. Arabic here was understood to unite Muslims, through the authoritative words of the Qur'an and other sacred texts, including the hadith collections. On the other hand, other parents contested the necessity of Arabic for their children, arguing that it potentially undermined the mission of Webb to create a seamless American Islam resonant with the realities of everyday life, in which Arabic is not spoken. From their perspective, Arabic should be maintained in specific ritual contexts, such as salat, but beyond that, it served few other functions in social life. Moreover, these parents objected to the ongoing use of Arabic in occasional sermons at mosques, which they argued led to the exclusion of Muslims who could not understand, and therefore could not benefit, from its message. Such uses of Arabic reflected mosques' continuing disregard for the needs of its actual constituents. These parents did not want Webb to perpetuate these forms of exclusion. Whatever their outcome, these debates over language ideology and use demonstrate the dynamic and highly contingent conceptions of belonging on which the Webb community is based.

Claiming American Muslim Space

These debates over language, authenticity, and spirituality come together in Webb's justification of the *mawlid* as a vital expression of American Islam. The *mawlid*'s contested status in modern taxonomies of religion takes on distinct valences in the US context. Imaginings of Sufism and Islam within the US context have made the *mawlid* a prime candidate for Webb's project to inculcate an "indigenous" American Islam. Like many late nineteenth- and early twentieth-century religious seekers, M. A. R. Webb was drawn to the poetry of the Persian Sufi masters, who appealed to his quest for a universal faith. Theosophists and other American spiritual nomads of this period devoured British Orientalist translations of poetry and other writings that unmoored Sufism from the Qur'an and sharia. Ernst explains how scholars such as Sir William Jones "discovered" Sufism as an ancient philosophical tradition of Persian and Indian origin that they believed had little or nothing to do with the Qur'an, ritual practice, or Muslim scholarship.[41] Indeed, M. A. R. Webb found spiritual inspiration and universal wisdom in the "pure and perfect esoteric dimension" of such writings.[42]

This detachment of Sufism from Islam continued in the twentieth-century United States. Many countercultural American Sufi movements in the 1960s and 1970s practiced Sufism as a universal, "Eastern" reservoir of universal religion.[43] These non-Muslim Sufi movements appealed to baby boomers seeking authentic religious experiences through dancing, music, and meditation.[44] Such Sufi movements promised its members a universal "spirituality" in the place of staid, formal offerings of institutional religion. Although some Sufi organizations remained entirely separate from Islam, Marcia Hermansen has argued that throughout the twentieth century, Sufi organizations in the United States have created spaces of "hybridization" for "Islamic and American elements."[45] Some of the largest groups, such as the Bawa Muhaiyaddeen based in Philadelphia, include both Muslim and non-Muslim members. In these contexts, Sufism has created positive images of Islam for those Americans who were initially drawn to what they understood as its universal qualities, often unaware of its Muslim lineages. In the 1990s, Hermansen has argued that Sufi organizations' role in "Islamisizing Americans seems greater than its role in Americanizing Muslims."[46] Since 9/11, however, Sufism has taken on new significance in the American national project.

Today, Sufism is frequently cited as a potential counterweight to Islamic extremism. This view relies on the persistent dissociation of Sufism from "real" Islam, especially the (inaccurate) view that Sufism is antithetically opposed to norms established in sharia.[47] G. A. Lipton calls this ideology "secular Sufism," a construct of the American security establishment, conservative think tanks, and the media, which have sought to remake Sufism into the paragon of moderation, tolerance, and political quietism, uniquely capable of being melded with "Christo-centric" religion based on belief, faith, and the separation of church and state.[48] This discursive configuration depends on its inaccurate portrayal as an inherently individualistic, mystical, universal orientation, and its opposition to the rigid, unchanging, and potentially violent dictates of the sharia. Among other things, these representations obviate numerous historical examples of Sufi political involvement, the long tradition of Sufi engagement with *fiqh* and other Islamic sciences, and the communal dimensions of Sufi practice, including the foundational role it has played in Muslim devotion.

Webb organizers implicitly replicate this idea by claiming that the *mawlid* can help to undermine Islamic extremism. They want to offer Chicago Muslims activities and rituals to express love, tolerance, and to cultivate a benign "spirituality."[49] Webb participants' use of the term "Wahhabi" reinforces the notion that certain forms of Islamic practice constitute an external, foreign threat that must be vigorously challenged from within the Muslim community. While a range of Muslim intellectuals and groups, encompassing a variety of theological and legal positions, have contested the efficacy and permissibility of the practice, Webb participants focus exclusively on Wahhabi opposition and its potential threats to "good" Muslims. The political context of the War on Terror provides additional urgency to the revival of the *mawlid*, as a ritual that not only promotes the practice of "real" faith, but that also contests a religious orientation that *mawlid* participants find both religiously and politically threatening. Like many other Americans, Webb members see "Wahhabism" as a problem that must be contained, and as Muslims, they have religious knowledge, financial resources, and cultural acumen to defend against it. Rather than being relegated to the dustbin of "backward" religion, in the context of Webb's third space, the *mawlid* is a flexible practice, adaptable to American culture (as well as many others), and consonant with the broader demands of American religious pluralism.

Although the *mawlid* is potentially amenable to the demands of secular Sufism, it also subverts the assumption that authentic religion ought to transcend the law, ritual, and community.[50] Instead, Webb members ground the *mawlid*'s efficacy and authenticity in the sharia and assert it as a foundational ritual specific to Islam. They affirm the *mawlid*'s power to create an embodied, direct relationship with the Prophet, attest to its continuity with premodern forms of practice built on ritual exchange, and seek the Prophet's intercession in their lives. The *mawlid* suggests the ongoing desire for a physical, material connection to the Prophet Muhammad through recitation and other embodied forms of ritual practice. All of these ritual goals indicate the ongoing relevance and importance of the presence of "special suprahuman beings" in modern religious life.[51] When Rahma and other Webb members seek *him* in a "physical manifestation," they do more than affirm the ritual's legality, its pedagogical benefits for children, or its commensurability with modern life.

However, as I explore below, the best way to bring this embodied relationship with the Prophet and with other *mawlid* participants into being is far from clear. These uncertainties point us toward other ways that the *mawlid* generates ambivalence about identity, language, and piety. The practice is not so easily subsumed into a familiar teleology toward a secular conception of religion defined by individual belief, private devotions, and text-based religion. In fact, Webb participants maintain key aspects of the *mawlid* that modernists and Western observers have found objectionable. As we have seen, participants understand themselves to be developing relationships to the Prophet, through embodied experience, not through the discursive knowledge gained through the study of texts. By emphasizing these dimensions of piety, Webb participants seek to maintain continuity with other generations of Muslims.

Contesting the Boundaries of Islam

As we have seen, Webb members observed a rise in Salafi and revivalist influences in their mosques during the 1980s, when they say that *mawlids* "disappeared" or became "forbidden." That is, they witnessed the practice being relegated to domestic spaces, instead of being visible, public, and large-scale gatherings. Before the Webb *mawlid* in 2014, I spoke to Jamila, a Pakistani second-generation immigrant who grew up celebrating *mawlids* in friends' and relatives' homes. She described how Chicago Muslims came to doubt the practice's legitimacy:

> *Mawlids* were unheard of in the Chicago area before Webb started doing them. This is because Wahhabis made people afraid to perform them and so mosques never did them. But we know that Muslims throughout history did them, in all societies. This means we can and should perform them.[52]

Here, Jamila articulated three overlapping narratives I frequently heard about the *mawlid*: one, that it has been performed throughout Muslim history; two, that Wahhabis are its main opponents; and three, that Wahhabis succeeded in practically eliminating the practice from Chicago.

This sense that *mawlids* have recently come under attack stems from late twentieth-century legal and theological disputes, which were short-lived but intense debates. During the 1980s, Saudi-based scholars, such as the Grand Mufti Abdul Aziz Ibn Baz, issued a series of fatwas condemning its performance as a deviation from the prophetic Sunna. He argued that obedience to the Sunna took priority over the type of emotional cultivation that Muslims seek through the *mawlid*. His fatwa elicited a number of responses from prominent scholars, including Yusuf al-Qaradawi, the al-Azhar trained mufti with a large global following, and Shakyh Hisham al-Kabbani, the influential Naqshbandiyya-Haqqani Sufi leader based in the United States.[53] These fatwas then prompted further responses from a variety of institutions and thinkers, including Al-Azhar. Al-Azhar issued a fatwa in defense of the *mawlid* in 1993, which argued that songs, praise litanies, and serving food were all permissible.[54]

In an online fatwa published in 1998, Kabbani offered a lengthy defense of the practice, celebrating it as a legitimate expression of joy and gratitude for the birth of the Prophet Muhammad:

> His greatness reflects the Greatness of His Creator, and his purity outshone that of angels, mankind and spiritual beings. His advent on this earthly sphere was accompanied by extraordinary signs and miraculous occurrences, harbingers of the inestimable effect our perfect leader, the Prophet of Islam, the Guide of the believers, was to have on history.[55]

Kabbani presents *mawlids* as opportunities to mark the "independence day of the Muslim nation," analogous to existing patriotic holidays honoring the founding of nations:

> Everywhere the birth of a nation is commemorated by means of dazzling displays, parades, lights, decorations, fireworks, and military processions, as in America on the 4th of July. *Subanallah*, no objections are made to the commemoration of Muslim national holidays. Therefore does it not behoove the Muslims to commemorate the one who brought us independence from other than Allah, who took us from unbelief to faith, from idolatry to monotheism, founded our Nation and gave us our identity as Muslims? He gave us more than a nation—he gave us an *ummah*![56]

The *mawlid* thus serves a unifying function for Kabbani, strengthening communal bonds among Muslims and solidifying their common religious identity. Like similar large-scale celebrations, the *mawlid* commemorates a foundational event like the birth of a nation. He points out that states such as Saudi Arabia host similar events regularly, even though such events are technically *bid'a*. He also compares the *mawlid* to national conferences organized by the Islamic Society of North America and the Islamic Circle of North America, which are "dedicated to reviving and supporting the spirit of Islam," but which have no obvious precedent in the practice of the Salaf. Kabbani called on Muslims to celebrate the *mawlid* of the Prophet as a national holiday, suggesting that participants call the *mawlid* "1472 Annual Global Conference for Commemorating the Birth of the Prophet."[57] Distancing the *mawlid* here from its cosmological significance, Kabbani portrays it as an occasion to reflect on Islam as a religion of progress and the locus of identity for contemporary Muslims.[58]

By comparing the *mawlid* to other religious and political gatherings of which the *mawlid*'s opponents take part, such as fundraising dinners and a week dedicated to Muhammad ibn Abdul Wahhab in Saudi Arabia, Kabbani probes what he saw as the hypocrisy of the ritual's detractors. For Kabbani, the commemoration of the birth of the Prophet binds contemporary Muslims together and connects them to prior generations of Muslims. He goes to great lengths to demonstrate the early origins of *mawlid* performances during the time of the Prophet, stressing the cosmic importance of Muhammad's birth and citing classical scholars to elucidate the benefits and rewards of honoring the Prophet's birth. Kabbani affirms the *mawlid* as a foundational Muslim ritual, confirmed in its practice by continuous generations who performed it.[59]

Webb narratives of the *mawlid*'s marginalization echo many of these themes, including al-Kabbani's observation of "extremist" influence in the 1990s. He made the controversial claim that this influence extended to organizations such as the Islamic Society of North America. At the time, these statements prompted direct rebuke from ISNA and many other Muslim leaders. Since 9/11, however, scholars such as Abd al-Hakim Murad, the British convert who frequently appears with Abd-Allah and Yusuf and shares their project of reviving classical scholarship as a counterpoint to Salafi influence, has stated that al-Kabbani was too easily dismissed. Such comments confirm what Webb members have observed about the marginalization of certain forms of piety in their mosques.

Moreover, Kabbani represents the *mawlid* as a practice entirely compatible with liberal democracy. Contrary to early twentieth-century modern portrayals of the *mawlid* as regressive, Kabbani argues that *mawlids* are in fact commensurate with modern religion and politics. *Mawlid* opponents, with their dangerous anti-American (or anti-Western) ideologies, such as religious intolerance, violent jihad, and puritanical morality, represent false religion, retain attachments to arcane ideology, and constitute the real threat to contemporary society. Whereas the *mawlid* was once an example of Islam's incompatibility with modernity, for Kabbani it embodies the faith's progressive potential.

Alongside Kabbani's intellectual production, his Naqshbandiyya-Haqqani community became active in reviving large-scale *mawlids* in Chicago during the 1990s. From 1994 to 2000, the Naqshbandi Foundation for Islamic Education also held regular, large-scale *mawlids*. By the 1970s, the Naqshbandiyya had established a viable presence in the United Kingdom under the leadership of the Turkish shaykh Nazim 'Adil al-Haqqani. The "Haqqani" branch expanded to North America, as well as many parts of Asia in the 1980s and 1990s, bolstered by its successful media campaigns, network of professional followers, educational initiatives, and charitable activities. The shaykh's nephew, the aforementioned Kabbani, established a network of American branches in multiple states, including in the Midwest. In his historical examination of the Naqshbandiyya, Itzchak Weismann characterizes the western Naqshbandi branches as ideologically conservative but pragmatically accommodating to religious pluralism, eschatological universalism, and encouraging the growth of non-Islamic-based Sufi spirituality.[60]

The *mawlid* conferences displayed the Naqshbandis' organizational prowess and its appeal to a broad network of devotees. In its inaugural year, the event garnered 1,200 attendees, including notable participants such as Muhammad Ali. The event featured performances in Urdu, Persian, and Arabic by several Pakistani performers, and included participation from a variety of Chicago religious leaders from a variety of Sufi-related organizations, including the Islamic Cultural Center, which caters primarily to Bosnian immigrants, Tijani shaykhs, and various Naqshbandi leaders. Unlike the silent *dhikr* typical of most Naqshabandi performances, these festivals included vocalized performance that appear to be linked to this branch's particular conception of the *mawlid*. Called "*mawlid* conferences," the *mawlids* also included talks by prominent American and British scholars of Islam, including Marcia Hermansen, Alan Godlas, and Abdul Hakim Murad. In addition to their ritual functions, then, these *mawlids* also served pedagogical aims and were designed to educate Chicago's Muslims about the aspects of Islamic theology, law, and ritual practice. That is, these events featured not just the expected ritual elements, but also lectures and reflections on the history and importance of these events for the audience. That is, they combined ritual performance and pedagogy, a structure that the Webb Foundation also follows.

In interviews, Webb members made no mention of these *mawlids*. Instead, their narratives focused on the rarity of *mawlids* throughout the early 2000s. This claim is understandable when we consider that *mawlids* largely did not take place in ethnically oriented, suburban mosques, which as we have seen were the locus of their religious practice as children and young adults. One notable exception is the Islamic Center of Chicago, a mosque in the northern suburbs that has historically catered to Bosnian immigrants and that hosted regular *mawlids* during this period.[61] The Webb social and familial networks, which by and large did not include Sufi associations, perhaps prevented them from becoming aware of these large-scale *mawlids*.

Fulfilling Spiritual Needs

The *mawlid* is part of Webb's broader mission to challenge forms of religious and racial exclusion by creating a welcoming and inclusive community. In the case of the *mawlid*, Webb members want to meet what they see as the pressing needs of affluent, second-, and third-generation immigrants and converts who have found their spiritual lives wanting because practices such as the *mawlid* and *dhikr* have been marginalized. Webb measures its success in part by citing examples of the *mawlid*'s increased performances, some of them sponsored by mosques, usually held in hotels or community centers. Its members credit their community with transforming what was once a marginal practice and restoring it as a legitimate, rewarding Islamic practice. They cite numerous examples of this growing influence, from mosques sponsoring them in suburban banquet halls to informal groups who perform monthly in their members' homes.

Like Kabbani, Webb participants seek to place the *mawlid* in a continuous, authentic Muslim tradition. Whereas *mawlid* detractors have sought to exclude the practice as beyond the pale of normative Islam, Webb organizers insist on its legitimacy as a matter of historical fact (that Muslims have performed *mawlids* in a variety of times and places) and as a matter of normative intent (that the Prophet Muhammad found *mawlids* praiseworthy and rewarding).[62] Although the ritual performance of the *mawlid* varies at Webb depending on the year, its organizers persistently articulate this common theme: up until the contemporary period, the *mawlid* was a uninterrupted, rewarding performance, encouraged by the Prophet himself and sanctioned by prior generations of Muslim scholars, including the Prophet's companions. Their physical proximity to the Prophet Muhammad and the emulation of his example in everyday life mirror the association that the Webb community strives to achieve through the *mawlid*. But most importantly, the reference to the origins of Islam provides an important mechanism through which to sanction this performance. The companions or successors of the Prophet need not have performed the specific ritual components of the *mawlid* that Webb follows. Rather, Malika invests the veneration and celebration of the Prophet as a foundational and original form of Islamic piety, even as the particulars of that veneration have shifted over time.

This is an essential distinction in the context of American Muslim debates over the practices of the original Muslim community, its authoritative influence over future generations, and the parameters of the Islamic tradition. Webb leaders unequivocally assert that *mawlids* are not only permissible but also meritorious. Indeed, participants eagerly discuss the fact that *mawlids* have become an object of contestation between Salafis and their opponents. They revive the practice against the theological orientation of other Muslims seeking to impose their own (and in their eyes, deficient) normative conceptions of piety.

To justify this view of the *mawlid*, Webb members draw inspiration from a group of American Muslim intellectuals who have called for its revival alongside a nexus of devotional practices. These scholars—Hamza Yusuf, Abdul Hakim Murad, and most importantly for our purposes, Abd-Allah—sustain transnational networks of followers outside of the historical *tariqa* orders and activities, and they promote such practices as part of a return to "traditional" or "classical" Islam. Despite these intellectuals' formal and informal connections with Sufi scholars and networks, they do not mention or emphasize them frequently. Whatever Abd-Allah's private affiliations with Sufi orders and shaykhs, he does not usually make them known in interviews or lectures. Like Hamza Yusuf, he draws upon what Zareena Grewal calls a "vague, unspecified sufi spirituality" alongside "traditional" markers of authority that appeal to a broader Muslim audience who are largely not members of formal Sufi organizations or networks.[63]

Historically, *mawlid* and *dhikr* are tied to Sufi devotional practice, but they were never wholly subsumed within Sufism's institutional frameworks.[64] Even as *mawlids* have mystical components that derive from and resonate within a Sufi context, such as saint veneration, they have wider devotional appeal. Abd-Allah promotes the *mawlid* as an essential practice of the authoritative classical Sunni thought that lends the practice essential legitimacy and merit. Instead, Abd-Allah steeps the practice in Sunni traditionalism and broader Muslim ideals. *Mawlid* performance as promoted by Abd-Allah and

Yusuf professes love, mercy, tolerance, and authentic experiential knowledge over and against what they view as the narrow-minded, shallow, and ignorant Safafi ideologies. In a recent talk, Abd-Allah reiterates many of the themes in Kabbani's defense, focusing on its continuous practice, legal permissibility, and locus of consensus among Muslims:

> The celebration of the birth of the Prophet, this is a festival, this is a festive occasion, that Sunni Muslims have celebrated for thousands of years in the world, in India, Pakistan, in Egypt, in Mecca, everywhere. And no scholar ever said that it was haram. None whatsoever. Even Ibn Taymiyya, who is a Hanbali and one of the strictest of the Hanbalis, and one of the greatest of the Hanbalis, even he, in volume 23 of his fatwas talks about the *mawlid* as a very good thing to do and as a means to approaching God. . . . No Hanafi scholar, no Maliki scholar, no Shafiʿi scholar, no Hanbali scholar in a thousand years ever said anything about the *mawlid*, but that it is one of the greatest things that we do. But you should not do it only once a year. You should not limit it to twelfth day of Rabiʿa al-Awwal, but that you should do it all the time. All of creation takes joy in the birthday of the Prophet. . . . So where are these teachings coming from? Who is saying this? These are not Sunnis. I know this will offend them deeply but it is the truth and it has to be said. They have an innovation. They are the people of the innovation.[65]

Abd-Allah reinforces the cosmological significance of the *mawlid*, bringing contemporary Muslims not just closer to God and the Prophet, but helping to unify all of creation in remembrance and gratitude for the gift of revelation. Similar to Kabbani, Abd-Allah inverts the usual charge of *bidʿa*, accusing the *mawlid*'s opponents of unlawful innovation because they reject the authority of the classical Sunni schools of law. Invoking the principle of scholarly consensus (*ijmāʿ*), he aims to establish the *mawlid* as a fundamental practice, originating with the Prophet, linked to divine creation, and endorsed over the centuries.

Abd-Allah claims Ibn Taymiyya to make his case for the *mawlid*'s legitimacy, taking him out of the genealogy of Salafism with which he has become associated in the contemporary world.[66] As we have seen, *mawlid*s have historically produced no small degree of scholarly ambivalence. Both supporters and detractors of the *mawlid* have appropriated Ibn Taymiyya to back their positions. Ibn Taymiyya conceived of *bidʿa* as a reprehensible innovation, and the *mawlid*, as a practice originating after the time of the Prophet, falls into that category. At the same time, he elucidated the different intentions behind performing different religious festivals, constructing a hierarchy that took into account the pious or impious aims. He conceded that the *mawlid* and other festivals included good (*khayr*) and evil (*sharr*) components.[67] Raquel Ukeles has argued that Ibn Taymiyya's concession that the *mawlid* produced rewards for some practitioners ultimately served his greater goal: to redirect Muslims from innovative rituals to those that he considered orthodox, such that Muslims' "spiritual needs" mirror "devotional norms." Ibn Taymiyya's work has been read in multiple, often competing ways by later interpreters in order to serve the particular needs of their specific audiences.[68] Here, Abd-Allah downplays Ibn Taymiyya's efforts to purify Islam and instead highlights his place within an authoritative, authentic line of madhab-based Sunni scholars.

For Abd-Allah, the *mawlid* functions as a boundary marker to delineate between the people of "innovation" and the people of the continuous tradition of Islam. Against the charge that the *mawlid* represents a deviation from the practice of the Prophet, Webb members rely on the notion of consensus of the Muslim community. According to this narrative, even if the companions did not perform *mawlids*, they agreed that honoring the Prophet Muhammad and conferring blessings on him were valid and obligatory things to do. But more importantly, all of my conversation partners stress that the *mawlid* has been performed across Muslim societies for centuries. The continuous weight of that practice gives them the confidence that the practice has tangible benefits and rewards for those who perform them. By emphasizing a very short but effective period of intense opposition on the part of Salafis, Webb members maintain that their viewpoint represents historical Muslim consensus.

Abd-Allah has also facilitated other devotional practices since his return to the United States in the early 2000s, which have increased interest in reviving different forms of Sufi piety. He began leading *dhikr* sessions in his followers' homes, including those of Webb members. Once a week, several dozen participants gathered on their living room floor, with children on their laps, to perform *dhikr*. Over time, these sessions attracted many middle-class, professional devotees of varying ethnic and racial backgrounds from broad swaths of the Chicagoland community. Much like his Nawawi classes, many interviews described the great effort they took to attend these sessions, rushing home from work, packing up their kids in the car, and braving over an hour or more of traffic to make the sessions. Eventually, these sessions were broadcast online to accommodate those who could not make it but who wanted to participate virtually.

Other American Muslim intellectuals see the *mawlid* as promoting forms of piety that are difficult to access in contemporary Europe and the United

States. Hamza Yusuf acknowledges that scholars disagree about the practice's legitimacy, but he argues that the practice's benefits for American Muslims outweigh lingering concerns about its permissibility. In particular, Yusuf says that the *mawlid* provides American Muslim children with exemplars of "real" faith:

> The majority of scholars felt that it was a good thing. If you have an alarm clock that gets you up for *fajr*, that's a *bidʿa*, that's an innovation. But if that's what you need, then that's what you do to get up for *fajr*. If you're living a life in which the qualities of the life of the Prophet Muhammad are absent, which is the case for the Islamic *ummah*. We don't have even have exemplars anymore. . . . We don't even have *'ulema* who remind us of the practice of the prophet Muhammad. You have to teach them to love the Prophet. . . . The *ṣaḥāba* [companions of the Prophet Muhammad] on the day of Uhud, they were jumping up and trying to stop the arrows from hitting the Prophet. So that level of love, you know, that's what you want people to have. You can't teach that. . . . He [The Prophet] was more precious to them than their own selves. And he said you have not tasted the sweetness of faith until Allah and his messenger are more beloved to him than his own self. That's the sweetness of faith. And that's when faith is real. Other than that, it's just, it's not real. We can have faith, but it's more like a just lip service. That's why teaching our children, especially in these lands, like in Europe and America. . . . When do they see the beauties of Islam? To deny the importance of these things is really insane. That's my opinion.[69]

For Yusuf, the *mawlid* has specific connotations and benefits in the United States. Because they live outside of the times and places with access to these authorities, American Muslims lack models for authentic faith and practice.[70] Yusuf views contemporary American society as devoid of profound spirituality; the *mawlid* offers the possibility of cultivating a faith through embodied connections with traditional exemplars who lived this kind of faith. The *mawlid* provides access to these models of self-denial and self-sacrifice. Here Yusuf implies that a scholar appropriately trained in classical Islamic knowledge must guide American Muslims in their devotions by sharing his wisdom of a life devoted to the Prophet. But crucially, he offers the ritual as an accessible act of piety, available to everyone who cultivates an embodied, selfless relationship to the Prophet, exemplary companions, scholars, and ultimately God. This is what Rahma meant when she said it is about "loving the Prophet more than yourself."[71]

Yusuf, Abd-Allah, and Kabbani use a series of inversions to challenge arguments made against the *mawlid*'s permissibility and efficacy. If its opponents have railed against it as "backward," Kabbani asserts its potential as a modern festival and celebration. Others have called it an innovation, beyond the pale of Islam; Abd-Allah argues not just for its legality, but for its centrality—as a continuous, legitimate ritual sanctioned by the Prophet himself. Critics have charged that it plays into base emotions; Yusuf celebrates the *mawlid* as a reservoir of a more pure and authentic Islam. Webb members share with Yusuf the perception that American Muslims need to build what he calls the "sweetness of faith" or "real" faith. This "real" faith is what many Webb members feel is lacking in their spiritual lives, and thus it must be actively and explicitly rebuilt in their American context. For many of them, Webb is the only place where they can be their "real" religious selves. But Webb participants do not express similar concerns about the lack of pious examples in contemporary America. Instead, *mawlid* practices represent a ritual opportunity to remake American Islam as an "indigenous" faith, interweaving Sunni traditionalism, Sufi piety, and American culture, and reconfiguring gendered authority. For Webb participants, there is every reason to believe that the United States can become the site of authentic, if not ideal, Islamic practice.

Conclusion

As the organization's paradigmatic American Muslim ritual, Webb members see the *mawlid* as fulfilling its mission of bringing a wider swath of Chicago's Muslims back into devotional practice and into the fold of a Muslim religious and social community. Like leisure practices, the *mawlid* produces belonging and community in a number of ways: by facilitating the participants' connections to the Prophet Muhammad and God, including women in ritual and leadership roles, incorporating experimental cultural forms, such as spoken word poetry, and facilitating friendships among *mawlid* participants.

Recovered from its marginalization, the *mawlid* showcases what Webb members see as the exceptional aspects of American culture, which have facilitated their recovery of the *mawlid* and reinfused the Chicago Muslim community with a renewed "spirituality." In this way, the *mawlid* offers an alternative narrative of Islam as a flexible, uplifting, and celebratory faith.

At the same time, the *mawlid* generates no small amount of ambivalence among its participants. Much of this ambivalence stems from the contingent and dynamic aspects of ritual performance that takes place in the third space at Webb. Even as Webb members celebrate the success of the *mawlid*, they return to foundational questions: *What does the* mawlid *do? Which communities are we trying to reach? How should one relate to the Prophet? To God?* Rooted in enduring notions of ritual exchange, oral performance, and the transmission of *baraka*, the *mawlid* unsettles modern, secular conceptions of religiosity. Although the Webb community seeks to make American Islam align with many of these conceptions, the *mawlid* also challenges paradigms of religion as individual, private faith.

This ambivalence also mirrors global debates over the practice's legitimacy and authenticity in contemporary Islam. A focal point in enduring conversations over the role of innovation and authenticity in the Islamic tradition, the *mawlid* brings practices of exclusion back to the fore. The Webb community seeks to bring the *mawlid* out of the margins into the center of Sunni Islam. In doing so, Webb members, supported in their assertions by scholars such as Abd-Allah and Kabbani, relegate other Muslims to the margins of Islam, or, as Abd-Allah refers to them, as the "people of innovation." The *mawlid*, then, enables the Webb community to lay claim to an authentic Sunni spirituality, one that is itself invested in marking the boundaries of the Islamic tradition.

5

"I Want to Know the Context"

DEBATING RELIGIOUS PLURALISM IN THE QUR'AN

THE NEXT THREE chapters focus on American Muslim engagement with texts, broadly conceived. Communal reading and discussion of texts are one of Webb's core activities, central to its self-understanding of an open and welcoming space for Muslim debate and ritual exploration. Far from an isolated act, reading in this context is eminently social, bringing Webb participants in conversation not only with each other, but also with various other interlocutors who emerge from the readings. The conversations thus include a range of "voices around the text": historical and contemporary; imagined and physically present; Muslim and non-Muslim.[1] To get at these multiple layers of conversation, I employ what Jonathan Boyarin has termed the "ethnography of reading" in order to trace how the students engage, contest, and generate interpretations in dialogue with each other, alongside their dynamic readings of texts within familial, educational, and media contexts.[2] In this chapter, I examine debates about soteriological pluralism in the Qur'an, a conversation into which Webb students brought multiple motivations: devotional study; determining what God requires of them as individuals and as a community; and establishing boundaries and connections among other Muslim and non-Muslim communities.[3]

Finding American Religious Pluralism in the Qur'an

As a text, the Qur'an occupies polarized positions in American cultural discourses. Groups embracing divergent agendas claim to have captured its essential message. Right-wing pundits rail on the text for its purportedly violent and oppressive character. Secular critics decry its incompatibility with modern individualism and freedom. Interfaith activists attest to the Qur'an's peaceful and tolerant ethos. American Muslim communities like Webb find themselves at the center of these wider representations, which neither capture the rich dimensions of Muslim devotional practice, nor attest to the dynamic and diverse ways that Muslims have historically approached the interpretation of the Qur'an.

Indeed, the US Protestant discourse of religious pluralism has profoundly shaped the ways that American Muslims read and interpret the Qur'an.[4] In particular, Muslims face increasing pressure to affirm, through Qur'anic interpretation and exegesis (*tafsīr*), that Islam recognizes Judaism and Christianity as salvific faiths and to downplay Islamic claims to superiority. The embrace of the "Abrahamic faiths" has become another test of national belonging. The demands of religious pluralism mean that non-Muslim readings of the Qur'an necessarily influence, structure, and add a particular urgency to Webb participants' engagement with the text. Webb participants employed multiple hermeneutical strategies in order to challenge broader culture discourses that have vilified the text (and by extension, Islam) as oppressive and antithetical to American religious pluralism. In doing so, they both affirmed and challenged the logic of pluralism.

Seeking to uphold ecumenicism in the Qur'an, Webb students appropriated a hermeneutical lens developed by classical Muslim exegetes known as the *asbāb al-nuzūl* (circumstances of revelation). They used and modified this concept under the rubric of "context," in order to make the case for the commensurability of Islam and religious pluralism, even as they disagreed about the terms under which those circumstances could be applied. Webb students employed these interpretative lenses selectively, revealing that their desire to open up engagement with other faiths sometimes foreclosed dialogue with fellow American Muslims who did not share their worldview. While Webb members invested authority in what they deemed "our tradition," the students also resolutely upheld the viability of individual interpretation. The ethnographic dialogues presented here demonstrate not only the rich and vibrant hermeneutics that contemporary Muslims bring to the Qur'an, but also the ways that pluralism both opens up and restricts forms of religious engagement.[5] Verses that defied the students' conceptions of religious pluralism required a discussion of context, while verses that confirmed contemporary practices of religious pluralism did not. This is because, while students sought a more "academic" and "historical" approach to the Qur'an, they also invested authority in their embodied knowledge.[6] That is, their relationships with non-Muslim American neighbors, coworkers, and friends informed how they conceived of religious pluralism in the Qur'an.

Constructing Islamic Knowledge through Peer Discussion

The dynamics of Webb's adult education classes reflect the community's efforts to promote peer discussion and debate. Unlike religious instruction offered in mosques or other education foundations, which tend to offer separate classes for men and women, Webb classes include both genders, with enthusiastic participation from female students.[7] Between twenty and thirty participants regularly attended Sunday classes that I observed. Although students followed loose gender separation in seating, husbands and wives or fathers and daughters frequently sat next to each other in combination chairs and desks. Men and women talked before class and responded directly to each other during lively discussions. Facilitated by the close relationships that these families had with each other, Webb encouraged its adult students to enact gender integration as an alternative to the Islamic spaces to which most of them were accustomed.

At the time, Webb typically offered one adult course per semester. This particular class, held in the spring of 2012 in a suburban high-school classroom, focused on the second chapter in the Qur'an, "Surat al-Baqara" ("The Cow"). This pedagogical choice facilitated far- reaching discussion, due to its range of material, including narratives, polemics, and legal directives. The wide array facilitated discussion of contemporary social concerns, sometimes to the point that the text itself remained peripheral to the discussion. This is not to say that the meaning, syntax, and context of verses were ignored entirely, but rather that reading the Qur'an in English translation served as a springboard for discussions about how to apply the verses to everyday situations. These discussions about the proper application of the Qur'an produced strong reactions from the students, who frequently disagreed with the instructor, questioned each other's comments, and expressed exasperation when the conversation went in unanticipated directions. The class brought out very impassioned differences of opinion about the nature of tradition, cultural diversity, gender norms, and the relationship between Muslims and non-Muslims. Some students were frustrated by this open format, hoping for more definitive answers to their questions. Tensions often erupted between students searching for clarity and students seeking to debate the questions that mattered most to them. In this space, participants constructed Islamic knowledge through peer discussion and debate, while privileging individual interpretation and experience. As a result, these third-space discussions produced multiple interpretations, rather than consensus or certainty, over the meanings of the Qur'an.

The course instructor, Omer Mozaffar, encouraged disagreement and debate. In addition to being the instructor for most of Webb's adult classes—Mozaffar's interstitial role at Webb underscores the community's third-space location and exemplifies its members' goal of being both fully Muslim and full American—Mozaffar intentionally cultivates a classroom dynamic in order to facilitate Webb's goal of constructing a "seamless" American Islam. His signature sweater vest and jeans are deliberate sartorial choices, designed to put his students at ease and to emphasize his role as facilitator. As he put it, "I just do what I can to help. I deliberately try to avoid cultivating that image. That's what the vest is all about."[8] He wants his students to feel comfortable raising any topic or question, and he seeks to avoid being viewed as the repository of authoritative knowledge. Instead, he wants to act as a guide, one who does not necessarily have all the answers. To do so, he maintains an easy, joking manner in the classroom, insisting that his students call him by his first name.

Despite his unassuming manner, students told me that he is a "big name" in the Chicago Muslim community, underscoring the growing demand for his services as a teacher, preacher, and counselor. Mozaffar's popularity as a teacher—and the reason why the Webb community sought him out—is that he has broad involvement in multiple networks and institutions in Chicago. In the last decade, he has amassed a diverse set of religious and social relationships, which have, in turn, led him to acquire the knowledge and experience that the Webb community recognizes as beneficial to their mission. Mozaffar left his IT career in the late nineties to enter the graduate program in Near Eastern Languages and Civilizations at the University of Chicago. He concurrently studied the Qur'an, theology, and law with Muslim scholars in the Chicago area, including Abd-Allah and Shaykh Amin Kholwadia at Darul Qasim, an educational foundation that primarily serves the Deobandi-oriented community. Mozaffar regularly logs hundreds of miles a week in his Toyota Prius, teaching courses as an adjunct professor at Loyola University, giving sermons at Friday prayers, speaking at Muslim Students Association events, and contributing to interfaith panels. He devotes seven days a week to his teaching and speaking obligations, embracing his role as an increasingly popular figure among the city's college students and middle-class devotees.

Mozaffar's role as an informal spiritual advisor is particularly valuable for the many members of the Webb community who have experienced spiritual doubt, marginalization from their religious institutions, and have felt anxious about the status of Muslims in the United States:

> It started with my office hours. People would come with Islamic questions, and my office hours became four hours long. Now people come

> all the time. Usually a question about faith or practice turns into a discussion about an eating disorder, or suicide. I sometimes refer them to professional help, but 90 percent of what I do is listen. Many of them don't feel comfortable talking to parents, chaplains, or scholars. They turn to people they trust, and maybe those people aren't completely trained. But it's probably better they come to me than the Internet.[9]

Initially, undergraduate students approached him with their questions about prayer or fasting, as well as medical and psychological issues such as anorexia and depression. Over time, he attracted people from all age groups who came to ask him questions, and his reputation as a Muslim authority grew accordingly. Growing numbers of students have attested to the depth of his knowledge and the efficacy of his guidance.

When Malika started searching for an instructor for Webb's adult community, she knew that she wanted to find someone who could guide Webb members through the specific challenges of being American Muslims, who would facilitate relationships among Webb members, and who embodied the Webb mission of being fully American and fully Muslim. For Malika, Mozaffar has all the necessary attributes: a Chicago native, steeped in both traditional and academic knowledge of Islam:

> We said, "Let's have adult classes at a high caliber, and have someone who can teach at a college level and knows our community." Omer is critical in this. We had a couple teachers who were really detached. Sure, we're learning the material, but not really connecting with each other or the teacher. It's a different dynamic with Omer. He knows the background of the question. It's a pivotal Islamic concept. You take a teacher from among your community, and who knows your context, and the environment. We're constantly looking for that.[10]

Other students echoed Malika's observations that Mozaffar possesses insight and sensitivity to the particular issues facing suburban Muslims. As one student told me, "He really knows the community and always has his ear to the ground."[11] Another student, Jamila, explained Mozaffar's appeal to her community:

> There are a lot of reasons why Brother Omer is appealing. He knows a lot of people in the community and he is Pakistani. His appearance helps, too, like his beard. All of that gives him the authority to set the stage for discussion about controversial things. Very few people could

> do that. For example, you couldn't teach us [laughs]. You know a lot about Islam, for sure, but there would be certain objections. You don't have the history.[12]

This familiarity with the suburban Muslim community enables him to broach topics that are typically not up for discussion in other settings. My presence made explicit for Jamila that Mozaffar's ethnicity and gender also help to construct his authority as a teacher of religious knowledge and arbiter of debate. As Fauzia relayed, "Omer went to Sunday school here, so he knows what was taught here. He can actually uproot misconceptions I don't even know that I have. That's what makes him unique."[13]

Like Abd-Allah, Mozaffar appeals to his students' desire for "academic" knowledge of Islam. The Webb curriculum has since adopted a more formal structure and regularized content, but during my fieldwork, Mozaffar and Malika determined the topics and texts on a per-semester basis. Mozaffar structures Webb classes like a graduate seminar, where he draws individual students into debate around shared texts. Multiplicity is his desired result. Within these seminars, he affirms the individual students as *sources* of religious and cultural knowledge, by encouraging them to interpret texts with reference to their specific challenges as American Muslims. This pedagogy created a collaborative environment for his professional, adult students, enabling them to draw on the very same practices of critical reading and debate that they honed in the university environment. He thus encourages Webb students to draw on their individual life histories and professional expertise as they discuss the Qur'an, *fiqh*, devotional practice, and ethical questions. This approach enables students to articulate, indeed to inhabit, multiple positions by engaging their experiences as lived encounters with Muslim history and theology.

Seeking Guidance and Meaning

Before proceeding to the students' engagement with American religious pluralism, it is important to recognize that the class functioned as a setting for religious devotion.[14] Though broader political concerns often framed class debates, they cannot simply be reduced to those interests. Instead, students also raised concerns and questions that have recurred in Islamic traditions of exegesis, recitation, and devotional study. When I asked students about the role of the Qur'an in their lives, the students confirmed the central role of oral recitation in daily practice.[15] Through recitation, Muslims embody and internalize the Qur'an, which they believe will bring immense rewards in the afterlife. As Carl Ernst puts it, "[R]eading or reciting the Qur'an is a direct engagement with the divine speech, not to be confused with ordinary acts of reading, nor to be dismissed as a meaningless repetition."[16] For the students, studying on Sunday mornings augmented this nexus of devotional practices centered on the Qur'an. The opportunity to address difficult and challenging issues in Qur'anic interpretation augmented the class's vital role in enhancing participants' devotional lives.

In addition to supplementing these ritual aspects of Qur'anic devotion, the students wrestled with other foundational questions, namely the limitations of human reason and knowledge in the interpretation of the divine word. These reflections demonstrate the multiple meanings produced even within a group of students who consider themselves to be "like-minded":

MOZAFFAR: The more important conversation is the role of revelation in our own lives. Is our goal to practice the entire Qur'an?

MARY: I struggle with your phrasing, "to practice the Qur'an." We should engage the Qur'an and find its meaning in our lives. We should use it as a source of guidance. "Practice" it implies that you know what it means. And we don't always know that.

YASMIN: I like "heed the Qur'an" better.

MOZAFFAR: Is this our goal? To heed the Qur'an?

SANA: We should submit to the will of Allah. "Practice" means different things to different people.

HUSNA: The Prophet is the walking Qur'an. He is the embodiment of everything in it. If we emulate him, then yes, we are following the whole book.

HUSSEIN: We need to look at the context and how the Prophet practiced.

SANA: If you have decided there are fallacies in the Qur'an, you can still be a Muslim, even if you don't follow everything. There are people who say this. Can you "practice" the Qur'an or "heed, take lessons" from it? It's really complicated.[17]

Mary's comment reiterated the text's self-description as a source of guidance for humanity and articulated a central theological point—that the Qur'an is the direct manifestation of divine speech. Because the Qur'an is perfect and inimitable, human understanding of its meaning is necessarily limited and provisional. To address Husna's concerns, Hussein pointed to the possibility of using the Sunna, and the Prophetic example embodied in the hadith, to clarify the meaning of the text and to develop rulings based on Qur'anic verses.[18] This approach was also reflected in Husna's understanding of the Prophet as the "walking Qur'an." From this perspective, the Prophet, as God's perfect servant, is the exemplary human model. Having embodied the Qur'an through revelation and through his actions, the Prophetic example becomes a source for Muslims to understand how to enact scriptural norms in daily life.[19]

In the midst of perspectives that one might expect from a practicing group of Muslims, Sana's statement snapped everyone to attention. She suggested that the Qur'an contained errors, implying that it is a human product or perhaps that God himself had erred. She recognized that holding such a view potentially excluded her from the Muslim community, and she distanced herself from the claim by attributing the view to "some people." Indeed, her remarks drew rebukes from the class, some of whom condemned this suggestion as that of an insignificant fraction of Muslims. To be sure, hers was a minority opinion even within this ostensibly open environment. Yet Sana's comment serves as an important reminder that there are no stable meanings in the Qur'an (or any sacred text). Sana was fully aware of the "dominant" view among her classmates; she chose to disregard it. Ethnographies are thus essential for discerning how Muslims construct varied meanings from their scripture in historically situated contexts.

Unfortunately, some scholars of Islamic studies have attributed viewpoints such as Sana's to the legacy of Western Orientalism, making her perspective potentially impossible for a true Muslim to hold. To take one example, Frederick Denny has argued the following:

> It is painful for Muslims to witness certain types of historico-critical, philological, and otherwise "Orientalist" scholarly treatment of their sacred book . . . unsympathetic or historical analyses of the Qur'an, amount to invasions of a Muslim's sense of identity and meaning.[20]

Denny is right that many Muslims consider critical academic approaches that take the human origins of the Qur'an as a historical assumption—especially those perceived as external attacks on Islam or Muslims—as threatening to the Qur'an's status as the final and complete revelation of God. But this is by no means universal. For Sana, however, questioning the Qur'an and considering critical approaches to it served as a means to strengthen rather than to undermine her identity as a Muslim. Here, human involvement in the Qur'an was perceived less as an "external attack," and more as a historical possibility incumbent upon devout Muslims to take into consideration.

Moreover, Sana's comment elucidates an important dimension of American Muslim *tafsīr*—that it necessarily is informed by, and in turn shapes, broader US histories of race, gender, and class. As Carolyn Rouse has ably demonstrated, the ideological boundaries of Sunni Islam are contested within American Muslim communities through exegesis. In the case of the women she observed, reading the Qur'an through the frames of racial and gender justice offered a powerful means for African American women to shape their Islamic and female subjectivities.[21] Interpretative communities produce meanings and interpretations steeped in ambivalence and uncertainty, suggesting the continuous making and remaking of Qur'anic guidance in their everyday lives. The historical-critical approach to scriptures, including the Bible and the Qur'an, constitutes an important hermeneutical frame for these educated students. Many Webb students have studied religion in secular university contexts. Some of these courses started their processes of becoming Muslim. Moreover, as we have seen, university credentials are a key basis of authority for this group. That is, academic approaches to the Qur'an offer a pathway to a more authentic and historically accurate view of Islam. They cannot be easily dismissed. These interpretations—and the limits placed on them—thus help to create, broaden, and often solidify boundaries within and among Muslim communities.

Seeking Context through *Asbāb al-Nuzūl*

This brief sketch establishes that while the students approached the Qur'an from their contemporary positionality, their conversations also reflect an intention to ground their individual interpretations in the tradition of *tafsīr*. Webb students invested tremendous authority in *tafsīr* to validate interpretations that, in turn, resonated with their individual and collective experiences. Here, I take *tafsīr* to be a broad and inclusive category of Muslim exegesis and engagement with the Qur'an, both by trained scholars and "lay" individuals and communities. In particular, Webb students celebrated the varied interpretations contained within classical commentaries. The fact that *tafsīr* literature historically generated multiple meanings was far more important to the students than the specific content of these commentaries.

Their insistence on the relevance of classical *tafsīr* speaks to the genre's ongoing cumulative weight. As Walid Saleh has argued, at its heart, *tafsīr* is a genealogical tradition; it functions as an authorizing force for future interpretations and provides a reservoir of meanings that contemporary communities continue to draw upon.[22] Given the vast number of interpretations advanced by classical exegetes, none of the interpretations advanced by the students were entirely novel. Rather, the students, like their classical predecessors, brought their own set of epistemological, political, and ethical concerns to bear on the text in order to produce new meanings, with their concomitant political and religious implications.[23] To be sure, the students' oral interpretations bear little structural resemblance to the textual characteristics and epistemological assumptions that defined classical *tafsīr* as a genre. Only a couple of Webb students possessed the requisite knowledge of Arabic to read classical works of exegesis. I point out these differences not to discount the Webb students as less authentic or outside of a normative conception of tradition. Instead, I do so with an eye toward analytical precision of the elements Webb participants seek to recover and which aspects they do not see as foundational to Islam or relevant to their experiences as American Muslims.

In this way, the class contributed to what Karen Bauer describes as the "meaning- creation" efforts at the heart of *tafsīr*, as "each scholar's attempt to relate his world to the world of the Qur'an . . . is his attempt to relate his intellectual, political, and social contexts to the Qur'an's text. It is a process of meaning-creation, because what the scholars read into the text is not always explicitly there: interpretation does not always respect the Qur'an's grammar or its context."[24] The class's attempts to emplace their interpretations in their historical context situated them within this continuous tradition of meaning-making.

The students particularly homed in on the *asbāb al-nuzūl*, or the circumstances of revelation. Exegetes used the context and conditions in which a verse was revealed to clarify its meaning and application. For example, scholars wanted to know whether a verse was revealed in response to a specific question posed to the Prophet Muhammad, and they relied on the hadith or *sīra* literature to provide the narrative context surrounding verses. Andrew Rippin has shown how the circumstances of revelation fulfilled the scholars' need to situate disparate Qur'anic events in a coherent narrative framework.[25] Rippin also observes that commentators used the *asbāb al-nuzūl* to construct a "*jāhilī* foil," a polemical device that highlighted the moral failings of the People of the Book prior to Islam and upheld the Muslim community as the renewal of God's covenant.[26] Commentators looked to the *asbāb al-nuzūl* to set Islam apart from other faith traditions and to position the Qur'an in the temporal frame of pre- and post-*jāhilī* epochs. The class thus called upon the context surrounding polemical verses, but to different theological and political ends.

Furthermore, Webb students used the *asbāb al-nuzūl* to explore legal and ethical dimensions of exegesis. By enabling exegetes and legal scholars to differentiate between the general and specific applications of each verse, the *asbāb al-nuzūl* also functioned as the starting point for discerning the legal implications of the Qur'an.[27] Like premodern scholars, the class employed the *asbāb al-nuzūl* to make the case for limiting the scope of certain Qur'anic verses while expanding the application of others to contemporary situations. This interest in the circumstances of revelation resulted from their efforts to reconcile the Qur'an with contemporary norms with reference to "context." For them, the circumstances of revelation went hand in hand with discussions of whether verses were specific or universal in their application.[28] Webb students struggled with how to interpret seemingly anachronistic, strange, or confusing Qur'anic verses that contradicted what they understood as universal concepts upheld in the text, especially religious pluralism. To address this tension, they turned to modern exegetical appropriations of the *asbāb al-nuzūl*.

Modern *Tafsīr* and New Approaches to *Asbāb al-Nuzūl*

Although Mozaffar's class claimed to be reviving classical Sunni scholarship, they also drew upon a more recent but established tradition of modernist exegesis. Particularly important was the influence of what Charles Kurzman has labeled "liberal Islam," which he categorizes as a subset of Islamic modernism. Kurzman argues that liberal Islam is "the critique of both the customary and revivalist tradition for what liberals sometimes term 'backwardness' which in their view has prevented the Islamic world from enjoying the fruits of modernity. . . . [T]he liberal tradition argues that Islam, properly understood, is compatible with—or even a precursor to—Western Liberalism."[29] We have already seen how Webb participants locate many liberal ideals within Islam, such as their emphasis on "spirituality." I have so far traced this liberalism through a broader American genealogy.[30] Here, I highlight how students found in classical exegesis the affirmation of religious pluralism as a core value. In this way, pluralism functioned as a defining and mutually shared concept that linked Islam to American culture, enabling this group to construct their vision of American Islam with respect to other Muslims and non-Muslim Americans.

The *asbāb al-nuzūl* has taken on new valences in the work of modernist thinkers. The students' interest bears the indirect influence of Fazlur Rahman (1919–1988), the renowned Pakistani American scholar of Islamic studies who spent the last two decades of his career at the University of Chicago, and who trained Abd-Allah as a doctoral student. While students never referred to Rahman directly, their understanding of context attests to the ongoing significance of his ideas, especially as they have been extended through other American Muslim intellectuals.[31] Rahman believed that classical scholars had not fully realized the exegetical implications of the *asbāb al-nuzūl*. In order to fully grasp the meaning of Qur'anic verses, he proposed a "twofold movement":

> First one must move from the concrete case treatments of the Qur'an—taking the necessary and relevant social conditions of the time into account—to the general principles upon which the entire teaching converges. Second, from this general level there must be a movement back to specific legislation, taking into account the necessary and relevant social conditions then obtaining.[32]

Rahman's argument that the Qur'an expressed general principles through specific circumstances and events drew upon the work of important figures in Islamic modernism, such as the Egyptian reformer Muhammad ʿAbduh. For Rahman, the Qur'an had a clear, unified purpose—to promote social justice and "human Egalitarianism."[33] For example, Muslims ought to interpret verses on polygamy, which limited the number of wives to four, not as Qur'anic sanction of the practice, but rather as evidence of the text's general objective to promote justice and care for weaker members of society. In this way, Rahman maintained that the Qur'an retained its universal qualities even as it reflected the conditions of a particular time and place. Each successive generation must therefore consider the Qur'an "in its total and specific background, not just studying it verse by verse or passage by passage with an isolated 'occasion of revelation.'"[34] Like Rahman, many Webb students sought to reconcile specific verses with the ethical principles that they believed the text espoused. They relied on the idea that these Qur'anic principles were fully consonant with the political, social, and religious frameworks of contemporary modernity in the United States.

Does the Context Change the Meaning?

Students demanded to know the context when the text appeared to defy what they considered to be universal ethical principles: justice, pluralism, and rationality. In April 2012, Mozaffar projected an English translation of Q. 2:191 onto the screen of the high school classroom:

> Kill them wherever you encounter them, and drive them out from where they drove you out, for persecution is more serious than killing. Do not fight them at the Sacred Mosque unless they fight you there. If they do fight you, kill them—this is what such disbelievers deserve. But if they stop, then God is most forgiving and merciful.[35]

Muslim commentators have historically disputed the meaning of this and surrounding verses. According to the *asbāb al-nuzūl* typically designated to the preceding verse, Q. 2:190 concerns the truce of Hudaybiyya in 628 during the holy month Dhū'l-Qa'da, and declares, "Fight God's cause against those who fight you, but do not overstep the limits: God does not love those who overstep the limits." Although the Quraysh and the Muslim community in Medina had agreed to a temporary truce, the Muslims feared that they would not be able to return to the Ka'ba on pilgrimage as promised. The verse limited violence to aggressors and prevented the killing of noncombatants, rather than declaring general restraint or mercy.[36] Exegetes did not apply the same circumstances to Q. 2:191, which stipulates restrictions for when and where violence can take place against the Muslims' enemies, including the Masjid al-Haram. These and other verses surrounding war reflect considerable ambivalence among some Muslims toward fighting during sacred months and served to mediate disputes within the Muslim community concerning the Prophet's militaristic approach.[37]

Mozaffar stressed to his class that the contemporary political and social relevance of this verse required them to reflect further upon its implications:

MOZAFFAR: What about a specific injunction from the Qur'an? How aboutkill them—the *kuffār*—wherever you find them? How do you respond?
SANA: Where is that verse?
JAMILA: I'd want to know the actual content and context of the verse.

Here, Mozaffar constructed the conversation around an imagined non-Muslim interlocutor. The term *kuffār* is used in the Qur'an to describe a variety of peoples, from the Quraysh who rejected Muhammad's teachings to the Christians and Jews who received and then later ignored God's message. Mozaffar's translation also resembled that of Q. 9:5:

> When the [four] forbidden months are over, wherever you encounter the idolaters, kill them, seize them, besiege them, wait for them at every lookout post; but if they repent, maintain the prayer and pay the prescribed alms, let them go on their way for God is most forgiving and merciful.

In the Qur'an, *kufr*, the state of disbelief or ingratitude, stands diametrically opposed to the state of *īmān* (faith). In American public discourse, the term *kāfir* is often translated as "infidel" and usually used as evidence of Islam's supposed violent proclivity and intolerance toward members of other faiths.

It was this meaning, and its political implications, that Mozaffar wanted his students to confront.

Non-Muslim assumptions and interpretations thus figured prominently in this dialogue because they posed the most pressing challenge to the students' pluralist ethos. Western anti-Muslim pundits have latched onto the verse as a tool for dismissing the Qur'an as an intolerant text. Moreover, as Talal Asad claims, of the three Abrahamic scriptures, the Qur'an has been identified as uniquely authoritarian in the United States and Europe:

> Religion has long been seen as a source of violence and (for ideological reasons) Islam has been represented in the modern West as peculiarly so (undisciplined, arbitrary, singularly oppressive). . . . The present discourse about the roots of "Islamic terrorism" in Islamic texts trails two intriguing assumptions: (a) that the Qur'anic text will force Muslims to be guided by it; and (b) that Christians and Jews are free to interpret the Bible as they please.[38]

These readings became some of the many interpretations that the students considered, alongside those of premodern and modern Muslims, as well as their own individual interpretations. In fact, these non-Muslim readings urgently framed the direction of the conversation, causing students to confront negative perceptions of the Qur'an. These negative images were particularly problematic because they perpetually undercut the class's recurring hope that American society was moving away from the current climate of discrimination and diminished citizenship and toward increasing tolerance of Islam and Muslims. Mozaffar stressed to the students that the vilification of the Qur'an required them to understand its meaning because they needed to respond to Americans who were likely to assume that Qur'anic verses promote violence and intolerance, and that Muslims blindly act upon those meanings.

Webb students' demands for context revealed their skepticism that the verse had direct bearing on their contemporary relationships with Americans of various faiths. Like some classical exegetes, Jamila demanded to know the *asbāb al-nuzūl* for this polemical passage, and she used them to render unfamiliar or disparate episodes comprehensible. At the same time, she relied on the circumstances of revelation to abstract general principles from the text. The students believed that interpreting the Qur'an in light of its context—however they defined it—was essential to addressing their contemporary situation as American Muslims. For them, illuminating the *asbāb al-nuzūl* would render the potentially destabilizing implications of this verse moot.

The ensuing conversation revealed the political and religious stakes of invoking divergent notions of context:[39]

MOZAFFAR: The verse is in the Qur'an. We can't reduce everything tocontext and say that I don't have to pray because it wasn't revealed in Medina.
SANA: Yes, though some people say and believe that.
HUSSEIN: Traditionally, you should look at the timing of the verse.
MOZAFFAR: The Qur'an isn't universal if it can be explained by timing.
JAMILA: If you look at the actual text and its context, the meaning changes. If you're assaulted, or need to act in self-defense, then you can retaliate. But if you forgive, that is considered the higher action.
MOZAFFAR: I'm talking about real examples. I recently met a guy who decided that we must kill the *kuffār*. He had a terrible story. He had lost his daughter in a car accident and then lost his job. He was convinced that he needed to retaliate against the people who had wronged him.
HUSNA: He looked at one verse, but what about the other ones? What about our other obligations? Don't we have to take the book as a whole?
HUSSEIN: I'm taken aback by this strident view that we can just ignore verses. These people are wrong, and it's a reaction against conservative interpretations of the Qur'an. We have wide latitude to interpret verses, engage with them, and this is rewarding. People are turned off by ultraconservatives, and their views toward women and other cultures.[40]

For Jamila, the circumstances of revelation provided the means to distill general principles that she believed were relevant to contemporary social conditions. From the students' perspective, Q. 2:191 was further evidence of God's mercy and His disdain for violence. Husna made a related claim, arguing that Muslims ought to take the book "as a whole." That is, Qur'anic verses collectively place obligations on Muslims to act, but no single verse should be taken as universally incumbent. Generally, students expressed confidence that classical exegetes employed methods that were far more nuanced and closer to the intended meaning than what they called "ultraconservative" readings, that is, Salafi/Wahhabi interpretations that approached the Qur'an as a direct blueprint for action.

Although exegetes employed a number of arguments regarding the context of these verses, the students did not consider these arguments specifically. Instead, classical methods of interpretation enabled them to ground their interpretations in the Islamic tradition as they understood it. Sherman Jackson suggests that medieval Muslim scholarship on *jihād* may support modern Muslim claims that Qur'anic verses do not enjoin Muslims to fight non-Muslims; rather the context of the verses' revelation indicates a limited applicability to the contemporary world.[41]

Even as Mozaffar encouraged the classroom to engage in debate, he also pointed out occasions when he believed that the students' opinions contradicted the very tradition—that is, classical scholarship—they sought to revive. In this case, he interpreted Jamila's insistence on context as exceeding the limits of the text's possible meanings. The fact that a verse was revealed in a specific time and place did not impinge on its universality. Knowing the circumstances enabled jurists to know how and if they should apply Qur'anic norms. Notable contemporary exegetes, however, have understood the *asbāb al-nuzūl* differently, extending the concept in order to dispute the legal relevance of certain parts of the Qur'an. For example, the American feminist scholar amina wadud has argued, following Abdullahi An-Na'im and extending the work of Rahman, that Muslims ought to privilege the universal verses of the Meccan period, though she has acknowledged that some Medinan verses might also have universal application.[42] For those verses deemed specific in nature, wadud maintained that Muslims ought to read the Qur'an as a "history book in the limited sense of a record of events . . . without implying in any way a restriction of the Qur'anic principles to that context."[43] Although not explicitly, students embraced wadud's reliance on the text's general principles, and some considered, or at least raised the possibility of, the application of certain verses in light of those principles, while others insisted on the need to retain the relevance of individual verses. Just by virtue of engaging in these debates over context, the students enacted their understanding of classical *tafsīr*. That is, they understood themselves to have "wide latitude" to debate interpretative possibilities, though, as Hussein and Mozaffar asserted, proper Islamic exegesis placed outer limits on these possibilities. In their understanding, premodern exegetes had far more freedom to debate the meanings of verses, to produce multiple and sometimes conflicting interpretations, and to acknowledge the relationship between text and context. Here, Hussein imagined a "conservative" Muslim interlocutor, who possessed insufficient knowledge of classical scholarship or chose to disregard it altogether, leading him to erroneous interpretations about the status of women and other religions and cultures.

During these Sunday morning debates, the class thus staked out an alternative hermeneutical ground in which they affirmed the internal plurality of the Islamic tradition and sought to demonstrate the commensurability of Islam and American religious pluralism.

The Politics of Literalism

The Qur'an students' concern with context reflected broader concerns about the plethora of competing voices around the Qur'an, both Muslim and non-Muslim. It re-emerged during the class's discussion of Q. 2:65–66:

> You know about those of you who broke the Sabbath, and so We said to them, "Be like apes! Be outcasts! We made this an example to those people who were there at the time and to those who came after them, and a lesson to all who are mindful of God."[44]

This passage narrates the consequences for a Jewish community that disobeyed the command to observe the Sabbath. Mozaffar described the story as a tale about a Jewish community that devised a plan to trap fish in a lake, but then waited until Sunday to actually remove the fish from the nets. By passively trapping the fish, the community attempted to circumvent their obligations on a technicality. In the end, their actions provoked divine wrath all the same. Mozaffar projected the verse on the screen and asked the class whether it should be interpreted metaphorically or literally:

MOZAFFAR: God turned the Children of Israel into apes because they trapped fish in a lake on Saturday, but then killed them to eat on Sunday. Is this a literal event or did Allah simply curse them?

SAID: I was always taught that it was literal. Allah turned the Children of Israel into apes.

TARIQ: The leader of Hamas says that the Jews were actually turned into apes. That's what my parents taught me, too.

FATIMA: I think it means that they might as well have been apes.

JAMILA: I don't know, seems pretty literal to me in the Arabic.

HUSSEIN: Early scholars interpreted it as metaphysical and allegorical.

ALI: Either way, it's bad. You either are animals or are acting like animals.[45]

This last comment drew laughter from the class, but then some students accused Mozaffar of selecting an unrepresentative example of the Qur'an's treatment of Jews and Christians. Hussein's statement pointed to historical debates within the *tafsīr* tradition about which group of people was turned into apes, as well as the possibility of an allegorical reading. A first-generation Egyptian immigrant, Hussein was one of the only class members to have formally studied *tafsīr* and other Islamic disciplines. Mozaffar described the punished people as the "Children of Israel," but commentators have assigned them various identities.[46] On the question of their crime, classical exegetes typically concurred that the Children of Israel were punished for circumventing the divine prohibition on labor during the Sabbath. Some classical interpreters disagreed about whether God actually transformed the Children of Israel into apes, or if they became like apes in their turning away from the covenant with God.[47] Exegetes have also understood this transformation to be physical but specific to this particular group of Jews.[48] This and similar episodes helped classical interpreters to establish a distinct moral boundary between the pre-Islamic and post-Islamic periods.

Such interpretations disrupted the students' assumptions regarding the text's affirmation of Judaism and Christianity. They were troubled because the idea that the punishment actually occurred had the potential to reinforce popular media images of Islam as intolerant and God in the Qur'an as tyrannical and despotic. Tariq referred to the now-deceased Hamas leader Nizar Rayyan, who publicly invoked the verse as evidence that Allah continues to punish the Jews as a cursed people.[49] In a 2009 interview with the *Atlantic*'s Jeffrey Goldberg, Rayyan declared, "Some of the ancestors of Jews were transformed into pigs and apes, and it is true that Allah continually makes the Jews pay for their crimes in many different ways. They are a cursed people."[50] In order to alleviate the class's concerns that God singled out the Jews for special and ongoing punishment, Mozaffar invoked the *asbāb al-nuzūl*, reminding them that the verse served a particular purpose during Muhammad's negotiations with Jewish tribes in Medina. While he affirmed the literal meaning of the verse, Mozaffar rejected Rayyan's idea that the punishment somehow extended through history to include contemporary Jews.

The class's discomfort was also linked to political disputes involving the Qur'an and American military power. The conversation then shifted to the disposal and subsequent burning of Qur'ans by US soldiers stationed at the Bagram Air Force Base in Afghanistan in February 2012, sparking waves of violent protests that resulted in several deaths. Many of the Webb students expressed dismay at the protestors' actions. Mary declared, "They worshipped the Qur'an as a thing. People get excessively upset when the Qur'an is burned, but it's just a physical thing. You can't burn the word of God."[51] Here, she distinguished between the Qur'an as a material object and the Qur'an as a message. Mozaffar responded to Mary's claim by differentiating between reverence and worship, and by reminding her that Muslims have traditionally imbued the written Qur'an with theological significance through, for example, the art of calligraphy. Indeed, it is possible to interpret Mary as affirming dual Islamic understandings of the Qur'an as a recitation, the form in which Muhammad received the text from the angel Gabriel, and as a manuscript written in Arabic, the *muṣḥaf*. From this perspective, her comment upheld the recited Qur'an as the original word of God and distinct from, though of course related to, its materiality.

At the same time, Mary's comment reflects normative assumptions about religion that are rooted in Protestant conceptions of modernity. For Mary, who grew up as a liberal Protestant and converted to Islam a couple of decades ago, the "word of God" superseded the linguistic and aesthetic features of the Qur'an as a material object. She hesitated to identify with the protestors because of her particular understanding of the proper place of religion in the modern world. From her vantage point—as a middle-class American citizen—true religious convictions should never result in violence and must be actively contained.[52]

Other moral judgments about scripture and materiality were also at work in this discussion. Here, Mary critiqued what she saw as excessive, dangerous, and erroneous attachment to the Qur'an as a text. This is how Mozaffar understood Mary's comment, as a critique of Muslims who understand the Qur'an-as-object to be religiously significant, to have a special status beyond that of simply a "thing." Webb Keane has argued that this devaluation of materiality is an important hallmark of what he calls the "Protestant semiotic ideology."[53] Keane uses the term to explore how moral claims are constructed through the relationships between words and things; for him, this semiotic ideology has had far-reaching effects on the construction of secular modernity, in which conceptions of individual freedom and social progress hinge on the subordination of things to human (and sometimes divine) agency. Mary's attempts to render the protestors' action comprehensible relied on a similar logic. For her, the protestors misrecognized the physical Qur'an for the word of God because they failed to see that the "true" word was immaterial. Elevating the status of the *muṣḥaf* was akin to "worship," a serious moral error that had problematic consequences, namely indulging in irrational, irreligious impulses. Not only did their actions lead to the loss of life, but it also reinforced representations of Muslims as uniquely submissive and passive to the power of the Qur'anic text.[54]

Evoking these multiple historical trajectories, some of the students developed their hermeneutics through a distinct understanding of revelation and modernity. One sunny March morning, Mozaffar turned the class's attention to Q. 2:72–74, which contains the set of verses for which the sura is named, in which God instructed the Children of Israel to sacrifice a cow. He described how instead of obeying the order, the community stalled by asking a series of questions. They eventually slaughtered the cow, but their hearts were subsequently "hardened" by God. In 2:72–73, the same community found a man dead in the fields. God then brought the man back to life:

WHEN YOU [ISRAELITES] killed someone and started to blame another—although God was to bring what you had concealed to light—We said, "Strike the body with a part of it": thus God brings the dead to life and shows His signs so that you may understand.[55]

MOZAFFAR: A man has been killed. Who was the murderer? Allah says strike the man with a part of the cow that has been sacrificed. Allah then brings the man back to life and the man identifies his killer. This seems unbelievable, and so this verse raises the question of reason versus revelation in our tradition. Can you think of other examples?

FARID: How about the sacrifice of Ismail?

MOZAFFAR: Yes—but can you think about anything in law? No, you can't, because our tradition conforms to reason. We have *tawfiqī* matters that are handed down to us that are beyond reason, like why we fast during Ramadan and not another month. But this is a tiny part of our tradition, even though it's a big part of our daily practice. But let's suppose a guy said, "I saw visions, and Allah told me that I have to slaughter my son." What would you do?

MARY: We would report him to DCFS [Department of Child and Family Services].

HUSNA: Is this person harmless or just crazy? A professional needs to evaluate people like him in our community and others. Are they going to harm themselves or others?[56]

In this exchange, Mozaffar constructed a dichotomy between the Qur'an as revelation and Islamic law as rational discourse, noting that the Qur'an served as the basis for commands considered exempt from argumentation, as in the case of fasting for Ramadan.[57] As the word of God, parts of the Qur'an transcended the dictates of established moral dictums. At the same time, Mozaffar gestured to legal traditions that permitted the modification of rulings originally set forth in the Qur'an. The students willingly accepted that aspects of the Qur'an exceeded rational explanation but rejected claims of contemporary prophecy or revelation. This hesitance reflected the common Muslim understanding that the Qur'an occupies unique status as the final revelation. From the Qur'an students' perspective, the claim of privileged communication with God provided evidence of insanity and criminality rather than divine inspiration. Notably, they embraced the role of the state in managing religious subjectivities that exceeded these boundaries, suggesting that religion must conform to liberal parameters. As we will see, the regulation of religion re-emerged in participants' critiques of other Muslims' use (and misuse) of the Qur'an as students opened up spaces of religious engagement with Jews and Christians, while foreclosing possibilities of engagement with Muslims whose perspectives they deemed irrational or dangerous.

When the Qur'an Is Clear: "The Interfaith Aya"

We have seen how Webb students employ multiple strategies and contexts to confront verses that posed problems for their modern conceptions of religiosity. Conversely, verses that conformed to participants' expectations required no such recourse to context. Instead, students eschewed the *asbāb al-nuzūl* when they understood the text to endorse their pluralistic convictions. This contrast demonstrates the ways in which readers of the Qur'an (and other religious texts) often prioritize their particular expectations and interests in the text over a consistent interpretive approach. The students' strategic use of hermeneutics became apparent in the discussion of Q. 62, which Mozaffar referred to as "the interfaith aya." Commonly cited as the basis for interfaith programs within US Muslim institutions, Q. 2:62 reads,

> The [Muslim] believers, the Jews, the Christians, and the Sabians—all those who believe in God and the Last Day and do good—will have their rewards with their Lord. No fear for them, nor will they grieve.

MOZAFFAR: I ask you: Can a non-Muslim go to paradise?

ZAYNAB: Yes, it's possible. Like Mother Teresa, she has to go to heaven.

YASMIN: I think the verse is very clear. Those who believe in God and the after-life, and do good, will go to heaven. We can't judge.

MARY: If we don't have Islam, Qur'an, religion, we can still know God. So, yes.

SAID: God sent the same message, so we all have the opportunity to go to *janna* [paradise].

MOZAFFAR: We need to be able to answer this question confidently. We might want to say yes to be accepted in society. But we don't know. Only Allah knows. Think about your own families, you have relatives who aren't Muslim. If non-Muslims can't go to heaven, then we should convert them. If I'm not doing this, then something is wrong with my humanity.[58]

This passage actually preceded the verse referring to the apes, and both its meaning and the circumstances of revelation were a matter of dispute among classical commentators. The verse appears to privilege belief in God and the afterlife as the criteria for salvation, rather than membership in a particular ethnic or even religious group. Mahmoud Ayoub notes that exegetes limited the scope of Q. 2:62's application and in some cases called for its abrogation. For example, some scholars maintained that the verse only applied to those groups who had faith in God prior to the coming of Islam, and were therefore granted salvation, but that the verse was no longer applicable after the revelation of the Qur'an.[59]

Disputes about the meaning of Q. 2:62 partially stem from the range of statements within the Qur'an concerning the fate of Jews and Christians, or the *ahl al-kitāb* (People of the Book). Some Qur'anic passages support the students' proposals that God's plan included different religious paths potentially capable of attaining salvation. For example, the text refers to the chosen nature of the Jews and confirms the Torah as God's revelation.[60] Moreover, the students clearly recognized provisions in Islamic jurisprudence that provided protection for Christian and Jewish minorities living under Muslim rule. By contrast, verses such as Q. 3:19 and Q. 3:85 suggest supercessionism, attesting to Islam as the only true *dīn*. However, even in these verses, many exegetes did not gloss "islām" as referring to the religion followed by Muslims. Thus, they left open the possibility of earlier recipients of scripture (including Jews and Christians) submitting to God. In other verses, the Qur'an castigates many Jews for turning away from God's message, refusing to join Muhammad, and for corrupting their sacred texts. Many Qur'anic passages concern the early Muslim community's conflicts with Jewish tribes, while others deal with Jews as a people with whom God maintained a special relationship.[61] This array of Qur'anic statements produced historical and contemporary debates among Muslims about the fate of non-Muslims and about the eternality of hell.[62]

Despite their earlier insistence on the context of revelation, the students expressed little interest in *asbāb al-nuzūl* when it came to the interfaith verse. Here, they read the Qur'an as a self-evident text with clear meanings. This illustrates how the group used exegetical tools as they saw fit and in order to confirm their conceptions about revelation, the Qur'an, and indeed about Islam generally.[63] In this case, the historical application of the circumstances of revelation would have undermined the students' expectations and confounded their attempts to assert the Qur'an's role in testifying to the unity of the Abrahamic faiths.

Mozaffar's last statement produced skeptical looks and a few scoffs from the class. He urged the students to consider whether their desire to be accepted by American society motivated this quick dismissal of the possibility of converting non-Muslim Americans. On the one hand, he insisted that the class needed to be confident in their reading of this verse. On the other, he maintained that the students lacked a definitive interpretation because only "Allah knows," a formulaic caveat often invoked by Muslims scholars to denote the provisional nature of their understanding. For Mozaffar, students should (somewhat paradoxically) confidently embrace this position of uncertainty as the closest approximation of classical Sunni scholars. But the students rejected the conversion of non-Muslims because the idea potentially undermined their project of creating an American Muslim identity predicated on the mutual recognition of Islam, Christianity, and Judaism as not just equal religions, but also equally deserving of the ability to practice their faiths unencumbered by incursions by members of the other faiths. Although not all students agreed that each faith was similarly capable of attaining salvation, they concurred that Islam's (not wholly realized) entrance into the American pluralist landscape required the rejection of certain practices, like conversion efforts, that would publicly and directly assert Islam's superiority and undermine the progress of American Muslims who were seeking full citizenship.

However, this rejection did not entail that the entire class embraced identical soteriologies with respect to Christians and Jews. Instead, individual comments actually reveal a diversity of perspectives found within Muslim thought regarding the fate of non- Muslims.[64] Mohammad Khalil's typology delineates various positions that Muslim scholars have taken historically, which include pluralist, inclusivist, and exclusivist orientations. He argues that Muslim scholars rarely embraced pluralist or exclusivist positions before the modern era. Instead, they held a number of positions under the rubric of "inclusivism."[65] Mozaffar and the students articulated different stances with regard to the salvation of non-Muslims. Using Khalil's taxonomy, Mozaffar's position belongs to the category of "liberal inclusivism," in which Muslims should encourage non-Muslims to actively engage with Islam, with the potential to convert them, in order to bring God's mercy upon them.[66] Liberal inclusivists acknowledge the prospect that ethical non-Muslims who have heard the message of Islam, but nonetheless do not convert, still may be saved. Yasmin articulated the pluralist worldview, that Christianity, Judaism, and Islam are in fact equally capable of leading their followers to salvation.[67] Mary's point relied on a different justification, arguing that those who have not heard the message of Islam could still be saved. Like limited inclusivists, she argued for the possibility that some contemporary communities simply had not been exposed to the true message of Islam. Her statement left open the possibility that those who were exposed to the Qur'an but who subsequently rejected or ignored it could be subject to harsher treatment in the afterlife. Finally, Said reiterated a pluralist position that claimed the essential sameness of Islam, Christianity, and Judaism as ontologically equal. They challenged public perceptions that Islam condemns nonbelievers to damnation and marked out opposition to exclusivist positions within their own communities.

This range of comments also demonstrates how this particular verse has taken on new meanings and significance in the contemporary United States. In response to a hostile public culture that portrays Islam as damning non-Muslims to eternal hellfire, Muslim communities have increasingly turned to interfaith efforts to present Islam as accepting of other faiths, especially Christianity and Judaism. This verse has been used by interfaith groups and invoked by religious studies scholars to underscore the shared heritage of the Abrahamic faiths. The mere suggestion that Muslims ought to actively convert Jews and Christians to Islam is anathema to the pluralist ethos in which the students' interpretative lenses had been formed.[68]

For many contemporary American Muslims, interfaith is not just an ideal, but a necessity for representing Islam as an acceptable and equal faith in the American political and religious landscape. These issues speak further to the tremendous pressures that individual American Muslims face to be "good Muslims" who present their faith as peaceful and tolerant.[69] Mozaffar's line of questioning further alluded to how individual Muslims have been made into spokespersons, speaking for the entire *umma*. In the decade since 9/11, many American Muslims have enrolled in classes at mosques and at educational institutions because, as Louise Cainkar explains, "they needed to understand Islam better—not only for their own sakes but because they could not explain or defend Islam to others when their state of knowledge was inadequate."[70] Engagement with the Qur'an and Muslim exegetical traditions thus also address the representational demands placed on Muslims. By developing confident answers to the questions posed by non- Muslims, the students sought to mark out an acceptable place for Islam in American pluralism.[71]

Confronting Exclusivism

In addition to addressing non-Muslim interlocutors, Mozaffar frequently urged the class to consider how to respond to Muslims who embrace exclusivism or a very limited inclusivism. To do so, he once invoked the case of Abū Ṭālib, the Prophet's paternal uncle, who is known for protecting Muhammad from hostile members of the Quraysh. Despite serving as the Prophet's confidante and supporter until his death, according to several hadiths, Abū Ṭālib never converted to Islam, though some reports attest to his internal sympathy for the emerging faith. Below, Mozaffar referred to a report in which he was spared the deepest reaches of hell because the Prophet interceded on his behalf.[72] Mozaffar reminds his students that many narratives confirm that Abū Ṭālib still met a horrible fate:[73]

MOZAFFAR: Think about the case of Abū Tālib. He helped the cause of Islam more than anyone. But he's going to the lightest point in hell, where the coals boil your brain.

SANA: I learned this as a child in Sunday school and it terrified me.

MOZAFFAR: Yes, and one of my teachers said if you lie, you'll go to hell where scissors will cut off your tongue.

HUSSEIN: Abū Ṭālib refused the opportunity to become Muslim. He was really close to the Prophet and helped the Muslims, but he still rejected Islam.

MOZAFFAR: Yes, this is one justification for his punishment. Abū Ṭālib had the Prophet to call him to the faith, and he still said no.

YASMIN: We shouldn't be having this conversation. We need to use our hearts. We can't apply Abū Ṭālib's example to everyone. People can do good things and not recognize the Prophet. You deny what's in your heart if you say that other people can be good and not go to paradise.

LAYLA: It's completely ignorant to say that if you don't do what I do, you're going to hell.

MOZAFFAR: But what if it's right?[74]

This dialogue typified the students' negative recounting of their childhood Islamic education, in which they remembered an overarching emphasis on punishment and judgment over mercy and forgiveness. In spite of students' objections, Mozaffar persisted in pursuing the fate of Abū Tālib. The discussion of hellfire clearly upset many of the students, especially Yasmin and Layla, who strenuously protested Mozaffar's line of argument. Yasmin's statement, "We need to use our hearts," echoed throughout our discussions about Christians and Jews. Relying on the "heart" rather than discursive study of texts, Yasmin argued, will help Muslims to see that non-Muslims who are moral can still be recipients of God's mercy.[75] From this perspective, reading the Qur'an was more than an intellectual exercise; it was also an affective one, developed through emotional attunement to God and His attributes, and through the relationships that one develops in the various communities in which American Muslims live and work.

Moreover, Yasmin asserted the primacy of her experiential knowledge of the divine will, formed by living as a member of a minority faith in the United States. She knows her Christian and Jewish neighbors are good people who will find a place in paradise. For her, Q. 2:62 was "straightforward" in meaning because it resonated with her personal experiences. Jews and Christians could in fact enter the garden if they submitted to God and accepted His message. In this way, she affirmed the integrity of her individual experience over and against the weight of textual interpretation. That Yasmin insisted on her point shows how the relevance of certain texts is not predetermined; rather, members of specific communities must attest to their significance and application in their everyday lives. Indeed, interpretation is always bound, at least in part, to the embodied experience of the interpreter.

Yasmin and other students' strong rejection of the interpretive implications of Abū Ṭālib's punishment also resulted from their objections to the perceived rise of exclusivism among American Muslims. Although premodern scholars tended to embrace inclusivism, revivalist currents ushered in a renewed embrace of supercessionism through the writings of influential thinkers such as Sayyid Quṭb (1906–1966).[76] Articulated as part of their attempts to reassert Islam as the superior salvific and political path, revivalists affirmed Islam as the sole path to salvation. Khalil points to the example of the Indian authority Zakir Naik. When faced with the question of Mother Teresa's salvation, he responded that she, too, faces eternal hellfire for committing *shirk*, or associating partners with God.[77] These exclusivist sentiments did not resonate with the students' encounters with their neighbors, whose beliefs and practices largely confirmed their understanding of the universal message of the Qur'an as tolerant of the Abrahamic faiths.

Layla's disdain for exclusivist Muslims reinforced the primacy of individual experience undergirding the students' pluralist assertions. Her emphatic rejection of Muslim superiority over other faiths was rooted in her experience growing up as the only Muslim in her neighborhood:

> Growing up, I wanted to know what the Qur'an had to say about people of other faiths because I had a lot of friends who were Jewish or Christian or atheists or all sorts of things. I refused to believe that they weren't good, worthy people as anyone who was Muslim. . . . And that I always believed in God, but it was never a personified or anthropomorphized being, it was more akin to the life force that binds everything. Now I realize that's an entirely accurate description within Islam, within the words of the Qur'an.[78]

Layla's theology evoked a naturalistic perspective in which God is observable through His creation. She claimed that she arrived at her conceptions of God not through the Qur'an but as a scientist trained in empirical methods, only later realizing that the Qur'an confirmed her understanding that God worked not through the "mundane" details of everyday life, but through broad strokes in the natural world. For her, God remained above the particulars of human social life and sanctioned the creation of different social, political, and religious institutions. The assertion that anyone who doubted the salvation of the People of the Book was simply ignorant reflected the combination of factors that made up Layla's interpretative lens. She derived religious truths from her relationships with non-Muslims, her everyday experiences as an American Muslim, and her university education. For her, the Qur'an provided divine justification for pluralism, scientific empiricism, and individualism. Although she sought out religious engagement with non- Muslims who shared her pluralistic principles, she resisted engaging with Muslims who embraced alternative soteriologies. These classroom conversations thus reveal the ways in which pluralism opens up possibilities of religious engagement with non-Muslims while foreclosing dialogue with other Muslims who are either unwilling or unable to adopt their understanding of pluralism.

On Interpretation, Modernity, and Sacrifice

Despite this overarching project of constructing religious pluralism through the Qur'an, some classmates expressed discomfort with a wholesale adoption of pluralism as defined by American (Protestant) liberalism. One morning, Jawad speculated about how the group fit into the denominational structure of American Judaism and worried about the implications of adopting "Western" interpretations of the Qur'an:

> I worry that we're using a Western perspective on scripture that reflects Jewish and Christian readings. I was at a Seder recently. The Reform Rabbi held up leg of lamb and said, almost apologetically, back when we used to be a sacrificial faith, we would actually kill the lamb. He felt the need to say that this didn't apply anymore. We feel like we need to say this, too, as Western Muslims. But sacrifice does matter.[79]

The conversation had turned back to the sacrifice of Ismāʿīl, a Qur'anic event that Muslims honor on ʿĪd al-Aḍḥā, typically through the ritual sacrifice of a goat. Anthropologists John Bowen and Elaine Combs-Schilling have shown that the practice and meanings of Muslim sacrifice vary over time and space. In Indonesia and Morocco, where Bowen and Combs-Schilling conducted fieldwork, respectively, the ritual has assumed different gendered and political connotations. Both of their studies demonstrate that the performance of sacrifice was not simply the implementation of scriptural dictates, but rather reflected relationships among humans and between humans and God that were inextricably connected to the cultural contexts that produced them.[80]

Jawad's musings point to the ways in which these different conditions have affected ritual slaughter among Western Muslims. Especially in Europe, Muslim sacrifice has been construed as a problem for secular society, due to the logistical challenges of slaughtering large numbers of animals and the ways in which sacrifice confirms suspicions about religion as threatening to the public order. Moreover, environmentalists have exhorted Muslims to reduce the number of animals killed on ʿId for health reasons and out of concern for animal welfare. As he noted, animal sacrifice has also been perceived as contradictory to conceptions of sacrifice that privilege the symbolic rather than the actual spilling of blood, as in Reform Judaism and some strains of Protestant Christianity. He read these renderings as emblematic of "Western" conceptions of ritual that transcend any particular religious community.

The example of sacrifice demonstrates that some American Muslims have both embraced the terms of American pluralism and attempted to stake out an alternative religious space in which its terms could be debated and contested. Throughout their discussions about the Qur'an, students were keen to find common ground among Jews and Christians and to establish the commensurability of Islam and American religious pluralism. And yet, as the discussion about sacrifice demonstrated, some students sought to demarcate theological differences between Muslims and the other Abrahamic faiths, worrying that Reform Jews—and implicitly their own community—had given up "too much" in their quest to promote their faith within the constraints of living as a minority religious community. Even as this group of Muslims worked toward similar goals, they also affirmed the possibility that the path as laid out in the Qur'an was ritually efficacious, obligatory, and potentially superior.

These tensions were ultimately left unresolved in student discussions. Rather than attempt to reconcile them, they should be understood as foundational to everyday interpretative acts, shaped through the messy contours of contemporary conversations around pluralism and exclusivity. Rather than producing a definitive resolution, the class sometimes augmented tensions between texts and contexts, a process that resulted in uncertainty and ambivalence among participants. Ultimately, these tensions point to the ongoing work that local communities perform in working out the implications of soteriological pluralism in the contemporary United States.

Conclusion

Webb's Sunday morning Qur'an classes, structured around guided peer discussions of the text, are central to the construction of an American Islam at Webb. Students come to these classes to raise doubts about interpretations they have encountered in other Muslim settings, to articulate alternative readings, to challenge broader representations of the Qur'an, and to think through the implications of these multiple interpretations in their lived experiences. The positions and interpretations that the students raised were not necessarily stable; that is, it was difficult to discern a specific hermeneutics or approach for an individual student. Although "context" was a common thread in these discussions, students used this context variously, depending on the verse in question, as well as in relation to their embodied experience and the other forms of knowledge they brought to the study of the Qur'an. The many voices present in Webb conversations make for creative engagement while also providing the limits of what can be said about the Qur'an and its statements on the status of other faiths.

These conversations also have implications for approaching the Qur'an through the lens of its social life. By attending to the rich and robust hermeneutics of Muslims in their everyday lives, the ongoing relevance, as well as transformation, of hermeneutical methods originally developed among scholarly elites, both premodern and modern, become readily apparent. Among some American Muslims, the "classical tradition," as they variously define it, becomes an authorizing vehicle through which they seek to render their religious practices "authentic." Making the Qur'an authoritative is an ongoing process of interpretation and practice, the results of which are by no means inevitable. Instead, these processes are marked by various tensions that cannot necessarily be resolved. In conversational and devotional spaces, Webb participants at once confirm the authority of classical Islam, while also embracing methods and assumptions that would have been unrecognizable to premodern scholars. They celebrate traditional authorities while uplifiting the primacy of individual experience. They affirm pluralism within the Islamic tradition and foster relationships with non-Muslims, while also excluding those Muslims who do not conform to their vision of Islam.

Exegesis—performed orally and through daily life—thus figures centrally in defining the limits and contours of Muslim communities and the Islamic tradition. These lay acts of exegesis are framed by, and in turn shape, extant hermeneutical frameworks. Most significantly, this chapter has demonstrated the interplay between Muslim and non- Muslim interpretations of the Qur'an in the United States. Public perceptions of the Qur'an form part of the constellation of lenses through which American Muslims attempt to work out the relationship between their sacred text and their cultural context. Many American Muslims sincerely embrace the ecumenical spirit of the Qur'an, in part, because of tremendous societal pressure to demonstrate Islam's commensurability with liberal Protestant discourse. Although this ideology of religious pluralism is in many ways specific to the contemporary United States, it is also part of broader colonial and postcolonial discourses that have profoundly affected the methods through which contemporary Muslims engage with their sacred texts. We know far more about these effects among Muslim intellectuals, less so about these issues in Muslims' everyday encounters with the Qur'an. By studying Muslim and non-Muslim exchanges over the status and meaning of the text, it is possible to trace the contours of contemporary Muslim discourses of modernity, the formation of overlapping identities, and the relationship between scripture and action.

6

"Islam Is More than Halal and Haram"

NAVIGATING *FIQH* AND SHARIA

THIS CHAPTER FOCUSES on Webb debates about Islamic law and ethics. In 2011, during a flurry of proposed anti-sharia legislation across the United States, the Webb community held an adult class focused on *fiqh* (Islamic jurisprudence). The conversations I track here occurred during the *fiqh* class as well as the many conversations I had with Webb members about how to live according to God's will as American Muslims. Students rarely talked about or engaged *fiqh* as a body of Islamic jurisprudence (as it is commonly defined in academic literature). Instead, as with ritual performance, the Webb interest in *fiqh* derived its urgency from its members' dual goals to raise their children to have "seamless" American Muslim identities *and* to improve the public image of Islam. In particular, Webb parents want their kids to understand that Islamic ethics is not a rigid, narrow set of guidelines, but rather everyday processes of normative reflection and action, negotiated within families and among individuals, religious scholars, and God. Seeking a flexible, adaptive ethical framework, they attempted to reclaim Muslim normativity as embedded in relationships and everyday experience, rather than defined by a set of rules and regulations articulated by scholars. Their practices reveal how American Muslims enact sharia as a much broader nexus of normative practices, ethical deliberations, and engagement with a wide range of ideological resources than the term "Islamic law" implies.

Webb conversations about *fiqh* show the possibilities and uncertainties that emerge within this third space. In addition to addressing parenting dilemmas, the class engaged in perennial debates about ritual practice, namely daily prayer (salat), and enduring questions about the nature of authority and tradition. For Omer Mozaffar and his *fiqh* students, consensus on these issues, like so many at Webb, remained elusive and, perhaps, undesirable. Instead, these robust conversations demonstrate the tensions inherent in Webb's attempt to construct an American Islam that is at once distinctive and continuous with the Islamic tradition as they define it.

Fiqh and Parental Authority

Webb members conceive of the nuclear family as the moral center for American Islam. As such, they embed constructions of Islamic ethics within these familial relationships, especially between parents and their children. Malika described how the *fiqh* class came about, namely as a way for parents to help their children understand some of the basic concepts in Islamic law. In particular, she noted several problems that she detects with kids' use of the terms "halal" and "haram."

> There's this subculture among Muslim kids, they throw around words like "haram" and "halal" at each other. It's their growing up crisis as Muslim youth. But if we don't get a handle on it pretty quickly, it can give them wrong ideas. Their parents don't have enough classical training or knowledge to correct their kids.[1]

It was this longer phrase, "crisis of Muslim youth," and not the political and media frenzy around sharia, that prompted Malika to suggest that Mozaffar teach the fall 2011 course on *fiqh*. As I discuss below, the anti-sharia legislation did have an effect on the ways that Webb members talked about sharia, but it was not the immediate impetus. In everyday parlance, "haram" refers to what is bad, wrong, and forbidden, whereas "halal" refers to what is permissible. These categories appear in the Qur'an in reference to specific behaviors such as dietary restrictions.[2] Malika observes that these terms have also become ubiquitous among American youth, used as kind of shorthand to delineate behaviors that they consider to be acceptable (halal) and those considered to be un-Islamic (haram). She understands this "crisis of Muslim youth" as part of their kids' identity formation and a way for different groups of kids to tease, mock, and maintain the boundaries of their various cliques. Webb parents also believe that these terms reveal something deeply amiss in American Muslim communities. In particular, many parents express anxiety that using the term "haram" promotes a rigid and inflexible understanding of Muslim ethics.

Malika's assessment of kids' use of haram and halal demonstrates the highly contextual and relational ways in which American Muslims go about moral deliberation. Kambiz GhaneaBassiri rightly maintains that "normativity" is more helpful than "law" for analyzing the ways that American Muslims live in accordance with sharia.[3] He focuses on the "triangular relationship between the individual, community, and God."[4] The advantage of this approach is that it emphasizes the *production* of normativity, rather than the articulation of ethical ideals or standards.[5] As he argues, "[T]he ways in which the relationship between the individual, God, and community could be normatively configured are as diverse as Muslims' varying understandings of what God demands of them individually in different communal settings."[6] Malika is attuned to the obligations and moral logics of multiple communities, including the nuclear family, groups of friends, and the broader American Muslim community. These contexts create different demands and expectations on kids and their parents, who in turn respond to these expectations with different motivations. For example, at school, kids want to fit in with their peers. As Malika muses, they might use "halal" and "haram" to tease each other or produce conformity. By contrast, she and other Webb parents worry about the negative perception of Islam that their kids' use of "haram" may produce.

Webb parents understand themselves as correcting and replacing deficient, harmful, and potentially dangerous conceptions of normativity and ethics that circulate in their local communities. In contrast to this polarity between forbidden and acceptable actions, Malika wants her kids to have an awareness of what she sees as the more flexible approach of "classical," premodern Sunni scholarship. Premodern jurists assessed actions on a scale of five categories, such that behavior was classified as one of the following: *wājib/farḍ* (obligatory); *mandūb* (recommended); *mubāḥ* (permissible); *makrūh* (abominable); and haram (forbidden). Under this framework, halal fell under the category of *mubāḥ*.[7] Haram actions, such as *zinā* (adultery) resulted in punishment if committed, and conversely, *wājib* acts were punishable if not performed.[8] With the decline of *madhhab*-based jurisprudence, especially in the United States, these categories are invoked less frequently in everyday Muslim practice. This is, in part, due to the popularity of scholars who do not ascribe to a particular school and the modern practice of combining rulings from various schools (*talfīq*).[9] Webb parents looked to classical scholarship because they wanted a way to move beyond what they saw as the narrow confines of the halal/haram dichotomy. It was important for Webb parents to have the religious knowledge to correct their children and to provide a more nuanced framework.

Such efforts to revive classical frameworks hinged on an underlying unease over divine and parental authority. Malika and other parents at Webb worried that their children (incorrectly) assumed that anyone, including their peers, possessed the authority to pronounce a behavior, idea, or object "haram." In the first place, Webb parents wanted to impress upon their kids that this authority certainly did not rest with them. These concerns surfaced when kids applied the term "haram" to areas of culture that their parents believe are not just permissible but also ought to be encouraged as authentic expressions of American Islam. Patricia, whom we met in chapter 2, relayed a particularly challenging incident:

> My husband wanted the kids to go to Islamic school, and I said, "OK." That was the best way they would get an Islamic education, but this set up major issues in our relationship because some of the things they learned there were not the best for our family. They learned the word "haram," which means bad or wrong. They started coming home and telling me what I was doing wrong as a mother. And I said, "We're drawing the line here." They would tell me everything was haram, like watching TV or music, any movie, and gossiping. Not that I'm a gossiper, but if I said anything about anyone, my seven-year-old would tell me that I'm going to hell, that I'm going to burn in hell for doing things wrong. I found myself doing my daughter's hair while she was studying for a test and learning about the Quraysh, the nonbelievers or the idolaters. As she's reading this stuff, I was connecting more with the Quraysh as opposed to the Muslims [laughs]. But that's not right. I didn't appreciate that my kids saw me as a bad person.[10]

As a convert who expresses uncertainty about her knowledge of Islam, this exchange only augmented Patricia's existing anxieties about her acceptance in the broader Muslim community. She had a difficult time giving up aspects of her Christian faith, particularly the celebration of Christmas. Patricia referred to the term "idolatry" several times in reference to the divinity of Jesus and to her dismay upon conversion that the family would no longer have a Christmas tree. Even though she now views praying to Jesus or having a Christmas tree as *shirk* (associating partners with God), she also conveyed the profound sense of loss that she experienced when she gave up rituals and objects that once connected her to her extended family. She identified with the Quraysh because she previously embraced "idolatrous" acts. Moreover, the perceived intolerance of contemporary Muslims contributed to her hesitation to affiliate with the early community, even though presumably her daughter was studying the Islamic traditions that narrated the injuries Muslims endured at the hands of the Quraysh. At that point, Patricia told me, she was so fed up at hearing the words "haram" and "*shirk*" that she found herself sympathizing with the unbelievers. And it was then that she knew something had to change. She asserted her parental authority, telling her children that listening to pop music did not make her a bad Muslim. This situation, alongside others, led her to re-enroll the kids in public schools.

Patricia expressed a robust understanding of the theological stakes involved in applying the term "haram." By invoking "*shirk*," she signaled that there was more at stake than just asserting her parental authority, but rather that her kids misunderstood the nature of God. As we have seen, Webb participants are concerned with uplifting divine attributes such as mercy. I interviewed many parents who doubt that God would inflict such harsh punishments for listening to pop music or having non-Muslim friends. They worry instead that their children use improper meanings of "haram" and do not fully grasp its eschatological implications.[11] Indeed, because the term had specific connotations and applications within *fiqh*, Patricia wants her kids to understand that "haram" should be applied discretely, carefully, and cautiously.[12] This view echoes the consensus among premodern thinkers that haram acts resulted in divine punishments that were far more damning than any human penalty.[13] While Patricia lacks familiarity with the nuances of these scholarly arguments, her comments nonetheless reveal an understanding of "haram" that conforms to this emphasis on divine rather human punishment of forbidden acts.

Patricia's encounter with her kids is also refracted through debates over permissibility and authority in American Muslim communities at large that intersect with essential questions surrounding religious and cultural authenticity.[14] For example, many American Muslims are broadly familiar with a hadith that prohibits the use of particular musical instruments, drinking alcohol, and illicit sexual intercourse, among other things.[15] It is a commonly held view that some, if not all, forms of music are haram.[16] As Su'ad Abdul Khabeer shows with respect to hip hop artists, however, American Muslims engage in robust debates about music and its permissibility. Some artists reject legal opinions they believe are based on foreign cultural norms and assert the authenticity of musical genres that are indigenous to the United States. Others artists place their craft in a continuous tradition of poetic expression.[17] Such complexities are far from unique to the United States. Despite the broad circulation of the idea that certain forms of music are haram, a flourishing secular and religious music industry exists in many Muslim-majority societies, though many Arab states censor the production of particular types of music.[18] Patricia similarly maintains the validity of her musical preferences and practices against some opinions that music is impermissible. But she find different ground on which to argue for the authenticity of American music. She claims the authority of her embodied *experience*, which guides her conviction that Islam ought to reflect the culture in which it is practiced.[19] As a parent, she is the arbiter of culture.

Haram and Halal Are Forbidden

Webb members' opposition to the overuse of the term "haram" are part of the community's ongoing attempts to construct an alternative vision for American Islam. In particular, parents conveyed shock and dismay when their children came home from Sunday school regaling them with stories about punishment and damnation. Mary told me about her decision to remove her daughter from an Islamic school:

> On the first day of kindergarten, the teacher told my daughter that when she dies, she will be put on a ladder. If you haven't done anything bad, then the ladder leads to heaven, but if you have done something wrong, then the ladder will turn to knives and cut you, as you fall into the burning fire of hell. I was livid. She never went back.[20]

Nearly every parent I spoke to at Webb had a story like this one to tell, which prompted them to seek alternative sites of religious education, eventually enrolling at Webb. They rejected what they saw as an understanding of Islam that emphasized Allah's punitive qualities and encouraged moral absolutism, where even the slightest deviation from established ethical norms conjured up images of hell.

Safiya, who helps run the Webb Sunday School, sees the haram/halal distinction as part of a bigger problem, namely the unnecessary religious regulation of children's behavior. For her, kids instead need to develop "character":

> We don't use the terms "haram" and "halal." That is forbidden. The kids hear it so they need to understand what it really means instead of just throwing it out there. It's more about character. . . . We need to switch everything around to good character. We don't get into things like stepping into the mosque with your left foot. Or they say that *shaytan* [Satan] is in the bathroom. The kids don't need to know that yet. It's usually just one or two people that ruin it for the kids at other programs. They're trying to do their best, and what they've learned is important. But I don't want them teaching my kids.[21]

Like Safiya, many Webb parents portray teachers who told such stories as well intentioned, but ultimately misguided. According to Safiya, the small number of teachers who are committed to obedience and conformity have had an outsized negative influence. Through their reliance on rules and punishments, these "immigrant" approaches neglect the development of "character" and the affirmation of individual choice in religious faith.

In order to encourage reflection and moral discernment, Safiya asserted that teachers should avoid introducing themes of retribution at a young age because of their potentially damaging psychological effects. Moreover, many Webb parents see fear as ineffective for promoting piety because it only engenders a superficial adherence to the faith that would not endure beyond childhood, when, presumably the fear of parents and Sunday School teachers wanes. Instead, they hope that one day their children will choose Islam freely. Webb parents believe that for their vision of American Islam to flourish, their children must themselves be able to recognize Islam as a faith that epitomizes universal values and is rooted in a flexible moral framework unmoored from the rigid constraints of halal and haram.[22]

From parents, I heard time and again that while it was too late for their own American Muslim identity to be "seamless," they expect that their kids would be model American Muslims (as well as Muslims generally). These high hopes resonate with the expectations of other American immigrant communities as they invest their children in the project of building an American faith. Among twentieth-century American Catholics, Robert Orsi argues that children in fact were looked to as model "Americans and as *American* Catholics."[23] Similarly, with respect to American Jews, Jonathan Sarna demonstrates how American synagogues transformed from "adult-centered" to "child-centered" institutions as Jews moved with increasing numbers to the suburbs and built synagogues to serve as a primary site for their children's moral formation.[24] Prema Kurien has documented the ways that American Hindus have dedicated tremendous intellectual and financial resources in shaping the formation of their children's knowledge of Hinduism and India. She shows how these efforts are predicated on the development of an American Hinduism that seeks to be "more" Hindu than the practice of the faith in India. American Hindu institutions attempt to meet the demands of American multiculturalism and religious pluralism by simultaneously preserving Hinduism's distinctiveness and affirming its universal, interreligious values.[25]

The term "character" signals Webb parents' commitment to inculcating an ethical approach that is less exclusively Muslim and more recognizable to non-Muslim Americans, one that is less focused on embodied action and more focused on universal values. Such values—namely tolerance, mercy, and respect—cohere with liberal, modern conceptions of religiosity as voluntary, individualized, and inclusive. Safiya's children may choose to step into the mosque with their left feet as adults, but for now, Safiya's priority is to minimize their exposure to practices that she sees as unduly rigid. As a result of her efforts, she hopes that the next generation will embrace an Islamic ethics rooted in choice rather than compliance.

Sharia and the Public Image of Islam

The parents' other overriding concern in these discussions of haram was the public image of Islam. Many saw these stories as proof of the influence of Salafi preachers and members in Chicago Muslim institutions.[26] For these parents, teaching love and mercy is vital for their children's moral formation, but they also seek to ensure that their kids are properly attuned to the demands of American religious pluralism. As we have seen, Webb members link claims of Muslim superiority to negative representations of their faith. One family pulled their son from a Muslim elementary school after he announced to his neighbors that he was not allowed to play with non-Muslims because they were unbelievers. Their children now attend a Catholic school, where they can learn to be pious but without being exposed to Muslim supercessionism. Adult Muslims are not the only ones expected to be representatives of Islam; children also bear this responsibility.

As we have seen in Qur'an discussions, Webb participants criticize other Muslims who emphasize God's wrath at the expense of his mercy. As an alternative, they seek to restore attention to divine attributes such as benevolence and forgiveness. This rhetoric resonates with the discourses of many national Muslim intellectuals and leaders, who similarly emphasize mercy as foundational to Islam. In an op-ed following the April 2013 bombings at the Boston marathon, Suhaib Webb, a prominent Muslim intellectual and the imam of the Islamic Center of Boston, declared:

> If the center of Judaism is the law, and the heart of Christianity is love, what Islam requires, above all else, is mercy. And whether on display in health care provided for the poor at South Los Angeles's UMMA Community Clinic, or in a patiently handled Arabic lesson that will one day lead a new convert into the fullness of the tradition, Islamic mercy, preached and practiced within the community, allows no room for radicalization.[27]

Suhaib Webb (who, as far as I know, is not related to M. A. R. Webb) calls attention to Islam as one of the Abrahamic faiths, attesting to its essential nature as a religion of mercy, just as Christianity and Judaism contribute their distinctive yet positive essences to the fabric of American pluralistic society. Such statements also help to naturalize the association of American mosques with extremism, confirming the need for surveillance of Muslim institutions that do not properly conform to this essence of Islam.

The veneration of God's mercy represents another instance in which generational struggles and broader discourses of extremism converge. Safiya acknowledges that many Sunday School teachers are well-intentioned "aunties" who replicate the teachings that they had learned in their childhood.[28] Yet she tries to prevent her children from being exposed to these views because for her, they represent a potentially dangerous and subversive path that potentially leads young children toward marginalization in American society. By stressing "good character" over restrictive and punitive measures, Safiya maintains that American Muslim children will be better positioned to lead ethical lives unmarred by the disdainful and "scary" elements. Safiya's approach affirms Islam as a "spiritual" faith sustained by individuals who freely choose to embrace its flexible and accommodating worldview and its inherently liberal ethos. Parenting anxieties thus dovetail with broader concerns over authority and representation, in particular the perceived lack of trustworthy and authentic Muslim American intellectuals, scholars, and imams, who are capable of shifting public discourse on Islam. Parents step in to fill this absence.

Anti-Sharia Initiatives and the Objectification of Sharia

The intense political attention on sharia made these Webb conversations about *fiqh* all the more urgent. In 2010, sharia became a lightning rod for anti-Islamic sentiment, which had previously not entered into American political discourse.[29] The anti-sharia movement in the United States originated with David Yerushalmi, a Hasidic Jew who had worked in commercial law and contributed to conservative think tanks.[30] In 2006, Yerushalmi joined forces with Frank Gaffney, Director of the Center for Security Policy at the Hudson Institute. Together they mounted a concerted lobbying campaign to draft bills outlawing sharia in various states.[31] By the end of 2011, more than twenty-five states had introduced over fifty anti-sharia bills. Media reports and various think tank exposés fueled hysteria over sharia as an insidious, "creeping" influence, implying that it threatened the survival of American democracy and its security abroad. Explicitly linking sharia to terrorism and fundamentalism, these reports claimed that sharia had successfully taken root in the United States by masquerading as a set of religious beliefs and practices and hiding under the protections of the First Amendment. According to this logic, Muslims took advantage of their Constitutional rights in order to conceal their true nefarious purpose, namely to undermine American legal and moral frameworks from within.[32]

Gaffney's report, "Shariah: The Threat to America," denounced sharia as "a comprehensive and totalitarian system of laws, an aggressive military doctrine, an all-encompassing socio-economic program and a ruthless enforcement mechanism. It is, in short, a complete way of life."[33] By this account, sharia is both spiritually and morally impoverished because it ultimately limits the expression of individual freedom and ethics. The ensuing media frenzy has gained traction in an environment in which Muslim citizenship was called increasingly under suspicion in overt and subtle ways. Additionally, these and other inflammatory claims about sharia coincided with the toxic public discourse surrounding the building of Park 51 in Lower Manhattan, the so-called Ground Zero Mosque.[34] These campaigns, which are ongoing, draw on this familiar set of tropes that depicted Islam as a regressive, antimodern, and oppressive religion that was inherently incompatible with the liberal values of Western modernity: individualism, capitalism, and democracy. This broader discourse flags sharia as the cornerstone of Islam's presumed antipathy toward the West.[35]

Beyond the negative associations that this controversy generated about sharia, they also contained another misconception—that sharia is a unified, singular set of laws and guidelines to which all Muslims are uniquely bound. Sharia encompasses relationships between humans and the divine through acts of worship (*ʿibādāt*), and it governs social relationships of various kinds, including family and economic transactions (*muʿāmalāt*). Indeed, *ʿibādāt* and *muʿāmalāt* are inextricably bound to each other because they both originate with God, the lawgiver. There is no book of sharia. Instead, Muslims rely on the intellectual and devotional practice of *fiqh* to try to know God's will. *Fiqh* means "discernment" or "understanding."[36] The term refers to the vast discourses of Islamic jurisprudence, including the opinions and rulings written by Muslim jurists.[37]

Islamic legal theory traditionally had two main goals: rule-creation and rule-justification, which were elaborated primarily through the four Sunni schools of law and the Shi'a Jafari school (sing. *madhhab*; pl. *madhāhib*).[38] Within the four Sunni schools, scholars recognized the validity of opinions issued by the other schools, underscoring the contingency of human interpretation in contrast to the definitive and supreme rulings of God. The Webb class focused on the ways that Muslims have sought to understand and fulfill the will of God through *fiqh*.

In media and public discourses, however, sharia has become "Islamic law," understood as an authoritative and authoritarian set of rules governing Muslim behavior. Its moral dimensions have been almost entirely subordinated to this rhetoric. Such a misunderstanding puzzled many American Muslims, including Webb members, for whom sharia is predominantly enacted through everyday practice. Ultimately, higher courts overturned the vast majority of anti-sharia legislation, but as I explore below, these laws have had important effects, which in turn have sparked numerous efforts among American Muslims to confront and resolve this dissonance.

The anti-sharia campaigns engendered a new wave of fear and concern among American Muslims about the public image of Islam and a redoubling of efforts to present Islam as compatible with secular American civic engagement and the demands of religious pluralism. Muslim organizations like the Council on American-Islamic Relations (CAIR) mounted national campaigns to educate Muslims about sharia with an eye toward presenting an alternative view of Muslim divine law. At the 2011 Islamic Society of North America conference, Corey Saylor, a CAIR representative, urged attendees to "reclaim the terminology" by providing this framing of sharia to other Americans:

> Sharia is the way I live my life. It's how I pray, how I marry, and how I invest. Sharia is what guides my faith, and tells me to be merciful, compassionate, and tolerant. The Constitution is the law of the land, and my faith dictates me to follow the law of the land.[39]

Muslim corporations also looked to rebrand sharia. For example, Soundvision, a Chicago-based media and production company that specializes in educational products, developed a sharia pamphlet designed to help Muslims to explain what sharia is to non-Muslims.[40] All of these efforts worked to place sharia squarely in the domain of personal piety. Through these campaigns, Muslim activists sought to assuage conservative political and religious concerns that adhering to sharia somehow compromised American Muslims' political loyalties. Instead, they cast it as a nonthreatening system of personal ethics that was fully commensurate with American pluralism. "Reclaiming the terminology" required reconfiguring sharia to conform to contemporary understandings of religion that have become naturalized in American politics as requirements for achieving full citizenship.[41] Muslim leaders replaced one reified view of sharia with another, representing Islam as religion of peace rather than a religion of oppression.[42]

It was in this climate in 2011 that Webb created a course to study *fiqh* and to explore its commensurability with American democracy.[43] But unlike CAIR and Soundvision, Webb students struggled to define sharia in a manner that could be easily digested by the American public *and* that accurately reflected the complex ethical negotiations around which they organize daily life. As these debates were ramping up, I discussed the anti-sharia campaigns with Webb founder Nadia. She responded, "The Constitution is sharia. Everything in it is sharia compliant."[44] Nadia understands sharia to be both compatible with, but also equivalent to, in some sense, the United States Constitution. That is, the obligations that sharia places on her are not qualitatively different from the social contract undergirding American democracy. American Muslims like Nadia thus continue to work out the complexities of these issues in the context of a shifting political terrain in which they were trying to bridge the perceived gap between negative representations and lived experiences of their faith.[45] In other words, while Nadia and her fellow Webb students see no conflict between their religious affiliation and their loyalty to the American nation-state, they nevertheless find themselves responding to charges against Islam in an objectified way that diverges from the role of sharia in their daily lives.

Indeed, Webb members noted that before the public scrutiny of sharia, they never felt pressure to explain sharia, much less define it to their neighbors as a discreet discursive object. The Webb community had only recently begun to think consciously about defining sharia and *fiqh* as means to defend Islam against charges of extremism and authoritarianism. Webb members attribute what they see as an inadequate American Muslim response to a lack of suitable educational opportunities to study the Islamic tradition; in part, the *fiqh* class was intended to remedy this perceived gap. My conversation partners conveyed that sharia figured prominently in their daily practices, but they hesitated to *explain* it in a politically viable way. I sometimes asked my interviewees what sharia was and usually received puzzled looks and responses such as, "sharia is just what we do," and another explained, "It's not like we use those terms around the house." These comments underscore the inadequacy of defining sharia as "Islamic law" or as an established set of rules that dictate behavior; rather, this community conceives of sharia to be what they *do* to fulfill their obligations to God, however imperfectly they may accomplish that aim.[46]

Meanings of Salat

Indeed, one of the primary actions through which Muslims fulfill these obligations to God is daily ritual prayer. Despite, or perhaps because of, prayer's foundational role in constructing the triangular relationship between the individual, society, and God, it continues to figure prominently in contemporary Muslim discourse concerning ethics, culture, and subjectivity. Webb conversations about prayer exemplify the multiple meanings that the practice evokes as well as the specific contours these meanings take in the United States. Prayer has to be fit into work and school routines that do not always accommodate the practice. As a result, American Muslims frequently grapple with how to fulfill what many understand as a universal obligation.

The Qur'an states that salat, daily ritual prayer, is a requirement; hadith and classical *fiqh* works then stipulate the specific requirements, such as bodily postures, timing, and exceptions. In the Qur'an, salat represents human obedience to Allah. Through their performance, Muslims remember God and give thanks for the blessings he has bestowed upon humanity. The Qur'an details many benefits for those who perform daily prayer, including the protection against evil and vice as well as spiritual rewards in the afterlife.[47] While Muslims perform salat out of obedience for God, the Qur'an suggests that ritual prayer is itself productive of a religious subjectivity that more fully encompasses the meaning of "Muslim" as one who submits to God.

Although salat is frequently glossed as a ritual that unifies the *ummah*, Webb discussions highlight divergence among Muslims about the obligations and meanings of prayer.[48] Far from achieving consensus about the effects and mechanics of prayer, the *fiqh* students disagreed about whether prayer produced unity among American Muslims and the wider *ummah* or whether different prayer practices affirmed Islam's cultural diversity. In this section, I contrast the perspectives of two Webb members, Hussein and Sana, to underscore the different ways that Muslims conceive of the relationship between individual, community, and God by anchoring conceptions of tradition in hierarchies of space. Hussein is a second-generation Arab immigrant in his early forties and the father of three young children. During one class, he announced to his classmates,

> Prayer is so crucial. It means a specific thing in the Qur'an and the hadith. Not everything can be reinterpreted. Some people want to reinterpret everything. Look at our prayer spaces and the way we pray. It's the same as in Muslim countries.[49]

Hussein's response evokes the importance of salat as an expression of piety performed by the global Muslim *ummah*. He maintained that prayer practices in "Muslim countries" confirm that American Muslims are part of a continuous and unified community. Because US Muslims pray like other Muslims, they can be confident that they are fulfilling their obligations correctly. Hussein located "authentic" Islam outside of the United States, where one can be surer that practices of prayer are efficacious, correct, and authentic, and one can therefore assess the validity of American Muslim practice against them.

Although Webb conceives of itself as an inclusive third space, this discursive move illustrates live tensions around inclusion and exclusion, and the ways that these tensions are contested through peer discussion. Students like Hussein contend with variations in practice among American Muslims that result from ethnic and cultural traditions as well as the range of theological and sectarian viewpoints represented in major urban centers like Chicago. In response to this fragmentation, Hussein conceives of prayer as an expression of Muslim unity, one that reinforces boundaries of correct practice.[50] Moreover, he expressed concern that Webb debates possibly exceeded the limits placed by the Qur'an and hadith. For him, these texts are self-evident, independent of the commentaries and works of jurisprudence that have accompanied them or the many views that his peers voice in the classroom.

By contrast, Sana, whom we met in the chapter on the Qur'an, affirmed the internal plurality of Islam through her prayer practices and ventured a view that again proved controversial among her classmates. She acknowledged the variations in the times and mechanics of ritual prayer elaborated differently by the four Sunni and Shi'a schools of law. For example, Muslims who follow the Maliki *madhhab*, in regions such as North Africa, pray with their hands at their sides, rather than in the folded position. Sana affirmed that this variation is God's intention and therefore essential to the Islamic tradition:

> There are many ways to pray. Allah said that he wants to make things easy on us. I've told the children they can combine the prayers. My daughter can pray in short sleeves and capris, and a scarf. I take an unorthodox approach, and I know that a lot of people at Webb don't even take the approaches I take. There's a hadith that says that the Prophet (may God be pleased with him) said that religion will one day be split into seventy-two and some people take that as horrible that we will be split along seventy-two lines. But I think there's beauty in diversity. The Ismailis combine prayers all the time. So you pray just once in the morning, midday, and night. You don't even cover your hair. At mosque that's not going to work. If we're in a mosque, then we have to follow the proper way. Out of respect for my family who are Hanafis, we follow their way when we visit them.[51]

Sana's views on the Hanafi *madhhab* reveal that while many American Muslims continue to be familiar with the ritual prescriptions of the Sunni schools, they also consciously modify those rules. Moreover, in the modern period, fewer Muslim scholars are affiliated with a particular *madhhab*.[52] In the course of my research, I only met a few people who followed a particular school. As with Sana, many Indian and Pakistani immigrants mentioned that they followed the Hanafi school, the dominant *madhhab* in that region, as part and parcel of their familial practice. Sana folded Hanafism into a set of cultural norms rather than as Islamic jurisprudence per se.[53] She teaches her children the Hanafi method of prayer out of respect for her parents and extended family, but only requires them to follow those prescriptions in their family's presence and in spaces she understands as governed by these cultural norms. The daughter of Indian immigrants, Sana often bristles at what she called the "immigrant restrictions" placed on young women. She wants to avoid placing a similar burden on her daughter. Sana's experiences demonstrate that as individuals inhabit different spaces and communities, they rework normative frameworks, adapting them to accommodate the normative expectations of these varying spaces. In the third space at Webb, Sana feels at liberty to discuss how she embraces this kind of variation by seeking guidance from Sunni and Shi'a practices alike.

Combining prayers is not without precedent. For example, premodern jurists permitted combining prayers under certain circumstances such as travel.[54] Sana has made this practice part of her daily routine and conceptualizes her method as the "Ismaili" way. Ismailis are the second-largest global Shi'a community, and its largest subgroup follows the Nizari line of Aga Khan imams whose decrees in recent decades have focused on responding to the social conditions of modernity.[55] In the nineteenth century, for example, Aga Khan III encouraged women's education and professionalization by permitting interactions between men and women in public.[56] Sana's ability to reference a singular Ismaili approach to prayer reflects the globalization of this movement's institutional structures.[57] Beginning in the mid-twentieth century, Nizari Ismailis standardized the frequency of prayer (known as *du'a* instead of salat) to three times a day, rather than the five daily prayers performed by Sunni Muslims. Additionally, Ismailis dispensed with using vernacular languages in prayer, adopting Arabic as the universal language of a pan-Ismaili religious practice.[58]

In addition to grounding her practice in Ismaili norms, Sana justified her reduction of the daily prayers pragmatically and in the context of meeting the demands on a busy mother. She commonly combines the final two daily prayers to accommodate her kids' activity schedules and to ensure that her children pray regularly. Sana believes that combining prayers is far better than abandoning the practice completely, and as such finds that the Ismaili accommodations of modern, Western norms has much to offer. Ismailis, she told me in our conversation, see Islam as compatible with Western culture, unlike many Muslims she knows. She acknowledges that some Sunni Muslims see Ismailis as outside the fold of normative Islam. Sana conceptualizes Islam as a broad umbrella under which a range of theological and ritual orientations are accepted and valid. From Sana's perspective, Ismaili and Hanafi methods of prayer are equally permissible. Her kids should know how to pray the Hanafi way not because it is superior, but in order to honor and participate in the traditions of their families.

Sana's attitudes toward prayer reflect a capacious understanding of Muslim normativity, which requires her to explore multiple ways of fulfilling her obligations to God. As a mother, she understands that one of these obligations is to inculcate in her children a celebratory view of Muslim diversity. She once took her kids to the Ahmadiyya mosque, even though "most Muslims don't think they are Muslim," because "there is beauty in diversity, and these divisions are what make our community great."[59] At the same time, Sana's matter-of-fact demeanor and confident tone belie her uneasiness with the theological and ritual positions she has staked out for herself and her family. She admitted, "I would never talk about this at the Webb Foundation, oh no, I know most people wouldn't approve. People say they [members of the Ahmadiyya] aren't Muslims, but I want them to go there to see how they do things. I'm too old to worry about what other people think of me."[60] Many Muslims understand key Ahmadi tenets as heretical, especially the claims of prophecy by the movement's founder, Ghulam Ahmad (d. 1908), who adopted the title "*masih-i ma'ud*" (promised messiah) and claimed to be *muhaddath* (the recipient of divine revelation). Both of these claims appropriated and refigured traditional Muslim understandings of these titles, as the former was usually assigned to Jesus, and the latter to Muhammad ibn 'Abd Allah.[61] The Ahmaddiyya came to the United States through the missionary efforts of Mufti Muhammad Sadiq in the 1920s, who started al-Masjid in Chicago, which then attracted many African American converts.[62] Over the next couple of decades, the organization grew to thousands of members and promoted a message of overcoming racial inequality through Islam.

Sana consciously included the Ahmadiyya because so many in her familial and social circles cast it beyond the pale of Islam. Contrary to the familiar charges of "heterodoxy," Sana's visit to the Ahmadiyya mosque reveals her conviction that the group is an authentic path to God. Rather than view plurality as problem for the *umma*, Sana thinks that God wants multiple ways of being Muslim. Acting on this conviction, she has familiarized her children with the history of American Islam and the variety of theological perspectives and ritual variations in American Muslim institutions. They attend a mosque Sunday school because "it's my duty as a parent to give them a community, and later on, they can choose whether to continue . . . and they like the misbehavior that is going on over there, pretty much unchecked."[63] In this case, her parental duties coincided with her children's desires for a particular social setting, showing how religious concerns dovetail with negotiations between parents and children about the benefits of religious education. For Sana, it is in fact these mundane challenges that govern her religious choices, enabling her to piece together Muslim normativity in creative and unexpected ways.

In her efforts to normalize internal diversity, Sana challenges extant interpretations of the hadith that she cites from the collection of Abu Dawud. The hadith, which is narrated by Abu Hurayra, a Companion of the Prophet, reports, "The Jews were split up into seventy-one or seventy-two sects; and the Christians were split up into seventy-one or seventy-two sects; and my community will be split up into seventy-three sects."[64] Other versions of the hadith stress its eschatological dimensions, portraying the division into seventy-three sects as a harbinger of the End of Days. For example, the report narrated by al-Tirmidhi says that seventy-two sects will go into the hell-fire and only one sect, the true Muslims, will go to paradise. Sana asserted that while other members of her community take a negative view toward these divisions, she viewed them as a sign of Islam's "beauty."

Through prayer, Sana and Hussein provide contrasting constructions of tradition. Here, it is important to see tradition as an "open-ended" discourse, the "unfolding of arguments over time," one that is animated by the political, social, and religious concerns of Muslims who enmesh themselves in it.[65] This is why even a foundational ritual like prayer continues to produce such vigorous debate. While drawing upon the Qur'an and hadith to justify their particular prayer practices, Sana and Hussein discover expressions of God's intentions for communities and individuals; that is, they orient tradition in different locations. According to this logic, Hussein and Sana both take prayer practices as proof of God's intentions, but they arrive at divergent moral assessments of homogenous and heterogeneous practices, respectively. These processes illuminate what Talal Asad calls the "domain of orthodoxy" or the relations of power through which Muslims seek to "regulate, uphold, require or adjust correct practices, and to condemn, exclude, undermine, or replace incorrect ones."[66] Both appropriate tradition along this inclusion and exclusion axis. Hussein's narrative of uniformity bridges American communities and Muslim-majority contexts, reflecting the ties he seeks with Muslims in distant yet potentially more authentic places. Asserting the homogeneity of prayer enables him to address the disorienting array of American Muslim practices and to assert limits over some of the opinions voiced in Webb spaces, like those of Sana. By contrast, Sana celebrates diversity through her discovery of the American Muslim past, investing the historical entanglements of immigrant and black Muslims in urban areas like Chicago with the authority of God's intentions. Rather than linking her to Muslims abroad, prayer connects Sana with other Chicago Muslims, whom she feels have been unduly marginalized, as well as with her immigrant family. Prayer facilitates her mobility and the religious options she wants to provide for her children. Her conviction that diversity lies at the heart of Islam was rooted in her understanding of hadith but also is the product of her embodied knowledge, attained through her experiences as an American Muslim. Like her classmates who believe that their non-Muslim neighbors will be saved, Sana claims that groups such as the Ahmadiyya represent an authentic path to God. Her experience guides her as much as the Qur'an and hadith, upon which she voiced her convictions.

The Intentions and Purposes of Prayer

In addition to exploring prayer as constituting boundaries among Muslim communities, these conversations also precipitated further reflection on the ways that prayer mediates the relationship between individuals and God.

MOZAFFAR: Do I focus on *taqwá* [God-consciousness] or worship?
SALWA: I think they're inseparable, in the same category.
MOZAFFAR: Suppose I don't feel connected to God. If I pray then it wouldn't be sincere. Should I still pray?
HUSNA: Yes. If we based our actions on feeling, then we wouldn't do it.
SANA: Life is long and praying five times every day is a fallacy. It just doesn't happen.
JAMILA: If you're doing ritual right, then it should develop consciousness and allow us to be present. It's our nature to yearn for that connection. If we don't then we are being distracted by the other things in our lives.
YASMIN: This sets the bar really high for people who are struggling. They should keep trying to do it. I could be praying perfectly and still have no connection. I don't always feel it; I just keep practicing.[67]

These students considered the relationship between *taqwá* and prayer, asking whether God-consciousness is a necessary precondition to perform salat. A Qur'anic term, *taqwá* appears in conjunction with a range of ritual acts, including prayer, zakat (almsgiving), and the hajj. The Qur'an tells its readers to strive toward *taqwá* because the condition protects humans from committing sin, and ultimately guards against eternal damnation.[68] Although salat is often glossed as a communal ritual, these dialogues demonstrate the importance of ritual prayer in developing one's interior convictions and intentions. The students imply that while desiring a relationship with God is an innate part of human nature (*fitra*), *taqwá* is actually not a natural condition. It must be produced through salat.[69] Jamila understood ritual prayer in relation to nonritual aspects of life, because the demands of mundane existence potentially disrupt the development of the God-conscious self. Jamila called these activities "distractions" that take her away from the acquisition of *taqwá*. In her study of the women's mosque movement in Cairo, Saba Mahmood shows how her informants' viewpoints challenge ritual theories that rely on a demarcation between ritual and "pragmatic action" and rather reflect a sophisticated engagement with the "Islamic interpretative tradition of moral discipline."[70] This sophistication also emerges among Webb students, despite the very different political and cultural contexts separating these two communities.

Not all Webb participants saw prayer as producing piety. Instead, they emphasized intentions and "feelings" that precede salat:

MARY: I struggled for years coming from a liberal tradition in Christianity of prayer. If I didn't feel it, then it had no meaning. I didn't do it if I didn't feel the spirit of the prayer. My Muslim family didn't press the point, *hamdullilah* [praise God], because it would have turned me off. It took me years and it took the original community time too. Prayer took a while to take root.

FARID: I was in Saudi Arabia and just prayed because everyone did. Here you pray as a child because of your parents. Later, you need a connection because American culture makes it easier not to pray. We have to make a connection; otherwise prayer isn't sustainable.

MOZAFFAR: One of my friends, a teacher from Karachi, said that if someone in America is able to pray five times a day, then they are *walī Allah* [friend of God; saint]. He had only been in the US for a week and saw how difficult it was to complete prayers. And he's a conservative Deobandi![71]

As in the conversations about the Qur'an, non-Muslim theologies figure prominently here. Mary, whom we met in the previous chapter, privileges prior connections to God. For her, salat is meaningless in the absence of an individual's preexisting connection with the divine. Without the "spirit" of prayer, the ritual has no meaning. Mary's views suggest the highly mobile and spiritually focused prayer of twentieth-century liberal Protestants, who, like contemporary Muslims, grappled with questions of how to perform prayer amid the constraints of work and leisure routines.[72]

These theologies of prayer also have deeper resonance in Islamic thought. Premodern scholars differentiated between those requirements necessary for a prayer to be considered valid before Allah, and the engendering of dispositions that extend beyond these basic elements. *Niya* (proper intention) was essential for removing worldly distractions and demarcating the ritual time and space for prayer. But Muslim thinkers have understood salat to encompass "a deep and mutual relationship between spiritual and physical postures and dispositions," as Marion Katz puts it.[73] Mary's yearning for a deeper connection with the divine echoes the longer tradition of the *fiqh* of prayer.

Webb students also cast the nature of these obligations and rewards as specific concerns for American Muslims. Students attest to the difficulties they encountered in performing salat. Obstacles include taking a break from the normal workday, finding a suitable space, and performing ablutions under less-than-ideal conditions. From this point of view, in societies where Muslims are the majority, they pray as a matter of course, as the practice is built into the patterns of daily life.[74] Webb participants imagine that in these places, prayer comes easily and naturally. As a result, some students wondered whether American and European Muslims ought to be given some leeway, recognizing that even the Prophet Muhammad learned and fulfilled his obligations to God over time.

This discussion of prayer illustrates the moral weight that students attach to individual choice in religious and cultural practices. In making sense of their position as a minority religious community, the Webb students transform the challenges of performing salat into moral opportunities. Normative claims about the modern religious subject also figures implicitly into this conversation. In contrast to Muslims living in majority contexts, who perform prayer out of obedience, habit, or social conformity, this dialogue turned on the assumption that Muslims in the West pray by choice. From this perspective, American Muslims exceed the minimum requirement by finding individual meaning and purpose in the act. Insofar as the Webb participants distance themselves from other Muslims who merely perform ritual by rote, they recognize the culturally mediated meanings assigned to prayer. At the same time, they celebrate Muslims who choose salat more than those who pray because they are socialized to do so. In this way, America becomes a privileged site of ethical practice, in which the obstacles to prayer facilitate spiritual rewards.

Appropriating Tradition, Authenticating Experience

Webb classes on the Qur'an and *fiqh* aimed to familiarize students with the "classical" tradition as a vital source for the construction of culturally resonant American Islam. To access this tradition, Mozaffar assigned Abd-Allah's essay "Living Islam with Purpose" to guide Webb discussions of *fiqh*.

> Islamic law is a set of priorities, not a list of do's and don'ts. All answers have to be decided based on time and place. Islamic law is focused on relevance, on how to practice wholly in accordance with our tradition and wholly within the environment in which we live. Culture has spirituality. Culture is good in our tradition.[75]

Intended for a North American audience, the essay sets out "five operational principles" to guide Muslim practice in the United States. Ideally, Abd-Allah envisions these principles as universal, though not necessarily exhaustive, and belonging to a "rich communal heritage."[76] The five principles are Trusting Reason, Respecting Dissent, Stressing Societal Obligations, Setting Priorities, and Embracing Maxims.[77] Abd-Allah offers the principles as a "bridge" between "Islam and the ideals and values of other cultures and religions. Muslims who understand them can speak coherently about their faith in any setting. They can make themselves relevant in diverse cultural surroundings, especially those of the West, and lay the foundations of a vibrant indigenous Muslim presence wherever they may be."[78] For Abd-Allah, the classical tradition has much to offer contemporary American Muslims because of what he perceives as its reliance on reason, its internal pluralism, its emphasis on promoting the common good, and its guidance for setting ethical priorities and core maxims, all of which for Abd-Allah constitute the "spirit of Islamic law in its entirety." In this way, "Islamic law" (the term he uses in this article) is foundational to the project of creating an "indigenous American Islam and to build a "sound understanding" of the "Islamic tradition" among American Muslims."[79] Here, Abd-Allah reinforces the imperative that American Muslims ought to act in accordance with God's will but also that they must be able to *explain* their faith to others. The representation and practice of American Islam is here, as elsewhere, deeply intertwined.

Like many contemporary scholars in Europe and North America, Abd-Allah turns to the *maqāsid al-sharia* (objectives of Islamic law). Scholars working under this framework argue that prior legal rulings work toward a common set of principles that promote human interests (*masālih*). Political theorist Andrew March contends that this approach "allows Muslims to ask not whether a given norm has been expressly endorsed as compatible with the texts, but whether it is compatible with the deeper good and interests which God wants to protect through the Law."[80] These efforts to ground normativity in universal principles are connected to the shifting cultural and political terrain upon which these judgments are based. Kathleen Moore refers to this practice as "diasporic jurisprudence," which she defines as the "transformation-through-relocation that occurs in law and in the perspectives of persons who perform the interpretation of law in various locations. Persistent transformative conditions in diaspora make possible the translation of the incomprehensible (i.e., seemingly culture-bound ways of thinking) into legible forms for political ends."[81] Abd-Allah's work is oriented toward these translocations with the aim of providing a portable, essential guide to ethical practice for American Muslims.[82]

Webb students used Abd-Allah's arguments about the principles of Islamic jurisprudence to evaluate how the resources of the classical tradition can help them to navigate everyday challenges. Abd-Allah also argues that, in addition to its technical meaning as a system of logic, Islam must "make sense, but to make sense, it requires intelligent followers with sound understanding."[83] As we have seen, Abd-Allah uplifts M. A. R. Webb as a model American Muslim for whom both American culture and Islam "made sense." That is, Muslim practices must resonate with common-sense knowledge and experience. Conversely, it is problematic to compel someone to engage in a practice that does "make sense." One "knows" culture by living it.

Moreover, Webb members appropriate Abd-Allah's ideas about internal disagreement and difference within the classical tradition to invest individuals with the authority to adjudicate the permissibility of cultural practice. Abd-Allah stresses that Muslim scholars permitted and encouraged divergent interpretations of religious texts as long as they were grounded in rational argumentation such that "traditional Islamic scholarship did not regard it an impropriety to raise difficult questions about the religion or ask about one's doubts; rather it was a sin *not* to ask."[84] In contrast to modern Muslim communities, which Abd-Allah says discourage dissent, early scholars created an environment of divinely sanctioned intellectual inquiry, which in turn laid the basis for rigorous scientific debate and a vibrant, pluralistic religious environment. According to this narrative, modernity ushered in a period of political, religious, cultural, and moral decline brought on by an ill-conceived emphasis on uniformity and purity.[85] Cast in this light, Webb invests its emphasis on rigorous discussion as the revival of pre-modern practices.

This dual emphasis on cultural fluency and internal disagreement has many implications. One of the most important is that "lay" practitioners may be better equipped to build an American Islam than, for example, an imam. Abd-Allah exhorts his American readers not to displace the norms, habits, and institutions already in place in the United States, save for the practices that are explicitly forbidden, such as drinking and selling alcohol. Nor should American Muslims be persuaded by Salafi calls to purify Islam of its local cultural practices. Well aware of the challenges many of his students face to accomplish such a task in their daily lives, Mozaffar affirmed to his students that their undertaking—discovering that sharia is compatible with American culture—is not only possible but a divine imperative. Mozaffar tried to impress upon his students that contingency and variation within the Islamic tradition is an asset that Muslims bring to American society, not a problem. Conversely, the United States offers the context in which Muslims could restore their faith to its rational, pluralistic foundations. As we have seen, Webb members pride themselves on their privileged access to a singular American culture and lifestyle. In this way, they interpret Abd-Allah's approach as validating their embodied experience as one source for Islamic knowledge.

These legal arguments concerning culture have direct relevance to how Webb leaders conceive of the work that rituals such as leisure activities and the *mawlid* do. We have already seen how Webb participants understand the particularity of local cultures as a marker of Islam's universality. Taking up Abd-Allah's idea that the "Islamic tradition" allows for wide latitude unless an action is explicitly forbidden, members see "American" practices as challenging what many see as the restrictive environment of their local institutions. Over the five years I conducted fieldwork, I heard many times that "Wahhabis" have made people afraid to do "American" things like going kayaking, camping, or playing football. Webb members implicitly use what Abd-Allah calls the "presumption of permissibility" to justify their leisure activities.[86] Abd-Allah castigates Muslims who "regard Islam as little more than a list of do's and don't, and, generally, the don'ts outnumber the do's . . . prohibition is made Islam's default position, and the religion is given the appearance of permitting very little and prohibiting everything else."[87] From this point of view, following cultural norms, such as shaking hands, "require no proof of permissibility," nor do they necessarily require consultation with scholars. Quite the opposite, such practices, according to Abd-Allah, are "societal obligations of the highest order."[88] Webb members take up Abd-Allah's argument and apply it with broad latitude in their leisure practice. So long as they do not conflict with obvious prohibitions, such as drinking alcohol, the Webb community has come to see the rituals of Americanness they perform as part of this wide latitude that Islamic ethics—as articulated by classical scholars, as mediated through Abd-Allah—affords them. Far from seeing these rituals as simply permissible, Webb members implicitly perform these rituals as obligations.

The Landscape of *Fiqh* in Chicago

The *fiqh* class raised lingering questions over the basis of religious authority that are emblematic of global debates among contemporary Muslims.[89] Students frequently asked Mozaffar how they could find trustworthy scholars from whom to seek opinions. As we have seen, many Webb members distrust imams and other local scholars, save for Abd-Allah. These conversations reveal considerable ambivalence about individual interpretative authority at Webb and its relationship to extant models of Muslim authority. In the following dialogue, the class considered the fragmentary and diverse field of Muslim authority in Chicago:

JAWAD: Competition pushes you to become better and to pursue excellence.

HUSSEIN: It produces creativity. Maybe someone will have a better idea than me.

SAID: You also risk pandering to people in order to get them to think like you do.

MALIKA: We also end up being fragmented, into our little bubbles, and we don't talk to each other.

MOZAFFAR: This is a real problem. I made a Deobandi scholar my teacher. We need to bridge the gap between the madrasa and the university. So you need to do things like this, to go out and embrace people who are different from you and learn from them.[90]

In contrast to his treatment of Salafism, Mozaffar always gave more credence to Deobandi scholars. In the landscape of American *fiqh*, the Webb students see the Deobandis as preferable to "Wahhabis" because they are perceived as laying legitimate claim to classical scholarship. Deobandi scholars are among the most prominent in Chicago. One is Navlur Rahman, who has founded several institutions specializing in the administration of *fatwa* and counseling on legal matters such as marriage and mortgages.[91] Additionally, through Tablīghī Jamāʿat missionary efforts in American mosques, and because many members are of South Asian descent, Webb members are generally familiar with Deobandis as major players in Chicago, even if they have not spent much time interacting with these scholars. Another is Shaykh Amin Kholwadia, whom some Webb members refer to as another trustworthy scholar. During one of my first interviews with Jawad, a founding board member, he mentioned that he had consulted with Kholwadia in the early years of the Webb project. Kholwadia directs the Darul Qasim Foundation, an educational institution also located in the western suburbs, which primarily hires scholars who have been trained at a Deobandi madrasa on the subcontinent or in South Africa. Darul Qasim offers classes in Quranic studies, Islamic theology, *fiqh*, and the Arabic language, modeled on a madrasa curriculum. To contrast its approach to that of Webb, Darul Qasim's *tafsīr* class is typically a lecture delivered by one of the organization's scholars, not a discussion among students. Similar to Abd-Allah, Kholwadia lays claim to an "academic" approach to Islamic knowledge, emphasizing scholarly expertise in classical sources alongside cultural fluency.[92]

Some Webb members have participated in Darul Qasim's classes because of their devotion to Abd-Allah, underscoring the interpersonal ties that construct religious authority among Webb members. Regardless of the institutional auspices in which he operates, Abd-Allah attracts a sizeable audience, in this case over a hundred and fifty people, to hear technical lectures on fine-grained distinctions between the categories undergirding Sunni theology. As I looked around the room, I noticed many people I recognized from Webb Foundation events, especially the *mawlid*. This fluidity of institutional boundaries hints at the ways that individual Muslims seek out different approaches to Muslim learning. Although we might be tempted to see Darul Qasim and Webb as different, perhaps even incompatible models, it is clear that many Chicago Muslims find potential benefit in both approaches. This does not necessarily entail a staunch commitment to one or the other, suggesting again that as scholars we should be cautious about labeling the individuals we study in our quest to describe and analyze. Thus, while members may engage in more open conversations at Webb, they may also during that same week participate in different pedagogical approaches to the Islamic tradition.

Among other Webb members, however, the Deobandis are synonymous with narrow traditionalism, patriarchy, and conservatism.[93] Despite Mozaffar's suggestion that the students learn from scholars who hold different perspectives, the students remained anxious about what they perceived as a lack of qualified scholars who shared their cultural and theological outlook:

MAHA: Is there a website I can go to for answers?

MOZAFFAR: Don't go to a website [laughter], but this is how a lot of us feel. Look, you can go to the USC website and look up the hadith and try to self-diagnose the problem. hadith are the raw material of our tradition, but they don't tell us what to do. And then you wind up diagnosing everything under the sun, with no guidance.

MALIKA: It's important who you take as a teacher. You need to know where the teacher gets their information, and that they have a good chain of transmission.

JAMILA: These are very personal issues. And we're ignoring the broader issue of taking hadith out of context. They are misused and used to oppress women on a larger front. I find it really hard and confusing to find answers.

AISHA: My heart is diseased, and I don't trust it, so I need to attach myself to teachers and scholars.

MOZAFFAR: Clearly. You're learning from me! [laughter]

NICK: You can't blindly follow a scholar. Humans are biased.

LISA: We can't just do what we think because we are also biased. Scholars have more knowledge that we can learn from.

FARID: You need to seek a qualified scholar with your cultural worldview. Seek a scholar who is American and informed by civil rights, feminism. If you're in Chechnya, you need a scholar who is familiar with certain parts of life, like war.[94]

The class's laughter evoked the uneasiness many of the students feel as they faced the proliferation of Muslim authority without clear direction of how to assess the qualifications of these scholars or the merit of the knowledge that they produced. The documented proliferation of Islamic authorities on the Internet is part of the now well-documentated fragmentation of Muslim authority in the modern period, as Muslim scholars who lack training in traditional Islamic sciences have assumed large followings through mass media.[95] Other classically trained Islamic scholars have also established a vibrant Internet presence. Alongside the growth of options to interact with scholars and other Muslims on the Internet, Islamic sources are more widely available, free of cost. Here, Mozaffar refers to the University of Southern California's hadith database, which provides searchable Arabic and English texts of the authoritative hadith collections. Mozaffar warns that consulting the "raw materials" of Islam is dangerous because individual Muslims might be led astray by their own interpretations. What American Muslims require is the availability of qualified scholars to actually produce "the tradition" from the divine sources, namely the Qur'an and hadith.

Students find themselves caught between this growth of Internet authority and their desire to find trustworthy scholars with whom to build personal relationships. Abd-Allah is their model scholar, conversant in American culture and steeped in traditional Islamic learning. In the absence of trustworthy scholars, to whom should one turn? Often, the answer is to rely on one's family and one's individual experience and knowledge. The broadening of the Islamic field of authority to include autodidacts and non-traditionally trained scholars produces disagreements among the students about the reliability of contemporary Muslim authorities and the potential fragmentation that results from relying on individual opinions, like those often voiced in Webb discussions. Malika believed they had strayed too far from "traditional" Islam and sought to create boundaries around the tradition as she understood it. In these discussions, she often reminded the class that the Webb project reflects an authentic Islam, linked to authoritative knowledge and sound transmissions from teacher to student, mainly through Abd-Allah. As I explore in the next chapter, she often invokes this continuity to distance Webb from labels such as "feminist" and "progressive." Yet this model of transmitting knowledge from teacher to student is not the pedagogical method that Webb implemented through Malika's leadership as the director of adult education. Rather, during her tenure, the Webb community constructed a space in which guided discussion among peers was the primary method through which students constructed and appropriated the Islamic tradition.

This highlights one of the central tensions within the Webb class on *fiqh*: does the affirmation of individual authority potentially undermine the project of reviving classical scholarship? This question is not about the compatibility of "Islamic tradition" and American life, though as we have seen, students often come up against this question through their specific challenges and situations as American Muslims. Rather, it is about the very basis of interpretative authority, a question that, as Grewal has shown, is of global Muslim concern.[96] Making tradition relevant to contemporary life is an ongoing, dynamic process, one that returns Muslims to the most foundational rituals, like prayer, and their practice. In the third space of Webb, this question, like many others, was held in tension, not because American Muslims are somehow more separated from their tradition as religious minorities. Rather, the community provided a space in which to negotiate, challenge, and creatively explore the nature of God's ethical obligations in daily life. Although Abd-Allah's thought, mediated through Mozaffar, guided and framed these debates, many students did not fully accept or follow their views. They also looked to their embodied experience as a vital resource in striving to live according to God's will.

Conclusion

This chapter has focused on the Webb's community's engagement with *fiqh* during a period in which sharia had become a highly politicized marker of Islam's purported incompatibility with American liberal democracy. Although members of the Webb community expressed the need to explain sharia, the main focus of Webb conversations about *fiqh* centered on daily ethical struggles. As parents, Webb members want to instill in their children a sufficiently flexible ethical framework that would ensure good "character" and American cultural fluency, while limiting the influence of what Webb members see as the narrow and overly restrictive labeling of actions as haram. Moreover, the locus of sharia is the nuclear family. Webb parents invest themselves with the obligation to obtain the necessary classical knowledge to educate their children, but also with the cultural fluency to determine the acceptability of certain behaviors.

Even under the immense pressure to explain sharia as a definable set of rules or an identifiable object, the Webb community instead remains heavily invested in sharia as a set of daily actions through which they fulfill their obligations to God. As individual religious practitioners committed to the devotional practice of salat, Webb members also engage in highly contested and dynamic conversations about the intentions and purposes of prayer. That is, Webb engagements with *fiqh* demonstrate the much broader rubric of normativity under which Muslim enactments of sharia ought to be understood. These conversations reveal the enduring importance of cultivating individual relationships to God for the Webb community as it navigates the particular meanings that prayer evokes in the American context.

The *fiqh* class also demonstrates broader trends in how middle-class, educated Muslims construct religious authority. Webb members rely on Dr. Umar Faruq Abd-Allah and Omer Mozaffar because they have received "authentic" knowledge from "traditional" scholars abroad and in the United States, earned credentials in Islamic Studies in American institutions of higher learning, and possess what Webb members see as a fluent understanding of American culture and the needs of the Chicago Muslim community. Many American Muslim intellectuals build their appeal on this same set of characteristics, including those who occupy different positions on the ideological spectrum, from Hamza Yusuf to Amin Kholwadia to Abd-Allah. Although these scholars maintain various institutional ties, their authority is not necessarily dependent on a single institution or audience. Moreover, these scholars rely on different pedagogies and sources, but they manage to draw audiences across these boundaries, through their embodied (and "authentic") experience of American culture. These claims to cultural and academic knowledge has helped them to earn the trust and affinity of deeply skeptical and marginalized Muslims such as those at Webb.

Moreover, it is from this embodied experience that Webb members sometimes draw their own authority to eschew the opinions and guidance of local Muslim authorities. When confronted with an opinion or approach with which they disagree, Webb members often turn to their individual judgment. That is to say, we have observed how Webb members objectify and parse religion and culture as separate and distinct domains. Here we see how culture and religion are inseparable in the practices through which American Muslims fulfill their obligations to God and their communities. The third space of Webb provides them with a vital context through which to pursue the implications of the inevitable tensions that arise from these relational processes of ethical action.

7

"Reading for Kernels of Truth"

THE WEBB BOOK CLUB

ON A WARM Wednesday morning in May, six women gathered around a table in a public library conference room. They were there for Webb's monthly book club meeting, and the book of the month was Gerd Gigerenzer's *Gut Feelings: The Intelligence of the Unconscious*. The women used the pop psychology text as a springboard to discuss intimate issues of faith, family, and identity:

AMINA: I want us to think about how we use our gut feelings in the three most important areas of our lives: education, marriage, and being Muslim.

MARY: My marriage was entirely irrational. We knew we wanted to be married after only four days. Now our gut feelings cause problems. My husband and his family believe that talking about negative things makes them happen. In Arab culture, this applies to everything, like whether to get a colonoscopy, whether to write a will, and whether to wash your fruit.

TINA [ETHNOGRAPHER]: Wash your fruit?

MARY: If you wash the apple, you're admitting there might be pesticides that could hurt you. But I was raised to look at all possible outcomes, to get all the information in order to avoid a negative outcome, which makes my husband crazy. Eventually, we could just see the fights happening ahead of time. It took us years to learn to prevent them.

KAMILA: This is another time when culture overrides Islam. Under Islam, you should have a will. It's like this in India and Pakistan too, with all the superstition. Or not having a baby shower. In Jewish culture, you shouldn't even have anything in the house for the baby, which is definitely not practical or rational.

SANA: These ideas come from the hadith that says angels are always saying *Ameen*. If you say something bad, then it might get an *Ameen* and come true.

AMINA: I've heard this hadith. During Friday prayers, you want your prayer to coincide with an *Ameen* and then it becomes a big point *Ameen*. I'm not so sure about that.[1]

The book club provided a space for this small group of women to take on questions they could not address elsewhere: exclusive male authority, homosexuality, marriage norms, and the surveillance of female bodies in order to imagine a more inclusive and egalitarian Muslim community. As in other book clubs, Webb women made sense of these injustices and exclusions through the narratives and characters of the texts they read. The Webb book club thus exemplifies how the community facilitates religious belonging for its members.

The Webb book club offers a crucial window into the generative possibilities and limitations of religious third spaces. In the book club, members explored feminism explicitly, sometimes claiming it as an identity and at other times distancing themselves from the category. This is because, as Aysha Hidayatullah puts it, Muslim feminists do their work at the "edge, a place of animated charge and the avowal and disavowal of tradition—a place home to many 'Muslims in spiritual quandary,' including, but not only, Muslim feminists."[2] The book club occupies this "edge," in the women's playful engagement with feminism, particularly their challenges to what Hidayatullah calls the "interpretative privilege" of male authority.[3] In the book club, the women claimed their own interpretative privilege to challenge forms of religious and social injustice and to explore possibilities for change. The women experimented with a variety of views depending on the author and text in question, reveling in the different possibilities for identity and subjectivity that their readings evoked. Through the "silent production" of reading, the women rendered the texts "habitable."[4] In the process, they constructed alternative visions for a more egalitarian Islam.[5]

As we have seen, Webb members consciously claim a marginal position in their third space, through which they both critique dominant religious orientations in local mosques and imagine alternative possibilities for American Islam. That is, their marginality is both imposed from the outside and asserted as an empowering, even advantageous, position. The women in the book club challenge male authority, probe heteronormativity, and explore links between gendered and racial inequalities. The group also took on a broader range of gendered concerns, including male sexuality, sartorial choices, spatial configurations of mosques, the status of homosexuality in Islam, the governance of religious institutions, and the relationships among family members. In all of these conversations, book club members recognized gender and sexuality as crucial to how religious power is deployed, often unjustly, against individuals and communities that do not conform to normative religious expectations. Gender provided the entry point through which they critiqued other Muslim communities for a variety of shortcomings, especially the failure to embody what the women understood to be core Muslim ideals, such as equality and tolerance. At the same time, the contested status of feminism in the broader Webb community illustrates the constraints of third spaces, as members sought to construct boundaries around normative Islam.

Claiming Female Interpretative Authority

Although Webb invited all of its members to join the book club, by scheduling the meetings for 10:00 a.m. on Wednesdays, they practically guaranteed that participants would be women who had flexible schedules and financial security. The core book club members from 2011 to 2014 were amina, a white convert in her forties; Sana, a stay-at-home mother of Indian descent also in her early forties; Kamila, a second-generation Pakistani journalist in her thirties; Mary, a white convert in her sixties married to an Egyptian physician; and Hind, an Indian immigrant by way of Britain in her fifties. With the exception of Kamila, who is single, all of the members were comfortably middle-class mothers. Sana and Mary were also regular participants in the Qur'an class, and their perspectives were also discussed at length in chapter 5.

Like most Webb programs, the book club began at the initiative of one of its members. amina started the group in 2011 because, as she put it, "I participated in Muslim reading groups in the past, but no one ever read the books. I hoped Webb people would be more committed."[6] She selected the book list with her husband, a Pakistani immigrant who had spent part of his childhood in Nigeria and Germany. As a result, the first book list had a decidedly German flavor, including varied titles such as Herman Hesse's *Demian* and Eric Metaxas's biography of Dietrich Bonhoeffer. amina included books such as the aforementioned *Gut Feelings*, Chinua Achebe's *Things Fall Apart*, and Greg Epstein's humanist manifesto, *Good without God*, in order to engage a variety of literary genres and to go beyond books that are explicitly devotional in content. As she said during our first meeting, "You can get all that religious stuff at your Muslim book clubs. Here, I want us to read more widely, and to shake things up a bit."[7] Some of the books dealt with Muslim themes, among them Kurban Said's *Ali and Nino*, Paul Kriwaczek's *In Search of Zarathrustra*, Leila Aboulela's *Minaret*, Ali Eteraz's *Children of Dust*, and *The Bread of Angels* by Stephanie Saldana. These titles reflected the women's intentions to read together *as Muslim women* and an explicit goal to expand their cultural repertoire. However, their conversations resembled other Webb conversational spaces, insofar as book group texts became the ground on which broader concerns over authority, belonging, and authenticity emerged.

These book selections initially ignited some controversy within the Webb community. In response to amina's online invitation, a couple members worried that some of these books were haram.[8] Others wanted to know whether a recognized Muslim scholar or imam had approved any of the books. When I asked amina about the situation, she responded, "Why does everyone in Chicago need their shaykh's approval to do anything? Can't we just get together and talk?"[9] She consciously crafted the list anticipating that titles such as *Good without God* would unsettle certain members. She did not want book club attendees who would potentially challenge the interpretative work she envisioned this group accomplishing. As I got to know amina better, we often talked about her frustration with Muslims who are, in her view, uncritically deferential to the authority of certain texts and scholars. She believed that many Webb members fell into this category; amina no longer attends Webb adult classes because she finds them too "conservative."[10]

The book club offered amina the opportunity to guide discussions among a group that she described as "like-minded" women.[11] For her in particular, open discussion of timely and contentious subjects is central to her spiritual formation as a Muslim and a form of devotional practice that she wants to foster among her peers.[12] Despite the consternation that the book club created, the influence that several group participants exerted at Webb—as board members and long-standing participants—ensured that the event stayed on the calendar. From the beginning, I was also an active member. When I first told the women who I was and what I was doing there, Hind exclaimed, "Ooh—a spy!" amina, who has her PhD in biology, reiterated the marginal position of the club: "I guess we can be your lab rats. I'll warn you, though, I think this group will throw off your bell curve."[13] She and Mary, who also has her PhD, were at once encouraging and suspicious, indicating several times that they knew what I was up to when I jotted down notes during our sessions. Despite their initial hesitations, I was expected to participate fully (and I gladly obliged). In the course of our meetings, they asked me about my college choices, how I came to study Islam, and my religious preferences. The book club members hosted me for meals in their homes, introduced me to their friends and families, invited me on outings to downtown Chicago, and shared their life stories. When I brought my newborn son to the group, he sat on their laps, playing with the toys and books they brought him.

Reading Religiously in America

The book club approached reading as a practice of self-formation, or what Kathryn Lofton has termed the practice of "reading religiously."[14] That is, they read in a communal setting with a particular set of moral expectations and agreed-upon ritual conventions. Exemplifying the recent growth of book clubs in the United States, all of the women had participated in reading groups prior to joining the Webb book group. Despite their busy schedules, like many educated, middle-class American women, they seemed to always find the time to read. And beyond the confines of Webb, they read for many reasons: for pleasure; to lessen the boredom of feeding an infant in the middle of the night; to seek guidance for marital problems; and to discover new and different parts of the world. Their reading practices reflect an ideology of reading as a refuge from the demands of everyday life in which women control their surroundings and engage in practices of self-fulfillment.[15] Every month, we gathered in a library conference room, settling into the cushy office chairs around an oval, cherry-stained table. amina always started the conversation with a series of questions, first asking for individual impressions of the texts (what did you like about the book?), and then moving to more specific themes, always reminding us to reflect on how the book related to events in our lives. Books in hand, notebooks close by, we offered customary apologies for not having read the book as carefully as we should have and then relayed such personal narratives through which it became clear that not only had we all "done" the reading, but also that each of us had begun to read the text into our own lives.

In addition to being avid readers, many of the women were also dedicated writers. In the past, amina, Hind, and Kamila had each been members of various writing groups. amina penned short stories, while Hind composed what she calls "creative nonfiction" about her childhood and her experiences as schoolteacher at a Muslim elementary school. She and Kamila, a journalist, were regular bloggers. Here, I also fit in, having plenty of experience to offer about writer's block and narrative choices. Already close enough to share their work with one another, these women came to the book club with prior familiarity with each other's literary sensibilities, religious proclivities, and political orientations. On our first day together, the writers shared their struggles to get published and to find the energy to write regularly. For this group of highly educated women, reading and writing provided a crucial intellectual and creative outlet distinct from the rote demands of their jobs, childcare, and other social obligations.

As time went on, the women expressed gratitude that the book club was an all-female space where they could engage in open, frank, and spirited discussion. Mary frequently contrasted the Webb group to her prior experiences in another Muslim book club, which she described as dominated by men. In spite of her grievances with this other group, it remained one of the most important religious experiences of her life. She confided that, before finding Webb, it had been the only Muslim space where she and her Egyptian husband had felt comfortable "to be themselves."[16] amina and Hind similarly observed that women's voices were sidelined in the other book clubs to which they had belonged.

Indeed, the Webb book club is part of a growing number of cross-ethnic female Muslim communities in Chicago, where women collectively negotiate their differences and commonalities as Muslims. Like many of the women in Jamillah Karim's study, the Webb book group served as a space for women to confront inequalities of class, ethnicity, and gender within American Muslim communities, to imagine alternatives and to confront their limitations in addressing them.[17] In this respect, the books' contents were less important than the self-reflection and possibilities of dissent that they inspired.[18] The women cherished their books as material objects, boasting of having entire shelves devoted to "heresy." In this way, the group embodied what Lofton has called the "reforming" history of "figures and commentaries that organized other fights for popular dissent and spiritual debate."[19] Reading is far from a passive consumer activity, but rather, as Elizabeth Long puts it, "quite literally productive."[20] The Webb women reveled in this opportunity to experiment with and challenge predominant understandings of gender, sexuality, and authority in their communities.

The Webb book group also reflects other characteristics of women's reading groups in the United States, especially their role in providing women a site of agency and thus possible dissent. Long contends that book clubs have the potential for altering their participants' worldviews, leading members "toward creative and expansive appraisals of social others as well as their own historical situation and life choices."[21] And Jenny Hartley argues, "[I]t might be said that the reading group is a forum for the kind of talk associated with women: co-operation rather than competition, the model of 'emotional literacy' which values teamwork, listening, and sharing over self-assertion."[22] The women asked each other probing personal questions, challenged each other's opinions, and teased one another gently. They fostered friendships with new Webb members and strengthened existing ones, based on their shared reading and writing practices.[23]

Webb's book club likewise follows the history of religious reading as a devotional practice of encountering various "others" and the cultivation of modern religious selves. Matthew Hedstrom demonstrates how twentieth-century book clubs and reading consumer culture helped to create "practices of spiritual cosmopolitanism," in which key practices within American religions emerged, namely the ideology of religious pluralism in the wake of the communist threat.[24] In this vein, the women used the books' characters to explore different religious worlds, pushing back against received teachings about "other" faiths and their salvific potential, and to frame Islam in terms of universal religious tenets. Moreover, the book club is a community through which to engage questions of justice and inequality. In the process, these women attempted to make sense of their own everyday challenges as American Muslims.

Contesting Feminism

amina, Mary, and Hind all self-identified as feminists in the course of our conversations. They claimed this label with full knowledge of feminism's contested place within the Webb community, among American Muslims more broadly, and in the United States writ large. This ambivalence also has a long history. Many scholars and activists hesitate to identify their work as feminist because of the term's fraught historical entanglements.[25] Colonial-era projects carried out in the name of women blamed Islam for what they observed as the oppression of women, thereby justifying imperialism in the name of, as Gayatri Spivak has famously put it, "white men saving brown women from brown men."[26]

For their part, Muslim women take a variety of theological and ideological stances in relation to the categories of feminism and Islam.[27] In postcolonial societies during the 1970s and 1980s, many feminist activists continued to criticize Islam for being patriarchal and sought to rectify gender hierarchies through their engagement with liberal understandings of individual autonomy, freedom, and secularism.[28] By contrast, many women who have participated in Muslim revival movements reject the label "feminist" as a Western import inextricably linked to colonialism and the ongoing exercise of US "soft power" in Muslim-majority societies.[29] This ideological linkage between Western dominance and the liberation of the "Muslim woman" continues in the contemporary geopolitical context, in which the wars in Afghanistan and Iraq have been justified in terms of liberating Muslim women.[30] These political complexities extend to Muslim feminist scholars working in the United States, on the one hand providing them with a privileged position through which to advance their projects, while also potentially limiting their appeal to Muslim women in other parts of the world.[31]

For these women, being either a pious Muslim or a secular feminist is a false choice. Neither the identification "Muslim" nor "feminist" captures the multifaceted modes of reading and interpretation that took place in the book club. Rather, they brought a variety of texts, personal histories and experiences, and ideological resources into our conversations. As Juliane Hammer has argued, "[R]eligious feminisms are a product of and in constant conversation with the concerns and investments in secular America and the secular feminist movement."[32] For example, book club conversations about the obligations of women to uphold norms of gender, sexuality, and family took place against the backdrop of particularly heated public debates about insurance coverage of contraception and the defunding of Planned Parenthood.[33] The book group demonstrates how this seeming divide between secular feminists and religious practitioners is a misleading dichotomy, based on an assumed delineation between the religious and the secular that fails to adequately capture how women actually navigate gender roles and expectations in historically situated contexts.[34]

Feminism and the Boundaries of Tradition

Other Webb women who identify as feminists experience these ambiguities acutely. One unusually warm June afternoon, I sat with Aisha at Starbuck's. We sipped iced teas on the patio, trying to ignore the oppressive humidity as she explained what feminism means to her. A college-educated, second-generation Arab immigrant, Aisha is all too familiar with the critiques that presume that being Muslim and feminist are mutually exclusive:[35]

> As a Muslim feminist, I am on the margins. Some people think that being a Muslim feminist is an impossible thing. Most people aren't ready for my views. I want the prayer space to be divided 50/50 in the mosque. More importantly, I want Muslim women to have the power to make their own choices. Actually, I think American women in general don't have the freedom to choose.[36]

Aisha's comments reveal the centrality of individual choice at Webb, and the self-understanding of the group as on the "margins" of the Muslim community. They are also simultaneously closer to the "mainstream" of American culture (as they define it) than other American Muslims, namely immigrants. She recently participated in debates about gender separation when her mosque underwent renovations. Passionate about changing architectural elements of the masjid to reflect her views on gender equality, she signed up enthusiastically for the renovation committee, but eventually resigned out of frustration. Aisha hesitated to withdraw completely from the mosque because she continues to believe that mosques played an essential role in facilitating female leadership and gender equality, even if these changes occur more slowly than she would like. Her story recalls many elements of the Webb critique of local mosques, centered on the construction of space, gendered authority, and intergenerational conflict.[37]

Aisha sees gender inequality as not simply a problem for Muslims, but for American society more broadly. Practices and expectations of modesty frame her understandings of female choice and subordination:

> I have a lot of problems with my daughter dressing in ways that I don't think are appropriate. There are so many pressures on really young girls. I can't believe what some of them wear. I try to teach my daughter that modesty is a norm for both men and women in Islam. I try to show my kids the reasoning of my decisions. Eventually I know these decisions will be up to them.[38]

Aisha's claims about the obligation of both genders to uphold modesty norms is rooted in her conviction that gendered sartorial practices function as sites for the unjust enactment of religious power, often to the disadvantage of women. For Aisha, Muslim women are entrusted (and burdened) with the task of preserving the sexual honor and dignity of the Muslim community.[39] At the same time, she expressed concerns about the ways that certain forms of dress eroticize young girls, echoing larger feminist concerns about the objectification of American women and the pressures to conform to a particular body image. Although Aisha approached these issues through the lens of Muslim modesty norms, her discussion suggests no obvious distinction between so-called secular and religious feminisms.[40] Aisha employs multiple experiences, observations, and resources in her critique of American sartorial practices.[41] While understanding modesty to be an obligation in Islam, Aisha ultimately conceived of her daughter's choices as circumscribed by the pressures from a wide range of social, religious, and familial directions.

Although some women at Webb identify as feminists, others explicitly sought to curb any affiliation between the organization and feminism. During one Sunday discussion, Malika, openly took on the labels "feminist" or "progressive":

> I want to distinguish us from progressives and feminists. Some would like us to be progressive Muslims. But Webb is grounded in traditional practices, authentically, in the four schools of law. We practice in continuity with earlier traditions. We present our faith in a different way. We

> follow scholars like Dr. Umar who have solid chains of transmission. We don't reinterpret things to mean that women should lead prayer.[42]

Malika intervened to draw boundaries between the Webb Foundation and progressives by insisting that Webb efforts are grounded in "tradition" as represented by classical pedagogies and modes of authority. As she saw it, progressive or feminist positions are outside of established texts and authority figures. Through Abd-Allah and his chain of transmission (*isnād*), Malika situated Webb practices in a continuous, authentic network of scholarly authority. Her assertions demonstrate the enduring power of what William Graham has called Islamic "traditionalism" or the particular importance Muslims have assigned to "personal connectedness" of knowledge transmission that can be traced to the Prophet Muhammad.[43] By framing Abd-Allah's authority through the *isnād*, Malika claims Webb's legitimacy in contrast to progressive or feminist frameworks that she deems to be outside of these established chains of transmission.[44]

Despite Malika's insistence on the irrelevance of progressivism for Webb, participants' ongoing concerns regarding gender and religious authority reflected the alignment of Webb with many views expressed by scholars who have identified, at one time or another, as progressive. In part, the term "Progressive Muslim" garnered notice following the publication of *Progressive Muslims* in 2003, a volume edited by Omid Safi, who is now the Director of the Duke University Islamic Studies Center. As Safi defines it, the term "progressive" denotes "an invitation to those who want an open and safe space to undertake rigorous, honest, potentially difficult engagement with tradition."[45] Although scholars and activists affiliated with the movement focus on a variety of issues, Safi argues they are united by three common commitments: social justice, pluralism, and gender equality.[46] This group of scholars helped to form the short-lived Progressive Muslim Union (PMU), which disbanded in 2006 following disagreements about the group's goals. The PMU and its website, the MuslimWakeUp, had publicized and served as a forum for the heated public debate over amina wadud's leading of Friday prayers at the St. John the Divine cathedral in New York City on March 18, 2005. The episode prompted heated exchanges about female authority, the proper interpretation of sacred texts, and media representations of Islam.[47] Safi's articulation of progressive Islam has much in common with Webb rhetoric, but its members overtly resist any identification with progressive thought, insisting on their engagement with premodern tradition.

For Malika, the Webb foundation engages in the vital project of *recovering* original forms of female leadership that she believes do not include female-led prayer. As we saw in chapter 4, Webb promotes other ritual roles for women through the *mawlid*. They also encourage women to take on other roles such as scholars and teachers as well as promoting equality between genders in all aspects of religious life. But its members are less concerned with the issue of female-led prayer. Instead, as we have seen, Webb promotes female religious authority in other ritual and educational contexts. In her capacity as the director of the adult theology program, Malika has broad authority over the curriculum at Webb and the structure of its classes. Indeed, Mozaffar often made an explicit point to defer to her judgment in the classroom, referring to her as the "boss."

The ambiguity toward feminism at Webb illustrates that the possibilities of third spaces are not limitless. Some participants viewed these discussions as traversing boundaries of tradition and authority. In constructing boundaries around the Islamic tradition, Malika also linked gender, space, and authority. Although she disagreed with efforts to institute female-led prayer, she also argued that mosques go against the practice of the Salaf by excluding women from other positions of authority such as boards of directors, where she believes that men and women should have equal representation. Categories mattered here. Malika wanted to ensure that Webb continues to construct its project along "traditional" rather than "progressive" lines.

Academic Sources of Religious Authority

In contrast to other Webb spaces, then, the women of the book club appropriated progressive and feminist thinkers and their work explicitly and frequently disregarded the opinions of scholars popular at Webb, such as Abd-Allah. As an alternative, they relied on texts that they deemed to have a more critical and academic perspective. The women used these intellectuals' work to challenge the relevance of classical Islam for the contemporary realities facing American Muslims.[48] Adamant about the need to reassess gender norms in light of modernity, amina frequently invoked American Muslim academics to support her opinions:

> We're talking about people who didn't have electricity. I'm sorry, but we can't find our answers from the past. To me, it was a certain time and place and you can't recapture that. You live now, here and today. What advice will you get from the tenth century? I've been reading Kecia Ali, because she puts it in the context of what was going on at the time. If the Prophet Muhammad says, I had sex with a nine-year-old girl, then sorry guys, that's what happened. The father gave permission and it was all OK. Childhood was different, and you should realize that.[49]

The Prophet's multiple marriages and in particular his marriage to the nine-year-old Aisha have been the basis for old and new polemics against Islam.[50] In our conversation, mina rejected what she considered apologetic explanations of seventh-century norms that are necessarily not in line with modern conceptions of marriage. Although she upheld Muhammad as the model of exemplary human behavior, she also maintained that he was a product of his time and as such, consummated his marriage with Aisha when she reached the age of puberty, probably at the customary age of nine years old. For her, gender relations during the seventh century reflected particular historical conditions, and as a result should not be emulated directly by the contemporary Muslim community. amina turned to the work of Kecia Ali, a scholar of Islamic Studies at Boston University, to advance her conviction that childhood and marriage were fundamentally "different" in the time of the Prophet.[51] Just as constructions of childhood, family, and socioeconomics have shaped marriage norms in contemporary America, so too the historical context shaped sexuality, gender roles, and marital customs of the Prophet Muhammad and his wives.

In amina's comments, we see that not everyone at Webb subscribes to the project of recovering tradition in the sense that Abd-Allah has defined it. In spite of Abd-Allah's unrivaled intellectual influence among Webb's founding members, his broader legacy at Webb is more ambivalent. For amina, classical hermeneutics have very little to offer contemporary Muslims because she sees their opinions as bound to the particular time and place in which they were articulated. And because they reflect specific historical conditions, they cannot serve as authoritative guidance for Muslims today. Speaking of Hamza Yusuf, she said, "It's been a spiritual journey for him, but the stuff he used to say about women. I'm totally underwhelmed by his Zaytuna Institute. I feel like, again, it's all Sufi texts, from the fourteenth century at most, God forbid you should quote anyone living in the twentieth or twenty-first century."[52] Instead, amina admires Ziauddin Sardar, the British author who has called for Muslim reform projects based on a "critical" interpretation of the Qur'an and hadith in their historical, contextual setting. The implication of such a reading, Sardar argues, is that certain portions of Muslim sacred texts are shown to be time-bound and specific, while others remain universal.[53] amina knows that many Muslims, including fellows "Webbies," do not subscribe to these approaches. Far from diminishing these thinkers' appeal, amina likes the view from the feminist "edge." She wants to confront the boundaries of the tradition because it is the only way she can imagine being Muslim.

Communities like the Webb book club represent an important space through which to track the influence, however limited, of academic work on gender and sexuality in Islam and the authority of feminist scholars among educated American Muslims. As we have seen, many Webb members look to scholars with an "academic" perspective gained through training in Islamic studies in US universities as well as informal study with Muslim scholars abroad. This is why Abd-Allah and Mozaffar serve as essential guides for Webb's engagement with "tradition." This particular group of women privileges university credentials over classical training, such that at book club we often engaged in discussions of authors in the academy, such as Kecia Ali, as well as Ebrahim Moosa, Farid Esack, and amina wadud. This group of women admired how these scholars question and deconstruct received narratives, especially ones that the women see as undergirding gender inequality and exclusion. For them, academic methods provide a more rigorous, accurate, and (by implication) authentic window into the Muslim past. Rather than seeking legitimacy in classical Muslim scholars and communities, amina invests authority in modern thinkers, believing they provide her access to superior epistemologies, scientific sensibilities, and cultural fluency.

Muslim Versus muslim: Debating the Universal and the Particular

As in other Webb discussions, book-club conversations frequently turned to the limits and possibilities of religious pluralism. During our first session, the book of the month was Stephanie Saldana's *Bread of Angels*, a young divinity student's memoir of living in the Jewish quarter of Damascus. The group immediately compared the author's description of religious oppression under the Syrian state to their experiences of governmental surveillance after 9/11:

AMINA: How do you think it would feel to live like the Jews in Damascus, under that kind of oppression?

ZEENAT: After 9/11, the FBI came to our house, wanting to talk with our son. They were perfectly polite, but it made me so afraid for my boys, who were teenagers at the time. They hadn't done anything wrong, but they had attended some events at the masjid. As Muslims, we know what it's like to be afraid of the government.[54]

In the aftermath, their most immediate and pressing concern was for the safety of their children, especially their bearded sons, who, they feared, would be branded as terrorists if they looked or acted "too" Muslim:

ZEENAT: I told them, "I don't want you to wear a beard, it's too dangerous right now."

AMINA: I said to my boys, "The last thing I want you to do is fight some jihad in Afghanistan or Chechnya!" But then, I don't want them to join the army either. Just no guns and shooting at all, please.[55]

The women's narratives resonated with the experiences of many American Muslims after 9/11. In her study of discrimination against Arab Americans, Louise Cainkar demonstrates that many Muslims endured a level of uncertainty and fear akin to refugees living in war zones during the years following the attacks on the World Trade Center.[56]

This experience of "de-Americanization" has been deeply gendered. Women, especially those who wore the hijab, have endured more public harassment, while men have been subject to more government surveillance, such as interrogation and bodily searches.[57] Only Kamila and Hind wear a hijab regularly, and perhaps as a result the other women encountered less personal harassment. As white converts, Mary and amina are also not immediately marked as Muslim by their appearance. As wives and mothers, they mostly feared for their male family members, all of whom were recognizable as potentially "dangerous others."

The women also noted that, in the aftermath of the 9/11 attacks, they felt a growing need to confront injustice and promote justice in their own communities. Such efforts became apparent during our discussion of Paul Kriwaczek's *In Search of Zarathustra*, which explores the persistence of Zoroastrian symbols and practices despite Muslim attempts over the centuries to stamp them out. The book club focused on Kriwaczek's descriptions of how orthodoxy is often constructed by delegitimizing competing faiths:

AMINA: This book raises really interesting questions about orthodoxy. How do we define orthodoxy? Wahhabis are telling us what to think. They are funded by Saudi money, which just gives them more power. They pick and choose hadith and Qur'an passages to justify whatever they want. We are fooling ourselves if we think we don't have priests. Everyone says there are no priests in Islam, but that's not true. We have scholars who tell us who is Muslim and who isn't.

ZEENAT: I just read this report on Daniel Pearl. He was the muslim in that situation, not his kidnappers. I believe his religion was truth. I also tell my kids that I think Nelson Mandela is the greatest muslim alive today, and they laugh at me.[58]

As we have seen elsewhere, amina's anxiety over Wahhabi influence mirrors public speculation in the United States that American mosques have been infiltrated by a Wahhabi-inspired extremism and fueled by Saudi government money.[59] Here amina reduced Salafi orientations to illegitimate claims of "orthodoxy," which have fostered divisions within the *umma*, unjustly excluded believers from the Muslim fold, used sacred sources to consolidate patriarchal power in the hands of male Muslim *ulema* (priests), and ignored the social realities of contemporary life.

Although amina cited Wahhabism as the source of her anger, her use of the term indexes a broader nexus of exclusionary practices that she experiences within the Muslim community. From her perspective, religious authorities in the United States have marginalized certain Muslims, like herself, for refusing to adhere to their normative understandings of proper religious practice, such as wearing the hijab. amina has often encountered restrictive religious spaces that have left her feeling that she does not belong. For her, limiting female access to mosque spaces and prescribing certain forms of dress are culturally based norms that are not foundational to Islam. She has often clashed with imams and board members in local masjids, particularly those who she believes are stuck in what she calls an "immigrant mentality."[60] It is thus not altogether clear whether the immigrant ("cultural") mentality or Wahhabism are responsible for the marginalization she feels. For her, the sources matter less than the gendered consequences: a religious environment in which she believes Muslim sources and practices are used to place women in an inferior position to men.

Zeenat affirmed amina's belief that Muslims ought to rethink boundaries of inclusion and exclusion. She redirected the discussion to the case of the Daniel Pearl, the *Wall Street Journal* reporter who was kidnapped and beheaded in Pakistan by an Al-Qaeda-affiliated group in 2002. Zeenat denied the designation of "muslim" to the kidnappers and instead conferred the identification of "muslim" on Pearl, a Jew. Zeenat argued that true Muslims embraced universal truths such as justice, rather than adhering to a set of specific doctrines or practices. Here I use the lowercase "muslim" to denote the more universal meaning of the term upon which Zeenat drew. In doing so, she called to mind the use of the term "muslim" in the Qur'an, which does not connote being a follower of the religion of Islam, but rather one who submits to the will of God. She insisted on a more expansive definition of "muslim" to include anyone who submits to God's will by working for justice. In this way, she appropriated conceptions of prophethood that apply to messengers who lived before the establishment of Islam. For example, the Qur'an portrays Abraham and Jesus as paragons of submission and faith in God even though they never heard God's message as revealed by the Prophet Muhammad. Similarly, Zeenat designated Pearl and Mandela as "muslims"; that is, they embodied and enacted Islamic teachings and norms even though they never professed to be "Muslim," or a follower of Islam. In doing so, Zeenat also asserted that violence committed in the name of Islam is outside the fold of the faith. Instead, the term "Muslim" signifies what all of the Abrahamic faiths share: foundational values such as mercy, tolerance, and truth. Born of their anxieties about the direction of their community, amina and Zeenat's comments thus illustrate the women's persistent interest in contesting Muslim exclusivity in favor of a more universal Islam that conforms the dominant paradigm of American religious pluralism, in which Abrahamic faiths converge around universal values. Rather than claim Islam's distinctiveness, the women marked its status as a true religion through its universality.

9/11 as a Turning Point

Like others at Webb, the women constructed a history of Islam in Chicago in which Salafi orientations came to dominate mosques in the latter part of the twentieth century. On a crisp October morning, Nadia, the founding board member, joined the conversation:

AMINA: 9/11 was a huge wake-up call about stuff like this. Before that, we were fundraising for jihad. We just thought it was Islam, not Wahhabism.

SANA: We didn't know. How could we know?

NADIA: At least it was a blessing that the leadership was shaken up after 9/11. Muslims are pluralists in their hearts. But before 9/11 Hamza Yusuf used to spew hatred. How was that ok? It was so wrong, all those college kids who listened to him and others, and then he did a 180. Or you had Zaid Shakir telling Muslims not to vote! At MCC [a mosque in the northern suburbs], it was very pluralistic in the '70s when I was growing up, and then became increasingly marginalized in the 1990s. We wore shorts and short sleeves to the masjid, *mashallah*. Now Brother Zaid says you must vote. This should have been the message all along because a lot of what you heard about ten to fifteen years ago as teenagers, we have to undo. They should have known better.

MARY: I couldn't even be part of the community in the '90s; we just weren't accepted.

SANA: Unless you wore hijab and *shalwar kamiz*.

HIND: Things just got crazy. Yusuf Islam stopped playing the guitar. It seems unthinkable. Thank goodness he plays the guitar again because his children are teenagers. We all know how that goes.[61]

amina linked jihad, violence, and Wahhabism. She thus took up tropes prevalent in some Muslim circles, but especially in broader public discourses that have equated the spread of Wahhabi ideology with terrorist acts. Jihad had different connotations in the 1980s, when the US government supported the *mujāhidīn* in Afghanistan. By supporting this foreign cause, many American Muslims affirmed their support of their coreligionists while demonstrating their patriotism. Despite amina's and Nadia's insistence on their community's withdrawal from politics during this period, it actually marked the growth of American Muslim involvement in US and global politics.[62] Because support for foreign causes now conferred suspicion on American Muslims, the women no longer saw these kinds of activities as acceptable forms of political action.

The women connected these political developments to transnational shifts in Muslim piety.[63] In the course of this conversation, the women argued that Wahhabism gained traction because American Muslims mistook it for a more authentic version of Islam and as a result relinquished their American cultural and artistic heritage. Hind used the example of Yusuf Islam, who converted to Islam in 1977 and was formerly known as Cat Stevens, to measure the extent of revivalist influence. She told us that Yusuf Islam stopped playing guitar during the 1990s because at the time he believed it was *bid'a*, or a harmful innovation. She relayed that when his son grew old enough to love the guitar, he then returned to the instrument that he had played for so long and taught his son how to play. In Hind's telling, this parental love transcended the narrow constrictions of "Wahhabism," leading him to embrace a more flexible, rich, and ultimately authentic expression of his faith. Becoming a parent made him a better Muslim. It required him to engage moral concerns with a range of emotional, aesthetic, and intellectual sensibilities that ultimately won out against the impoverished foundations of Wahhabi theology and practice.

The women were less emphathetic toward other prominent American Muslims. Nadia singled out Hamza Yusuf and Zaid Shakir, another important scholar and founder of Zaytuna College, castigating them for isolating Muslims from the rest of American society during the 1990s and making it more susceptible to extremist elements. Her statements echoed amina's criticism that Yusuf shifted his religious convictions in the wake of political pressures following the World Trade Center attacks.[64] Given Yusuf's popularity at Webb and the consonance of his mission with that of the organization, Nadia's unflattering portrayal came as a surprise. Scholars have noted how Yusuf's rhetoric shifted in the 2000s, in which he accepted responsibility for promoting "hate."[65] The women's comments mirror Yusuf's own statements of guilt, which center on his public acceptance of liberal democratic ideals as normative for American Muslims. Although they question his credibility, the book club members have also internalized Yusuf's narrative of self-transformation as their own, embracing his critique of immigrant traditions and asserting the moral obligation of Muslims leaders to shape American Muslim civic engagement.

In addition to placing responsibility on the Muslim community for failing to embrace civic commitments prior to 9/11, the women worried about how they might have contributed to the rise of Wahhabism:

NADIA: I feel like I should have done more, that I could have done more, but I felt alone.

AMINA: You were changing diapers, taking care of your babies; we all were. That was our job then.

MARY: What could you have done? You risk being a martyr if you had stood up and said something. It was dangerous. Look at Rushdie. No, you had to stay quiet. Only now can we speak up.[66]

The subsequent isolation of the Muslim community from broader American society coincided with an intensely demanding period in these women's family lives. In expressing regret, Nadia suggested that Wahhabism managed to take hold because she and like-minded peers—second-generation, American-raised and educated women—were preoccupied with fulfilling what many at Webb see as their primary moral obligation—taking care of their young children. Now, Nadia occupies prominent positions in Muslim institutions, being a founding board member of the Webb Foundation and a committee member at her local mosque, not to mention the positions she holds at her children's schools and at other nonprofit organizations. Her activism has instilled in her a sense of individual responsibility for the direction of the American Muslim community writ large. Her sense of accountability also stems from the conviction, common at Webb, that her demographic of Muslim immigrants plays a special role in the development of American Islam, as its "vanguards." She thus embraces broader cultural discourses linking certain Muslim practices and ideologies to radicalism, claiming that only her duties as a mother prevented her (and other women like her) from stopping the rise of destructive theological forces in their mosques.

In the women's telling, 9/11, while tragic for its loss of life and the ensuing foreign and domestic repercussions for Muslims during the War on Terror, laid bare the misconceptions and fallacies that they believed American Muslims had embraced for too long. During the last decade, the book group members noted that a wider variety of Muslim viewpoints and literature have become available, though as amina laughed, "You do have to pay for it, as opposed to the Saudi stuff."[67] The women perceived a greater openness to a diversity of opinions, gradual moves toward gender equality, and efforts to engage in American politics and culture. Most importantly, they have felt empowered to create and enact a different kind of American Islam through their participation in spaces like the book group. The post-9/11 period represents hope and possibility to reshape their religious community so that it resonates with the lived experiences of the majority of American Muslims and reflects a more authentic Islam.

Although the women seemed to make definitive, confident claims, the perspectives they articulated were highly contingent, produced within the unpredictable context of textual engagement. Mary's striking reference to Rushdie, an atheist, is a case in point. She used Rushdie to demonstrate the extent to which she has experienced complete alienation and withdrawal from American Muslim institutions at various points since converting in the 1980s. In this way, like Rushdie, Mary has struggled with what it means to be a Muslim.[68] As such, here Mary invoked him as an admirable figure. But subsequent conversations about Rushdie revealed her ambivalence toward him. The following year, the group read Rushdie's *Shalimar the Clown*, a 2005 novel set against the political conflicts of Kashmir. During that conversation, Mary ardently claimed that Rushdie should never have written *The Satanic Verses* because the ensuing fatwa controversy produced such negative public perceptions of Islam. She has refused to read the book because she fears the emotional repercussions on her as a believing Muslim.[69] Mary's shifting identifications demonstrate how the book group facilitated its members' articulation of multiple positions, none of which were wholly stable or predetermined. Instead, they retain the improvisational quality of "tactics" that respond to shifting situations in real time.[70] These multifaceted positions changed depending on events in the women's lives, the direction of individual conversations, and the content of the books under discussion. Rather than interpreting these shifts as inauthentic or superficial, we should understand them as constitutive of the American Muslim identity these women seek. This fragmentary experimentation was sometimes unsettling, but ultimately it fulfilled the women's need to create an American Muslim identity that was dynamic enough to respond to shifting political demands.

Sexuality as a "Litmus Test" for Good Muslims

At its heart, the book club gave this group of women the opportunity to engage questions surrounding gender and sexuality explicitly. Gender and sexuality commonly surfaced in the women's attempts to reconcile their individual experiences of exclusion with their conviction that Islam is an inclusive and tolerant faith. These tensions were especially evident during a special book club meeting to celebrate National Poetry Month. The meeting followed the group's field trip to the Poetry Foundation, which had recently opened a new library and performance space in downtown Chicago. Inspired by this trip, amina requested copies of *Poetry* magazine for each participant and invited us to her home for a poetry reading and discussion over brunch. Four women arrived to enjoy the spread of coffee, pastries, and casseroles on amina's dining room table:

HIND: I thought this might happen. Here we are, the core group, forging ahead with poetry. Good thing Zeenat isn't here so we can discuss all of the racy ones.

AMINA: Let's start with my favorite one, about the faggot dinosaurs. Can you imagine talking about this anywhere but here?[71]

These opening comments reveal how the women understood themselves and the book group to constitute the religious and cultural margins, a position that they embraced as a privileged one. While the women thought of themselves as marginal within most Muslim communities, they moved through other social institutions and cultural contexts with relative ease.

As Hind suggested, we were the self-selecting, elite group willing to take on sexuality and other topics considered scandalous, read obscure poetry, and explore unfamiliar social and religious worlds. amina echoed this sentiment in her response to a survey distributed by *Poetry* about the issue: "Wendy Videlock's poem was our naughty secret favorite, the poem in the brown paper bag." The poem, entitled "!" begins, "I think I should never fear, a brontosaurus that is queer." The women especially liked the last two lines, "but those who perfectly adhere, stay clear, stay clear, stay clear, stay clear."[72] In her e-mail to the magazine, amina observed, "This poem made us feel far more tolerant towards sexual deviants than rigid, religious-fundamentalist whack-jobs."[73] The women interpreted their enjoyment of Videlock's poem as evidence of their tolerance and openness. Yet as amina's tongue-in-cheek comment indicated, the women dismissed those Muslims (and other "fundamentalist" practitioners) who disapproved of homosexuality as both religiously and culturally suspect. Perhaps because she explicitly identified the book group as Muslim to a presumed non-Muslim audience, the *Poetry* staff, amina was particularly keen to distinguish between us, as culturally-savvy Muslims, and "fundamentalists."[74] She presented the group's willingness to discuss homosexuality as evidence that they espouse a good, liberal version of Islam—tolerant, peaceful, individualistic, and pluralistic—as opposed to other Muslims who are rigid, oppressive, and marginal to American society.

The concept of sexuality as a litmus test for "good" Muslims emerged during our discussion of Ali Eteraz's controversial memoir, *Children of Dust.*[75] Eteraz spent his early childhood in Pakistan and immigrated with his family to the United States while still a young boy. The book is a biting assessment of immigrant communities, replete with anecdotes depicting a narrow-minded emphasis on dress and physical appearance, increasing rigidity, and the repression of sexuality. Not surprisingly, book club members found much to like in *Children of Dust,* particularly for what the women saw as its frank and honest observations of American Muslim life. As Hind put it, "The whole thing was like my childhood. You can't make this stuff up."[76] During one episode Eteraz recalls how as a young boy, he castigated a young woman for dressing in a manner he found provocative. Eteraz uses this event as emblematic of the spiritual bankruptcy and moral hypocrisy that he detects among his coreligionists. Moreover, Eteraz builds on this and other awkward encounters with women to demonstrate how his sexuality has been repressed through social and religious norms, the results of which are only further attempts to control women and their bodies.

Like our discussion of Videlock's poem, book club members engaged Eteraz's sexuality to frame broader critiques of American Muslim communities:

SANA: For all his talk about girls, I don't think he's actually interested in a wife.

AMINA: He was married to a Pakistani woman, but now I believe he's divorced. After writing the book, he's now totally off the grid, which would make sense if he is gay.

SANA: I think the term is "bi."

TINA: Why would he need to be off the grid?

AMINA: Because being gay or accepting gay people is the litmus test in Islam. You are in or you're out based on that, and he would be totally discredited, even more than he already is.[77]

In this discussion, the concept of a "litmus test" functioned in two ways. As amina explained to me, sexuality served as a litmus test within Muslim communities, insofar as homosexuality was grounds for discrimination and exclusion. For amina, this explains why Eteraz no longer gives interviews or maintains his blog. More importantly, the women employed sexuality as their own litmus test in order to apprise Eteraz as a devout Muslim who has also correctly accepted and internalized certain liberal values. For them, the author's sexual orientation, far from discrediting him, made him an even more appealing critic of the Muslim community. His struggle for a unified identity parallels the women's own attempts to reconcile what they have been taught about Islam and their attempts to claim interpretative authority. The women evaluated whether Eteraz and other Muslims embrace the virtues of tolerance and pluralism that they view as essential to their own American Muslim identities. These efforts mirror political projects elsewhere that construct homosexuality as a problem for Muslim assimilation into Western cultures, in which the presumed incommensurability of Islam and homosexuality becomes yet another marker of Islam's incompatibility with the West.[78] For the book-club women, sexuality provided the discursive ground through which they assessed the authenticity and reliability of the authors that they read.[79]

The book group was not the only Webb space in which members discussed homosexuality. One of the first Webb classes I attended revolved around questions concerning the treatment of gay Muslims and the status of homosexuality in Islam.[80] At Webb, participants generally question the permissibility of homosexuality, but they also deplored the poor treatment they observed that gay Muslims endure at mosques and the lack of support they receive for their struggles with sexuality.[81] In the Webb conversation I observed, some also worried that taking a firm stance against homosexuality potentially aligned them with political and religious groups that tend to be openly anti-Muslim, especially conservative politicians and evangelical Christian communities in the western suburbs. Discussions surrounding homosexuality tended to confuse, rather than resolve, participants' positions on these questions.

This is not surprising, because it is impossible to determine "the" Muslim perspective on homosexuality. Following the mass shooting at an Orlando nightclub on June 12, 2016, in which Omer Mateen killed forty-nine people and wounded fifty-three others, there has been increased attention to Muslim positions on homosexuality and the status of LGBTQ Muslims in their communities.[82] Before 2016, however, homosexuality had been more visibly debated among progressive Muslim organizations and intellectuals, which have addressed the permissibility of homosexuality in an Islamic framework.[83] Academics such as Scott Siraj al-Hajj Kugle have sought to engage more fully with Islamic sources on the possible accommodation of contemporary homosexual and transgender identities.[84] In a 2011 poll conducted by the Pew Research Center, Muslims were more likely to report that homosexuality ought to be discouraged than the overall American population, though this percentage has declined significantly from an earlier survey.[85] While research is only beginning to emerge on homosexuality and Islam, the very broad picture in the United States is that most Muslims—like other Americans—construe heterosexual marriage as normative. As we have seen, this is the case at Webb, where the nuclear, companionate marriage is uplifted as the moral foundation for American Islam. For other American Muslims, homosexuality is morally suspect because it is potentially an act of *zinā*, or illicit intercourse.[86] Of course, not all Muslims ascribe to this view. At Webb, however, the question is less about the legal status of homosexuality within Islam and more about how to be welcoming of gay and lesbian Muslims, whose experiences of marginalization resonate with those of Webb members.

Using sexuality as their anchor, the group's discussion of Eteraz's memoir turned to broader critiques of the gendered expectations of women in the United States. Speculation about Eteraz's sexual orientation subsequently shifted to a discussion about the regulation of male and female sexualities:

AMINA: Why are conservative religions so afraid of female sexuality? It's not just us, but Christians and Jews too.

HIND: Female sexuality isn't the problem; it's male sexuality, actually.

AMINA: But no one is talking about getting rid of Viagra.

HIND: True. But focusing on women distracts from the real issue, which is men. Look, I'm taking the feminist, man-hating approach here. This covering up, putting us behind a curtain, it puts less emphasis on guys to do anything, and we don't scrutinize males as a result. And outside the Muslim community, we also place everything on women, like a girl who gets raped in the park, we think she was wearing a miniskirt and asked for it. Ok, maybe she shouldn't walk through the park alone, but rape was the crime here. The judgmentalness toward women, look at her, she's a slut, the nail polish, the short skirts. It's this whole postcolonial mentality and because of financial insecurity. You're judging other Muslims by their appearance.[87]

Hind attributed the control of female bodies to a variety of ailments in the Muslim community including collective sexual anxieties, postcolonial political humiliations, and economic failures. Even though she sometimes wears a headscarf, Hind here referred to the male enforcement of "covering up" as another instance in which women's choices are subordinated. Following Eteraz, Hind understood unhealthy male sexualities as the source of many problems facing Muslim communities. But in her experience, only female sexuality is subject to scrutiny, correction, maintenance, and restriction. This conversation underscores how Webb members construct gender and sexuality in relational terms. That is, Hind insisted on the inextricable connections between constructions of male and female subjectivities in Muslim communities, rooting them in broader histories of political and economic subjugation.

It is worth pausing to consider the work that Hind's invocation of the "feminist, man-hating approach" accomplishes. At first glance, she seemed to distance herself from feminism as one ideology among many others that she may adopt and potentially discard. She acknowledged the possibility of other positions and resources that were available to her. For Hind, women unjustly endure charges of promiscuity that lay blame at their feet rather than those of criminals who commit acts of sexual violence against women. That is to say, while she upbraided Muslims for their treatment of women, feminism provided her with the tools to take American society to task more broadly for what she understood as sexual double standards. Her comments suggest that while she and other book club members often singled out Muslim practices and beliefs for excluding women, they also identified a wider American culture in which women are blamed for sexual violence against them.

Kamila, the youngest of the group, chimed in to link female sexuality to socioeconomic realities, intergenerational conflict, and immigrant challenges:

> It's an order thing. I was talking to my mom and you know, you hear from the aunties, the women aren't falling in line, so they're getting divorced. But that's not it. They just won't put up with the stuff they would have in Pakistan, and men don't know how to deal with that because they've only seen how their mothers do things. But no American woman is going to put up with what her mom did, with a crazy mother-in-law telling her what to do. American women are succeeding, and men don't know how to deal with that.[88]

Referring to the common practice in her extended Pakistani family in which young wives move in with their in-laws, Kamila echoed Hind's assertion that female sexuality is actually a reflection of male anxieties. She observed Muslim women thriving in American society, becoming educated and securing good jobs. Curiously, by placing American and Pakistani women into opposing categories, Kamila implied that there are few professional, educated women in Pakistan. Rather than bowing to the expectations of their mothers-in-law, according to Kamila, American Muslim women insist on greater autonomy to pursue their individual career goals, and in some cases to be more professionally successful than their husbands. In her assessment, female professional success threatens older women's authority and leads to the unsettling of relationships between mothers and sons. Muslim husbands, Kamila maintained, only exacerbate the problem by taking their mothers' side and leaving their wives feeling left out to dry. Furthermore, her comment suggests that the task of changing gender roles largely falls on young wives, who struggle to navigate a whole host of religious, familial, and workplace expectations.

For amina and Mary, articulating a feminist position is particularly important for them, because they are converts who have experienced acute periods of marginalization and exclusion. Mary's first response to *Children of Dust* captured the strong emotions produced by what miriam cooke calls the "difficult double commitment"[89] to their faith and women's rights:

> As a feminist free agent, converting was relatively easy, but entering the community was like a constant assault to reason. I thought, "Where is the kernel of truth in this religion? How I do I negotiate everything? What are these people thinking? It's so restrictive. How can they live in the West?"[90]

Mary converted after marrying her husband in the 1980s, but as she reminds the group, it took her more than two decades to join Webb, the first community where she has felt welcome. For her, the expectations placed on her as a woman—to cover her hair, to sit in a separate part of the mosque, and to act demurely—affronted her standards of "reason." Mary's rattled off a slew of familiar critiques against Islam as incompatible with individualism, democracy, and equality. Here, "reason" indexed the ways that she believed that gender norms, as practiced in local mosques, defied her deeply held faith in individual choice, autonomy, and freedom. Yet Mary's critique resulted from her desire for acceptance and the pain of her subsequent rejection. These comments also reflected Mary's deeply felt conviction about the essence of Islam. She converted to Islam because she found universal truths in the Qur'an that improved upon, but that were simultaneously consonant with, her liberal Protestant background. In mosques, Mary continues to encounter narrow, culturally inflected dictates imposed on her as religiously normative. Perhaps more importantly, these experiences have made her question the universal message that she discovered in Islam, a sacred foundation built on reason and tolerance.

In response to Mary's story, amina offered her early experiences of marginalization:

> I was once scolded by an eight-year-old for wearing nail polish. I was told I would be going to hell without my toenails if I prayed with nail polish on. She was well trained, knew her stuff. The worst part was I got mad at this kid for telling me I couldn't wear nail polish. It wasn't her fault.[91]

amina's eight-year-old interlocutor unwittingly participated in the ongoing debate among contemporary Muslims about whether wearing nail polish invalidates ritual ablutions and the subsequent performance of salat. For example, nail polish is a frequent topic of discussion on legal websites; some scholars argue that any form of ornamentation on the feet and hands that prevents water from touching the skin negates ablutions' purifying effects. amina's humiliation at being scolded by a young child underscored her feeling that she was being constantly monitored and corrected as a female convert, even by children.

Conclusion

Centered on gendered concerns, the Webb book club demonstrates the possibilities and constraints of religious third spaces. On the one hand, the book club members reveled in this third space of deconstruction, critique, and doubt, where they took comfort in sharing experiences of pain and marginalization, claimed "interpretative privilege," addressed topics openly that they believed could not be raised elsewhere, and experimented with a range of ideological positions. The improvisational nature of the women's encounter with these diverse texts shows the fluidity of third spaces, and the tension and ambivalence that define them. The Webb book club has since dissolved officially, as the group of friends found it more convenient to meet informally. Small and impermanent as they are, the Webb book group and the many other reading groups like it provide indispensable perspectives into the construction of selfhood and meaning in contemporary America.

On the other hand, the women of the book club desire significant change within American Muslim institutions and in American society more broadly, but it is not at all clear whether their efforts will come to fruition. Even in a third-space commitment to greater inclusion, other Webb conversations around feminism and progressivism suggest the tenuous nature of these identifications, which continue to generate ambivalence around authenticity and authority among American Muslims. Such ambivalence is by no means limited to Muslim communities, but rather indicative of how gender and sexuality become the contested and often polarizing ground on which questions of ultimate meaning are engaged.

Conclusion

THIRD SPACES AND ETHNOGRAPHIC ENTANGLEMENTS IN THE AGE OF OBAMA

AS A CASE study, the Webb community demonstrates that third spaces are key sites for studying lived religion in the twenty-first century. Third spaces provide a vital window into the convergence of institutional and everyday religion, the creative uses and contestations of space, and the generative potential of devotional practice.

Moreover, third spaces are essential for incorporating a much broader spectrum of marginal spaces into religious studies scholarship. These emerging communities are often numerically small, short-lived, and difficult to recognize in diffuse geographic landscapes such as those of suburban America. Their lack of visibility is a product of their marginal position both within American Islam and in American society in general. Across the United States, dynamic and creative forms of religious practices are taking place in the ex-burbs of the Midwest, which have long been associated with conformity and conventionality and dismissed as "fly-over country." Looking beyond more visible institutions and dense urban neighborhoods enables us to track the ways in which communities are formed, how they seek to create a space of belonging for their members to inhabit, and how these attempts to create community simultaneously reinforce discourses of exclusion and marginalization.

As generative sites, third spaces thus highlight the contingency and unpredictability of lived religious practice. Religion is too often presented as an integrative force that facilitates greater acceptance in American society and the ultimate fulfillment of individual selves. Although Webb members share a commitment to creating a "seamless" American Muslim identity, their discussions and ritual performances show how constructing American Islam is an ongoing process, the outcome of which is uncertain. The Webb community rarely reaches consensus on theological or ritual questions. Instead, its emphasis on peer conversation and ritual experimentation produces new ambiguities and unresolved tensions. For all the "comfort" that Webb elicits in its members, my ethnography reveals enduring anxieties and instabilities around authority, authenticity, and belonging.

Third spaces underscore how relationships structure contemporary religious practice. Indeed, the Webb community is bound together not by any defined theological program or set of beliefs, but rather by its relationships: among parents and children, among friends, and among its members, God, and the Prophet Muhammad. Shared consumer sensibilities, education levels, and multiethnic family structures undergird its members' claim that the Webb community is "like-minded." These relationships, embedded as they are in gendered, classed, and racial hierarchies, orient us toward the contingencies through which religious subjectivities are produced.

Focusing on third spaces also has important implications for the study of American Islam in particular. In the twentieth and twenty-first centuries, third spaces have been created to serve American Muslims who have, for a variety of reasons, remained outside the fold of American mosques. These American Muslims, who account for roughly half of the Muslim population in the United States, fit uneasily into the ethnic particularism that has defined many of America's mosques in metropolitan areas. The Webb community is just one type of community that imagines itself as an alternative to the ethnic particularism in which new forms of belonging and community are possible. Such groups deserve further study to account for the diverse rituals, theologies, structures of authority, and communal relationships that structure the religious and social lives of this large constituency of "unmosqued" Muslims. As American Muslim families (like American families writ large) become ever more ethnically and racially diverse, this group also fits uneasily into extant narratives of American religious history that have focused on ethnicity as an analytical frame.

This internal critique of ethnic Muslim communities has animated the Webb project, producing forceful dissent against extant authority structures, on the one hand, and efforts to ensure continuity with an authentic Islamic tradition, on the other. This interplay between dissent and continuity is nowhere more evident than in Webb's attempts to provide ritual roles and leadership opportunities for women, while also distancing itself from feminist or progressive trends in American Islam. Although events such as amina Wadud's 2005 leading of a mixed-gender prayer have attracted significant media and scholarly attention, attending to American Muslim third spaces demonstrates how many women (and men) are more focused on building female authority in areas such as communal governance, pedagogy, and other forms of public ritual such as the *mawlid*. These possibilities do not portend a teleological progression toward egalitarianism, nor do they suggest enduring forms of patriarchal authority. Rather, Webb's gendered practices demonstrate ongoing, unpredictable efforts among American Muslims to reorient spatial, pedagogical, and ritual contexts to more closely align with diverse visions of American Islam.

In addition to imagining possibilities for a postethnic American Muslim community, I have also shown how third spaces serve as vital sites for civic and political engagement. In the wake of surveillance and discrimination after 9/11, the Webb community has sought to make Islam recognizable and visible as a good religious faith in America's pluralistic religious landscape. These efforts come from the bottom up. Webb's efforts to realize a culturally robust American Islam take place outside of the more visible institutional efforts of mosques and national organizations such as the Islamic Society of North America. The Webb community seeks to change not only how Islam has been represented in the broader discourse, but perhaps more importantly, it has challenged the capacity of those Muslim leaders who have spoken for American Islam in the past.

The post-9/11 moment has made ordinary American Muslims into spokespeople for Islam, charging them with the task of teaching their neighbors and friends that Islam is a "good" American religion. Third spaces are one context through which some American Muslims confront and take up this obligation explicitly in order to prove their loyalty to the American state and to make Islam recognizable to other Americans *as American*. The Webb community provides its members with the confidence to say to their non-Muslim friends that yes, just such an American Islam exists.

A Fragile Optimism: American Islam in the Age of Obama

Although it is tempting to see Webb as representative of some "future" American Islam, it is more helpful to understand its significance within the political and religious context of the Age of Obama. In contrast to the deep uncertainty with which the Webb community described the immediate post-9/11 moment, the Obama presidency, during which I conducted fieldwork, was a time marked by a fragile optimism in the American political project. This fragile optimism opened up certainly possibilities of religious and political engagement, while foreclosing others.

To be sure, the Obama administration largely kept intact governmental surveillance of American Muslims, though with some effort to curb the most blatant abuses of their civil rights. Unlike the "countercitizenship" forged in some American Muslim communities, such as those described in Grewal's and Khabeer's studies, by and large, Webb members do not seek to challenge dominant representations of "America."[1] They contest their "outsiderhood" even as they occupy a position on the margins. The Webb community's activities and programs have been consistently aimed at rectifying the negative image of Islam by uplifting positive images of Muslim families engaged in recognizable American leisure and community service activities. Participants talked about these ritual enactments primarily in religious terms, as part of their obligations as Muslims to produce an indigenous, vibrant American Muslim culture.

Of course, in their attempts to make themselves recognizable as Americans, the Webb community is by no means unique. Many other American religious communities have undertaken similar constructions in the past and crafted ritual performances to align with political and religious demands. Immigrant communities of all kinds have waged generational conflicts over culture, language, and authority. Moreover, members of the Webb community draw on persistent and enduring narratives of other immigrant and religious communities, looking to white Catholics and Jews as models for achieving the recognition that they seek.

The appropriation of these white ethnic immigrant narratives, however, is discursively constructed on complex racial hierarchies. To be clear, the Webb community does not represent a good/moderate Islam. On the contrary, this study treats American Muslims as historically situated actors who use, appropriate, and challenge cultural and religious discourses and practices. And they do so in conscious and unconscious ways, such that the community reproduces certain inequalities and exclusions, sometimes against other Muslims. Webb members deliberately and sometimes unwittingly select certain American, Muslim, and American Muslim pasts over others, for example, by uplifting the heteronormative nuclear family, and celebrating the contributions of white converts such as M. A. R. Webb over those of American Muslims such as Malcolm X.

By the early 2010s, Webb practices had come to reflect a tentative hope in the capacity of the American political project to move toward greater inclusion, however gradual and uneven the path that this progress took. One indication of this optimism was Webb's reaction to the anti-sharia initiatives. By and large, Webb participants did not view the anti-sharia bills as an indication of widespread public animosity toward Islam and American Muslims. Rather, they saw it as an aberration that required self-reflection and study among Webb members about sharia and *fiqh* as well as a more intentional attempt to ensure that their kids had a more robust ethical framework with which to navigate the boundaries of religion and culture. They also looked inward, assigning blame to American Muslims for isolating themselves from the American cultural "mainstream" and for inculcating ethical norms and prescriptions that did not sufficiently allow for cultural context and embodied experience.

At the same time, Webb members expressed concern that lawmakers and the broader public had failed to grasp the fundamental aspects of Islamic ethics. They articulated alarm at the persistence and intensification of Islamophobic rhetoric. But I also observed a robust faith that American political institutions would protect them. As the Council on American-Islamic Relations and other civil rights organizations successfully won court challenges to the legislation, their hope seemed justified.

Late in the Obama presidency, other Webb members like Zaid grew increasingly worried about the international political context and directed their community service efforts to improving the lives of Muslims abroad. Drone attacks surpassed the pace of the Bush years, directed against terrorist targets in Afghanistan, Iraq, and Yemen, among many other places, often with significant civilian casualties. Many Webb members, especially those of Syrian descent, became distraught over the lack of international intervention in the worsening civil war, the deepening of the humanitarian crisis, and the unwillingness of Obama to make good on his promises to act. Still, Zaid and others placed their faith in their own capacities to improve the lives of less fortunate Americans and less fortunate Muslims abroad, doubling down on their service efforts and committing their time and financial resources where they saw gaps in their government's capacities.

The 2016 presidential campaign and election marked a moment in which many Americans, Muslim and non-Muslim alike, came to doubt whether such an optimistic narrative of American politics would hold. If the first months of Donald Trump's administration are any indication of the future (and surely it is difficult to predict what direction that administration will take), many American Muslims now fear that white nationalist discourse, government surveillance, and the curtailing of their civil rights, along with those of immigrants, racial minorities, and gay and transgendered communities, will only intensify.

In response, some Webb members have been shifting their service commitments toward direct political action. A recent *Atlantic* article featured several west suburban Chicago Muslims who have decided to stand for local elections in the wake of the 2016 election. Among them was Asma Akhras, one of Webb's longstanding members and an ongoing participant in its programs. Photographed against the backdrop of a Downers Grove housing subdivision, Akhras explained why she decided to run for the board of the Indian Prairie Library: "Trump's election has exponentially reaffirmed the need to be civically engaged. This is my way in my little neighborhood."[2] She spoke further about local elections as paving the way for midterm congressional elections, mobilizing suburban Muslim campaigning skills and ultimately, solidifying American Muslims as a voting bloc.

I came across the *Atlantic* article quite by accident, and initially it put a smile on my face. Indeed, here was evidence of Webb's success, a display of the community's political and social capital. They have the contacts and networks necessary to make themselves visible representatives of American Islam. What is more, their educational level, middle-class status, and suburban milieu have made them highly desirable symbols of American Muslim success. Moreover, I reflected on Asma's campaign as an obvious outgrowth of Webb's emphasis on American Muslim cultural and civic engagement. Like the profound shock of 9/11, which spurred the creation of the Webb community, Trump's election seems to have similarly prompted Webb members to take matters into their own hands, this time to run for public office.

As I finished the article, however, I grew uneasy over the representational work that the *Atlantic* was doing for its readers. The *Atlantic* appeals to urban liberals, many of whom would find Asma's candidacy an encouraging sign, as I did. And yet, the *Atlantic* piece underscores the hegemonic, enduring pressures placed on American Muslims to prove that they conform to narrow conceptions of Americanness. These pressures arise from across the political spectrum. It is worth noting that in this instance, this pressure does not come from right-wing media outlets like Fox News, which have become ever more invested in the narrative of Islam's incompatibility with American liberal democracy. Rather, scrutiny of American Muslim political commitments remains rooted in lingering doubts over their commitment to secular modernity. As long as the American discourse demands it, American Muslims will have to demonstrate their capacity for the "good" or "moderate" kinds of religious and political action.

Entanglements of American Islam

The *Atlantic*'s coverage of Asma's candidacy is an important reminder that scholars are often much closer to their conversation partners than they often pretend. This is what Courtney Bender calls the "entanglements" of American religious history.[3] Bender observes how as an ethnographer she was often "caught" in the "imaginative webs" of the practitioners she studied.[4] Despite her efforts to prevent such entanglements, Bender's conversation partners often interpreted her statements and actions as evidence of "mystical" experiences and past lives.[5] In the research and writing of this project, I too became ever more aware of the multiplying webs of relationality in which scholars of American Islam find themselves.

As we have seen, the representation of Islam is of prime importance to many Webb members, who have taken on the responsibility of crafting an alternative narrative and portrayal of their faith. Aware of the role that scholars have in shaping these representations, many American Muslim communities are highly invested in what scholars write about them. Moreover, technology has augmented the opportunities for communities who are the subjects of ethnographies to respond to what is written about them. Scholarship is now more widely available in a variety of forms: on blogs, social media, open access journals, and databases such as ProQuest, the online depository for dissertations. Whatever our preferences as scholars, our writing reaches beyond strictly academic publics. Additionally, many Webb members seek out and look to academic works on Islam for guidance and for what they see as a more sound understanding of their history.

All of these factors have contributed to the fact that, over the past several years, some members of the Webb community have been among my most consistent interlocutors. My conversation partners have understandably been very interested in what I write about them. Not only does this group understand the nature of the academic enterprise, but they also understand that academic work has a life outside the academy. I have come to see these ongoing conversations as essential to the direction my work has taken. Webb members read this work in its various instantiations: the dissertation in partial and complete form, published articles based on my ethnography, new and revised chapters, and a review of the dissertation published online. Their reactions have ranged from questions about the academic frames I have chosen to employ; surprise and curiosity of Webb being the subject of an academic book; specific questions about and challenges to claims that I make; and observations of how my arguments have developed over the years. Webb members know all too well that the construction of American Islam is not, and has never been, the preserve of Muslims alone. They are also acutely aware of the political implications of these non-Muslim perceptions and representations of Islam and how, in various ways, these images have shaped the development of contemporary Islam.

Whether they want to acknowledge it or not, scholars, through their research and public intellectual activities, are shaping the direction of

American Islam. As a non-Muslim and an "outsider," I initially hesitated to acknowledge this reality. But the inadequacy of this perspective became gradually apparent. In 2013, I gave a conference paper on Webb conversations and engagements with the Qur'an. After I finished, a colleague asked whether I had participated in Webb conversations on the Qur'an. I explained that I did not want to alter the tenor and content of the discussions and so had remained an observer. My colleague asked for further clarification, "Why not? Don't you know the kinds of things about the Qur'an they want to know? Aren't you the kind of academic expert they look to?" I responded by saying that because I am not Muslim, I lacked the embodied experience that Webb members saw as an essential foundation for authority.

While I do not share a Muslim identity with my interlocutors, as my fieldwork progressed I began to observe the many things we have in common. Among them is a shared faith in the production of expert knowledge in the university setting. Surely this is an important entanglement, for it suggests a common epistemology and construction of authority. As a teacher-scholar, I share their conviction in the transformative potential of conversations around texts and the interpretative authority of individuals. For members of the Webb community and myself, these conversations are embodied practices with profound moral implications that bridge a false divide between "ethnographer" and "subject."

As readers have likely noticed, these entanglements extend to the sources I cite and the American Muslim intellectuals whom Webb members engage as they attempt to construct an alternative American Islam. I often found myself in unexpected conversations about the academic works and authors that I engage in my own work. My conversation partners and I also discussed authors whom I later cited to analyze the Webb community. For example, Dr. Sherman Jackson is an inspiration to Webb members. He has spoken at Webb events and is often invoked as a model American Muslim. His academic work on American Islam is also indispensable, especially his observations regarding the enduring power of the "immigrant" ideology and his call for the critical study of race and religion. Perhaps the most important intellectual entanglement involves Dr. Umar Faruq Abd-Allah. Like Jackson, Abd-Allah is an astute observer of American Muslim life, bringing anthropological theory to bear on the challenges facing his followers. At the same time, Abd-Allah's primary aim is to shape the American Muslim community according to his "cultural imperative."[6]

The implications of these overlaps and boundaries should indeed give us pause. Is it even possible for scholarship on contemporary Islam to extricate itself from the normative interests and political projects that it seeks to disentangle? Edward Curtis argues that while scholars might wish to resist the political implications of their work, there is no escaping them. He writes, "So many different people and institutions with so many different goals are *interested*—so many people have something at stake. Practitioners of Islamic studies experience their work as a form of local, national, and/or international politics, whether they like it or not."[7]

Indeed, this book is enmeshed in the interested politics of representing American Islam. It is not disinterested in these politics. Rather, my work is animated by intellectual and ethical concerns about how American Muslims and Islam are constructed in the twenty-first century, and it seeks to provide a more complex, critical, and historically situated portrayal. In particular, it attunes us to the multiple ways in which academic works are read, and how different audiences read them, in ways that authors do not (and sometimes cannot) anticipate. My ongoing conversations with Webb participants have illuminated this shared representational politics.

This is precisely why scholars need to be rigorously attentive to the potential effects of our narratives, categories, and modes of analysis. We should be aware of how, for instance, scholarly investments in religious pluralism have both positive and negative effects on Muslim communities. As we have seen, despite the celebratory cast usually accorded to religious pluralism, its discursive practices are never wholly positive; they both restrict and open up possibilities of religious engagement in unanticipated ways. Religious pluralism excludes certain practitioners while including others. These dynamics require us to allow for new challenges and subversions of these pluralistic logics, to attend to their exclusions, rather than celebrating one path over another.

The Webb community is embedded in a whole host of historical and cultural developments of which its members are only partially aware. My task in this book has been to account for how this community enables its members to challenge dominant representations of Islam, from within and beyond the Muslim community, and in the process to enact an alternative space of belonging. Even as it serves as a place of inclusion, Webb also produces its own set of exclusions that have less to do with the organization per se and more to do with the practice of religion more broadly. Some of these tensions come from the demands placed on American Muslims; others are embedded in deeply entrenched racial, gendered, and classed inequalities of the United States; still others relate to global Muslim debates over authority and tradition. It is impossible to study a community like Webb and conclude that religious communities are wholly liberating, integrative, and transcendent. Instead, we must focus on the shifting ground upon which religion, culture, nation, community, and selfhood are constructed.

Notes

INTRODUCTION

1. "Remarks by the President at Islamic Society of Baltimore," The White House, February 3, 2016, https://www.whitehouse.gov/the-press-office/2016/02/03/remarks-president-islamic-society-baltimore.
2. For accounts of the hypervisibility of American Muslims, see Zareena Grewal, *Islam Is a Foreign Country: American Muslims and the Crisis of Islam* (New York: New York University Press, 2013); Amaney Jamal and Nadine Naber, eds. *Race and Arab Americans before and after 9/11* (Syracuse: Syracuse University Press, 2013), 1–5. Shabana Mir, *Muslim American Women on Campus: Undergraduate Social Life and Identity* (Chapel Hill: The University of North Carolina Press, 2014), 40–5.
3. Sunaina Marr Maira, *Missing: Youth, Citizenship, and Empire after 9/11* (Durham, NC: Duke University Press, 2009), 80–85.
4. Maira, *Missing*, 80–85. Maira expands on the term as coined by Renato Rosaldo, "Cultural Citizenship and Educational Democracy," *Cultural Anthropology* 9, no. 3 (1994): 402–11.
5. As Sylvester Johnson has shown, the racialization of Islam predates 9/11. See Sylvester Johnson, *African American Religions, 1500–2000: Colonialism, Democracy, and Freedom* (New York: Cambridge University Press, 2015), 377–99. This particular community, however, experienced the consequences of racialization after the September 11 attacks in ways they had not previously felt before.
6. For analyses of the mainstreaming of these anti-Muslim discourses, see Rosemary R. Corbett, *Making Moderate Islam: Sufism, Service and the "Ground Zero Mosque" Controversy* (Palo Alto, CA: Stanford University Press, 2016); Nadia Marzouki, *Islam: An American Religion* (New York: Columbia University Press, 2017).
7. Trump's campaign promises to prevent Muslims from entering the United States have materialized in the form of two executive orders. The Executive

Order 13769, Protecting the Nation from Terrorist Entry into the United States, was issued on January 27, 2017 and barred the entrance of citizens from Muslim-majority countries: Sudan, Libya, Iran, Iraq, Syria, Somalia, and Yemen; it suspended Syrian refugees indefinitely, and it temporarily suspended the US refugee program, while making provisions for the entry of Christian refugees. Following large-scale protests and the court challenge *Washington v. Trump*, which was upheld by the United States Court of Appeals Ninth Circuit on February 9, 2017, the Trump administration issued Executive Order 13780, which removed Iraq from the list and removed the dispensation for Christians.

8. Melissa Etehad, "After Nice, Newt Gingrich Wants to 'Test' Every Muslim in the U.S. and Deport Sharia Believers," *Washington Post*, July 15, 2016, https://www.washingtonpost.com/news/morning-mix/wp/2016/07/15/after-nice-newt-gingrich-wants-to-test-every-american-muslim-and-deport-those-who-believe-in-sharia/.
9. Carl Ernst, "Introduction: The Problem of Islamophobia," in *Islamophobia in America: The Anatomy of Intolerance*, ed. Carl Ernst (New York: Palgrave MacMillan, 2013), 1–10.
10. Zain Abdullah, "American Muslims in the Contemporary World: 1965 to the Present," in *The Cambridge Companion to American Islam*, ed. Juliane Hammer and Omid Safi (New York: Cambridge University Press, 2013), 81.
11. "Our History, Vision, and Mission," Mohammed Alexander Russell Webb Foundation, www.mohammedwebb.org/about.
12. "Our History Vision, and Mission," Mohammed Alexander Russell Webb Foundation, www.mohammedwebb.org/about.
13. One notable exception is Mir's *Muslim American Women on Campus*, which explores how a variety of leisure practices (drinking, dating, and sartorial choices) frame constructions of what it means to be young, Muslim, and American. Sunaina Maira also discusses consumerism at length in the fifth chapter of *Missing*, but not in conjunction with her interviewees' religious identities.
14. Here I draw on the now vast literature on lived religion, especially two groundbreaking volumes that have set in motion this field of inquiry. See Nancy Ammerman, ed., *Everyday Religion: Observing Modern Religious Lives* (New York: Oxford University Press, 2007); David D. Hall, ed., *Lived Religion in America: Toward a History of Practice* (Princeton, NJ: Princeton University Press, 1997).
15. Edward Curtis IV explores this tension between the universality of Islam and the particularity of American Muslims in Black Muslim thought. See Edward Curtis IV, *Islam in Black America: Identity, Liberation, and Difference in African-American Islamic Thought* (Albany: State University of New York, 2002).
16. Corbett, *Making Moderate Islam*, 3.
17. For a historical account of institutionalization of American Islam, see Sally Howell, "Laying the Groundwork for American Muslim Histories," in *The*

Cambridge Companion to American Islam, ed. Juliane Hammer and Omid Safi (New York: Cambridge University Press, 2013), 45–64.

18. Grewal, *Islam Is a Foreign Country*, 57–78. Grewal adopts Talal Asad's now ubiquitous definition of Islam as a "discursive tradition" to described ongoing global debates among Muslims about authenticity, knowledge, and authority. See Talal Asad, "The Idea of an Anthropology of Islam" *Qui Parle* 17, no. 2 (Spring/Summer 2009): 1–30.
19. Grewal, *Islam Is a Foreign Country*, 76–78.
20. Grewal, *Islam Is a Foreign Country*, 7.
21. Juliane Hammer and Omid Safi, "Introduction: American Islam, Muslim Americans and the American Experiment," in *The Cambridge Companion to American Islam*, ed. Juliane Hammer and Omid Safi (New York: Cambridge University Press, 2013), 9–12.
22. More recently, scholars have taken up these historical engagements to undercut the assumption that Islam is new to the United States. See Sophia Rose Arjana, *Muslims in the Western Imagination* (New York: Oxford University Press, 2015); Sylviane A. Diouf, *Servants of Allah: African Muslims Enslaved in the Americas* (New York: New York University Press, 1998); Kambiz GhaneaBassiri, *A History of Islam in the United States: From the New World to the New World Order* (New York: Cambridge University Press, 2010), 6; Timothy Marr, *The Cultural Roots of American Islamicism* (Cambridge: Cambridge University Press, 2006); Denise Spellberg, *Thomas Jefferson's Qur'an: Islam and the Founders* (New York: Alfred A. Knopf, 2013).
23. In the 1980s and 1990s, works by Yvonne Haddad, Jane Smith, and John Esposito focused on immigrant Muslim communities in order to theorize the extent to which Muslims were "becoming American." These scholars pioneered the study of Islam in America and produced valuable case studies. But they also consistently reified the dichotomy between immigrant and black Muslims by representing Islam as a newcomer in the United States. See Yvonne Yazbeck Haddad and Jane I. Smith, *Muslim Communities in North America* (Albany: State University of New York Press, 1994); Yvonne Yazbeck Haddad, *Becoming American?:The Forging of Arab and Muslim Identity in Pluralist America* (Waco, TX: Baylor University Press, 2011); Yvonne Yazbeck Haddad, *Not Quite American?: The Shaping of Arab and Muslim Identity in the United States* (Waco, TX: Baylor University Press, 2004); Yvonne Yazbeck Haddad, ed., *Muslims in the West:From Sojourners to Citizens* (Oxford: Oxford University Press, 2002), 7–8; Yvonne Yazbeck Haddad and John L. Esposito, eds., *Muslims on the Americanization Path?* (New York: Oxford University Press, 2000).
24. Aaron Hughes, "The Study of Islam before and after September 11: A Provocation," *Theory and Method in the Study of Religion* 24 (2012): 324. Aaron Hughes goes so far as to suggest that US scholars of Islam avoid studying terrorist organizations such as al-Qaeda *as religious* because we as a field have all

too readily presumed that such communities are distortions of authentic Islam and "good" religion. According to Hughes, we have also been biased in our hermeneutics, uplifting only those texts and practices that conform to liberal standards of democracy and pluralism.

25. Mahmood Mamdani, *Good Muslim, Bad Muslim: America, the Cold War, and the Roots of Terror* (New York: Pantheon Books, 2004).
26. G. A. Lipton, "Secular Sufism: Neoliberalism, Ethnoracism, and the Reformation of the Muslim Other," *Muslim World* 101, no. 3 (2011): 427–40.
27. GhaneaBassiri, *A History of Islam in America*, 377.
28. GhaneaBassiri, *A History of Islam in America*, 8.
29. Johnson, *African American Religions*, 377–99.
30. Mir, *Muslim American Women on Campus*, 11, 125.
31. Mir, *Muslim American Women on Campus*, 41.
32. Edward W. Soja, *Thirdspace: Journeys to Los Angeles and Other Real-and-Imagined Places* (London: Blackwell Publishing, 1996), 5, 22.
33. Homi Bhabha, *The Location of Culture* (London: Routledge, 2004), 3.
34. Michel de Certeau, *The Practice of Everyday Life*, trans. Steven F. Rendall (Berkeley: University of California Press, 1984), 31.
35. Barbara Metcalf, ed., *Making Muslim Space in North America and Europe* (Berkeley: University of California Press, 1996), 2–3.
36. Robert A. Orsi, "Everyday Miracles: The Study of Lived Religion," in *Lived Religion in America: Toward a History of Practice*, ed. David Hall (Princeton, NJ: Princeton University Press, 1997), 11.
37. Courtney Bender and Pamela E. Klassen, eds., *After Pluralism: Reimagining Religious Engagement* (New York: Columbia University Press, 2010), 1–3.
38. Kevin Schultz, *Tri-Faith America: How Catholics and Jews Held Postwar America to Its Protestant Promise* (New York: Oxford University Press, 2011). For a historical overview of pluralism in the United States, see William R. Hutchison, *Religious Pluralism in America: The Contentious History of a Founding Ideal* (New Haven, CT: Yale University Press, 2003); and Stephen J. Stein, *Communities of Dissent: A History of Alternative Religions in America* (New York: Oxford University, 2003). For a theoretical discussion of secularism and pluralism from the perspective of American literature, see Tracy Fessenden, *Culture and Redemption: Religion, the Secular, and American Literature* (Princeton, NJ: Princeton University Press, 2006).
39. Pew Forum, "Religious Landscape Survey," 2008, http://www.pewforum.org/religious-landscape-study/. Muslim responses are comparable to Christian evangelicals. Nationally, 70 percent of survey participants supported the statement that many religions lead to eternal life.
40. See Asma Afsaruddin, "The Hermeneutics of Interfaith Relations: Retrieving Moderation and Pluralism as Universal Principles in Quranic Exegesis," *Journal*

of Religious Ethics 37, no. 2 (2009): 331–35; Khaled Abou El Fadl, *The Place of Tolerance in Islam* (Boston: Beacon Press, 2002); Jerusha Lamptey, *Never Wholly Other: A Muslima Theology of Religious Pluralism* (New York: Oxford University Press, 2014); Abdulaziz Sachedina, *The Islamic Roots of Democratic Pluralism* (New York: Oxford University Press, 2001).

41. For example, see Reza Shah-Kazemi, *The Spirit of Tolerance in Islam* (Occasional Papers Series 4. London: Institute for Ismaili Studies, 2012).
42. Justine Howe, "Invocations of Early Islam in US Discourse(s) of Muslim Pluralism," in *The Routledge Handbook of Early Islam*, ed. Herbert Berg (London: Routledge, 2017), 374–88.
43. Marcia Hermansen, "Two-Way Acculturation: Muslim Women in America between Individual Choice (Liminality) and Community Affiliation (Communitas)," in *The Muslims of America*, ed. Yvonne Hazbeck Haddad (New York: Oxford University Press, 1991), 177–201.
44. Kathryn Lofton, "Religion and the Authority in American Parenting," *Journal of the American Academy of Religion* (June 2016): 4. Lofton points to the numerous studies showing that women continue to do the majority of child care and household labor in nuclear family households.
45. Rachel Newcomb, an anthropologist of urban life in Morocco, recently declared, presumably tongue-in-cheek, that had she known the positive effects of being a mother for her ethnography, she would have had children much earlier. Rachel Newcomb, "Fieldwork in Morocco with Sofia (Age 1)," in *The Chronicle of Higher Education*, February 14, 2011.
46. This discussion of the embodied experiences of fieldwork was inspired by my reading of Kristy Nabhan-Warren, *The Virgin of El Barrio: Marian Apparitions, Catholic Evangelizing, and Mexican American Activism* (New York: New York University Press, 2005); Kristy Nabhan-Warren, "Embodied Research and Writing: A Case for Phenomenologically Oriented Religious Studies Ethnographies," *Journal of the American Academy of Religion* 72, no. 2 (2011): 378–407.
47. Ruth Behar, *The Vulnerable Observer: Anthropology That Breaks Your Heart* (Boston: Beacon Press, 1996).

CHAPTER 1

1. Interview with the author, October 13, 2011, Darien, IL. To preserve the anonymity of my conversation partners, I do not provide their names. All future citations will include the date and location of the interview.
2. Interview with the author, October 13, 2011, Darien, IL.
3. This phrase is taken from the Webb Foundation's mission statement. "About Us," Mohammed Alexander Russell Webb Foundation, www.mohammedwebb.org/about.

4. I use the terms "mosque" and "masjid" (its Arabic equivalent) interchangeably, as did my informants.
5. Jamillah Karim, *American Muslim Women: Negotiating Race, Class, and Gender in the Ummah* (New York: New York University Press, 2009), 14. In another ethnography on Chicago's Muslim communities, *Islam in Urban America: Sunni Muslims in Chicago* (Philadelphia: Temple University Press, 2004), Garbi Schmidt goes so far as to imbue Chicago with theological significance, idealizing it as a contemporary Medina in which the global Muslim community comes together. See Schmidt, *Islam in Urban America*, 1–2. To be sure, Medina is a sacred Muslim site for the reasons Schmidt outlines. Thereafter, the city was known as Medina, shorthand for *medinat al-nabi*, or the city of the prophet. Medina is also the second-most important pilgrimage destination next to Mecca. But we must not conflate the specific site of Medina with the category of urban metropolises. Even if we know less about Islam in more remote areas, Muslims have created vibrant communities in every possible geographic location. There is no empirical reason to afford "the city" a special status in the study of Islam as such. Moreover, as Karim argues, and this study affirms, Chicago is a site of creative religious activity built on pervasive race, gender, and socioeconomic inequality.
6. Ihsan Bagby, *The American Mosque 2011: Basic Characteristics of the American Mosque, Attitudes of Mosque Leaders* (New York: Council on American Islamic Relations, 2012), https://www.cair.com/images/pdf/The-American-Mosque-2011-part-1.pdf. For population estimates, see Su'ad Abdul Khabeer, *Muslim Cool: Race, Religion, and Hip Hop in the United States* (New York: New York University Press, 2016), 10.
7. Karim, *American Muslim Women*, 49.
8. Ibid., 239–41. Karim's conclusion demonstrates her normative interest in mapping *ummah* spaces in Chicago. As a Muslim woman who moves between various Islamic communities, she believes Muslims can begin to overcome the hierarchies she identifies by embracing a common project of social justice and civic engagement in the United States.
9. One notable exception is Abdo Elkholy's sociological comparison of Toledo and Detroit's suburban Muslim communities. Contrary to Will Herberg's claims in *Protestant, Catholic, Jew: An Essay in American Religious Sociology*, Elkholy maintained that being Muslim was not necessarily an impediment to acceptance in American society. Elkholy found that Toledo's Muslims were more assimilated than those in Detroit because "religion in Toledo has been pursued as a means of emulating, and being accepted by, the American socioeconomic middle class." Although Elkholy maintained the stigma that African American Muslims had "distorted" Islam, his study avoided many of the value-laden assumptions about the incompatibility of Islam and American culture that plagued subsequent studies. His conclusions also anticipated one of the core findings of my research, namely the importance of class and residence for the construction of

competing American Muslim identities and the perception of these constructions by non-Muslim Americans. See Abdo A. Elkholy, *Arab Moslems in the United States: Religion and Assimilation* (New Haven: College & University Press, 1966), 16; Will Herberg, *Protestant, Catholic, Jew: An Essay in American Religious Sociology* (Garden City: Doubleday, 1955).

10. Joel Garreau, *Edge City: Life on the New Frontier* (New York: Doubleday, 1991); Eileen Luhr, *Witnessing Suburbia: Conservatives and Christian Youth Culture* (Berkeley: University of California Press, 2009); Justin G. Wilford, *Sacred Subdivisions: The Postsuburban Transformation of American Evangelicalism* (New York: New York University Press, 2012).
11. Dolores Hayden, *Building Suburbia: Green Fields and Urban Growth, 1820–2000* (New York: Vintage Books, 2004).
12. Robert A. Orsi, *Gods of the City: Religion and the American Urban Landscape* (Bloomington: Indiana University Press, 1999), 35–36.
13. Khabeer, *Muslim Cool*, 11–12. In this section, I rely on Khabeer's excellent discussion of race, class, and residence among Chicago's Muslims.
14. Khabeer, *Muslim Cool*, 11.
15. Judith Weisenfeld, *New World A-Coming: Black Religion and Racial Identity During the Great Migration* (New York: New York University Press, 2017), 5.
16. GhaneaBassiri, *A History of Islam in the United States*, 208–9.
17. Khabeer, *Muslim Cool*, 10–12.
18. Karim, *American Muslim Women*, 54.
19. Interview with the author, October 13, 2011, Darien, IL.
20. Wilford, *Sacred Subdivisions*, 61. Wilford argues that this isolation and fragmentation is a key feature of postsuburban life.
21. "About Islamic Foundation, Villa Park, IL," Islamic Foundation, http://www.islamicfoundation.org/index.php/about-ifs,
22. I use the terms "mosque" and "masjid" interchangeably, reflecting the usage of my conversation partners.
23. Marion Holmes Katz, *Prayer in Islamic Thought and Practice* (Cambridge: Cambridge University Press, 2013).
24. Marcia Hermansen, "Two-Way Acculturation: Between Individual Choice (Liminality) and Community Affiliation (Communitas)," in *The Muslims of America*, ed. Yvonne Hazbek Haddad (New York: Oxford University Press, 1991), 188–203. Hermansen argues that American Muslims experience racial and religious differences acutely in the diverse spaces of American Muslim communities.
25. Zareena Grewal documents this shift in second- and third-generation Muslims' understandings of marriage in her article "Marriage in Colour: Race, Religion, and Spouse Selection in Four American Mosques," *Ethnic and Racial Studies* 32, no. 2 (February 2009): 323–45.
26. Ibid, 325.

27. Fieldnotes, July 3, 2011.
28. Interview with the author, October 19, 2014, Naperville, IL.
29. Karim, *American Muslim Women*, 238.
30. Metcalf, *Making Muslim Space*, 3.
31. The Webb Foundation moved yet again in the fall of 2012 to a small private Muslim elementary school. From informal conversations with students, I heard that the space was less than ideal for adult members, who had to sit in desks and chairs designed for children.
32. Metcalf, *Making Muslim Space*, 3–4.
33. Barbara DeLollis, "Marriott Conference Center in Lisle, Ill., to Close," *USA Today*, September 30, 2011.
34. I take up the themes of experimentation and controversy in chapters 3 and 4.
35. Interview with the author, October 13, 2011, Darien, IL.
36. Here, Malika refers to journalist Genevieve Abdo's *Mecca on Main Street: Muslim Life in America after 9/11* (New York: Oxford University Press, 2006). The book documents younger Muslims' attempts to construct an American Muslim identity after 9/11. She focuses on the itineraries of prominent Muslim leaders and activists such as Shaykh Hamza Yusuf, Asra Nomani, Rami Nashashibi, and amina wadud.
37. The suburban strip mall could be seen as the counterpart to the Chicago storefront church, which emerged as a distinct institution in the early twentieth century. As Wallace Best demonstrates, while storefront churches were initially conceived as temporary spaces, they eventually became permanent institutions serving black migrants. See Wallace D. Best, *Passionately Human, No Less Divine: Religion and Culture in Black Chicago, 1915–1952* (Princeton, NJ: Princeton University Press, 2005), 51–61, 147–58.
38. Kathleen M. Moore, *Al-Mughtaribun: American Law and the Transformation of Muslim Life in the United States* (Albany: State University of New York Press, 1995), 117–33.
39. Ibid., 119–20.
40. Ernst, "Introduction: The Problem of Islamophobia," 3–4.
41. Joseph Ruzich, "MECCA Champions Willowbrook Mosque," *Chicago Tribune*, August 18, 2010; Bob Goldsborough, "DuPage Board Rejects Dome and Minaret for Mosque near Willowbrook," *Chicago Tribune*, March 13, 2012.
42. Corbett, *Making Moderate Islam*, 183–203.
43. Ibid.
44. Eric Lutz, "Walsh: Muslims Trying to Kill Americans," *Salon*, August 9, 2012.
45. I address the anti-sharia discourse in greater detail in chapter 6.
46. Interview with the author, March 20, 2011, Oak Brook, IL.
47. Karim, *American Muslim Women*.
48. In this account of Abd-Allah's biography, I rely on the lengthy interview he recently gave on the *Diffused Congruence* podcast: See *Diffused Congruence*,

Episode 32, "Dr. Umar Faruq Abd-Allah," http://diffusedcongruence.podbean.com/e/episode-32-dr-umar-faruq-abd-allah. Over the course of this project, I corresponded with Dr. Abd-Allah over e-mail and met him briefly at Webb events. Due to his extensive speaking commitments and time spent out of the country, I was unable to interview him for this project.

49. Abd-Allah recently published his dissertation as an academic monograph, *Malik and Medina: Islamic Legal Reasoning in the Formative Period* (Leiden: Brill, 2013).
50. "About Us," Nawawi Foundation, http://www.nawawi.org/?page_id=7.
51. For an analysis of the Deen Intensive program, see Karim, *American Muslim Women*, 144–48. Karim notes that many Deen Intensive participants were skeptical of Dr. Umar's approach, in particular his claim that American Muslims should take the "best of" American culture.
52. Interview with the author, October 23, 2011, Evanston, IL.
53. Interview with the author, October 15, 2014, Darien, IL.
54. Interview with the author, October 17, 2011, Burr Ridge, IL.
55. Interview with the author, October 13, 2011, Darien, IL.
56. Umar F. Abd-Allah, "Islam and the Cultural Imperative," Nawawi Foundation, 2007.
57. In the book's acknowledgments, Abd-Allah thanks various Webb board members for their assistance.
58. To avoid confusion, I refer to "M. A. R. Webb" to distinguish him from the foundation, which I refer to as simply "Webb" throughout.
59. Umar F. Abd-Allah, *A Muslim in Victorian America: The Life of Alexander Russell Webb* (New York: Oxford Unviersity Press, 2006), 276–77.
60. Abd-Allah's biography of Mohammed Alexander Russell Webb is considered the definitive academic work. Unless otherwise noted, I rely on Abd-Allah's account for M. A. R. Webb's biographical details, as many other scholars do. Cf. Ghanea Bassiri, *A History of Islam in the United States*, 113–22. There were both tensions and opportunities created by this and other overlaps between my field sources and the academic field of American Islam, a point that I discuss further in the conclusion.
61. Abd-Allah, *A Muslim in Victorian America*, 83.
62. Ibid., 53–61.
63. Ibid., 47–49. Abd-Allah provides a detailed and lengthy account of Webb's conversion to Islam, noting that it was a gradual process.
64. On the history of *The Moslem World*, see Brett D. Singleton, "*The Moslem World*: A History of America's Earliest Islamic Newspaper and Its Successors," *Journal of Muslim Minority Affairs* 27, no. 2 (August 2007): 297–307.
65. For an account of the downfall of M. A. R. Webb's missionary efforts, see Brett D. Singleton, "Brothers at Odds: Rival Islamic Movements in Late Nineteenth Century New York City," *Journal of Muslim Minority Affairs* 27, no. 3 (December 2007): 473–86.

66. On the ideologies of world religions at the World's Parliament, see Tomoko Masuzawa, *The Invention of World Religions* (Chicago: The University of Chicago Press, 2005).
67. Interview with the author, October 13, 2011, Darien, IL.

CHAPTER 2

1. Rogers Brubaker, "Categories of Analysis and Categories of Practice: A Note on the Study of Muslims in European Countries of Immigration," *Ethnic and Racial Studies* 36, no. 1 (January 2013): 4.
2. Brubaker argues that the objectification of Islam is particularly acute among Muslims in minority contexts. See Brubaker, "Categories of Analysis and Categories of Practice," 3.
3. Junaid Rana, *Terrifying Muslims: Race and Labor in the South Asian Diaspora* (Durham, NC: Duke University Press, 2011), 5.
4. Dale F. Eickelman and James P. Piscatori, *Muslim Politics* (Princeton, NJ: Princeton University Press, 2004), 38–39; Gregory Starrett, *Putting Islam to Work: Education, Politics, and Religious Transformation in Egypt* (Berkeley: University of California Press, 1998); Dale F. Eickelman, *Knowledge and Power in Morocco: The Education of a Twentieth-Century Notable* (Princeton, NJ: Princeton University Press, 1985). The extraction of religion from culture has a long history in colonial and postcolonial contexts. Dale Eickelman and James Piscatori argue that a central feature of modern Muslim discourses is what he calls the "objectification" of Islam, a shift that occurred as Muslims reflected on questions imbricated in modern conceptions of the self, such as "What is my religion? Why is it important in my life?" See Eickelman and Piscatori, *Muslim Politics*, 38. Muslim thinkers across the ideological spectrum have produced a host of responses to these questions, but they share a common concern for authenticity and the notion that Islam is a discernible religion that can be differentiated from other faiths. The objectification of religion is also closely connected to questions of religious pluralism and normative judgments between and among religions. For a critique of Eickelman and Piscatori's theory of objectification, see Hussein Ali Agrama, *Questioning Secularism: Islam, Sovereignty, and the Rule of Law in Modern Egypt* (Chicago: University of Chicago Press, 2012), 10–17.
5. Rogers Brubaker, *Ethnicity without Groups* (Cambridge, MA: Harvard University Press, 2004), 28–63.
6. Interview with the author, January 9, 2015, La Grange, IL.
7. On this anxiety, see Zareena Grewal, *Islam Is a Foreign Country*, 7.
8. Sylvia Chan-Malik, "Common Cause: On the Black-Immigrant Debate and Constructing the Muslim American," *Journal of Race, Ethnicity, and Religion* 2, no. 8 (May 2011): 1–39; Zareena Grewal, *Islam Is a Foreign Country*, 133; Karim, *American Muslim Women*, 4–11.

9. Khabeer, *Muslim Cool*, 15.
10. Zareena Grewal, *Islam Is a Foreign Country*, 132.
11. Interview with the author, January 9, 2015, La Grange, IL.
12. Sylvester A. Johnson, "The Rise of Black Ethnics: The Ethnic Turn in African American Religions, 1916–1945," *Religion and American Culture: A Journal of Interpretation* 20, no. 2 (2010): 130.
13. Chan-Malik, "Common Cause," 1–39; Shalini Shankar, *Desi Land: Teen Culture, Class, and Success in Silicon Valley* (Durham, NC: Duke University Press, 2008).
14. Johnson, "Rise of Black Ethnics," 127–28. Johnson argues that ethnicity is a "thoroughly historical construction," which "articulated difference among whites through the vocabularies of culture rather than biology."
15. Johnson, "Rise of Black Ethnics," 127.
16. Zareena Grewal, *Islam Is a Foreign Country*, 133; Karim, *American Muslim Women*, 4–11; Sunaina Maira, *Desis in the House: Indian American Youth Culture in New York City* (Philadelphia: Temple University Press, 2002); Bandana Purkayastha, *Negotiating Ethnicity: Second-Generation South Asian Americans Traverse a Transnational World* (New Brunswick, NJ: Rutgers University Press, 2005).
17. Rana, *Terrifying Muslims*, 45.
18. Chan-Malik, "Common Cause," 24.
19. Chan-Malik, "Common Cause," 25.
20. Prema A. Kurien, *A Place at the Multicultural Table: The Development of an American Hinduism* (New Brunswick, NJ: Rutgers University Press, 2007), 189–90.
21. Interview with the author, September 19, 2011, Chicago, IL.
22. Zareena Grewal, *Islam Is a Foreign Country*, 130. Grewal notes that the employment of foreign imams mirrors twentieth-century Catholic practices of hiring German, Irish, or Polish priests.
23. Ihsan Bagby, *Report Number 2 from the American Mosque Survey: Activities, Administration and Vitality of the American Mosque* (New York: Council on American Islamic Relations, 2012).
24. Marion Holmes Katz, *Women in the Mosque: A History of Legal Thought and Social Practice* (New York: Columbia University Press, 2014).
25. Masooda Bano and Hilary Kalmbach, "Introduction: Islamic Authority and the Study of Female Religious Leaders," in *Women, Leadership and Mosques: Changes in Contemporary Islamic Authority*, ed. Masooda Bano and Hilary Kalmbach (Leiden: Brill, 2012), 18.
26. Bano and Kalmbach, "Introduction," 23–24.
27. A fuller discussion of Webb engagement with "progressive" scholars appears in chapter 7.
28. Interview with the author, September 19, 2011, Chicago, IL.
29. Warner, Martel, and Dugan, "Islam Is to Catholicism as Teflon Is to Velcro," 50. In their focus groups of college-aged women, the authors found that

Latina Catholic women invoked the religion/culture distinction far less than their Muslim counterparts, a difference that they attributed to the fact that Catholicism is more "mainstream" in the United States than Islam. Muslims thus attempt to universalize Islam in order to accommodate and attain acceptance in American society. The language of "best of American culture" can be found on "Our History, Vision, and Mission," Webb Foundation, www.mohammedwebb.org/about.

30. For an insightful discussion of everyday uses of the term "FOB" among South Asian (both Hindu and Muslim) youth and their parents, see Shankar, *Desi Land*, 119–41.
31. Fieldnotes, May 22, 2011.
32. As I explore in chapter 4, Webb leaders make a deliberate point to start the organization's events at the designated hour, an implicit condemnation of social events in immigrant communities that tend to start late in the evening.
33. See Henri Lauzière, *The Making of Salafism: Islamic Reform in the Twentieth Century* (New York: Columbia University Press, 2016). For an overview of debates concerning the origins of Salafism and its taxonomization, see Ovamir Anjum, "Salafis and Democracy: Doctrine and Context," *The Muslim World* 106, no. 3 (July 2016): 448–73.
34. Lauzière, *Making of Salafism*, 28.
35. Natana J. DeLong-Bas, *Wahhabi Islam: From Revival and Reform to Global Jihad* (New York: Oxford University Press, 2004), 5. DeLong-Bas offers a detailed examination of Ibn Abd Al-Wahhab's thought, but in her effort to contest the negative image of Wahhabism, her account devolves into a celebration of her subject's accomplishments.
36. Roel Meijer, "Introduction," *Global Salafism: Islam's New Religious Movement* (New York: Oxford University Press, 2013), 5.
37. Lauzière, *Making of Salafism*, 201.
38. GhaneaBassiri, *A History of Islam in the United States*, 262; Edward Curtis IV, "Islamism and Its African American Muslim Critics: Black Muslims in the Era of the Arab Cold War," *American Quarterly* 59, no. 3 (September 2007): 683–709.
39. I have yet to find an ethnographic or historical study of these currents in the United States. Most of the literature comes from policy circles, is sensationalist, or is written by ex-Muslims. Post-9/11, some *Chicago Tribune* journalists investigated charges against the Mosque Foundation in Bridgeview to determine the extent of Saudi influence and terrorist accusations against imams. Noreen S. Ahmed-Ullah et al., "Hard-liners Won Battle for Bridgeview Mosque," *Chicago Tribune*, February 8, 2004.
40. Scholars are beginning to study Salafi trends within American Islamic institutions, but as I discuss in the conclusion, far more research among religious studies scholars is needed in this area to avoid the politicized

assumptions embedded in current studies. For a fairly balanced account of the transnational Salafi networks in Europe and the United States, see Roel Meijer, ed., *Global Salafism: Islam's New Religious Movement* (New York: Columbia University Press, 2009). For a discussion of Islamism and revivalism in US mosques, see Zareena Grewal, *Islam Is a Foreign Country*, 136–39.

41. In his study of Salafism in Nigeria, Alexander Thurston defines Salafism in terms of its "canon," calling attention to the complex intellectual origins of the Salafi approach. See Alexander Thurston, *Salafism in Nigeria: Islam, Preaching, and Politics* (Cambridge, UK: Cambridge University Press, 2016), 5–11.
42. GhaneaBassiri, *A History of Islam in the United States*, 229.
43. GhaneaBassiri, *A History of Islam in the United States*, 229.
44. For a discussion of these transnational changes, see Lila Ahmed, *A Quiet Revolution: The Veil's Resurgence from the Middle East to America* (New Haven, CT: Yale University Press, 2011). I take up the themes of gender and ritual practice in greater detail in chapter 4.
45. Interview with the author, February 8, 2014, Darien, IL.
46. Interview with the author, May 25, 2011, Naperville, IL.
47. Mahmood Mamdani, *Good Muslim, Bad Muslim: America, the Cold War, and the Roots of Terror* (New York: Three Leaves Press, 2004), 17–62.
48. Ernst, "Introduction: The Problem of Islamophobia"; Bruce B. Lawrence, *New Faiths, Old Fears: Muslims and Other Asian Immigrants in American Religious Life* (New York: Columbia University Press, 2002).
49. For an important essay on the historical surveillance of American Muslims, starting with the Nation of Islam, see Edward Curtis IV, "The Black Muslim Scare of the Twentieth Century: The History of State Islamophobia and Its Post-9/11 Variations," in *Islamophobia in America: The Anatomy of Intolerance*, ed. Carl Ernst (New York: Palgrave Macmillan, 2013), 75–106.
50. Louise Cainkar, *Homeland Insecurity: The Arab American and Muslim American Experience after 9/11* (New York: Russell Sage Foundation, 2011); Juliane Hammer, "Center Stage: Gendered Islamophobia and Muslim Women," in *Islamophobia in America: The Anatomy of Intolerance*, ed. Carl Ernst (New York: Palgrave Macmillan, 2013), 107–44.
51. "History, Mission, and Vision," Mohammed Webb Foundation, www.mohammedwebb.org/about.
52. I return to constellations of culture and choice at length in chapter 3.
53. Interview with the author, October 19, 2014, Naperville, IL.
54. Interview with the author, October 19, 2014, Naperville, IL.
55. Interview with the author, May 17, 2012, Chicago, IL.
56. Interview with the author, May 17, 2012, Chicago, IL.
57. Converts in the Webb book group shared similar stories; cf. chapter 7.
58. Sherman Jackson, *Islam and the Blackamerican: Looking Toward a Third Resurrection* (New York: Oxford University Press, 2011), 137–38.

59. For a theoretical discussion of "mapping" of the "Muslim World," see Zareena Grewal, *Islam Is a Foreign Country*, 4–11.
60. Interview with the author, October 17, 2014, Willowbrook, IL.
61. Zareena Grewal, *Islam Is a Foreign Country*, 62–63.
62. Marcia Hermansen, "Cultural Worlds/Culture Wars: Contemporary American Muslim Perspectives on the Role of Culture," *Journal of Islamic Law and Culture* 11, no. 3 (2009): 187–90. Islamist thinkers such as Sayyid Qutb (d. 1966) and Abu'l A'la Mawdudi (d. 1979) answered these questions by calling for the Islamization of social life in opposition to the encroachment of secular modernity characterized by a new state of ignorance and depravity. By contrast, modernist thinkers have argued that Muslims must embrace new political and economic realities, which for some require new ways of approaching Islamic sacred sources.
63. Interview with the author, October, 17, 2014, Willowbrook, IL.
64. Interview with the author, July 22, 2012, Oak Brook, IL.
65. Interview with the author, July 22, 2012, Oak Brook, IL.
66. Interview with the author, July 22, 2012, Oak Brook, IL.
67. American dating rituals were a common parenting concern among my female interviewees, many of whom had dated prior to converting to Islam, and now struggled to prohibit their daughters from doing the same.
68. Interview with the author, July 22, 2012, Oak Brook, IL.
69. Zareena Grewal, *Islam Is a Foreign Country*, 60–61, 136.
70. Interview with the author, July 22, 2012, Oak Brook, IL.

CHAPTER 3

1. Sophia Arjana, *Muslims in the Western Imagination* (New York: Oxford University Press, 2015).
2. Kathryn Lofton, *Oprah: The Gospel of an Icon* (Berkeley: University of California Press, 2011).
3. David Chidester, *Authentic Fakes: Religion and American Popular Culture* (Berkeley: University of California Press, 2005), 4.
4. Wilford, *Sacred Subdivisions*, 6. Historian Bethany Moreton theorizes how consumer capitalism became intertwined with "family values" and evangelical Christianity. As she writes, "The Wal-Mart mode of shopping removed several traditional stumbling blocks for Christian devotees of consumption. As long as mass buying could mean procuring humble products for the 'family,' as long as men could perform women's work without losing their authority . . . consumer capitalism could be born again." See Bethany Moreton, *To Serve God and Wal-Mart: The Making of Christian Free Enterprise* (Cambridge, MA: Harvard University Press, 2010), 89. In the aisles and the checkout counters, managers,

clerks, and (mainly female) consumers produced a vibrant and activist evangelical movement that transformed everyday acts of consumerism into meaning-laden activities.

5. Chidester, *Authentic Fakes*, 4–6. Historian of religion David Chidester argues that the "national religious impulses" that Robert Bellah identified as the cornerstones of American civil religion are now largely produced, disseminated, and contested within the realms of consumer and popular culture. That is, the ways that individuals and communities consume material goods, media representations, and experiences constitute contemporary American culture.
6. Inderpal Grewal, *Transnational America: Feminisms, Diaporas, Neoliberalisms* (Durham, NC: Duke University Press, 2005), 205.
7. Ibid., 9.
8. Interview with the author, May 22, 2011, Naperville, IL.
9. Sean McCloud, "Putting Some Class into Religious Studies: Resurrecting an Important Concept," *Journal of the American Academy of Religion* 75, no. 4 (December 2007): 842–43.
10. "About Us," Webb Foundation, http://www.mohammedwebb.org/about/.
11. Fieldnotes, March 20, 2011.
12. Shankar, *Desi Land*, 1–25.
13. Interview with the author, October 19, 2014, Naperville, IL.
14. For a discussion of "normal" and its relationship to leisure, see Mir, *Muslim American Women on Campus*.
15. "About Us," Webb Foundation, 2016, www.webbfound.org/about.
16. Courtney Bender, *The New Metaphysicals: Spirituality and the American Religious Imagination* (Chicago: The University of Chicago Press, 2010), 182–83.
17. Leigh Eric Schmidt, *Restless Souls: The Making of American Spirituality* (San Francisco: HarperSanFrancisco, 2005), 10–12.
18. GhaneaBassiri, *A History of Islam in the United States*, 118.
19. Schmidt, *Restless Souls*, 184. Schmidt argues that Webb exemplifies the "struggle at the heart of liberal spirituality" between the "firmness and fragility of religious identity."
20. Robert A. Orsi, *Between Heaven and Earth: The Religious Worlds People Make and the Scholars Who Study Them* (Princeton, NJ: Princeton University Press, 2005), 187–88.
21. Ibid.
22. On the history of the "spiritual" in American religious history, see Bender, *The New Metaphysicals*.
23. Lara Deeb and Mona Harb, *Leisurely Islam: Negotiating Geography and Morality in Shi'ite South Beirut* (Princeton, NJ: Princeton University Press, 2013), 9.
24. Interview with the author, January 9, 2015, La Grange, IL.
25. Interview with the author, May 25, 2012, Chicago, IL.

26. In this appropriation of (Protestant) middle-class identity, Webb Muslims are far from unique. Edward Curtis shows how the Nation of Islam appropriates these same ideals as Islamic. See Edward Curtis IV, *Black Muslim Religion in the Nation of Islam, 1960–1975* (Chapel Hill: The University of North Carolina Press, 2006), 9.
27. Interview with the author, October 17, 2014, Oakbrook, IL.
28. I draw on Shabana Mir's apt description of the condition of being American Muslim here. See Mir, *American Muslim Women on Campus*, 8–14.
29. Zareena Grewal, *Islam Is a Foreign Country*, 340.
30. Chidester, *Authentic Fakes*, 1–2.
31. Art Remillard, "Steelers Nation and the Seriously Religious Side of Football," *Marginalia*, August 28, 2013, http://marginalia.lareviewofbooks.org/steelers-nation-and-the-seriously-religious-side-of-football/.
32. Interview with the author, January 9, 2015, La Grange, IL.
33. Mahdi Tourage, "Performing Belief and Reviving Islam: Prominent (White Male) Converts in Muslim Revival Conventions," *Performing Islam* 1, no. 2 (2012): 212–14.
34. I do not presume any natural connection between whiteness and middle-class identity. Rather, I draw attention to the ways that Webb participants assume this connection in their understanding of mainstream America. The construction of whiteness is the product of historically contingent material and ideological processes that have produced shifting representations of "white" and "black" and their relationship to classed and gendered inequalities in the United States. As David Roediger has argued, nineteenth-century constructions of whiteness were inextricably linked to working-class identity. See David R. Roediger, *The Wages of Whiteness: Race and the Making of the American Working Class*, rev. ed. (London: Verso, 1999).
35. Marcia Hermansen,"Muslims in the Performative Mode: A Reflection on Muslim-Christian Dialogue," *Muslim World* 94, no. 3 (2004): 387–96; Tourage, "Performing Belief and Reviving Islam," 211.
36. Tourage, "Performing Belief and Reviving Islam," 212–14. Mahdi Tourage argues that white male converts are celebrated for "hyper-performing their muslimness" such that "the performative power of their idealized Muslim subjectivities is augmented by the advantages derived from their whiteness," 213, 217. Tourage argues that these performances enact belief among North American Muslims. He also relies heavily on the insights of Marcia Hermansen regarding the anxiety surrounding the authenticity of converts. See Hermansen, "Muslims in the Performative Mode," 392.
37. Zareena Grewal, *Islam Is a Foreign Country*, 105.
38. Tourage argues that Malcolm X offers a different conversion model, one in which the individual overcomes a childhood marred by dysfunctional families, poverty, and drugs to embrace Islam.
39. "Dr. Umar Faruq Abd-Allah," *Diffused Congruence* podcast, January 8, 2016. http://diffusedcongruence.podbean.com/e/episode-32-dr-umar-faruq-abd-allah/.

40. R. Laurence Moore, *Religious Outsiders and the Making of Americans* (New York: Oxford University Press, 1987).
41. Etan Diamond, "Beyond Borscht: The Kosher Lifestyle and the Religious Consumerism of Suburban Orthodox Jews," in *Faith in the Market: Religion and the Rise of Urban Commercial Culture*, ed. John Michael Giggie and Diane Winston (New Brunswick: Rutgers University Press, 2002), 228.
42. The history of housing discrimination practices, in Chicago and other northern and Midwestern cities, buttressed by support of federal and local governments, is now extensive. Arnold R. Hirsch, *Making the Second Ghetto: Race and Housing in Chicago 1940–1960* (Chicago: The University of Chicago Press, 1998); Charles Lamb, *Housing Segregation in Suburban America since 1960* (New York: Cambridge University Press, 2005); Natalie Y. Moore, *The South Side: A Portrait of American Segregation* (New York: St. Martin's Press, 2016); Beryl Satter, *Family Properties: Race, Real Estate, and the Exploitation of Black Urban America* (New York: Henry Holt and Company, 2009).
43. Schultz, *Tri-Faith America*, 7–9.
44. Schultz, *Tri-Faith America*, 5.
45. Curtis, *Black Muslim Religion*, 127–30.
46. Zareena Grewal, *Islam Is a Foreign Country*, 85.
47. Ibid., 89.
48. Ibid., 149–50.
49. Ibid., 150.
50. Curtis, *Islam in Black America*, 122–27.
51. Paul Numrich has argued that historical trajectories of different Muslim racial and ethnic groups in Chicago determined whether and in what manner communities embraced the ideal of a unified Muslim community or *ummah* that transcends racial divisions. He argues that in the case of the Mosque Foundation, Chicago's oldest and largest Arab mosque, *ummah* rhetoric is a recent development. Paul Numrich, "The Emergence of the Rhetoric of the Unified Ummah among American Muslims: The Case of Metropolitan Chicago," *The Journal of Muslim Minority Affairs* 32, no. 4 (2012): 450–51.
52. Sylvia Chan-Malik, "'Common Cause': On the Black-Immigrant Debate and Constructing the Muslim American," *Journal of Race, Ethnicity and Religion* 2, no. 8 (May 2011): 17.
53. Sherman A. Jackson, *Islam and the Blackamerican: Looking Toward the Third Resurrection* (New York: Oxford University Press, 2005), 3–6.
54. Ibid., 78.
55. Ibid., 77–78.
56. Interview with the author, October 19, 2014, Naperville, IL.
57. Carolyn Chen notes that Taiwanese Christians use these activities to evangelize to non-Christians. See Carolyn Chen, "The Religious Varieties of Ethnic Presence: A Comparison between a Taiwanese Immigrant Buddhist Temple

and an Evangelical Christian Church," *Sociology of Religion* 63, no. 2 (2002): 224. Webb prides itself on the openness of its community to non-Muslims, though I never encountered any form of evangelization in the organization. As chapter 5 explores more fully, the prospect of converting non-Muslims to Islam was practically unthinkable among members of the Webb community.

58. Nancy F. Cott, *Public Vows: A History of Marriage and the Nation* (Cambridge, MA: Harvard University Press, 2000).
59. For an expansive history of companionate marriage, see Stephanie Coontz, *Marriage, a History: How Love Conquered Marriage* (New York: Viking, 2005).
60. Jennifer S. Hirsch and Holly Wardlow, eds., *Modern Loves: The Anthropology of Romantic Courtship and Companionate Marriage* (Ann Arbor: University of Michigan Press, 2009), 11.
61. Interview with the author, October 19, 2011, Chicago, IL.
62. Kathryn Lofton, "Religion and the Authority in American Parenting," 84, no. 3 (June 2016): 4.
63. Interview with the author, October 11, 2011, Willowbrook, IL.
64. Elaine Tyler May, *Homeward Bound: American Families in the Cold War Era* (New York: Basic Books, 2008).
65. Lofton, "Religion and the Authority in American Parenting," 20–21.
66. Marcia Inhorn, *The New Arab Man: Emergent Masculinities, Technologies, and Islam in the Middle East* (Princeton, NJ: Princeton University Press, 2012), 57. For a full description of the "hegemonic" construction of Middle Eastern masculinity, see 48–57.
67. Ibid., 49.
68. Ibid., 50.
69. Arjana, *Muslims in the Western Imagination*, 8–18.
70. For a discussion of masculinity and Muslim men in German, see Katherine Ewing, *Stolen Honor: Stigmatizing Muslim Men in Berlin* (Palo Alto, CA: Stanford University Press, 2008), 2–6.
71. Lila Abu-Lughod, *Do Muslim Women Need Saving?* (Cambridge, MA: Harvard University Press, 2013).
72. Inhorn, *The New Arab Man*, 1–2.
73. The scholarship on Muslim masculinities is now a burgeoning field of study. In addition to Ewing's work, in this discussion I draw especially on Inhorn, *The New Arab Man*. For a perspective on masculinity and Muslim sacred texts, see Arjana, *Muslims in the Western Imagination*; Amanullah de Sondy, *The Crisis of Islamic Masculinities* (London: Bloomsbury Academic, 2014). See also Farha Ghannam, *Live and Die Like a Man: Gender Dynamics in Urban Egypt* (Palo Alto, CA: Stanford University Press, 2014).
74. Interview with the author, October 19, 2014, Naperville, IL.
75. Interview with the author, January 9, 2015, La Grange, IL.

76. "Muslim Group Donates Turkeys to Needy Families," *ABC News*, November 12, 2009, http://abc7chicago.com/archive/6523354/.
77. Interview with the author, January 9, 2015, La Grange, IL.
78. Interview with the author, January 9, 2015, La Grange, IL.
79. See Khabeer, *Muslim Cool*, 16–17, 36–37. See also Garbi Schmidt, *Islam in Urban America*, 41–61. Schmidt focuses almost exclusively on immigrant communities, a scholarly omission that obscures the role of IMAN and similar community-based organizations oriented across this false divide between immigrant/black Muslims.
80. "Staff," Inner-City Muslim Action Network, http://www.imancentral.org/about/staff/.
81. For a discussion of IMAN's role in antiracism efforts and constructing "Muslim Cool," see Khabeer, *Muslim Cool*, 2–3, 38–40.
82. Khabeer, *Muslim Cool*, 2–3.
83. Ibid., 198.
84. Rosemary R. Corbett, "For God and Country: Religious Minorities Striving for National Belonging through Community Service," *Religion and American Culture: A Journal of Interpretation* 26, no. 2 (Summer 2016): 227–59.
85. Interview with the author, January 9, 2015, La Grange, IL.
86. Zareena Grewal, *Islam Is a Foreign Country*, 154–56.
87. Juan Perez Jr., "Study Looks at Aftermath of Chicago School Closings in 2013," *Chicago Tribune*, January 22, 2015, http://www.chicagotribune.com/news/local/breaking/ct-chicago-school-closings-study-met-20150122-story.html.
88. Interview with the author, October 19, 2014, Oak Brook, IL.
89. The Mosque Foundation in Bridgeview, which serves the well-established Arab community on the southwest side of the city, added solar panels and achieved LEED certification in 2008. Interview with the author, July 7, 2011, Chicago, IL. For a discussion of the mosque's environment in the context of interfaith environmentalism in Chicago, see Amanda J. Baugh, *God and the Green Divide: Religious Environmentalism in Black and White* (Berkeley: University of California Press, 2016), 79–82.
90. Baugh, *God and the Green Divide*, 81–2.
91. Corbett, "For God and Country," 243–4.
92. Ibid., 228–9.
93. Ibid., 247. See also Corbett, *Making Moderate Islam*, 205–9.

CHAPTER 4

1. Regula Burckhardt Qureshi, "Transcending Space: Recitation and Community among South Asian Muslims in Canada," in *Making Muslim Space in North America and Europe*, ed. Barbara Daly Metcalf (Berkeley: University of California

Press, 1996), 53–56. Qureshi's descriptions focus on South Asian immigrants, but they correspond to my informants' narratives of *mawlids* from their childhoods.

2. Despite the ritual's popularity, the scholarly literature on *mawlids* remains sparse. For historical accounts of *mawlids*, see N. J. G. Kaptein, "Materials for the History of the Prophet Muhammad's Birthday Celebration in Mecca," *Der Islam* 69 (1992): 193–246; *Muhammad's Birthday Festival: Early History in the Central Muslim Lands and Development in the Muslim West until the 10th/16th Century* (Leiden: Brill, 1993); Marion Katz, *The Birth of the Prophet Muhammad: Devotional Piety in Sunni Islam* (London: Routledge, 2007). For ethnographic accounts of the *mawlid*, see Marion Katz, "Women's 'Mawlid' Performances in Sanaa and the Construction of 'Popular Islam,'" *International Journal of Middle East Studies* 40, no. 3 (August 2008): 467–84; Samuli Schielke, "Hegemonic Encounters: Criticism of Saints-Day Festivals and the Formation of Modern Islam in Late 19th and Early 20th-Century Egypt," *Die Welt des Islams* 47, nos. 3–4 (2007): 319–55; *The Perils of Joy: Contesting Mulid Festivals in Contemporary Egypt* (Syracuse: Syracuse University Press, 2012); Nancy Tapper and Richard Tapper, "The Birth of the Prophet: Ritual and Gender in Turkish Islam," *Man* 22, no. 1 (March 1987): 69–92. For an Orientalist account of *mawlid* performances, see C. Snouck Hurgronje, *Mekka in the Latter Part of the 19th Century*, trans. J. H. Monahan (Leiden: Brill, 1970).
3. Fieldnotes, March 20, 2011.
4. Fieldnotes, March 20, 2011.
5. For this definition, see William Rory Dickson, *Living Sufism in North America: Between Tradition and Transformation* (Albany: State University of New York, 2015), 39; Carl W. Ernst, "Sufism, Islam, and Globalization in the Contemporary World: Methodological Reflections on a Changing Field of Study," in *In Memoriam: The 4th Victor Danner Memorial Lecture* (Bloomington, IN: Department of Near Eastern Languages and Cultures, 2009).
6. For an account of Muhammad's cosmological and theological significance, see Omid Safi, *Memories of Muhammad: Why the Prophet Matters* (New York: HarperCollins, 2009). On constructions and contestations over Muhammad, see Jonathan C. Brown, *Misquoting Muhammad: The Challenges and Choices of Interpreting the Prophet's Legacy* (New York: Oneworld, 2014).
7. Fieldnotes, October 11, 2014.
8. For a discussion of embodiment and knowledge in Islam, see Rudolph Ware III, *The Walking Qur'an: Islamic Education, Embodied Knowledge, and History in West Africa* (Chapel Hill: The University of North Carolina Press, 2014).
9. Interview with the author, October 17, 2014, Oak Brook, IL.
10. Interview with the author, October 13, 2011, Darien, IL.
11. Qureshi, "Transcending Space," 56.

12. Ibid.
13. Juliane Hammer, *American Muslim Women, Religious Authority, and Activism: More than a Prayer* (Austin: University of Texas Press, 2012).
14. For an excellent volume on female religious authority within mosques, focusing especially on contexts outside of the United States, see Masooda Bano and Hilary Kalmbach, eds., *Women, Leadership, and Mosques: Changes in Contemporary Islamic Authority* (Leiden: Brill, 2012).
15. Ingrid Mattson, "Can a Woman Be an Imam? Debating Form and Function in Muslim Women's Leadership," ingridmattson.org/article/can-a-woman-be-an-imam/. Last updated June 20, 2005.
16. Hammer, *American Muslim Women, Religious Authority, and Activism*, 144–46.
17. Katz, "Women's 'Mawlid' Performances in Sanaa," 468.
18. Fieldnotes, February 8, 2014.
19. Katz, *Birth of the Prophet Muhammad*, 63–102.
20. Schielke, "Hegemonic Encounters," 324.
21. Katz, *The Birth of the Prophet Muhammad*, 1–5, 169–201.
22. Katz, *Birth of the Prophet Muhammad*, 67. Katz uses the *mawlid* to dispute A. Kevin Reinhart's claim in *Before Revelation* that thanking God became "categorically different from thanking another human being." Katz argues that *mawlid* practices demonstrate the persistence of the transactional model. See A. Kevin Reinhart, *Before Revelation: The Boundaries of Muslim Moral Thought* (Albany: State University of New York Press, 1995).
23. Katz, *Birth of the Prophet Muhammad*, 198.
24. Ibid., 123.
25. Ibid., 130–31. Katz discusses how scholars differed on the question of whether standing was a spontaneous outpouring of emotion or a recognized social act of reverence and respect.
26. Ibid., 170–74. Katz pays less attention to new defenses of the *mawlid*, though she mentions some anti-Wahhabi polemics that claim the legitimacy of *mawlid* performances.
27. Schielke, "Hegemonic Encounters," 345.
28. Katz, *Birth of the Prophet Muhammad*, 174–82.
29. Ibid., 177.
30. Katz, "Women's 'Mawlid' Performances," 467–70. Katz shows how *mawlid* participants and scholars in Yemen describe the *mawlid* as a form of "popular Islam" distinct from that of scholarly practices. See Katz, "Women's 'Mawlid' Performances," 467. The term can be used to uphold certain forms of *mawlid* practice as legitimate and normative within the Islamic tradition while delegitimating other forms of practice.
31. Ibid., 470.
32. Katz, *Birth of the Prophet Muhammad*, 169.

33. Schielke, "Hegemonic Encounters," 327–28.
34. Schielke, *The Perils of Joy*, 53–80.
35. Event Program, Webb Foundation Grand Mawlid, February 8, 2014.
36. Fieldnotes, February 8, 2014.
37. Fieldnotes, February 8, 2014.
38. Mucahit Bilici, *Finding Mecca in America* (Chicago: The University of Chicago Press, 2012), 88.
39. Ibid., 83.
40. Zareena Grewal, *Islam Is a Foreign Country*, 150.
41. Carl Ernst, *The Shambhala Guide to Sufism* (Boston: Shambhala, 1997), 8–18.
42. Abd-Allah, *A Muslim in Victorian America*, 67.
43. Marcia Hermansen, "Hybrid Identity Formations in Muslim America: The Case of American Sufi Movements," *Muslim World* 90, nos. 1–2 (Spring 2000): 158–97.
44. Wade Clark Roof, *A Generation of Seekers: The Spiritual Journeys of the Baby Boomer Generation* (San Francisco: Harper San Francisco, 1994).
45. Hermansen, "Hybrid Identity Formations in Muslim America," 187.
46. Hermansen, "Hybrid Identity Formations in Muslim America," 189. See also Dickson, *Living Sufism in North America*, 7.
47. G. A. Lipton, "Secular Sufism: Neoliberalism, Ethnoracism, and the Reformation of the Muslim Other," *The Muslim World* 101, no. 3 (2011): 427–40.
48. Ibid., 434.
49. Ibid., 438.
50. Wendy Brown, *Regulating Aversion: Tolerance in the Age of Identity and Empire* (Princeton, NJ: Princeton University Press, 2006).
51. Robert A. Orsi, *History and Presence* (Cambridge, MA: Harvard University Press, 2016), 4.
52. Interview with the author, February 8, 2014, Darien, IL.
53. For further reading on Kabbani's advocacy on behalf of Sufism in the United States, see Dickson, *Living Sufism in North America*, 121–24.
54. Katz, *Birth of the Prophet Muhammad*, 188.
55. For the full text of Kabbani's and al-Qaradawi's fatwas, see "Mawlid," As-Sunna Foundation of America, http://www.sunnah.org/ibadaat/mawlid.htm.
56. Kabbani, "Mawlid."
57. Katz, *Birth of the Prophet Muhammad*, 191. Katz notes that Kabbani's suggestion was likely tongue-in-cheek.
58. Katz calls this move a "homogenization" of time, such that the *mawlid*'s timing is incidental to its pedagogical import. See Katz, *Birth of the Prophet Muhammad*, 153–63. Such a view of time is shared by both *mawlid* proponents and opponents. For a discussion of reconfigurations of time and modernity in colonial and postcolonial contexts, see Dipesh Chakrabarty, *Provincializing Europe: Postcolonial Thought and Historical Difference* (Princeton, NJ: Princeton University Press, 2007).

59. Katz argues that Kabbani's fatwa represents a "secularization" of *mawlid* performances. See Katz, *Birth of the Prophet Muhammad*, 191. This secularization seems to be connected to Kabbani's lack of emphasis on the cosmological significance of the *mawlid* and his comparison of the *mawlid* to patriotic celebrations. Here, though secular signals the privileging of the nation-state as the highest moral good, Katz does not use "secular" to separate economic from religious activity. Monetary exchange, festive elements, eating, and socializing in premodern *mawlid* performances are all part of the nexus of devotional practices that she explains.
60. Itzchak Weismann, *The Naqshbandiyya: Orthodoxy and Activism in a Worldwide Sufi Tradition* (London: Routledge, 2007), 166–70.
61. Personal correspondence, Jawad Qureshi, August 7, 2014.
62. Many of these ongoing debates over *mawlid* legitimacy take place online. See Jonas Svensson, "ITZ BIDAH BRO!!!!! GT ME??—YouTube Mawlid and Voices of Praise and Blame," in *Muslims and the New Information and Communication Technologies: Notes from an Emerging and Infinite Field*, ed. Thomas Hoffmann and Göran Larsson (New York: Springer, 2013), 89–111.
63. Zareena Grewal, *Islam Is a Foreign Country*, 163.
64. Schielke, *Perils of Joy*, 13.
65. Dr. Abd-Allah's talk was uploaded on August 26, 2012. https://www.youtube.com/watch?v=_Jb5GYkJxaY.
66. See Ovamir Anjum, *Politics, Law, and Community: The Taymiyyan Moment* (New York: Cambridge University Press, 2012); Yosef Rapaport and Shahab Ahmed,eds. *Ibn Taymiyya and His Times* (New York: Oxford University Press, 2010).
67. Raquel M. Ukeles, "The Sensitive Puritan? Revisiting Ibn Taymiyya's Approach to Law and Spirituality in Light of 20th-Century Debates on the Prophet's Birthday (mawlid al-nabī)," in *Ibn Taymiyya and His Times*, ed. Yosef Rapaport and Shahab Ahmed (New York: Oxford University Press, 2010), 319–27.
68. Ibid., 319–27.
69. Hamza Yusuf, "What is *Mawlid*?" https://www.youtube.com/watch?v=2x14RQLgB9s. Uploaded October 6, 2011.
70. Zareena Grewal, *Islam Is a Foreign Country*, 160–69.
71. Interview with the author, October 17, 2014, Oak Brook, IL.

CHAPTER 5

1. Jonathan Boyarin, ed., *The Ethnography of Reading* (Berkeley: University of California Press, 1993), 212–13; James S. Bielo, *Words upon the Word: An Ethnography of Evangelical Group Bible Study* (New York: New York University Press, 2009); *The Social Life of Scriptures: Cross-Cultural Perspectives on Biblicism* (New Brunswick, NJ: Rutgers University Press, 2009).

2. Boyarin, "Introduction," *Ethnography of Reading*, 3–4.
3. Bielo, *Words upon the Word*, 11. Bielo identifies similar motivations among participants in Protestant evangelical bible groups in the Midwest.
4. Bender and Klassen, *After Pluralism*, 1–3.
5. Ibid.
6. For an overview of other institutions of Muslim learning in the United States, see Zareena Grewal and R. David Coolidge, "Islamic Education in the United States," in *The Cambridge Companion of American Islam*, ed. Juliane Hammer and Omid Safi (Cambridge: Cambridge University Press, 2013), 246–65.
7. Islamic religious instruction takes place in a variety of settings in the United States, usually under the guidance of scholars, shaykhs, or other knowledgeable members of Muslim communities. For example, most mosques hold adult classes devoted to the Qur'an, usually on Sundays and weekday evenings. These classes focus on various topics, such as *tafsīr* (Quranic interpretation), *tajwīd* (rules of Quranic recitation), *fiqh* (Islamic jurisprudence), and the Arabic language. Like the Webb community, many educational foundations have grown out of less formal communities, and over time they have become more established institutions devoted to a particular theological worldview or institutional framework.
8. Interview with the author, May 9, 2011, Skokie, IL.
9. Interview with the author, May 9, 2011, Skokie, IL.
10. Interview with the author, October 10, 2011, Evanston, IL.
11. Interview with the author, May 9, 2011, Skokie, IL.
12. Interview with the author, March 28, 2011, Darien, IL.
13. Interview with the author, October 16, 2014, Willowbrook, IL.
14. Until recently, Western scholars working under the Orientalist tradition have primarily analyzed the literary features of the written Qur'an, tracing its philological features and situating its content within sociopolitical and religious developments of seventh-century Arabia. Among the "classic" works are Richard Bell, *Introduction to the Qur'an* (Edinburgh: University Press, 1953); and John Wansbrough, *Quranic Studies: Sources and Methods of Scriptural Interpretation* (Oxford: Oxford University Press, 1977). These early works stressed the formation of the Qur'an in a Jewish and especially Christian context and disputed the traditional Muslim account of the Qur'an's compilation during the early decades of Islam. Scholars such as Patricia Crone and Andrew Rippin similarly dispute the Muslim narrative of the Qur'an's origins; see Patricia Crone and Michael Cook, *Hagarism: The Making of the Islamic World* (Cambridge: Cambridge University Press, 1977); and Andrew Rippin, *The Qur'an: Formative Interpretation* (Brookfield: Ashgate, 1999). The excellent work of Michael Sells focuses on the connections between the textual and literary features and oral practices. See Michael A. Sells, *Early Islamic Mysticism, Early Islamic Mysticism: Sufi, Qur'an, Miraj, Poetic and Theological Writings* (New York:

Paulist Press, 1996); *Approaching the Qur'an: The Early Revelations* (Ashland, OR: White Cloud Press, 1999).

15. For the role of recitation in Muslim ritual life, see Anna Gade, *Perfection Makes Practice: Learning, Emotion, and the Recited Qur'an* (Honolulu: University of Hawai'i Press, 2004); Kristina Nelson, *The Art of Reciting the Qur'an* (Austin: University of Texas Press, 1986); Rudolph Ware III, *The Walking Qur'an: Islamic Education, Embodied Knowledge, and History in West Africa* (Chapel Hill: The University of North Carolina Press, 2014).
16. Carl Ernst, *How to Read the Qur'an: A New Guide* (Chapel Hill: The University of North Carolina Press, 2011), 59–60.
17. Fieldnotes, April 15, 2012.
18. Mohammad Hashim Kamali, *Principles of Islamic Jurisprudence* (Cambridge: Islamic Texts Society, 2003), 58.
19. Carl Ernst, *Following Muhammad: Rethinking Islam in the Contemporary World* (Chapel Hill: The University of North Carolina Press, 2003).
20. Frederick Denny, *An Introduction to Islam*, 2nd ed. (New York: Macmillan, 1994), 158.
21. Carolyn Rouse, *Engaged Surrender: African American Women and Islam* (Berkeley: University of California Press, 1998), 36. Rouse argues that African American Sunnī women oppose male patriarchy and US racial injustice by asserting their ability to perform *tafsīr*, a discipline usually reserved for educated males. The women maintain that the Qur'an promotes a model of gender equality. Expanding the term outside of its specific legal meaning, Rouse describes *ijmāʿ* as "authoritative community consensus" and "praxis." See Rouse, *Engaged Surrender*, 18–21, 164–9. Likewise, Webb participants do not employ the term "*asbāb al-nuzūl*," but I find it to be analytically useful to describe how they make sense of context in debating the meaning of the Qur'an.
22. Walid Saleh, *The Formation of the Classical Tafsīr Tradition: The Qurʾān Commentary of al-Thaʿlabī (D. 427/1035)* (Leiden: Brill, 2004), 14–16.
23. Karen Bauer, ed. *Aims, Methods, and Contexts of Qur'anic Exegesis: 2nd/8th–9th/15th Centuries* (London: Oxford University Press, 2013), 7–10.
24. Bauer, ed., introduction to *Aims, Methods, and Contexts*, 8.
25. Andrew Rippin, "The Function of Asbab al-Nuzul in Quranic Exegesis," *Bulletin of the School of Oriental and African Studies* 1 (1988), 1–20.
26. Rippin argues that the "jāhilī foil" both highlighted the depravity of the pre-Islamic era and preserved the continuity of the Abrahamic legacy by confirming the fulfillment of God's covenant through the revelation of the Qur'an and the establishment of the Islamic community. See Rippin, "The Function of Asbab al-Nuzul in Quranic Exegesis," 10.
27. Juan Campo, *Encyclopedia of Islam* (New York: Facts On File, 2009), 652–54.
28. Kamali, *Principles of Islamic Jurisprudence*, 24.

29. Charles Kurzman, ed., *Liberal Islam: A Source-Book* (New York: Oxford University Press, 2004), 6.
30. The term "liberal" in Kurzman's study has a very broad meaning, one that does not necessarily accurately apply to all of the authors in the edited volume. In the case of the Webb Foundation and M. A. R. Webb, however, we have seen the importance of many liberal principles as articulated in the US context, and that also have resonance for certain intellectual trends in modern Islam.
31. Hammer, *American Muslim Women, Religious Authority, and Activism*, 66–70. Hammer points out that Rahman likely would not have supported the feminist approaches that have drawn on his work.
32. Fazlur Rahman, *Islam and Modernity: Transformation of an Intellectual Tradition* (Chicago: University of Chicago Press, 1982), 20.
33. Ibid. Rahman argues here that it "is not difficult" to determine the "real point" of a Qur'anic verse.
34. Kurzman, *Liberal Islam*, 312.
35. M. A. S. Abdel Haleem, trans., *The Qur'an* (Oxford: Oxford University Press, 2004). All subsequent translations are taken from this text.
36. Mahmoud Ayoub, *The Qur'an and Its Interpreters* (Albany: State University of New York Press, 1984), 1:199–203.
37. Reuven Firestone, "Disparity and Resolution in the Quranic Teachings on War: A Reevaluation of a Traditional Problem," *Journal of Near Eastern Studies* 56, no. 1 (1997): 1–19.
38. Talal Asad, *Formations of the Secular: Christianity, Islam, Modernity* (Stanford, CA: Stanford University Press, 2003), 10–11.
39. Fieldnotes, April 15, 2012.
40. Fieldnotes, April 15, 2012.
41. Sherman Jackson, "Jihad and the Modern World," *The Journal of Islamic Law and Culture* 7, no. 1 (2002): 8.
42. amina wadud, *Qur'an and Woman: Rereading the Sacred Text from a Woman's Perspective*, 2nd ed. (New York: Oxford University Press, 1999), 30–31; ʿAbd Allah Ahmad Naʿīm, *Toward an Islamic Reformation: Civil Liberties, Human Rights, and International Law* (Syracuse, NY: Syracuse University Press, 1990)' Mahmūd Muhammad Tāhā, *The Second Message of Islam* (Syracuse, NY: Syracuse University Press, 1987).
43. wadud, *Qur'an and Woman*, 30. wadud argues that once the reason for revealing the verse no longer exists, then the "universal" or "extra-historical" nature of the Qur'an is removed.
44. This story also appears in Q. 5:57–59 and Q. 7.166.
45. Fieldnotes, March 29, 2012.
46. Ayoub, *The Qur'an and Its Interpreters*, 1:109–11.

47. Ibid., 1:110.
48. Farid Esack, "The Portrayal of Jews and the Possibilities for Their Salvation in the Qur'an," in *Between Heaven and Hell: Islam, Salvation, and the Fate of Others*, ed. Mohammad Hassan Khalil (Oxford: Oxford University Press, 2013), 220–21.
49. Jeffrey Goldberg, "Nizzar Rayyan on God's Hatred of Jews," *Atlantic*, January 2, 2009, http://www.theatlantic.com/international/archive/2009/01/nizar-rayyan-of-hamas-on-god-apos-s-hatred-of-jewsh/9278/.
50. Ibid.
51. Fieldnotes, April 15, 2012.
52. Fessenden, *Culture and Redemption*, 215. Fessenden argues that this containment of irrationality for the sake of democracy is a key feature of modern secularism in the United States. This reverence for rationality along these specific lines is derived from liberal Protestantism. See also Orsi, *Between Heaven and Earth*, 178–79, 183–85.
53. Webb Keane, *Christian Moderns: Freedom and Fetish in the Mission Encounter* (Berkeley: University of California Press, 2007), 16–21, 49–58. For a critique of liberal conceptions of agency and freedom, see Saba Mahmood, *Politics of Piety: The Islamic Revival and the Feminist Subject* (Princeton, NJ: Princeton University Press, 2005), 1–39.
54. Keane, *Christian Moderns*, 60. Keane draws on the previously cited quotation from Asad, *Formations of the Secular*, 10–11.
55. Fieldnotes, March 20, 2012.
56. Fieldnotes, March 20, 2012.
57. The command to fast during the month of Ramadan, during which the Qur'an was revealed to the Prophet Mohammed, is also found in Q. 2:185.
58. Fieldnotes, April 29, 2012.
59. Ayoub, *The Qur'an and Its Interpreters*, 1:109–16.
60. Q. 2:40; Q. 2:47; Q. 5:44; and Q. 46:16. See Esack, "The Portrayal of Jews," 207–8.
61. Esack, "The Portrayal of the Jews," 214.
62. Mohammad Hassan Khalil, *Islam and the Fate of Others: The Salvation Question* (New York: Oxford University Press, 2012).
63. Ernst, *Following Muhammad*, 45–46.
64. Khalil, *Islam and the Fate of Others*, 7.
65. Ibid., 20. All four thinkers in Khalil's study embrace different forms of inclusivism.
66. Ibid., 12–13.
67. Khalil points out that pluralists can still maintain that Islam is superior to Christianity and Judaism even as they recognize the salvific benefit of the other monotheistic traditions. For other work exploring these dimensions, see Shah-Kazemi, *The Spirit of Tolerance in Islam*.
68. Bender and Klassen, *After Pluralism*, 1.

69. Rosemary R. Hicks, "Religious Pluralism, Secularism, and Interfaith Endeavors," in *The Cambridge Companion to American Islam*, ed. Juliane Hammer and Omid Safi (New York: Cambridge University Press, 2013), 156–58.
70. Cainkar, *Homeland Insecurity*, 6.
71. Fessenden, *Culture and Redemption*, 215.
72. Fred Donner, "The Death of Abu Tālib," in *Love and Death in the Ancient Near East: Essays in Honor of Marvin H. Pope*, ed. John H. Marks and Robert M. Good (Guilford, CN: Four Quarters Publishing Company, 1987), 237–46.
73. Donner translates the hadith as follows: "Perhaps my intercession will help [Abu Tālib] on judgment day and make for him a shoal of fire reaching [only] to his heels, from which his brains will boil." See Donner, "The Death of Abu Tālib," 239.
74. Fieldnotes May 5, 2012.
75. Abu Tālib's fate has not always engendered debates about the fate of non-Muslims. Rather, as Donner shows, this hadith played a prominent role in contestations over religious leadership and early delineations of Sunni and Shi'i communities.
76. Jackson, "Jihad and the Modern World," 10. Jackson claims that Qutb's ideas are among the most widely read among contemporary Muslims.
77. Khalil, *Islam and the Fate of Others*, 134–35.
78. Interview with the author, July 24, 2012.
79. Fieldnotes, April 29, 2012.
80. John R. Bowen, "On Scriptural Essentialism and Ritual Variation: Muslim Sacrifice in Sumatra and Morocco," *American Ethnologist* 19, no. 4 (1992): 656–671; Elaine Combs-Schilling, *Sacred Performances: Islam, Sexuality, and Sacrifice* (New York: Columbia University Press, 1989).

CHAPTER 6

1. Interview with the author, October 13, 2011, Darien, IL.
2. See Q. 2:73; 5:3; 5:20; 6:145; 16:115. These guidelines are determined locally and are the subject of dispute. "Halal" refers to meat that Muslims consider to be permissible. The term "*zabīha*" refers to the specific technique of killing the animal by slitting its throat. But the specific means of halal are constructed at the local level. Many Muslims I met accept kosher meat as halal, while others maintain that it is necessary to find a grocery store that guarantees *zabīha* meat.
3. Kambiz GhaneaBassiri, "Religious Normativity and Praxis among American Muslims," in *The Cambridge Companion to American Islam*, ed. Juliane Hammer and Omid Safi (New York: Cambridge University Press, 2013), 208–28. Drawing on the work of John Bowen, Edward Curtis IV makes a similar claim regarding the Nation of Islam, arguing that religious expression is best understood

"not as abstracted windows into belief or as essential statements of religious truth, but as specific events of speaking, commenting, and reflecting, that help to illuminate what it meant, for the believers, to be members of a religious community, to perform religious acts, and to abide by religious rules." See Curtis, *Black Muslim Religion*, 6; John R. Bowen, *Muslims through Discourse: Religion and Ritual in Gayo Society* (Princeton, NJ: Princeton University Press, 1993).

4. GhaneaBassiri, "Religious Normativity," 208–9.
5. GhaneaBassiri, "Religious Normativity," 209. GhaneaBassiri acknowledges that Muslims idealize sharia as universal and timeless, even as communities and individuals implement local understandings of it according to political, economic, social, and cultural factors.
6. GhaneaBassiri, "Religious Normativity," 213.
7. Kamali, *Principles of Islamic Jurisprudence*, 323–35. Wael B. Hallaq, *Shari'a: Theory, Practice, Transformations* (Cambridge: Cambridge University Press, 2009), 84–85.
8. Hallaq, *Shari'a: Theory, Practice, Transformations*, 84.
9. The practice of *talfiq* became popular in legal codes developed after the colonial period.
10. Interview with the author, July 22, 2012, Oak Brook, IL.
11. Hallaq, *Shari'a: Theory, Practice, Transformations*, 85.
12. Kamali, *Principles of Islamic Jurisprudence*, 329–31.
13. Hallaq, *Shari'a: Theory, Practice, Transformations*, 84–85.
14. Su'ad Abdul Khabeer, "Rep That Islam: The Rhyme and Reason of American Islamic Hip Hop," *Muslim World* 97 (January 2007): 125–41.
15. Ibid., 128 and n. 13.
16. Ibid., 128.
17. Ibid., 128–30.
18. Jonas Otterbeck, "Battling Over the Public Sphere: Islamic Reactions to the Music of Today," *Contemporary Islam* 2, no. 3 (December 2008): 211–28.
19. The question of music also surfaced in the Webb book club, particularly around the case of Yusuf Islam.
20. Interview with the author, July 28, 2011, Oak Brook, IL.
21. Interview with the author, May 2, 2012, Naperville, IL.
22. Robert Orsi, *Between Heaven and Earth: Religious Worlds and the Scholars Who Study Them* (Princeton, NJ: Princeton University Press, 2005), 77.
23. Ibid., 85; original emphasis.
24. Jonathan Sarna, *American Judaism: A History* (New Haven, CT: Yale University Press, 2004), 284–85.
25. Kurien, *A Place at the Multicultural Table*, 67–71.
26. Interview with the author, May 2, 2012, Naperville, IL.
27. Suhaib Webb and Scott Korb, "No Room for Radicals," *New York Times*, April 25, 2013.

28. Interview with the author, May 2, 2012, Naperville, IL.
29. Kathleen M. Moore, *The Unfamiliar Abode: Islamic Law in the United States and Britain* (New York: Oxford University Press, 2010), 147. The United States is different in this respect than many European countries. In Britain, for example, anxiety over the sharia surfaced at various points during the 2000s about councils that enabled Muslims to obtain divorces according to Islamic principles. American courts have taken into account Islamic marriage contracts to rule on divorce cases, as they do with Jewish marriage contracts. The consideration given to Islamic marriage contracts varies widely, even at the county level. For example, in my conversations with lawyers who handle Muslim divorce cases, it is clear that Cook and DuPage County judges have taken different approaches to the *mahr* (marriage payment) question. In DuPage County, where judges tend to be more conservative, Islamic marriage contracts are often excluded from divorce proceedings because judges fear the impression of sharia "creeping" into American law.
30. Andrea Elliott, "The Man Behind the Anti-Shariah Movement," *New York Times*, July 30, 2011.
31. Ibid.
32. For an extensive analysis of the history and cultural logics behind the anti-sharia movement, see Marzouki, *Islam: An American Religion*, 106–37.
33. Center for Security Policy, *Shariah: The Threat to America: An Exercise in Competitive Analysis* (Washington, DC: The Center for Security Policy, 2010), 19.
34. For an extended discussion of the Park 51 controversy, see Corbett, *Making Moderate Islam*, 183–203.
35. For an analysis of Muslims family law in American courts, see Asifa Qureshi-Landes, "Rumors of the Sharia Threat Are Greatly Exaggerated: What American Judges Really Do with Islamic Family Law in Their Courtrooms," *New York Law School Review* 57, no. 2 (2012–2013): 244–57.
36. Muhammad Masud, Brinkley Messick, and David S. Powers, "Muftis, Fatwas, and Islamic Legal Interpretation," in *Islamic Legal Interpretation: Muftis and Their Fatwas*, ed. Muhammad Masud, Brinkley Messick, and David S. Powers (Cambridge, MA: Harvard University Press, 1996), 3–32.
37. See Masud, Messick, and Powers, "Muftis, Fatwas, and Islamic Legal Interpretation," 63. Wael B. Hallaq, *A History of Islamic Legal Theories: An Introduction to Sunni Usul al-Fiqh* (Cambridge: Cambridge University Press, 1997). Key for Webb's purposes are *usūl al-fiqh*, the sources of Islamic law, which legal scholar Wael Hallaq calls an "umbrella," as the "theoretical and philosophical foundation" of Islamic law. See Hallaq, *A History of Islamic Legal Theories*, vii. *Usūl al-fiqh* comprises legal theory or the principles through which jurists discern how to worship and live according to sacred texts, particularly the Qur'an and Sunna.

38. In addition to the four Sunni *madhāhib*, there are other legal schools devoted to Shi'i *fiqh*. Because Webb is primarily concerned with Sunni *fiqh*, the distinct history and practice of Shi'i *fiqh* need not concern us here, though research on Shi'i jurisprudence and practice in the United States is very much needed.
39. Fieldnotes, July 3, 2011.
40. "The Sharia that Muslim Americans Live," Sound Vision Foundation, 2011. https://drive.google.com/file/d/0B29ZlG_1jSGwSkNLbFY4YUpxRlE/view.
41. This effort also reflected what Omid Safi dubbed "pamphlet Islam." Omid Safi, ed., introduction to *Progressive Muslims: On Justice, Gender, and Pluralism* (New York: Oneworld, 2003), 22–23.
42. GhaneaBassiri, *A History of Islam in America*, 368.
43. *Pace* the anti-sharia pundits in the United States, most Muslim Americans are not advocating for sharia councils sponsored by the US government; see Kathleen Moore, *Unfamiliar Abode*, 103–28. Scholars of Islamic studies were also drawn into these debates, most notably Vincent Cornell and Sherman Jackson. The heated exchange between Jackson and Cornell demonstrates how personally invested many prominent scholars of Islamic studies have become in defining sharia and its obligations in the current climate. There are political dimensions to this debate as well, including the status of the US constitution in light of the history of slavery and Jim Crow. For Sherman Jackson's original arguments about the US constitution and sharia, see Jackson, *Islam and the Blackamerican*, 148. For the exchanges between Jackson and Cornell, see Sherman Jackson, "Soft Shari'a Fundamentalism and the Totalitarian Epistemology of Vincent Cornell," *The Religion and Culture Web Forum*, The University of Chicago Divinity School, https://divinity.uchicago.edu/sites/default/files/imce/pdfs/webforum/052011/Cornell_chapter.pdf, last updated May 2011; Cornell's essay was also published as Vincent Cornell, "Reasons Public and Divine: Liberal Democracy, Shari'a Fundamentalism and the Epistemological Crisis of Islam," in *Rethinking Islamic Studies: From Orientalism to Cosmopolitanism*, ed. Carl Ernst and Richard Martin (Columbia: University of South Carolina Press, 2010), 23–51.
44. Interview with the author, May 22, 2011.
45. GhaneaBassiri, *A History of Islam in America*, 377.
46. I provide a comprehensive discussion of sharia in the introduction, underscoring dimensions of Muslims' religious lives that have been marginalized in contemporary studies.
47. Q. 2:43.
48. Despite its centrality in Muslim practice and the extensive discursive tradition devoted to it, salat has received remarkably little attention in the anthropological literature. More recently, ethnographers John Bowen and Saba Mahmood have pointed to the ways that social structures, political configurations and moral disciplines inform communities' imaginings and performances of salat. See

John R. Bowen, "Salat in Indonesia: The Social Meanings of an Islamic Ritual," *Man* 24, no. 4 (1989): 600–19; Saba Mahmood, "Rehearsed Spontaneity and the Conventionality of Ritual: Disciplines of Salat," *American Ethnologist* 28, no. 4 (November 2001): 827–53.

49. Fieldnotes, April 15, 2012.
50. Asad, *The Idea of an Anthropology of Islam*, 20. In particular, I focus on this aspect of his definition: "A tradition consists essentially of discourses that seek to instruct practitioners regarding the correct form and purpose of a given practice that, precisely because it is established, has a history. These discourses relate conceptually to a past . . . and a future through a present."
51. Interview with the author, March 28, 2012.
52. Kathleen Moore, *Unfamiliar Abode*, 12.
53. As Grewal points out, seeking out classical knowledge became one way for American Muslims to attempt to resolve the crisis of authority in their mosques. For the student-travellers in her book, this involves seeking out scholars abroad. But for this group of Muslims, one need go no further than a suburban hotel for answers. See, Zareena Grewal, *Islam Is a Foreign Country*, 33–42.
54. Q. 2:239.
55. Jonah Steinberg, *Isma'ili Modern: Globalization and Identity in a Muslim Community* (Chapel Hill: The University of North Carolina Press, 2011), 11.
56. Zahra N. Jamal, "Ismaʿilis," in *Encyclopedia of Islam in the United States*, ed. Jocelyne Cesari, (Westport, CT: Greenwood Press, 2007), 2: 348–51; Zayn R. Kassam, "The Gender Policies of Aga Khan III and Aga Khan IV," in *A Modern History of the Ismailis: Continuity and Change in a Muslim Community*, ed. Farhad Daftary (London: I. B. Tauris, 2011), 257–59.
57. Steinberg, *Isma'ili Modern*, 8–12. Imami Shiʿis observe similar practices because the Qur'an only specifies three times for daily prayer. The Sunna specifies the requirement of praying five times a day.
58. Ali S. Asani, "From Satpanthi to Ismaili Muslim: The Articulation of Ismaili Khoja Identity in South Asia," in *A Modern History of the Ismailis: Continuity and Change in a Muslim Community*, ed. Farhad Daftari (London: I. B. Tauris, 2007), 112–13.
59. Interview with the author, April 25, 2012, Darien, IL.
60. Interview with the author, April 25, 2012, Darien, IL.
61. GhaneaBassiri, *A History of Islam in America*, 208.
62. Brannon Ingram, "Ahmadi Muslim Americans," *Encyclopedia of Muslim-American History*, ed. Edward CurtisIV (New York: Facts on File, 2010), 32–34. GhaneaBassiri, *A History of Islam in America*, 208–19.
63. Interview with the author, April 25, 2012.
64. "Partial Translation of Sunan Abu-Dawud," Center for Muslim-Jewish Engagement, 2017, http://www.cmje.org/religious-texts/hadithhadith/abu-dawud/040-sat.php.

65. Grewal, *Islam Is a Foreign Country*, 77.
66. Asad, "The Idea of an Anthropology of Islam," 22.
67. Fieldnotes, March 18, 2012.
68. Fazlur Rahman, "Some Key Ethical Concepts of the Qur'an," *The Journal of Religious Ethics* 11, no. 2 (Fall 1993): 170–85; *Major Themes of the Qur'an*, 2nd ed. (Minneapolis: Bibliotheca Islamica, 1994). I cite Rahman here because he has devoted a significant portion of his scholarly work to the concept of *taqwa*, arguing that it is a key ethical theme in the Qur'an.
69. Mahmood, "Rehearsed Spontaneity," 831–33.
70. Ibid., 832.
71. Fieldnotes, March 18, 2012.
72. Rick Ostrander, "The Practice of Prayer in a Modern Age: Liberals, Fundatmentalists, and Prayer in the Modern Age," in *Practicing Protestants: Histories of Christian Life, 1630–1985*, ed. Laurie Maffly-Kipp, Leigh Schmidt, and Mark Valeri (Baltimore: Johns Hopkins University Press, 2006), 159–76.
73. Marion Holmes Katz, *Prayer in Islamic Thought and Practice* (New York: Cambridge University Press, 2013), 44–74.
74. There are varying levels of observance in Muslim-majority contexts, and the relative ease with which prayer is performed depends on a range of personal and structural factors.
75. Fieldnotes, October 2, 2011.
76. Umar F. Abd-Allah, "Living Islam with Purpose," Nawawi Foundation, 2. http://www.nawawi.org/wp-content/uploads/2013/01/Article6.pdf.
77. Ibid. Abd-Allah notes that other operational principles might be better suited for other contexts.
78. Ibid.
79. Abd-Allah, "Living Islam with Purpose," 33–7.
80. Andrew March, "Islamic Legal Theory, Secularism, and Religious Pluralism: Is Modern Religious Freedom Sufficient for the Sharī'a 'Purpose' of 'Preserving Religion' [Hifz al-din]?," Islamic Law and Law of the Muslim World Paper No. 09-78; Yale Law School, Public Law Working Paper No. 208: 2. Uploaded August 15, 2009. https://papers.ssrn.com/sol3/papers.cfm?abstract_id=1452895.
81. Kathleen Moore, *Unfamiliar Abode*, 85.
82. Abd-Allah, "Living Islam with Purpose," 3. This passage provides an apt example of the recurring tension between universality and particularity that Edward Curtis identifies. See Curtis, *Islam in Black America*, 1–2.
83. Ibid., 34.
84. Ibid., 12.
85. For example, Abd-Allah claims that the conflict between religion and science was "unheard of" in classical Islam. See Abd-Allah, "Living Islam with Purpose," 4.

86. Abd-Allah, "Living Islam with Purpose," 26–7.
87. Abd-Allah, "Living Islam with Purpose," 27.
88. Ibid., 28.
89. Zareena Grewal, *Islam Is a Foreign Country*.
90. Fieldnotes, October 30, 2011. This is yet another example of religious studies scholarship filtering into the lived practices of this educated group of Muslims.
91. The most well-known of these institutions is the Shariah Board, run by a Deobandi graduate, Mufti Navalur Rahman. Located in the Devon Avenue area, in the far northern section of Chicago, the Shariah Board is part of larger organization, the Rahmat-e-Alam. The foundation lists *zabīha* -compliant slaughter houses, provides online fatwas, and information about counseling services.
92. "Leadership," Darul Qasim Institute. https://darulqasim.org/aboutus/leadership.
93. Zaman, *The Ulama in Contemporary Islam*, 30.
94. Interview with the author, October 19, 2014, Naperville, IL.
95. The literature on these new Islamic authorities is extensive. See for example, Dale Eickelman and James Piscatori, *Muslim Politics* (Princeton, NJ: Princeton University Press, 2004); Olivier Roy, *The Failure of Political Islam*, trans. Carol Volk (Cambridge, MA: Harvard University Press, 1998); Muhammad Khalid Masud and Armando Salvatore, *Islam and Modernity: Key Issues and Debates* (Edinburgh: Edinburgh University Press, 2009).
96. Zareena Grewal, *Islam Is a Foreign Country*, 31–78.

CHAPTER 7

1. Fieldnotes, May 23, 2012.
2. Aysha Hidayatullah, *Feminist Edges of the Qur'an* (New York: Oxford University Press, 2014), 3.
3. Hidayatullah, *Feminist Edges of the Qur'an*, 4.
4. De Certeau, *The Practice of Everyday Life*, xxi–xxii.
5. De Certeau, *The Practice of Everyday Life*, xxi.
6. Interview with the author, October 13, 2011, Willowbrook, IL.
7. Fieldnotes, July 27, 2011.
8. I explore Webb understandings of haram in the previous chapter.
9. Interview with the author, October 13, 2011, Willowbrook, IL.
10. Interview with the author, October, 13, 2011, Willowbrook, IL
11. Interview with the author, October, 13, 2011, Willowbrook, IL.
12. Amina misses the "freedom" that living in a small town afforded her family to explore Islam without being encumbered by what she perceives as the top-down approach of Chicago religious authorities. When she lived with her young family in Indianapolis, with its much smaller community of Muslims, they referred to their book club as a *halaqa*, or informal lesson group, which met semiregularly in private homes. The notion of *halaqa* here is quite different from the

traditional institution, which was led by a scholar who read a religious text to a group of students and sometimes provided commentary on it. The Indianapolis families met for *halaqa* on Friday nights. An adult would lead a brief lesson on the Qur'an or explore a religious topic, such as charity, which would then be followed by discussion. The focus of the group was on learning and growing as Muslims through open debate of religious texts. They also read nonreligious texts in order to debate timely social and ethical topics.

13. Fieldnotes, July 27, 2011.
14. Lofton, *Oprah*, 148. Lofton uses the phrase "reading religiously" to denote several ways (ritual, interpretative) in which Oprah's book club is "religious" and to point out the arbitrariness of categorizing cultural practices as such.
15. Ibid., 158–60.
16. Interview with the author, September 28, 2011, Oak Brook, IL.
17. Karim, *American Muslim Women*, 11–13.
18. Lofton, *Oprah*, 179–81.
19. Ibid., 170–71.
20. Elizabeth Long, *Book Clubs: Women and the Uses of Reading in Everyday Life* (Chicago: University of Chicago Press, 2003), 22.
21. Long, *Book Clubs*, xviii. Long is careful to point out that this is not always the case; not all women are similarly affected or transformed by their experiences.
22. Jenny Hartley, *The Reading Groups Book* (London: Oxford University Press, 2002), 137.
23. Christopher Cantwell, "Once a Member, Always a Member: Feeling, Faith, and Friendship in the Adult Bible Class Movement," paper presented at the *Annual Meeting of the American Historical Association*, New York, NY, January 4, 2009.
24. Matthew Hedstrom, *The Rise of Liberal Religion: Book Culture and American Spirituality in the Twentieth Century* (New York: Oxford University Press, 2013), 10.
25. Karim, *American Muslim Women*, 17–21.
26. Gayatri Chakravorty Spivak, "Can the Subaltern Speak?," in *Marxism and the Interpretation of Culture*, ed. Cary Nelson and Lawrence Grossberg (Urbana: University of Illinois Press, 1988), 296. For a full discussion of colonial projects concerning Muslim women, see also Leila Ahmed, *Women and Gender in Islam: Historical Roots of a Modern Debate* (New Haven, CT: Yale University Press, 1993).
27. Fatima Seedat, "When Islam and Feminism Converge," *The Muslim World* 103 (July 2013): 404–20; "Islam, Feminism, and Islamic Feminism: Between Inadequacy and Inevitability," *Journal of Feminist Studies in Religion* 29, no. 2 (2013): 25–45.
28. Mahmood, *Politics of Piety*, ix–xii. Mahmood's personal reflections on secular feminism's dismissal of Islam animate her arguments about the possibility for women's subject formation through the mosque movement.
29. Ahmed, *Women and Gender in Islam*, 150–55.

30. Lila Abu-Lughod, "Do Muslim Women Really Need Saving? Anthropological Reflections on Cultural Relativism and Its Others," *American Anthropologist* 104, no. 3 (September 2002): 783–90.
31. Hidayatullah, *Feminist Edges of the Qur'an*, 6–7.
32. Hammer, *American Muslim Women, Religious Authority, and Activism*, 8.
33. Passed into law on March 23, 2010, the Affordable Care Act prompted the Roman Catholic Church to issue statements arguing that the government was infringing on the free exercise of religion and claiming that Catholic-run charities and hospitals should not be required to pay for contraception, whose use the Catholic Church opposes. At the same time, the Susan G. Komen Foundation announced it would pull its financial support from Planned Parenthood, a policy that was later rescinded. This action led to a flurry of protests from feminists and renewed right-wing efforts to lobbying efforts to withdraw federal and state funding from the organization because it offers abortions in some of its clinics.
34. Seedat, "Islam, Feminism, and Islamic Feminism," 27.
35. Margot Badran, *Feminism in Islam: Secular and Religious Convergences* (New York: Oneworld, 2009), 1.
36. Fieldnotes, June 2, 2011.
37. Juliane Hammer has written extensively on this subject, in *American Muslim Women, Religious Authority, and Activism*, and in "Activism as Embodied *Tafsir*: Negotiating Women's Authority, Leadership, and Space in North America," in *Women, Leadership and Mosques: Changes in Contemporary Islamic Authority*, ed. Masooda Bano and Hilary Kalmbach (Leiden: Brill, 2012), 457–80.
38. Fieldnotes, June 2, 2011.
39. Cooke, "Multiple Critique: Islamic Feminist Rhetorical Strategies," 142–60.
40. Badran, *Feminism in Islam*, 4–5. Badran distinguishes between two distinct genealogies of secular and Islamic feminisms, arguing that secular feminism grew out of the experiences of modernization, nationalism, and the postcolonial condition of the early to mid-twentieth century, while Islamic feminism is a more recent phenomenon, grounded in a particular religious and intellectual endeavor, namely that of *ijtihād* (independent legal reasoning). She argues that secular feminism was willing to concede gender inequality in private spaces while advocating for parity in public spaces, whereas Islamic feminism advanced gender equality in all aspects of life.
41. Badran, *Feminism in Islam*, 5.
42. Fieldnotes, April 12, 2012.
43. William Graham, "Traditionalism in Islam: An Essay in Interpretation," *The Journal of Interdisciplinary History* 23, no. 3 (Winter 1993): 499–502. Graham distinguishes between traditionalism and modernism on social levels, arguing that traditionalism is not part of Western societies. But here, we see how traditionalism functions in an ostensibly "modern" setting.

44. As chapter 1 demonstrates, Abd-Allah's authority derives from a number of related sources and discourses.
45. Omid Safi, ed. Inroduction to *Progressive Muslims: On Justice, Gender and Pluralism* (Oxford: Oneworld, 2003), 18.
46. Safi, *Progressive Muslims*, 6.
47. See Hammer, *American Muslim Women, Religious Authority, and Activism*, esp. 36–55, for a detailed analysis of the ensuing debates.
48. Ibid., 13–55. Hammer outlines the various positions taken by American Muslim leaders, political pundits, and human rights activists in the lead-up and aftermath of the prayer event.
49. Interview with the author, October 13, 2011, Willowbrook, IL.
50. There is a long history of polemics against the Prophet Muhammad that caricature him as a womanizer. For contemporary scholarly responses from within the Islamic tradition to these demeaning portrayals, see Tariq Ramadan, *In the Footsteps of the Prophet: Lessons from the Life of Muhammad* (Oxford: Oxford University Press, 2007), x–xii; Omid Safi, *Memories of Muhammad: Why the Prophet Matters* (New York: HarperCollins, 2009), 1–6.
51. Kecia Ali actually concurs with the prevailing Muslim wisdom that although the Prophet married Aisha when she was six or seven years of age, he likely consummated the union a few years later. See Kecia Ali, *Marriage and Slavery in Early Islam* (Cambridge, MA: Harvard University Press, 2010), 31.
52. Interview with the author, October 13, 2011.
53. Ziauddin Sardar, *Reading the Qur'an: The Contemporary Relevance of the Sacred Text of Islam* (Oxford: Oxford University Press, 2011).
54. Fieldnotes, September 28, 2011.
55. Fieldnotes, October 26, 2011.
56. Louise Cainkar, *Homeland Insecurity: The Arab American and Muslim American Experience After 9/11* (New York: Russell Sage Foundation, 2011).
57. Cainkar, *Homeland Insecurity*, 3–5; Rana, *Terrifying Muslims*, 5; Juliane Hammer, "Center Stage: Gendered Islamophobia and Muslim Women," in *Islamophobia in America: The Anatomy of Intolerance*, ed. Carl Ernst (New York: Palgrave Macmillan, 2013),107–44.
58. Fieldnotes, October 26, 2011.
59. DeLong-Bas, *Wahhabi Islam*, 3–5. DeLong-Bas argues that after 9/11 Wahhabism and terrorism are routinely linked in American cultural discourse.
60. Interview with the author, October, 13, 2011, Willowbrook, IL.
61. Fieldnotes, October 26, 2011.
62. GhaneaBassiri, *A History of Islam in America*, 325.
63. I more fully elucidate the genealogies of "Wahhabism" in chapter 2.
64. Karen Leonard, "American Muslims and Authority: Competing Discourses in a Non-Muslim State," *Journal of American Ethnic History* 25, no. 1 (Fall 2005): 14.

65. Zareena Grewal, *Islam Is a Foreign Country*, 306–7.
66. Fieldnotes, October 26, 2011.
67. Fieldnotes, October 26, 2011.
68. Interview with the author, September 28, 2011, Oak Brook, IL.
69. Fieldnotes, October 26, 2012.
70. De Certeau, *The Practice of Everyday Life*, 38–39.
71. Fieldnotes, April 11, 2012.
72. Fieldnotes, April 11, 2012. Wendy Videlock, "!" *Poetry*, April 2012.
73. E-mail correspondence with the author, April 13, 2012.
74. In the *Poetry* survey, Amina also noted my presence as a Christian participant.
75. Ali Eteraz is a nom de plume, adopted by the author because he anticipated significant controversy to arise from his book and wanted to protect his family from scrutiny.
76. Fieldnotes, April 11, 2012.
77. Fieldnotes, April 11, 2012.
78. Tom Boellstorff, "Between Religion and Desire: Being Muslim and Gay in Indonesia," *American Anthropologist* 104, no. 4 (December 2005): 575–85. Cf. Juliane Hammer, "Studying American Muslim Women: Gender, Feminism, and Islam," in *The Cambridge Companion to American Islam*, ed. Juliane Hammer and Omid Safi (New York: Cambridge University Press, 2013), 331.
79. Steven Erlanger, "Amid Rise of Multiculturalism, Dutch Confront Their Questions of Identity," *New York Times*, August 13, 2011.
80. I discuss how Webb has become a space for these types of discussions in the introduction and chapter 1.
81. Fieldnotes, March 29, 2011.
82. Lizette Alvarez and Richard Perez-Pena, "Orlando Gunman Attacks Gay Nightclub, Leaving 50 Dead," *New York Times*, June 12, 2016, http://www.nytimes.com/2016/06/13/us/orlando-nightclub-shooting.html?_r=0.
83. For example, the al-Fatiha Foundation is dedicated to providing an "opening" for gay Muslims to express their identities.
84. Scott Siraj al-Haqq Kugle, *Homosexuality in Islam: Critical Reflections on Gay, Lesbian, and Transgender Muslims* (New York: Oneworld, 2010).
85. "Muslim Americans: No Signs of Growth in Support for Extremism or Alienation," Pew Research Center, 2011, http://www.pewforum.org/2011/08/30/muslim-americans-no-signs-of-growth-in-alienation-or-support-for-extremism/.
86. Omar Minwalla, Jamie Feldman, Christine Varga, and B. R. Simon Rosser, "Identity Experience among Progressive Gay Muslims in North America: A Qualitative Study within Al-Fatiha," *Culture, Health, and Sexuality* 7, no. 2 (March 2005): 113–28.
87. Fieldnotes, June 27, 2012.

88. Fieldnotes, June 27, 2012.
89. miriam cooke, "Multiple Critique: Islamic Feminist Rhetorical Strategies," in *Postcolonialism, Feminism, and Religious Discourse*, ed. Laura E. Donaldson and Kwok Pui-Lan (New York: Routledge, 2010), 142–60.
90. Fieldnotes, June 27, 2012.
91. Fieldnotes, June 27, 2012.

CONCLUSION

1. Grewal, *Islam Is a Foreign Country*, 82–83; Khabeer, *Muslim Cool*, 3–4.
2. Emma Green, "How American Muslims Are Trying to Take Back Their Government," *Atlantic*, April 16, 2017, https://www.theatlantic.com/politics/archive/2017/04/american-muslims-running-for-office/522585/.
3. Bender, *The New Metaphysicals*, 16.
4. Ibid.
5. Ibid., 188.
6. Abd-Allah, "Islam and the Cultural Imperative."
7. Edward Curtis IV, "Ode to Islamic Studies, Its Allure, Its Danger, Its Power," *Religion Bulletin*, May 2, 2014, http://bulletin.equinoxpub.com/2014/05/ode-to-islamic-studies-its-allure-its-danger-its-power-reflections-on-islamic-studies/.

Bibliography

Abd-Allah, Umar F. "Islam and the Cultural Imperative." *Nawawi Foundation*, 2007.

———. "Living Islam with Purpose." *Nawawi Foundation*, 2004.

———. *Malik and Medina: Islamic Legal Reasoning in the Formative Period*. Leiden: Brill, 2013.

———. *A Muslim in Victorian America: The Life of Alexander Russell Webb*. New York: Oxford University Press, 2006.

Abdo, Genevieve. *Mecca on Main Street: Muslim Life in America after 9/11*. New York: Oxford University Press, 2006.

Abdullah, Zain. "American Muslims in the Contemporary World: 1965–Present." In *The Cambridge Companion to American Islam*, edited by Juliane Hammer and Omid Safi, 65–82. New York: Cambridge University Press, 2013.

Abou El Fadl, Khaled. *The Place of Tolerance in Islam*. Boston: Beacon Press, 2002.

Abraham, Nabeel, Sally Howell, and Andrew Shyrock, eds. *Arab Detroit 9/11: Life in the Terror Decade*. Detroit: Wayne State University Press, 2011.

Abraham, Nabeel, and Andrew Shyrock, eds. *Arab Detroit: From Margin to Mainstream*. Detroit: Wayne State University Press, 2000.

Abu-Lughod, Lila. *Do Muslim Women Need Saving?* Cambridge, MA: Harvard University Press, 2013.

———. "Do Muslim Women Really Need Saving? Anthropological Reflections on Cultural Relativism and Its Others." *American Anthropologist* 104, no. 3. New Series (September 2002): 783–90.

Afsaruddin, Asma. "The Hermeneutics of Interfaith Relations: Retrieving Moderation and Pluralism as Universal Principles in Quranic Exegesis." *Journal of Religious Ethics* 37, no. 2 (2009): 331–54.

Agrama, Hussein Ali. *Questioning Secularism: Islam, Sovereignty, and the Rule of Law in Modern Egypt*. Chicago: University of Chicago Press, 2012.

Ahmed, Leila. *A Quiet Revolution: The Veil's Resurgence from the Middle East to America*. New Haven, CT: Yale University Press, 2011.

———. *Women and Gender in Islam: Historical Roots of a Modern Debate.* New Haven, CT: Yale University Press, 1993.

Ahmed-Ullah, Noreen S. et al. "Hard-Liners Won Battle for Bridgeview Mosque." *Chicago Tribune,* February 8, 2004.

Ali, Kecia. *The Lives of Muhammad.* Cambridge, MA: Harvard University Press, 2016.

———. *Marriage and Slavery in Early Islam.* Cambridge, MA: Harvard University Press, 2010.

———. *Sexual Ethics in Islam: Feminist Reflections on Qur'an, Hadith, and Jurisprudence.* 2nd ed. London: Oneworld, 2016.

Alvarez, Lizette, and Richard Perez-Pena. "Orlando Gunman Attacks Gay Nightclub, Leaving 50 Dead." *New York Times,* June 12, 2016. http://www.nytimes.com/2016/06/13/us/orlando-nightclub-shooting.html?_r=0.

Ammerman, Nancy, ed. *Everyday Religion: Observing Modern Religious Lives.* New York: Oxford University Press, 2007.

Anjum, Ovamir. *Politics, Law, and Community: The Taymiyyan Moment.* New York: Cambridge University Press, 2012.

———. "Salafis and Democracy: Doctrine and Context." *The Muslim World* 106, no. 3 (July 2016): 448–73.

Arjana, Sophia Rose. *Muslims in the Western Imagination.* New York: Oxford University Press, 2015.

Asad, Talal. *Formations of the Secular: Christianity, Islam, Modernity.* Stanford, CA: Stanford University Press, 2003.

———. "The Idea of an Anthropology of Islam." *Qui Parle* 17, no. 2 (Spring/Summer 2009): 1–30.

Asani, Ali S. "From Satpanthi to Ismaili Muslim: The Articulation of Ismaili Khoja Identity in South Asia." In *A Modern History of the Ismailis: Continuity and Change in a Muslim Community,* edited by Farhad Daftary, 95–128. London: I. B. Tauris, 2007.

Ayoub, Mahmoud. *The Qur'an and Its Interpreters.* Vol. 1. Albany: State University of New York Press, 1984.

Badran, Margot. *Feminism in Islam: Secular and Religious Convergences.* New York: Oneworld, 2009.

Bagby, Ihsan. *The American Mosque 2011: Basic Characteristics of the American Mosque, Attitudes of Mosque Leaders.* New York: Council on American Islamic Relations, 2012.

———. *Report Number 2 from the American Mosque Survey: Activities, Administration, and Vitality of the American Mosque.* New York: Council on American Islamic Relations, 2012.

Bano, Masooda and Hilary Kalmbach. "Introduction: Islamic Authority and the Study of Female Religious Leaders." In *Women, Leadership and Mosques: Changes in Contemporary Islamic Authority,* edited by Hilary Kalmbach and Masooda Bano, 1–30. Leiden: Brill, 2012.

———. eds. *Women, Leadership, and Mosques: Changes in Contemporary Islamic Authority*. Leiden: Brill, 2012.

Bauer, Karen, ed. *Aims, Methods, and Contexts of Qur'anic Exegesis: 2nd/8th–9th/15th Centuries*. London: Oxford University Press, 2013.

Baugh, Amanda. *God and the Green Divide: Religious Environmentalism in Black and White*. Berkeley: University of California Press, 2016.

Behar, Ruth. *The Vulnerable Observer: Anthropology That Breaks Your Heart*. Boston: Beacon Press, 1996.

Bell, Richard. *Introduction to the Qur'an*. Edinburgh: University Press, 1953.

Bender, Courtney. *The New Metaphysicals: Spirituality and the American Religious Imagination*. Chicago: The University of Chicago Press, 2010.

Bender, Courtney, and Pamela E. Klassen, eds. *After Pluralism: Reimagining Religious Engagement*. New York: Columbia University Press, 2010.

Best, Wallace D. *Passionately Human, No Less Divine: Religion and Culture in Black Chicago, 1915–1952*. Princeton, NJ: Princeton University Press, 2005.

Bhabha, Homi. *The Location of Culture*. London: Routledge, 2004.

Bielo, James S., ed. *The Social Life of Scriptures: Cross-Cultural Perspectives on Biblicism*. New Brunswick, NJ: Rutgers University Press, 2009.

———. *Words upon the Word: An Ethnography of Evangelical Group Bible Study*. New York: New York University Press, 2009.

Bilici, Mucahit. *Finding Mecca in America*. Chicago: The University of Chicago Press, 2012.

Boellstorff, Tom. "Between Religion and Desire: Being Muslim and Gay in Indonesia." *American Anthropologist* 104, no. 4 (December 2005): 575–85.

Bowen, John R. "Anthropology and Islamic Law." In *The Oxford Handbook on Islamic Law*, edited by Anver M. Emon and Rumee Ahmed. Oxford: Oxford University Press, 2015. http://www.oxfordhandbooks.com/view/10.1093/oxfordhb/9780199679010.001.0001/oxfordhb-9780199679010.

———. *Muslims through Discourse: Religion and Ritual in Gayo Society*. Princeton, NJ: Princeton University Press, 1993.

———. *On British Islam: Religion, Law, and Everyday Practice in Shari'a Councils*. Princeton, NJ: Princeton University Press, 2016.

———. "On Scriptural Essentialism and Ritual Variation: Muslim Sacrifice in Sumatra and Morocco." *American Ethnologist* 19, no. 4 (1992): 656–71.

———. "Salat in Indonesia: The Social Meanings of an Islamic Ritual." *Man* 24, no. 4 (1989): 600–19.

Boyarin, Jonathan, ed. *The Ethnography of Reading*. Berkeley: University of California Press, 1993.

Brown, Jonathan C. *Misquoting Muhammad: The Challenges and Choices of Interpreting the Prophet's Legacy*. New York: Oneworld, 2014.

Brown, Wendy. *Regulating Aversion: Tolerance in the Age of Identity and Empire*. Princeton, NJ: Princeton University Press, 2006.

Brubaker, Rogers. "Categories of Analysis and Categories of Practice: A Note on the Study of Muslims in European Countries of Immigration." *Ethnic and Racial Studies* 36, no. 1 (2013): 1–8.

———. *Ethnicity without Groups*. Cambridge, MA: Harvard University Press, 2006.

Cainkar, Louise. *Homeland Insecurity: The Arab American and Muslim American Experience after 9/11*. New York: Russell Sage Foundation, 2011.

Campo, Juan, ed. *Encyclopedia of Islam*. New York: Facts On File, 2009.

Cantwell, Christopher. "Once a Member, Always a Member: Feeling, Faith, and Friendship in the Adult Bible Class Movement." Paper presented at the *Annual Meeting of the American Historical Association*, New York, NY, January 4, 2009.

Center for Security Policy, *Shari'ah: The Threat to America. An Exercise in Competitive Analysis*. Washington, DC: The Center for Security Policy, 2010.

Chakrabarty, Dipesh. *Provincializing Europe: Postcolonial Thought and Historical Difference*. Princeton, NJ: Princeton University Press, 2007.

Chan-Malik, Sylvia. "'Common Cause': On the Black-Immigrant Debate and Constructing the Muslim American." *Journal of Race, Ethnicity, and Religion* 2, no. 8 (May 2011): 1–39.

Chen, Carolyn. "The Religious Varieties of Ethnic Presence: A Comparison between a Taiwanese Immigrant Buddhist Temple and an Evangelical Christian Church." *Sociology of Religion* 63, no. 2 (2002): 215–38.

Chen, Carolyn, and Russell Jueng, eds. *Sustaining Faith Traditions: Race, Ethnicity, and Religion among the Latino and Asian Second Generation*. New York: New York University Press, 2012.

Chidester, David. *Authentic Fakes: Religion and American Popular Culture*. Berkeley: University of California Press, 2005.

Combs-Schilling, Elaine. *Sacred Performances: Islam, Sexuality, and Sacrifice*. New York: Columbia University Press, 1989.

Cook, Michael, and Patricia Crone. *Hagarism: The Making of the Islamic World*. Cambridge: Cambridge University Press, 1977.

cooke, miriam. "Mulitiple Critique: Islamic Feminist Rhetorical Strategies." In *Postcolonialism, Feminism, and Religious Discourse*, edited by Laura E. Donaldson and Kwok Pui-Lan, 142–60. London: Routledge, 2010.

Coontz, Stephanie. *Marriage, a History: How Love Conquered Marriage*. New York: Viking, 2005.

Corbett, Rosemary R. "For God and Country: Religious Minorities Striving for National Belonging through Community Service." *Religion and American Culture: A Journal of Interpretation* 26, no. 2 (Summer 2016): 227–59.

———. *Making Moderate Islam: Sufism, Service, and the Ground Zero Mosque*. Palo Alto, CA: Stanford University Press, 2016.

Cornell, Vincent. "Reasons Public and Divine: Liberal Democracy, Sharīʿa Fundamentalism, and the Epistemological Crisis of Islam." In *Rethinking Islamic*

Studies: From Orientalism to Cosmopolitanism, edited by Carl Ernst and Richard Martin, 23–51. Columbia: University of South Carolina Press, 2010.

Cott, Nancy F. *Public Vows: A History of Marriage and the Nation*. Cambridge, MA: Harvard University Press, 2000.

Curtis, Edward, IV. *Black Muslim Religion in the Nation of Islam, 1960–1975*. Chapel Hill: The University of North Carolina Press, 2006.

———. "The Black Muslim Scare of the Twentieth Century: The History of State Islamophobia and Its Post-9/11Variations." In *Islamophobia in America: The Anatomy of Intolerance*, edited by Carl Ernst, 75–106. New York: Palgrave MacMillan, 2013.

———. *The Call of Bilal: Islam in the African Diaspora*. Chapel Hill: The University of North Carolina Press, 2014.

———. *Islam in Black America: Identity, Liberation, and Difference in African-American Islamic Thought*. Albany: State University of New York Press, 2002.

———. "Islamism and Its African American Muslim Critics: Black Muslims in the Era of the Arab Cold War." *American Quarterly* 59, no. 3 (September 2007): 683–709.

———. "Ode to Islamic Studies, Its Allure, Its Danger, Its Power." *Religion Bulletin*, May 2, 2014, http://bulletin.equinoxpub.com/2014/05/ode-to-islamic-studies-its-allure-its-danger-its-power-reflections-on-islamic-studies/.

De Certeau, Michel. *The Practice of Everyday Life*. Translated by Steven F. Rendall. Berkeley: University of California Press, 1984.

Deeb, Lara, and Mona Harb. *Leisurely Islam: Negotiating Geography and Morality in Shi'ite South Beirut*. Princeton, NJ: Princeton University Press, 2013.

DeLollis, Barbara. "Marriott Conference Center in Lisle, Ill., to Close." *USA Today*, September 30, 2011.

DeLong-Bas, Natana. *Wahhabi Islam: From Revival to Reform to Global Jihad*. New York: Oxford University Press, 2004.

Denny, Frederick. *An Introduction to Islam*. 2nd ed. New York: Macmillan, 1994.

De Sondy, Amanullah. *The Crisis of Islamic Masculinities*. London: Bloomsbury Academic, 2014.

Dey, Amit. "Bengali Translation of the Qur'an and the Impact of Print Culture on Muslim Society in the Nineteenth Century." *Societal Studies* 4, no. 4 (2012): 1299–1315.

Diamond, Eton. "Beyond Borscht: The Kosher Lifestyle and the Religious Consumerism of Suburban Orthodox Jews." In *Faith in the Market: Religion and the Rise of Urban Commercial Culture*, edited by John Michael Giggie and Diane Winston, 227–46. New Brunswick, NJ: Rutgers University Press, 2002.

Dickson, William Rory. *Living Sufism in North America: Between Tradition and Transformation*. Albany: State University of New York Press, 2015.

Diouf, Sylviane A. *Servants of Allah: African Muslims Enslaved in the Americas*. New York: New York University Press, 1998.

Donner, Fred. "The Death of Abu Talib." In *Love and Death in the Ancient Near East: Essays in Honor of Marvin H. Pope*, edited by John H. Marks and Robert M. Good, 237–46. Guiford, CN: Four Quarters Publishing Company, 1987.

Eickelman, Dale F. *Knowledge and Power in Morocco: The Education of a Twentieth-Century Notable*. Princeton, NJ: Princeton University Press, 1985.

Eickelman, Dale F., and James P. Piscatori. *Muslim Politics*. Princeton, NJ: Princeton University Press, 2004.

Elkholy, Abdo A. *Arab Moslems in the United States: Religion and Assimilation*. New Haven: College & University Press, 1966.

Elliott, Andrea. "The Man Behind the Anti-Shariah Movement." *New York Times*, July 30, 2011.

Erlanger, Steven. "Amid Rise of Multiculturalism, Dutch Confront Their Questions of Identity." *New York Times*, August 13, 2011.

Ernst, Carl. *Following Muhammad: Rethinking Islam in the Contemporary World*. Chapel Hill: The University of North Carolina Press, 2003.

———. *How to Read the Qur'an: A New Guide*. Chapel Hill: The University of North Carolina Press, 2011.

———. "Introduction: The Problem of Islamophobia." In *Islamophobia in America: The Anatomy of Intolerance*, edited by Carl Ernst, 1–10. New York: Palgrave MacMillan, 2013.

———. *Islamophobia in America: The Anatomy of Intolerance*. New York: Palgrave MacMillan, 2013.

———. *The Shambhala Guide to Sufism*. Boston: Shambhala, 1997.

———. "Sufism, Islam, and Globalization in the Contemporary World: Methodological Reflections on a Changing Field of Study." In *In Memoriam: The 4th Victor Danner Memorial Lecture*. Bloomington, IN: Department of Near Eastern Languages and Cultures, 2009. https://www.unc.edu/~cernst/pdf/danner.pdf.

Esack, Farid. "The Portrayal of Jews and the Possibilities for Their Salvation in the Qur'an." In *Between Heaven and Hell: Islam, Salvation, and the Fate of Others*, edited by Mohammad Hassan Khalil, 207–33. Oxford: Oxford University Press, 2013.

Etehad, Melissa. "After Nice, Newt Gingrich Wants to 'Test' Every Muslim in the U.S. and Deport Sharia Believers." *Washington Post*, July 15, 2016. https://www.washingtonpost.com/news/morning-mix/wp/2016/07/15/after-nice-newt-gingrich-wants-to-test-every-american-muslim-and-deport-those-who-believe-in-sharia/.

Ewing, Katherine Pratt. *Stolen Honor: Stigmatizing Muslim Men in Berlin*. Palo Alto, CA: Stanford University Press, 2008.

Fader, Ayala. *Mitzvah Girls: Bringing up the Next Generation of Hasidic Jews in Brooklyn*. Princeton, NJ: Princeton University Press, 2009.

Fessenden, Tracy. *Culture and Redemption: Religion, the Secular, and American Literature*. Princeton, NJ: Princeton University Press, 2006.

Firestone, Reuven. "Disparity and Resolution in the Quranic Teachings on War: A Reevaluation of a Traditional Problem." *Journal of Near Eastern Studies* 56, no. 1 (1997): 1–19.

Gade, Anna. *Perfection Makes Practice: Learning, Emotion, and the Recited Qur'an.* Honolulu: University of Hawai'i Press, 2004.

Garreau, Joel. *Edge City: Life on the New Frontier.* New York: Doubleday, 1991.

GhaneaBassiri, Kambiz. *A History of Islam in America: From the New World to the New World Order.* New York: Cambridge University Press, 2010.

———. "Religious Normativity and Praxis among American Muslims." In *The Cambridge Companion to American Islam,* edited by Juliane Hammer and Omid Safi, 208–27. New York: Cambridge University Press, 2013.

Ghannam, Farha. *Live and Die Like a Man: Gender Dynamics in Urban Egypt.* Palo Alto, CA: Stanford University Press, 2014.

Goldberg, Jeffrey. "Nizzar Rayan on God's Hatred of Jews." *Atlantic,* January 2, 2009. http://www.theatlantic.com/international/archive/2009/01/nizar-rayyan-of-hamas-on-god-apos-s-hatred-of-jewsh/9278/.

Goldsborough, Bob. "DuPage Board Rejects Dome and Minaret for Mosque near Willowbrook." *Chicago Tribune,* March 13, 2012.

Graham, William. "Traditionalism in Islam: An Essay in Interpretation." *The Journal of Interdisciplinary History* 23, no. 3 (Winter 1993): 495–522.

Green, Emma. "How American Muslims Are Trying to Take Back Their Government." *Atlantic,* April 16, 2017. https://www.theatlantic.com/politics/archive/2017/04/american-muslims-running-for-office/522585/.

Grewal, Inderpal. *Transnational America: Feminisms, Disaporas, Neoliberalisms.* Durham, NC: Duke University Press, 2005.

Grewal, Zareena. *Islam Is a Foreign Country: American Muslims and the Crisis of Islam.* New York: New York University Press, 2013.

———. "Marriage in Colour: Race, Religion, and Spouse Selection in Four American Mosques." *Ethnic and Racial Studies* 32, no. 2 (February 2009): 323–45.

Grewal, Zareena, and R. David Coolidge. "Islamic Education in the United States." In *The Cambridge Companion to American Islam,* edited by Juliane Hammer and Omid Safi, 246–65. New York: Cambridge University Press, 2013.

Haddad, Yvonne Yazbeck. *Becoming American?: The Forging of Arab and Muslim Identity in Pluralist America.* Waco, TX: Baylor University Press, 2011.

———, ed. *Muslims in the West: From Sojourners to Citizens.* New York: Oxford University Press, 2002.

———. *Not Quite American?: The Shaping of Arab and Muslim Identity in the United States.* Waco, TX: Baylor University Press, 2004.

Haddad, Yvonne Yazbeck, and John Esposito, eds. *Muslims on the Americanization Path?* New York: Oxford University Press, 2000.

Haddad, Yvonne Yazbeck, and Jane I. Smith, eds. *Muslim Communities in North America.* Albany, NY: State University of New York Press, 1994.

Haleem, M. A. S., trans. *The Qur'an.* Oxford: Oxford University Press, 2004.

Hall, David, ed. *Lived Religion in America: Toward a History of Practice.* Princeton, NJ: Princeton University Press, 1997.

Hallaq, Wael B. *A History of Islamic Legal Theories: An Introduction to Sunni Usul Al-Fiqh*. Cambridge: Cambridge University Press, 1997.

———. *Shari'a: Theory, Practice, Transformations*. Cambridge: Cambridge University Press, 2009.

Hammer, Juliane. "Activism as Embodied *Tafsir*: Negotiating Women's Authority, Leadership, and Space in North America." In *Women, Leadership and Mosques: Changes in Contemporary Islamic Authority*, edited by Masooda Bano and Hilary Kalmbach, 457–80. Leiden: Brill, 2012.

———. *American Muslim Women, Religious Authority, and Activism: More than a Prayer*. Austin: University of Texas Press, 2012.

———. "Center Stage: Gendered Islamophobia and Muslim Women." In *Islamophobia in America: The Anatomy of Intolerance*, edited by Carl Ernst, 107–44. New York: Palgrave MacMillan, 2013.

———. "Studying American Muslim Women: Gender, Feminism, and Islam." In *The Cambridge Companion to American Islam*, edited by Juliane Hammer and Omid Safi, 330–44. New York: Cambridge University Press, 2013.

Hammer, Juliane, and Omid Safi. "Introduction: American Islam, Muslim Americans, and the American Experiment." In *The Cambridge Companion to American Islam*, edited by Juliane Hammer and Omid Safi, 1–14. New York: Cambridge University Press, 2013.

———, eds. *The Cambridge Companion to American Islam*. New York: Cambridge University Press, 2013.

Hartley, Jenny. *The Reading Groups Book*. London: Oxford University Press, 2002.

Hayden, Dolores. *Building Suburbia: Green Fields and Urban Growth, 1820–2000*. New York: Vintage Books, 2004.

Hedstrom, Matthew. *The Rise of Liberal Religion: Book Culture and American Spirituality in the Twentieth Century*. New York: Oxford University Press, 2013.

Herberg, Will. *Protestant, Catholic, Jew: An Essay in American Religious Sociology*. Garden City: Doubleday, 1955.

Hermansen, Marcia. "Cultural Worlds/Culture Wars: Contemporary American Muslim Perspectives on the Role of Culture." *Journal of Islamic Law and Culture* 11, no. 3 (2009): 185–95.

———. "Hybrid Identity Formation in Muslim America: The Case of American Sufi Movements." *The Muslim World* 90, nos. 1–2 (Spring 2000): 158–97.

———. "Muslims in the Performative Mode: A Reflection on Muslim-Christian Dialogue." *The Muslim World* 94, no. 3 (2004): 387–96.

———."Two-Way Acculturation: Between Individual Choice (Liminality) and Community Affiliation (Communitas)." In *The Muslims of America*, edited by Yvonne Hazbek Haddad, 188–204. New York: Oxford University Press, 1991.

Hicks, Rosemary R. "Religious Pluralism, Secularism, and Interfaith Endeavors." In *The Cambridge Companion to American Islam*, edited by Juliane Hammer and Omid Safi, 156–69. New York: Cambridge University Press, 2013.

Hidayatullah, Aysha. *Feminist Edges of the Qur'an*. New York: Oxford University Press, 2014.

Hirsch, Arnold R. *Making the Second Ghetto: Race and Housing in Chicago 1940–1960*. Chicago: The University of Chicago Press, 1998.

Hirsch, Jennifer S., and Holly Wardlow, eds. *Modern Loves: The Anthropology of Romantic Courtship and Companionate Marriage*. Ann Arbor: University of Michigan Press, 2009.

Howe, Justine. "Invocations of Early Islam in US Discourses of Muslim Pluralism." In *The Routledge Handbook for Early Islam*, edited by Herbert Berg, 374–88. London: Routledge, 2017.

Howell, Sally. "Laying the Groundwork for American Muslim Histories." In *The Cambridge Companion to American Islam*, edited by Juliane Hammer and Omid Safi, 45–64. New York: Cambridge University Press, 2013.

Hughes, Aaron. "The Study of Islam before and after September 11: A Provocation." *Theory and Method in the Study of Religion* 24, nos. 4–5 (2012): 314–36.

Hurgronje, C. Snouck. *Mekka in the Latter Part of the 19th Century*. Translated by J. H. Monahan. Leiden: Brill, 1970.

Hutchison, William. *Religious Pluralism in America: The Contentious History of a Founding Ideal*. New Haven, CT: Yale University Press, 2003.

Ingram, Brannon. "Ahmadi Muslim Americans." *Encyclopedia of Muslim-American History*, edited by Edward Curtis IV, 32–34. New York: Facts on File, 2010.

Inhorn, Marcia. *The New Arab Man: Emergent Masculinities, Technologies, and Islam in the Middle East*. Princeton, NJ: Princeton University Press, 2012.

Jackson, Sherman A. *Islam and the Blackamerican: Looking toward the Third Resurrection*. New York: Oxford University Press, 2005.

———. "Jihad and the Modern World." *Journal of Islamic Law and Culture* 7, no. 1 (2002): 1–15.

———. "Soft Sharī'a Fundamentalism and the Totalitarian Epistemology of Vincent Cornell." *The Religion and Culture Web Forum*, University of Chicago Divinity School (May 2011).

Jamal, Amaney, and Nadine Naber, eds. *Race and Arab Americans before and after 9/11*. Syracuse: Syracuse University Press, 2007.

Jamal, Zahra N. "Ismaʿilis." In *Encyclopedia of Islam in the United States*, edited by Jocelyne Cesari, 2: 348–51. Westport, CT: Greenwood Press, 2007.

Johnson, Sylvester A. *African American Religions, 1500–2000: Colonialism, Democracy, and Freedom*. New York: Cambridge University Press, 2015.

———. "The Rise of Black Ethnics: The Ethnic Turn in African American Religions 1916–1945." *Religion and American Culture: A Journal of Interpretation* 20, no. 2 (2010): 125–63.

Kamali, Mohammad Hashim. *Principles of Islamic Jurisprudence*. Cambridge: Islamic Texts Society, 2003.

Kaptein, N. J. G. "Materials for the History of the Prophet Muhammad's Birthday Celebration in Medina." *Der Islam* 69 (1992): 193–246.

———. *Muhammad's Birthday Festival: Early History in the Central Muslim Lands and Development in the Muslim West until the 10th/16th Century*. Leiden: Brill, 1993.

Karim, Jamillah. *American Muslim Women: Negotiating Race, Class, and Gender in the Ummah*. New York: New York University Press, 2009.

Kassam, Zayn. "The Gender Policies of Aga Khan III and Aga Khan IV." In *A Modern History of the Ismailis: Continuity and Change in a Muslim Community*, edited by Farhad Daftary, 247–64. London: I. B. Tauris, 2011.

Katz, Marion Holmes. *The Birth of the Prophet Muhammad: Devotional Piety in Sunni Islam*. London: Routledge, 2007.

———. *Prayer in Islamic Thought and Practice*. New York: Cambridge University Press, 2013.

———. *Women in the Mosque: A History of Legal Thought and Social Practice*. New York: Columbia University Press, 2014.

———. "Women's 'Mawlid' Performances in Sanaa and the Construction of 'Popular Islam.'" *International Journal of Middle East Studies* 40, no. 3 (August 2008): 467–84.

Keane, Webb. *Christian Moderns: Freedom and Fetish in the Mission Encounter*. Berkeley: University of California Press, 2007.

Khabeer, Su'ad Abdul. *Muslim Cool: Race, Religion, and Hip Hop in the United States*. New York: New York University Press, 2016.

———. "Rep That Islam: The Rhyme and Reason of American Islamic Hip Hop." *The Muslim World* 97 (January 2007): 125–41.

Khalil, Mohammad Hassan, ed. *Between Heaven and Hell: Islam, Salvation, and the Fate of Others*. New York: Oxford University Press, 2013.

———. *Islam and the Fate of Others: The Salvation Question*. New York: Oxford University Press, 2012.

Korb, Scott. *Light without Fire: The Making of America's First Muslim College*. Boston: Beacon Press, 2013.

Kugle, Scott Siraj al-Haqq. *Homosexuality in Islam: Critical Reflections on Gay, Lesbian, and Transgender Muslims*. New York: Oneworld, 2010.

Kurien, Prema. *A Place at the Multicultural Table: The Development of an American Hinduism*. New Brunswick, NJ: Rutgers University Press, 2007.

Kurzman, Charles, ed. *Liberal Islam: A Source-Book*. New York: Oxford University Press, 2004.

Lamb, Charles. *Housing Segregation in Suburban America since 1960*. New York: Cambridge University Press, 2005.

Lamptey, Jerusha. *Never Wholly Other: A Muslima Theology of Religious Pluralism*. New York: Oxford University Press, 2014.

Lauzière, Henri. *The Making of Salafism: Islamic Reform in the Twentieth Century*. New York: Columbia University Press, 2016.

Lawrence, Bruce B. *New Faiths, Old Fears: Muslims and Other Asian Immigrants in American Religious Life*. New York: Columbia University Press, 2002.

Leonard, Karen. "American Muslims and Authority: Competing Discourses in a Non-Muslim State." *Journal of American Ethnic History* 25, no. 1 (Fall 2005): 5–30.

———. *Muslims in the United States: The State of Research*. New York: Russell Sage Foundation, 2003.

Lipton, G. A. "Secular Sufism: Neoliberalism, Ethnoracism, and the Reformation of the Muslim Other." *The Muslim World* 101, no. 3 (2011): 427–40.

Lofton, Kathryn. *Oprah: The Gospel of an Icon*. Berkeley: University of California Press, 2011.

———. "Religion and the Authority in American Parenting." *Journal of the American Academy of Religion* 84, no. 3 (June 2016): 1–36.

Loimeier, Roman. "Translating the Qur'an in Sub-Saharan Africa." *Journal of Religion in Africa* 35, no. 4 (2005): 403–23.

Long, Charles. *Housing Segregation in Suburban America since 1960*. New York: Cambridge University Press, 2005.

Long, Elizabeth. *Book Clubs: Women and the Uses of Reading in Everyday Life*. Chicago: The University of Chicago Press, 2003.

Luhr, Eileen. *Witnessing Suburbia: Conservatives and Christian Youth Culture*. Berkeley: University of California Press, 2009.

Lutz, Eric. "Walsh: Muslims Trying to Kill Americans." *Salon*, August 9, 2012. http://www.salon.com/2012/08/09/walsh_muslims_are_trying_to_kill_americans/.

Mahmood, Saba. *Politics of Piety: The Islamic Revival and the Feminist Subject*. Princeton, NJ: Princeton University Press, 2011.

———. "Rehearsed Spontaneity and the Conventionality of Ritual: Disciplines of Salat." *American Ethnologist* 28, no. 4 (November 2001): 827–53.

Maira, Sunaina. *Desis in the House: Indian American Youth Culture in New York City*. Philadelphia: Temple University Press, 2002.

———. *Missing: Youth, Citizenship, and Empire after 9/11*. Durham, NC: Duke University Press, 2009.

Mamdani, Mahmood. *Good Muslim, Bad Muslim: America, the Cold War, and the Roots of Terror*. New York: Pantheon Books, 2004.

March, Andrew. "Islamic Legal Theory, Secularism, and Religious Pluralism: Is Modern Religious Freedom Sufficient for the Shari'a 'Purpose' of 'Preserving Religion' [Hifz Al-Din]?" *Islamic Law and Law of the Muslim World Research Paper Series* (2009): 1–38.

Marr, Timothy. *The Cultural Roots of American Islamicism*. Cambridge: Cambridge University Press, 2006.

Marzouki, Nadia. *Islam: An American Religion*. New York: Columbia University Press, 2017.

Masud, Muhammad Khalid, and Armando Salvatore, eds. *Islam and Modernity: Key Issues and Debates*. Edinburgh: Edinburgh University Press, 2009.

Masud, Muhammad, Brinkley Messick, and David S. Powers, "Muftis, Fatwas, and Islamic Legal Interpretation." In *Islamic Legal Interpretation: Muftis and Their*

Fatwas, edited by Muhammad Masud, Brinkley Messick, and David S. Powers, 3–32. Cambridge, MA: Harvard University Press, 1996.

Masuzawa, Tomoko. *The Invention of World Religions*. Chicago: The University of Chicago Press, 2005.

Mattson, Ingrid. "Can a Woman Be an Imam? Form and Function in Muslim Women's Leadership." June 20, 2005. http://ingridmattson.org/article/can-a-woman-be-an-imam/.

May, Elaine Tyler. *Homeward Bound: American Families in the Cold War Era*. New York: Basic Books, 2008.

McCloud, Sean. "Putting Some Class into Religious Studies: Resurrecting an Important Concept." *Journal of the American Academy of Religion* 75, no. 4 (December 2007): 840–62.

Meijer, Roel, ed. *Global Salafism: Islam's New Religious Movement*. New York: Oxford University Press, 2013.

———. "Introduction." In *Global Salafism: Islam's New Religious Movement*, edited by Roel Meijer, 1–32. New York: Oxford University Press, 2013.

Metcalf, Barbara Daly, ed. *Making Muslim Space in North America and Europe*. Berkeley: University of California Press, 1996.

Minwalla, Omer, Jamie Feldman, Christin Varga, and B. R. Simon Rosser. "Identity Experience among Progressive Gay Muslims in North America: A Qualitative Study within Al-Fatiha." *Culture, Health, and Sexuality* 7, no. 2 (March 2005): 113–28.

Mir, Shabana. *Muslim American Women on Campus: Undergraduate Social Life and Identity*. Chapel Hill: The University of North Carolina Press, 2014.

Moore, Kathleen M. *Al-Mughtaribun: American Law and the Transformation of Muslim Life in the United States*. Albany: State University of New York Press, 1995.

———. *The Unfamiliar Abode: Islamic Law in the United States and Britain*. New York: Oxford University Press, 2010.

Moore, Natalie Y. *The South Side: A Portrait of American Segregation*. New York: St. Martin's Press, 2016.

Moore, R. Laurence. *Religious Outsiders and the Making of Americans*. New York: Oxford University Press, 1987.

Moreton, Bethany. *To Serve God and Wal-Mart: The Making of Christian Free Enterprise*. Cambridge, MA: Harvard University Press, 2010.

"Muslim Americans: No Signs of Growth in Alienation or Extremism." Pew Research Center, August 30, 2011. http://www.pewforum.org/2011/08/30/muslim-americans-no-signs-of-growth-in-alienation-or-support-for-extremism/.

Nabhan-Warren, Kristy. "Embodied Research and Writing: A Case for Phenomenologically Oriented Religious Studies Ethnographies." *Journal of the American Academy of Religion* 72, no. 2 (2011): 378–407.

———. *The Virgin of El Barrio: Marian Apparitions, Catholic Evangelizing, and Mexican American Activism*. New York: New York University Press, 2005.

Na'im, Abd Allah Ahmad. *Toward a Islamic Reformation: Civil Liberties, Human Rights, and International Law*. Syracuse: Syracuse University Press, 1987.

Nelson, Kristina. *The Art of Reciting the Qur'an*. Austin: University of Texas Press, 1986.

Newcomb, Rachel. "Fieldwork in Morocco with Sofia (Age 1)." *The Chronicle of Higher Education*, February 14, 2011.

Numrich, Paul. "The Emergence of the Unified Ummah Rhetoric among American Muslims: The Case of Metropolitan Chicago." *Journal of Muslim Minority Affairs* 32, no. 4 (2012): 450–66.

Orsi, Robert A. *Between Heaven and Earth: The Religious Worlds People Make and the Scholars Who Study Them*. Princeton, NJ: Princeton University Press, 2005.

———. "Everyday Miracles: The Study of Lived Religion." In *Lived Religion in America: Toward a History of Practice*, edited by David Hall, 3–21. Princeton, NJ: Princeton University Press, 1997.

———. ed. *Gods of the City: Religion and the American Urban Landscape*. Bloomington: Indiana University Press, 1999.

———. *History and Presence*. Cambridge, MA: Harvard University Press, 2016.

Ostrander, Rick. "The Practice of Prayer in a Modern Age: Liberals, Fundamentalists, and Prayer in the Modern Age." In *Practicing Protestants: Histories of Christian Life, 1630–1985*, edited by Laurie Maffly-Kipp, Leigh Eric Schmidt, and Mark Valeri, 159–76. Baltimore: Johns Hopkins University Press, 2006.

Otterbeck, Jonas. "Battling Over the Public Sphere: Islamic Reactions to the Music of Today." *Contemporary Islam* 2, no. 3 (December 2008): 211–28.

Painter, Nell Irvin. *The History of White People*. New York: W. W. Norton, 2010.

Patel, Eboo. *Sacred Ground: Pluralism, Prejudice, and the Promise of America*. Boston: Beacon Press, 2012.

Perez, Juan Jr. "Study Looks at Aftermath of Chicago School Closings in 2013." *Chicago Tribune*, January 22, 2015.

Purkayastha, Bandana. *Negotiating Ethnicity: Second-Generation South Asian Americans Traverse a Transnational World*. New Brunswick, NJ: Rutgers University Press, 2005.

Qureshi, Regina Burkhardt. "Transcending Space: Recitation and Community among South Asian Muslims in Canada." In *Making Muslim Space in North America and Europe*, edited by Barbara Daly Metcalf, 46–64. Berkeley: University of California Press, 1996.

Qureshi-Landes, Asifa. "Rumors of the Sharia Threat Are Greatly Exaggerated: What American Judges Really Do with Islamic Family Law in Their Courtrooms." *New York Law School Review* 57, no. 2 (2012–2013): 244–57.

Rahman, Fazlur. *Islam and Modernity: Transformation of an Intellectual Tradition*. Chicago: The University of Chicago Press, 1982.

———. *Major Themes of the Qur'an*. 2nd ed. Minneapolis: Biblioteca Islamica, 1994.

———. "Some Key Ethical Concepts of the Qur'an." *Journal of Religious Ethics* 11, no. 2 (Fall 1993): 170–85.

Ramadan, Tariq. *In the Footsteps of the Prophet: Lessons from the Life of Muhammad.* Oxford: Oxford University Press, 2007.

Rana, Junaid. *Terrifying Muslims: Race and Labor in the South Asian Diaspora.* Durham, NC: Duke University Press, 2011.

Reinhart, A. Kevin. *Before Revelation: The Boundaries of Muslim Moral Thought.* Albany: State University of New York Press, 1995.

Remillard, Art. "Steelers Nation and the Seriously Religious Side of Football." *Marginalia*, August 28, 2013. http://marginalia.lareviewofbooks.org/steelers-nation-and-the-seriously-religious-side-of-football.

Rippin, Andrew. "The Function of Asbab Al-Nuzul in Quranic Exegesis." *Bulletin of the School of Oriental and African Studies* 1 (1998): 1–20.

———. *The Qur'an: Formative Interpretation.* Brookfield: Ashgate, 1999.

Roediger, David R. *The Wages of Whiteness: Race and the Making of the American Working Class.* London: Verso, 1999.

Roof, Wade Clark. *A Generation of Seekers: The Spiritual Journeys of the Baby Boomer Generation.* San Francisco: HarperSanFrancisco, 1994.

Rosaldo, Renato. "Cultural Citizenship and Educational Democracy." *Cultural Anthropology* 9, no. 3 (1994): 402–11.

Rouse, Carolyn. *Engaged Surrender: African American Women and Islam.* Berkeley: University of California Press, 1998.

Roy, Olivier. *The Failure of Political Islam.* Translated by Carol Volk. Cambridge, MA: Harvard University Press, 1994.

Ruzich, Joseph. "MECCA Champions Willowbrook Mosque." *Chicago Tribune*, August 18, 2010.

Sachedina, Abdulaziz. *The Islamic Roots of Democratic Pluralism.* New York: Oxford University Press, 2001.

Safi, Omid. *Memories of Muhammad: Why the Prophet Matters.* New York: HarperCollins, 2009.

———, ed. *Progressive Muslims: On Justice, Gender, and Pluralism.* New York: Oneworld, 2003.

Saleh, Walid. *The Formation of the Classical Tafsīr Tradition: The Qur'ān Commentary of al-Tha'labī (D. 427/1035).* Leiden: Brill, 2014.

Sardar, Ziauddin. *Reading the Qur'an: The Contemporary Relevance of the Sacred Text of Islam.* Oxford: Oxford University Press, 2011.

Sarna, Jonathan. *American Judaism: A History.* New Haven, CT: Yale University Press, 2004.

Satter, Beryl. *Family Properties: Race, Real Estate, and the Exploitation of Black America.* New York: Henry Holt and Company, 2009.

Schielke, Samuli. "Hegemonic Encounters: Criticism of Saints-Day Festivals and the Formation of Modern Islam in Late 19th and Early 20th-Century Egypt." *Die Welt Des Islams* 47, nos. 3–4 (2007): 319–55.

———. *The Perils of Joy: Contesting Mulid Festivals in Contemporary Egypt*. Syracuse, NY: Syracuse University Press, 2012.

Schmidt, Garbi. *Islam in Urban America: Sunni Muslims in Chicago*. Philadelphia: Temple University Press, 2004.

Schmidt, Leigh Eric. *Restless Souls: The Making of American Spirituality*. San Francisco: HarperSanFrancisco, 2005.

Schultz, Kevin. *Tri-Faith America: How Catholics and Jews Held Postwar America to Its Protestant Promise*. New York: Oxford University Press, 2011.

Seedat, Fatima. "Islam, Feminism, and Islamic Feminism." *Journal of Feminist Studies in Religion* 29, no. 2 (Fall 2013): 25–45.

———. "When Islam and Feminism Converge." *The Muslim World* 103 (July 2013): 404–20.

Sells, Michael A. *Approaching the Qur'an: The Early Revelations*. Ashland, OR: White Cloud Press, 1999.

———. *Early Islamic Mysticism, Early Islamic Mysticism: Sufi, Qur'an, Miraj, Poetic and Theological Writings*. New York: Paulist Press, 1996.

Shah-Kazemi, Reza. *The Spirit of Tolerance in Islam*. Occasional Papers Series 4. London: Institute for Ismaili Studies, 2012.

Shankar, Shalini. *Desi Land: Teen Culture, Class, and Success in Silicon Valley*. Durham, NC: Duke University Press, 2008.

Singleton, Brett D. "Brothers at Odds: Rival Islamic Movements in Late Nineteenth Century New York City." *Journal of Muslim Minority Affairs* 27, no. 3 (December 2007): 473–86.

———. "*The Moslem World*: A History of America's Earliest Islamic Newspaper and Its Successors." *Journal of Muslim Minority Affairs* 27, no. 2 (August 2007): 297–307.

Soja, Edward W. *Third Space: Journeys to Los Angeles and Other Real-and-Imagined Places*. London: Blackwell Publishers, 1996.

Spellberg, Denise. *Thomas Jefferson's Qur'an: Islam and the Founders*. New York: Alfred A. Knopf, 2013.

Spivak, Gayatri Charkravorty. "Can the Subaltern Speak?" In *Marxism and the Interpretation of Culture*, edited by Cary Nelson and Lawrence Grossberg, 271–313. Urbana: University of Illinois Press, 1988.

Starrett, Gregory. *Putting Islam to Work: Education, Politics, and Religious Transformation in Egypt*. Berkeley: University of California Press, 1998.

Stein, Stephen J. *Communities of Dissent: A History of Alternative Religions in America*. New York: Oxford University Press, 2003.

Steinberg, Jonah. *Isma'ili Modern: Globalization and Identity in a Muslim Community*. Chapel Hill: The University of North Carolina Press, 2011.

Svensson, Jonas. "ITZ BIDAH BRO!!!!! GT ME??—YouTube Mawlid and Voices of Praise and Blame." In *Muslims and the New Information and Communication*

Technologies: Notes from an Emerging and Infinite Field, edited by Thomas Hoffmann and Göran Larsson, 89–111. New York: Springer, 2013.

Tāhā, Mahmūd Muhammad. *The Second Message of Islam*. Syracuse, NY: Syracuse University Press, 1987.

Tapper, Nancy, and Richard Tapper. "The Birth of the Prophet: Ritual and Gender in Turkish Islam." *Man* 22, no. 1 (March 1987): 69–92.

Tourage, Mahdi. "Performing Belief and Reviving Islam: Prominent (White Male) Converts in Muslim Revival Conventions." *Performing Islam* 1, no. 2 (2012): 207–26.

Ukeles, Raquel M. "The Sensitive Puritan? Revisiting Ibn Taymiyya." In *Ibn Taymiyya and His Times*, edited by Yosef Rapaport and Shahab Ahmed, 319–37. New York: Oxford University Press, 2010.

wadud, amina. *Qur'an and Woman: Rereading the Sacred Text from a Woman's Perspective*. 2nd ed. New York: Oxford University Press, 1999.

Wansborough, John. *Quranic Studies: Sources and Methods of Scriptural Interpretation*. Oxford: Oxford University Press, 1977.

Ware, Rudolph, III. *The Walking Qur'an: Islamic Education, Embodied Knowledge, and History in West Africa*. Chapel Hill: The University of North Carolina Press, 2014.

Warner, R. Stephen, Elise Martel, and Rhonda E. Dugan. "Islam Is to Catholicism as Teflon Is to Velcro." In *Sustaining Faith Traditions: Race, Ethnicity, and Religion among the Latino and Asian Second Generation*, edited by Carolyn Chen and Russell Jueng, 46–68. New York: New York University Press, 2012.

Warner, R. Stephen, and Judith G. Wittner, eds. *Gatherings in Diaspora: Religious Communities and the New Immigration*. Philadelphia: Temple University Press, 1998.

Webb, Suhaib, and Scott Korb. "No Room for Radicals." *New York Times*, April 25,2013.

Weisenfeld, Judith. *New World A-Coming: Black Religion and Racial Identity During the Great Migration*. New York: New York University Press, 2017.

Weismann, Itzchak. *The Naqshbandiyya: Orthodoxy and Activism in a Worldwide Sufi Tradition*. London: Routledge, 2007.

Wenger, Tisa Joy. *We Have a Religion: The 1920s Pueblo Indian Dance Controversy and American Religious Freedom*. Chapel Hill: The University of North Carolina Press, 2009.

Wilford, Justin. *Sacred Subdivisions: The Postsuburban Transformation of American Evangelicalism*. New York: New York University Press, 2012.

Yang, Fenggang, and Helen Rose Ebaugh. "Religion and Ethnicity among New Immigrants: The Impact of Majority/Minority Status in Home and Host Countries." *Journal for the Scientific Study of Religion* 40 (September 2001): 367–78.

Yusuf, Hamza. "What is *Mawlid?*" https://www.youtube.com/watch?v=2x14RQLgB9s. Uploaded October 6, 2011.

Zadeh, Travis. *The Vernacular Qur'an: Translation and the Rise of Persian Exegesis.* New York: Oxford University Press, 2012.

Zaman, Muhammad Qasim. *The Ulama in Contemporary Islam: Custodians of Change.* Princeton, NJ: Princeton University Press, 2002.

Index

CPSIA information can be obtained
at www.ICGtesting.com
Printed in the USA
BVHW090002080122
625567BV00001B/2

9 780197 558539